The Lesbian and Gay Movements

Dilemmas in American Politics

Series Editor: **Craig A. Rimmerman,** Hobart and William Smith Colleges

If the answers to the problems facing U.S. democracy were easy, politicians would solve them, accept credit, and move on. But certain dilemmas have confronted the American political system continuously. They defy solution; they are endemic to the system. Some can best be described as institutional dilemmas: How can the Congress be both a representative body and a national decision-maker? How can the president communicate with more than 250 million citizens effectively? Why do we have a two-party system when many voters are disappointed with the choices presented to them? Others are policy dilemmas: How do we find compromises on issues that defy compromise, such as abortion policy? How do we incorporate racial and ethnic minorities or immigrant groups into American society, allowing them to reap the benefits of this land without losing their identity? How do we fund health care for our poorest or oldest citizens?

Dilemmas such as these are what propel students toward an interest in the study of U.S. government. Each book in the *Dilemmas in American Politics Series* addresses a "real world" problem, raising the issues that are of most concern to students. Each is structured to cover the historical and theoretical aspects of the dilemma but also to explore the dilemma from a practical point of view and to speculate about the future. The books are designed as supplements to introductory courses in American politics or as case studies to be used in upper-level courses. The link among them is the desire to make the real issues confronting the political world come alive in students' eyes.

BOOKS IN THIS SERIES

The Lesbian and Gay Movements

Assimilation or Liberation?

Craig A. Rimmerman
Hobart and William Smith Colleges

A Member of the Perseus Books Group

To those teachers, scholars, and activists who paved the way.

Designed by Timm Bryson
Set in 11 point Minion

Library of Congress Cataloging-in-Publication Data

Rimmerman, Craig A.
    The lesbian and gay movements : assimilation or liberation? / Craig A. Rimmerman.
        p. cm. (Dilemmas in American politics)
    Includes bibliographical references and index.
    ISBN-13: 978-0-8133-4054-8
    ISBN-10: 0-8133-4054-3
    1. Gay liberation movement—United States. 2. Gay rights—United States. 3. Homosexuality—Political aspects—United States. 4. Assimilation (Sociology) 5. United States—Social conditions. 6. United States—Politics and government. I. Title.
    HQ76.8.U5R58 2008
    306.76'6—dc22
                                                                            2007034346

10 9 8 7 6 5 4 3 2 1

Contents

Illustrations

Preface

This book owes its existence to the wonderful 1992–1993 sabbatical year that I spent in Washington, D.C., as an American Political Science Association Congressional Fellow. I lived at Dupont Circle, the heart of Washington's vibrant gay community, and I witnessed firsthand the excitement, hope, and anticipation of the Democrats' return to power. And then like so many people in D.C.'s lesbian and gay community (and in the country writ large), I experienced immediate disappointment with President Clinton's handling of the gays-in-the-military fiasco. By day, I worked as a congressional fellow in the offices of Senator Tom Daschle (D-SD) and Representative Barbara Kennelly (D-CT), and I observed the early months of the Clinton presidency unfolding from the inside of Congress. And I met and socialized with lesbian and gay activists who embraced both the assimilationist and the liberationist perspectives that are at the core of this book's underlying dilemma.

Now some fifteen years later, I revisit some of the important issues and questions that grew out of my time living and working in the nation's capital. How much progress have the lesbian and gay movements made over the years in achieving larger movements' goals? And what are those goals? How have they changed over time? What political organizing strategies are the most effective, and which are the least effective? What are our criteria for "effectiveness"? Why is there such virulent opposition on the part of some to public policies that would support and explicitly value lesbians, gays, bisexuals, and those who are transgendered? And what would our society look like if we broadened our conception of citizenship to include sexual minorities?

The policy issues that are at the core of this book—HIV/AIDS, the military ban, and same-sex marriage—are among the most contentious public policy issues of our time, and as such they are an excellent set of issues for exploring the tensions between the assimilationist and liberationist political organizing strategies, which is the central dilemma of this book. With these questions and issues in mind, I hope that this book will be of

interest to those students, teachers, and activists who are particularly interested in American politics, public policy, social movements, and interest groups.

I have had the support and encouragement of so many people while writing this book. I especially wish to thank Westview's Dilemmas in American Politics editorial board, who encouraged me to "get this book done!"
And a huge thanks to Steve Catalano, Westview acquisitions editor, who
saw this book as a potentially important contribution and waited so patiently as I wrote ever so slowly when assuming my teaching and community responsibilities at Hobart and William Smith Colleges, where I have
taught since 1986. Steve personifies the best qualities that any author looks
for in an editor: patience, professionalism, and support every step of the
way. I also acknowledge the excellent copyediting of Annette Wenda and
the work of Laura Stine, Westview senior project editor, who was instru-
mental in moving the manuscript toward publication.

I am fortunate, honored, and privileged to hold the Joseph P. DiGangi
Chair in the Social Sciences at Hobart and William Smith Colleges. Thank
you to Joe DiGangi for his genuine commitment to quality undergraduate
teaching and to his many students who endowed this chair. I thank, as
well, my students over many years who have helped make Hobart and
William Smith a wonderful place to teach. And a special thank-you to
Jamie Smith, who completed an honors project with me on the lesbian
and gay movements during the 2006–2007 academic year and whose passion and commitment are an inspiration.

Thank you, as well, to an array of people who have been so supportive
of my work and kind to me over the years: Teresa Amott, Stewart Auyash,
Betty Bayer, Sheila Bennett, Scott Brophy, Val Bunce, Lynne Cohen, Dick
Dillon, Joyce Dillon, Zillah Eisenstein, Shawn Fitzgibbons, Alan Frishman,
Ronny Frishman, Mark Gearan, Jack Goldman, Robert Gross, Chris
Gunn, Susan Henking, James Henry Holland, Kim Kopatz, Steven Lee,
Derek Linton, Judith McKinney, Scott McKinney, Dunbar Moodie,
Meredith Moodie, Ilene Nicholas, David Ost, Eric Patterson, Don Spector,
Rich Szanyi, the late Deborah Tall, David Weiss, Clyde Wilcox, Stacia
Zabusky, and Patty Zimmermann. A special thanks to Ted Richards and
Bill Wears, friends extraordinare, who have recommended a treasure trove
in classical music, books, and movies to me over the years, and whose own
loving relationship is an inspiration.

I thank, too, the entire Hobart and William Smith library staff, especially Joseph Chmura, Sara Greenleaf, Michael Hunter, and Dan Mulvey, for their continued support. I am appreciative that the Hobart and William Smith Faculty Research and Awards Committee provided ongoing support for this and related projects.

And I am so grateful to the lesbian and gay activists who very generously agreed to sit down with me to talk about many of the ideas that are at the core of this book. I conducted interviews beginning in 1992, and they spanned across the United States: from Boston, New York, Los Angeles, and Philadelphia to Portland, Oregon, and Washington, D.C. I am inspired daily by the courage and commitment of the many teachers, scholars, and activists who paved the way. It is to them that I dedicate this book.

Ithaca, New York
July 2007

1

....

Introduction to the Core Dilemma

If we are to transform our state of virtual equality, evident in pervasive discrimination, ambivalent public opinion, and the persistence of the closet, we must begin with ourselves—both individually and as a movement. Coming out is the one step each gay, lesbian, or bisexual person can take to shatter virtual equality and move closer to the genuine equality with heterosexuals that is our birthright as moral human beings. Our challenge as a movement requires an examination of the strategies that have brought us to this troubling juncture.

—Urvashi Vaid, *Virtual Equality: The Mainstreaming of Gay and Lesbian Liberation*

Trying to find common ground for political mobilization among all these identities has become one of the most difficult tasks of what has come to be called the gay rights movement.

—Robert Bailey, *Gay Politics, Urban Politics: Identity and Economics in the Urban Setting*

Urvashi Vaid's and Robert Bailey's observations capture the challenges facing the contemporary lesbian and gay rights movements.[1] Vaid and Bailey point to the reality that all social movements, including the lesbian and gay movements, must constantly examine their broader political, social, and cultural approaches to change. The goal is to assess the difficulties and possibilities that have faced the movements over time with an eye toward what might be done in the future to expand the traditional notions of democracy and citizenship.

This is a particularly auspicious time to engage in the kind of critical examination that underlies this book, given the cultural visibility that lesbians, gays, bisexuals, and those who are transgendered have faced in recent years. This cultural visibility has been increasingly reflected in an array of popular television shows, including *The L Word*, *Queer as Folk*, *Six Feet Under*, *Will and Grace*, *The Sopranos*, *Rescue Me*, *Nip/Tuck*, *Buffy the Vampire Slayer*, *OZ*, *NYPD Blue*, and *The Shield*, to name a few. And when a moving, mainstream Hollywood film, *Brokeback Mountain*, receives considerable critical praise from reviewers and enthusiastic attention by the moviegoing public, one recognizes the sea change that has taken place since even the mid-1990s. But what does this visibility really mean in terms of people's daily lives? In recent years we have seen increased public tolerance and support for people coming out of the closet. The students I teach now are more likely to be supportive of their "out" peers than others were even ten years ago. And courses related to the lesbian and gay movements across academic disciplines are often among the most popular offerings on college campuses. This undoubtedly reflects the political organizing and education of earlier eras and the salience of these complicated and challenging issues for young people's lives.

At the same time, the lesbian and gay movements have achieved tangible accomplishments in the political arena at all levels of government, but especially in communities throughout the United States. For example, there are open communities of lesbians and gay men in urban areas throughout the United States. In addition, openly gay men and lesbians have been successful in the electoral arena, as they have been elected to city councils, state legislatures, and the U.S. Congress. Community organizations and businesses target the interests of the lesbian and gay movements. And some progress has been made through the legal system, most notably in the Supreme Court's 2003 *Lawrence v. Texas* decision that essentially ruled state sodomy laws unconstitutional.

But for all of the so-called progress, lesbians and gay men remain second-class citizens in vital ways. Fewer than one-tenth of 1 percent of all elected officials in the United States are openly lesbian, gay, or bisexual; very few transgendered people have been elected to public office. Lesbians and gay men are forbidden to marry, to teach in many public schools, to adopt children, to provide foster care, and to serve in the armed forces, National Guard, reserves, and the ROTC. If evicted from their homes, expelled from their schools, fired from their jobs, or refused public lodging, they usually are not able to seek legal redress. The topic of homosexuality is often deemed inappropriate for discussion in public schools, including in sex education courses. Many public school libraries refuse to own some of the many books that address the issue in important ways. Lesbians and gays are often reviled by the church and barred from membership in the clergy. They are the victims of hate crimes and targets of verbal abuse, and the possibility still exists that they will be beaten, threatened, attacked, or killed for simply loving another human being. And there is still no national hate-crimes legislation. Their parents reject them, and many gay youth have either attempted or contemplated suicide. Indeed, one political scientist concludes that "no other group of persons in American society today, having been convicted of no crime, is subject to the number and severity of legally imposed disabilities as are persons of same-sex orientation" (Hertzog 1996, 6).

What does all of this mean for how the contemporary lesbian and gay movements conceive of their political organizing strategies, especially given the determination by the Christian Right to use lesbian and gay issues, such as same-sex marriage, as wedge issues in elections at all levels of government? Should policy and cultural change reflect a top-down model, or should it be inspired by grassroots organizing in local communities throughout the United States? And should the goal be a more assimilationist, rights-based approach to political and social change, or should movement activists embrace a more liberationist, revolutionary model, one that might embrace a full range of progressive causes? This last question is the central dilemma of this book, given how the assimilationist and liberationist approaches have been integral to the lesbian and gay movements' organizing over the past sixty years.

Throughout their relatively short history, the lesbian and gay movements in the United States have endured searing conflicts over whether to embrace the assimilationist or liberationist strategy. This book explores this dilemma in both contemporary and historical contexts within a broader social-movement theoretical setting. The assimilationist approach typically embraces a rights-based perspective, works within the broader framework of pluralist democracy—one situated within classical liberalism—and fights for a seat at the table. In doing so, the assimilationists celebrate the "work within the system" insider approach to political and social change. Typically, they espouse a "let us in" approach to political activism, rather than the "let us show you a new way of conceiving the world" strategy associated with lesbian and gay liberation. Assimilationists are more likely to accept that change will have to be incremental and to understand that slow, gradual progress is built into the very structure of the U.S. framework of government. In this way, they typically embrace an insider approach to political change.

A second approach, the liberationist perspective, favors more radical cultural change, change that is transformational in nature and often arises outside the formal structures of the U.S. political system. Liberationists argue that there is a considerable gap between access and power and that it is simply not enough to have a seat at the table. For many liberationists, what is required is a shift in emphasis from a purely political strategy to one that embraces both structural political and cultural change, often through "outsider" political strategies. The notion of sexual citizenship embraced by liberationist activists and theorists is much more broadly conceived, as sociologist Steven Seidman describes: "Buoyed by their gains, and pressured by liberationists, the gay movement is slowly, if unevenly, expanding its political scope to fighting for full social equality—in the state, in schools, health-care systems, businesses, churches, and families" (2002, 24). Political theorist Shane Phelan claims that liberationists often "attempt to subvert the hierarchies of the hegemonic order, pointing out the gaps and contradictions in that order, thus removing the privilege of innocence from the dominant group" (2001, 32). As I will demonstrate, the assimilationist and liberationist strategies are not mutually exclusive.

FIGURE 1.1   **Social and Political Movements Compared**

Social Movements	Political Movements
Ideology	Lifestyle
Multiple Leaders	Single Leader Entrepreneur
Social and Political Spheres	Political Spheres Only
Have-Nots	Haves
Social Group Identity	Diverse Social Groups
Group Consciousness	Issue Positions

Source: Baer and Bositis 1993, 166. Reprinted by permission of Pearson Education, Inc., Upper Saddle River, New Jersey.

In order to better explicate the book's central dilemma, I will couch my analysis within the broader context of social-movement theory. First, it is necessary to understand how social movements differ from political parties, interest groups, and protests. They have three distinguishing features: they grow out of "a mass base of individuals, groups, and organizations, linked by social interaction"; they "organize around a mix of political and cultural goals"; and they "rely on a shared collective identity that is the basis of mobilization and participation" (Wald 2000, 5). Political scientist Sidney Tarrow extends this definition, stating that social movements involve "mounting collective challenges, drawing on common purposes, building solidarity and sustaining collective action" (1994, 3). They are also decentralized and comprise an array of organizations. They are often confused with political movements, but there are key differences between them, as figure 1.1 demonstrates.

Unlike political movements, which tend to represent middle-class interests, social movements represent those at the margins of American society, as defined by class, race, gender, or sexual orientation. Political movements are often defined through a single leader and her or his organization, whereas social movements are generally much more decentralized and sometimes have no real leader per se. Finally, social movements develop a comprehensive ideology, whereas political movements most often focus on narrow political objectives such as handgun control or the nuclear freeze. Often, social movements push for political change at the same time they seek structural change in the social, cultural, economic, and private spheres (Baer and Bositis 1993). At their core, social movements inspire participatory democracy.

They raise expectations that people can and should be involved in the decision-making process in all aspects of public life. They convert festering social problems into social issues and put them on the political agenda. They provide a role for everyone who wants to participate in the public process of addressing critical social problems and engaging official powerholders in a response to grassroots citizen demands for change. In addition, by encouraging widespread participation in the social change process, over time social movements tend to develop more creative, democratic, and appropriate solutions. (Moyer et al. 2001, 10)

The lesbian and gay movements certainly meet the criteria for an existing social movement. Lesbians, gays, bisexuals, and transgendered people have persistently occupied a place at the margins of society.

The vulnerability of groups at the margins of U.S. society permits elites to create serious obstacles to political participation and control of the political agenda (Scott 1990, 72). In response to their structural and cultural marginalization, groups outside the mainstream identify strategies that they perceive will meet their needs while challenging structures that constrain their life choices. These strategies commonly include developing alternative resources, constructing different ideological frameworks, and creating oppositional organizations and institutions. Such structures are most often "grounded in the indigenous or communal relationships of marginal groups" (Cohen 1999, 48). This is especially true for the lesbian and gay movements.

From the vantage point of marginalized groups, then, social movements are seen as vehicles for organization, education, and resistance. They are often galvanized when they perceive that there are "changes in political opportunities that give rise to new waves of movements and shape their unfolding." Successful social movements build on political opportunities by seizing and expanding them, thus turning them into collective action (Tarrow 1994, 7). I will examine how well the lesbian and gay movements have done so by studying the intersection between the assimilationist and liberationist strategies over time. We will see that social-movement politics are conflictual, messy, and complicated; they defy easy generalizations and often even explanations for various behaviors.

Chapter 2 places the development of the lesbian and gay movements within their proper historical context. Particular attention is devoted to the development of the assimilationist and liberationist approaches over the past sixty years by examining the creation and goals of the Mattachine Society and the Daughters of Bilitis (DOB) in the 1950s, the rise of the homophile movement in the 1950s and 1960s, and the connections between that movement and the movements growing out of the Stonewall Rebellion of 1969.

The assimilationist-accommodationist strategy prevailed within the broader movements until Stonewall. Despite various accomplishments, the mainstream homophile organizations were thrown on the defensive in light of Stonewall, as a new style of political organizing and leadership was demanded by newly energized lesbian and gay activists, many of whom were veterans of the various movements of the 1960s. This more confrontational liberationist approach embraced militancy and the unconventional politics associated with the antiwar, women's liberation, and civil rights movements. The modern gay liberation movement was soon born, built on some of the same ideas that undergirded the original Mattachine Society envisioned by Harry Hay and his cofounders almost twenty years earlier. For those who embraced gay liberation, a rights-based strategy was far too limited. Instead, the goal should be to remake, not merely reform, society. Chapter 2 explores these conflicts within the broader movements throughout the 1970s and 1980s, which were dominated by the rise of a conservative insurgency in society at large. The response of the Christian Right to various movements' gains in the 1970s and early 1980s is also examined in considerable detail.

Chapter 3 explores the tensions between those activists who embraced an insider assimilationist strategy and those who demanded an outsider liberationist strategy to political and social change, as reflected in broader movements' responses to public AIDS policy. As we explore this tension, we will devote considerable attention to AIDS policy and how AIDS activism in the 1980s, 1990s, and early twenty-first century altered the landscape of lesbian and gay politics, while mobilizing an array of newly politicized activists in the midst of a hideous epidemic that has so far claimed millions of lives the world over. Act Up, Queer Nation, and the Lesbian Avengers are all organizations that developed at the height of the AIDS crisis and demanded a liberationist organizing strategy. The role of the Treatment Action Group (TAG), which typically embraced insider assimilationist political strategies, will also be explained. As one would expect, the chapter discusses the responses of Presidents Reagan, Bush, and Clinton and Congress over time to HIV/AIDS policy and broader movements' demands, as well as how the movements have intersected with the Christian Right. Finally, the chapter examines in considerable detail the debates over the "degaying" and "regaying" of AIDS in the 1990s, debates that provide a window for assessing the contemporary landscape of lesbian and gay politics. This will all set a context for the discussion of the George W. Bush presidency and how that administration has addressed HIV/AIDS policy. A major goal of Chapter 3 is to assess the circumstances under which the assimilationist and liberationist strategies were effective, as well as how the Christian Right responded to these various strategies by using the threat of AIDS as a part of its successful grassroots fund-raising strategy.

At the core of recent social-movement theory is the belief that expanding political opportunities help to determine the overall strength of a social movement. With the election of President Clinton in November 1992, many members of the lesbian and gay movements perceived that after twelve long years of Republican Party control of the White House, the opportunities now existed for forceful presidential leadership that would be much more supportive of sexual minorities' interests. This is the broad context in which the military-ban issue appeared on the policy agenda soon after Clinton was elected. Chapter 4 assesses the original circumstances under which Clinton proposed to overturn the ban, how he attempted to do so once he became president, and why he fell short of his goal. The analysis interrogates the role of the lesbian and gay movements in interacting with the Clinton administration, Congress, and the Christian Right during the 1993 debate over the military ban. It explores broader movements' strategies and the debates between those who argued vigorously for overturning the ban (the assimilationist perspective) and those who argued that the movements need to transcend narrow rights goals and instead pursue broader political, social, and economic change (the liberationist perspective). The implementation of the "don't ask, don't tell" policy is also assessed in light of the lesbian and gay movements' goals and political strategies.

The campaign for same-sex marriage has depended on the courts for much of its success. It was inspired not through consensus among activists, but by a relatively small coterie of lawyers. Today the campaign is rooted in litigation, though it has now garnered the support of most major national lesbian and gay organizations, including the Lambda Legal Defense and Education Fund, National Gay and Lesbian Task Force, and

Human Rights Campaign. It has clearly become one of the leading issues of the mainstream assimilationist lesbian and gay movements. Chapter 5 will discuss how the issue has developed over time.

There are, however, vocal critics of same-sex marriage within the lesbian and gay movements. The arguments associated with the liberationist critique will be outlined in detail. These conflicts within the broader lesbian and gay movements are placed within a discussion of debates over the Defense of Marriage Act (codified into law in fall 1996). In addition, considerable attention will be devoted to same-sex-marriage policies and political organizing on the part of supporters and Christian Right opponents at the state level, with specific attention devoted to Hawaii, Vermont, and Massachusetts. The goal is to see the conflicts and tensions between the assimilationist and liberationist perspectives as played out within the context of a contentious public policy issue—same-sex marriage.

Chapter 6 explores the movements' futures in light of the analysis presented in this book. As this book will reveal, the goal of equal rights is the centerpiece of the contemporary lesbian and gay rights movements' strategies. This rights-based approach has dominated mainstream-movement thinking from the early years of the homophile movement to the debate over AIDS, the military ban, and same-sex marriage today. As we will see, a narrow rights-based perspective, rooted in identity politics, is largely unquestioned and unchallenged by mainstream contemporary lesbian and gay movements, especially those that dominate politics and public policy at the national level. It has led to heightened cultural visibility but also to what Urvashi Vaid calls "virtual equality."

This final chapter assesses the limitations of embracing either an assimilationist or a liberationist strategy exclusively. Instead, it argues that both approaches have worked in important and complementary ways throughout the movements' histories and are not mutually exclusive. In addition, both the assimilationist and the liberationist strategies are necessary for the future, as the movements attempt to navigate the aftermath of the George W. Bush presidency and a reinvigorated Christian Right movement at the national, state, and local levels. In the end, then, the dilemma presented throughout this book can be resolved by pursuing a dual organizing strategy, one that builds on the strengths of the assimilationist and liberationist strategies and one that recognizes the limitations of each approach to political and social change.

2

· ·

The Assimilationist and Liberationist Strategies in Historical Context

The emergence of gay liberation would not have been possible but for the long, lonely organizing efforts of the Mattachine Society and the Daughters of Bilitis and, indeed, of the pioneers to whom they looked for inspiration.

—Nicholas Edsall, *Toward Stonewall: Homosexuality and Society in the Western World*

••

HOW HAVE THE assimilationist and liberationist strategies developed over time? That is the prevailing question underlying this chapter. In answering this question, Chapter 2 places the development of the lesbian and gay movements within their necessary historical context. Like so many of the social movements that came of age during the 1960s and 1970s, the activism of lesbians and gays in this period was rooted in the events of previous eras. Popular lore has it that the contemporary lesbian and gay movements began with the Stonewall Rebellion of 1969. Historian George Chauncey (1994) has written of the extensive gay network that developed in the streets, apartments, saloons, and cafeterias of New York City in the late nineteenth and early twentieth centuries. When laws were enacted that prohibited lesbians and gays from gathering in any state-licensed public place, as a part of the virulent New York City crackdown of the 1930s, lesbians and gays fought for their rights in courageous ways—a precursor to the organized political resistance of the Daughters of Bilitis and Mattachine Society of the 1950s. Allan Berubé's pathbreaking work (1990) on lesbians and gays in the military during World War II found that the discriminatory and unjust treatment afforded them did not lead to an organized resistance movement per se, but it did inspire many lesbians and gay men to develop an all-important group identity. David K. Johnson's illuminating work (2004) on federal government policies during the cold war era in response to the so-called lavender menace provides concrete examples of individual and collective courage and resistance on the part of people who later organized for full citizen rights. John D'Emilio's important historical work (1983) chronicles the early years of the Mattachine Society and the Daughters of Bilitis, organizations that developed at the height of the McCarthy era, in the 1950s. And Barry Adam's study (1995) of the lesbian and gay movements focuses considerable attention on the rise of the homophile movement in the United States during the 1950s and the connections between that movement and the movements growing out of the Stonewall Rebellion of 1969. These themes will be explored throughout this chapter by making connections between the contemporary lesbian and gay movements and the organizing that preceded them.

The tensions between the assimilationist and liberationist perspectives are also developed in historical context. Much of the work of the contemporary national lesbian and gay organizations has relied on an insider assimilationist strategy, one that strives for access to those in power and is rooted in an interest-group and legislative-lobbying approach to political change. The strategy is centered on civil rights, legal reform, political access, visibility, and legitimation. It is an approach that reinforces the existing political and economic framework that is associated with classical liberalism. For those who embrace a liberationist approach, the assimilationist perspective is far too narrow. As Urvashi Vaid has argued, the assimilationist perspective is far too rooted in "virtual equality—a state of conditional equality based more on the appearance of acceptance of straight America than on genuine civic parity" (1995, xvi). Liberationists challenge "virtual equality" and emphasize the goals of cultural acceptance, social transformation, understanding, and liberation (ibid., 106).

One scholar of the movements believes that all of the organizing activity over the past fifty years or so "has had remarkable political effects" that resonate in the present (Eisenbach 2006, vi). What is his evidence for this claim? Looking back to the 2004 presidential election, David Eisenbach notes that "the news media focused on the gay marriage controversy and the debate over the Federal marriage amendment, but the presidential candidates themselves displayed a notable consensus in favor of gay rights" (ibid.). And this was particularly true of the candidates for the Democratic Party nomination, who all supported key elements of the contemporary assimilationist gay-rights agenda, including an increase in funding for HIV/AIDS research and services, the recognition of domestic partnerships, and sexual-orientation nondiscrimination laws. Three of the candidates supported same-sex marriage, but four opposed it, including John Kerry. Assimilationists would argue that all of this represents considerable progress, but liberationists would likely expect more concrete accomplishments that challenge the prevailing order of heteronormativity. As we will see, there are reasons for these differences in approaches to political and social change and how they have developed over time.

One of the central goals of the early lesbian and gay movements in the United States was to improve the media depiction of homosexuality. Indeed, before the development of the modern lesbian and gay rights movement that began in the 1950s, "the media commonly depicted homosexuals as insane deviants and sexual predators." With that in mind, movement activists recognized the importance of altering the media's portrayal of homosexuality and to ensure a more positive image, which was especially important as more people began to "come out of the closet." The hope was that positive press coverage would lead to the public recognizing that homosexuality was not a threat and that this, in turn, would lead to much greater "political and legal progress" (ibid., vii).

The Birth of the Homophile Movement and the Foundations for Contemporary Politics

The homophile movement arose within the context of a prevailing ideology that regarded lesbians and gays "as perverts, psychopaths, deviates, and the like." Lesbians and gays internalized these negative labels, which ultimately became stereotypes. As John D'Emilio points out, "whether seen from the vantage of religion, medicine, or the law, the homosexual or lesbian was a flawed individual, not a victim of injustice. For many, the gay world was reduced to a setting where they shared an affliction" (1983, 53).

In its early manifestations, the homophile movement embraced liberationist principles through the Mattachine Society. In 1951 Communist Party activist Harry Hay, then working at the Los Angeles People's Education Center as a music teacher, decided to form this organization along with several of his colleagues—Rudi Gernreich, Bob Hull, Dale Jennings, and Chuck Rowland. Hay and his coorganizers built the Mattachine Society based on communist principles of organizing and social change (Adam 1995, 67–68), a model that would soon lead to considerable controversy within the organization. Mattachine's founding statement of "Missions and Purposes" articulated the intended purposes of the new organization:

- "To unify" those homosexuals "isolated from their own kind. . . ."
- "To educate" homosexuals and heterosexuals toward "an ethical homosexual culture . . . paralleling the emerging cultures of our fellow-minorities—the Negro, Mexican, and Jewish Peoples. . . ."
- "To lead"; the "more . . . socially conscious homosexuals [are to] provide leadership to the whole mass of social deviates" and also

- To assist "our people who are victimized daily as a result of our oppression." (ibid., 68)

As the above principles suggest, the organizers wished to galvanize a large gay constituency, one that was cohesive and capable of militant activity (D'Emilio 1983, 63).

Mattachine emerged as the first effective gay political organization in the United States, one that in its early years devoted itself to challenging and repealing repressive legislation and altering public opinion. Out of a Mattachine discussion group emerged *One*, the first publicly distributed American homophile magazine. Two historians identify the important impact of *One*: "Against heavy odds in the midst of the reactionary McCarthy era, ONE made a considerable impact nationally, appearing on newsstands in several U.S. cities and selling about 5,000 copies a month, many of which passed through multiple hands" (Faderman and Timmons 2006, 116). The U.S. Post Office placed a ban on *One* in 1954 but was overruled in 1958 by the Supreme Court, which stated that the ban violated free-speech protections guaranteed by the First Amendment (Adam 1995, 68). This incident serves as a sobering reminder of the repressive nature of the times.

But the Mattachine Society was not immune to serious criticism. In 1953 the organizational structure and militant ideology of the Mattachine Society was challenged by rank-and-file organization members. A *Los Angeles Daily Mirror* columnist had identified Frank Snyder as the lawyer for the organization. Snyder had been an uncooperative witness when called to testify before the House Un-American Activities Committee. Given the repressive political and cultural climate associated with the McCarthy era, it is no surprise that rank-and-file Mattachine members grew increasingly concerned with the organization's possible association with communism (Hunt 1999, 129). The split that ultimately occurred between the organization's founders and its newer members reflected serious disagreements over assimilation and liberation, conflicts that have plagued the movements over the years. The Mattachine founders envisioned a separate homosexual culture, whereas other members worried that such a strategy would only increase the hostile social climate. Instead, they called for integration into mainstream society (D'Emilio 1983, 81). In the end, Harry Hay was expelled from the Mattachine Society in 1953, at the height of the McCarthy era, due to his Communist Party background and his unwavering support for more radical principles.

Hay's successors—Hal Call, Marilyn Reiger, and David Finn—and Phyllis Lyon and Del Martin, two lesbian activists who founded the Daughters of Bilitis in 1955, all embraced an assimilationist and accommodationist approach to political and social change. In practice, this meant the two groups sought to open a productive dialogue with an array of professionals or "experts" who had expressed views concerning homosexuality. Their strategy was to present themselves as reasonable, well-adjusted people, hoping that these heterosexual arbiters of public opinion would rethink their assumptions regarding homosexuality. This approach, rooted in dialogue, emphasized conformity and attempted to minimize any differences between heterosexuality and homosexuality. The activists hoped to de-emphasize sex, since the act of sex itself was the source of so much anger and fear directed at homosexuals. Ultimately, the architects of this assimilationist, accommodationist strategy hoped to reduce social hostility as a necessary precursor to the changes desired in both law and public policy (ibid., 109). They attempted to frame issues in ways that would accomplish this important goal.

The Daughters of Bilitis, San Francisco's second homophile organization, was founded by Lyon, Martin, and others in 1955. The organizers had no previous knowledge of the Mattachine Society. Their goal was to provide women an alternative to the bars in the form of a social club (Armstong 2002, 37). Although the Daughters of Bilitis eschewed much of the Mattachine Society's ideology and tactics, they agreed that publishing a newspaper was important and began distributing their own, the *Ladder*, in 1956. This paper came out regularly between 1956 and 1971 and garnered the DOB national attention. The Mattachine Society, the Daughters of Bilitis, and *One* and the *Ladder* were the central organized elements of the homophile movement until the 1969 Stonewall Riots. Both organizations, in their later stages, embraced public education as their primary assimilationist goal "because they believed that the source of prejudice is ignorance or a misinformed view of homosexuals as different and dangerous" (Seidman 2002, 175).

The assimilationist, accommodationist strategy prevailed within the broader movement until the 1969 Stonewall Rebellion. During that time the movement as a whole gained little ground and, in fact, experienced some significant setbacks. For example, a medical model of homosexuality gained currency in this period, one that equated homosexuality with mental illness. This made it even more difficult for lesbians and gays to come out of the closet and to enter mainstream American life. But there were challenges to the more mainstream homophile, assimilationist strategy by such activists as Barbara Gittings and Franklin Kameny. Gittings and Kameny began openly embracing unconventional politics and picketing for basic rights and human dignity. Kameny expressed the ideological foundations of the 1960s homophile movement by arguing that homosexuals did not suffer from mental illness, constituted 10 percent of the population at large, did not need medical experts to speak on their behalf, and had a right to live their lives free from discrimination (Clendinen and Nagourney 1999, 114). Several years later he commented on the appropriate use of various political tactics in light of the Stonewall Rebellion: "I don't believe in picketing until you've tried negotiation and gotten nowhere and then tried picketing and gotten nowhere, then . . . I'm perfectly willing to go along to the next step—which is probably some sort of confrontation that possibly mildly oversteps the bounds of the law. If that doesn't serve, I'm willing to draw the line further, although I do draw the line at violence" (Teal 1995, 73–74). Kameny's endorsement of a more radical political strategy was inspired by the African American civil rights movement. And Kameny was not the only one inspired by a rise in civil rights militancy. Indeed, as early as 1966, lesbian and gay activists adopted a symbol of the civil rights movement—a black and white civil rights lapel button with an equals sign on a lavender background, signaling their desire for more daring avenues to effect change. Kameny's endorsement of a more radical political strategy, with precedent in the African American civil rights movement, reflects some of the tensions that would soon be felt within the homophile movement as it came under increased criticism and scrutiny from more radically minded lesbian and gay activists who called for liberatory change in light of Stonewall. Such tensions have continued to pervade the movements.

At the time of Stonewall, the situation for lesbians, gay men, bisexuals, and transgender individuals was much different than it is today. For example, homosexual sex was illegal in all states except Illinois at the end of the 1960s. There were no laws on the book at *any* level of government that protected lesbians, gay men, bisexuals, or transgender individuals from being denied housing or fired from their jobs. In addition, no openly lesbian or gay politicians participated in politics anywhere in the United States. No political party had a gay caucus at that time. And there were few role models for young people who were struggling with their sexual orientation, as there were no openly gay or lesbian public school teachers, lawyers, doctors, or police officers. Unlike today, there were no television shows that had any identifiable lesbian or gay characters. Hollywood painted a particularly ugly view of gay life; most often, gay characters in movies killed other people or killed themselves (Carter 2004, 1–2). Those activists who were growing increasingly uncomfortable with more traditional forms of political organizing pointed to the lack of progress as evidence that a more radical, liberationist vision needed to be articulated.

But by the time of Stonewall, the lesbian and gay movements could also point to concrete accomplishments. The Supreme Court had affirmed the legality of lesbian and gay publications. A number of state court rulings afforded gay bars more security, and the homophile movement had won constraints on police harassment of lesbians and gays in New York and San Francisco. In employment discrimination cases, the federal court provided the first victories. A dialogue was established with members of the scientific community regarding whether homosexuality should be classified as a mental illness. The movements had begun to shift to occasional media visibility, largely as a result of the transition to public protest. At the time of the Stonewall Riots, there were perhaps some fifty lesbian and gay organizations nationwide. Finally, and perhaps most important, the notion that lesbians and gays were a persecuted minority had infiltrated not only the lesbian and gay subculture but also the larger society (D'Emilio 1992, 238–239).

Despite these accomplishments, the mainstream homophile organizations were thrown on the defensive in the wake of Stonewall, as a new style of political organizing and leadership was demanded by newly energized lesbian and gay activists, many of whom were veterans of the various social and political movements of the 1960s. This more confrontational, liberationist approach embraced the unconventional politics associated with the antiwar, women's liberation, and civil rights movements. What was the connection between the latter and the lesbian and gay movements? Grant Gallup, a priest who was active in the African American civil rights movement, makes the connection well: "Many of us who went south to work with Dr. King in the sixties were gay. A lot of gay people who could not come out for their own liberation could invest the same energies in the liberation of black people" (Kaiser 1997, 136). And veteran civil rights activist John Lewis makes important connections between the Mississippi Freedom Summer of 1964 and the movements that followed:

The atmosphere of openness and breaking down barriers that we developed
that summer extended far beyond issues of race. It extended into everything
from sexuality to gender roles, from communal living to identification with
working classes. And they live on today. I have no doubt that the Mississippi
Freedom Summer Project, in the end, led to the liberating of America, the
opening up of our society. The peace movement, the women's movement,
the gay movement—they all have roots that can be traced back to Mississippi in the summer of '64. (Lewis and D'Orso 1998, 273)

Lewis's observation reminds us of the important legacy that the African
American civil rights movement left for other rights-based movements
that developed throughout the decade of the 1960s.

Yet the rights-based strategy associated with the civil rights, women's,
and homophile movements came under increased scrutiny and criticism in
light of Stonewall. The modern gay liberation movement was soon born,
built on some of the same ideas that undergirded the original Mattachine
Society almost twenty years earlier. For those who embraced gay liberation,
a rights-based strategy was far too limited. In their view, the goal should be
to remake society, not merely reform it (Loughery 1998, 323).

The Stonewall Rebellion and Beyond

One way of thinking about the larger meaning of the Stonewall Rebellion
is that "political movements are not born fully formed; they require numerous acts of small-scale resistance." As we have already seen, there were
many small-scale acts of organizing, courage, and resistance in various
forms prior to Stonewall. One scholar believes that "without the prior activism, Stonewall might never have occurred, or rather, it might never
have been turned into a symbolic event of major importance" (Allyn 2000,
155). The Stonewall Rebellion not only escalated the call for a more activist posture within the lesbian and gay civil rights movement but also
fractured the movement into two distinct ideological strategic camps. On
June 27–28, 1969, scores of gay men, lesbians, and transvestites who fre-
quented a bar called the Stonewall Inn in New York City found themselves
in a dramatic confrontation with the police, who had decided to raid the
establishment that evening. The raid itself was not newsworthy, as the police routinely harassed gay men, lesbians, and transvestites wherever they
gathered, but the fact that they fought back this time was. The so-called

Stonewall Riot, which lasted on and off for six days, quickly threw the more mainstream organizations associated with the homophile movement on the defensive and led to the widely accepted conclusion that "these riots are widely credited with being the motivating force in the transformation of the gay political movement" (Carter 2004, 1).

It is in this broad context that the Gay Liberation Front (GLF) was founded in late 1969. Soon thereafter, similarly militant organizations were created in other countries, including Australia, Belgium, Britain, Canada, France, and the Netherlands, which is a testimony to how the Stonewall Rebellion had consequences for the international lesbian and gay rights movements. Toby Marotta captures the essence of the U.S. organization in its first few weeks of existence: "Radicals and revolutionaries shared the conviction that since every dimension of the existing system was bankrupt, a total transformation of society was desirable, and that to effect change, it was necessary to unite all oppressed minorities into a broad-based movement" (Loughery 1998, 324).

As it attempted to build the coalitions necessary for this movement, the GLF championed a broad New Left program. It attacked the consumer culture, militarism, racism, sexism, and homophobia. In challenging the latter, the GLF devoted considerable energy to how lesbians and gays were represented in the larger culture through language. With this in mind, the more widespread but clinical term *homosexual* was replaced by *gay,* "pride" became an important feature of liberation consciousness, and "coming out" was a crucial element of the liberatory experience (ibid., 321).

Within one year of the group's founding in New York, Gay Liberation Front organizations were born throughout the United States, including in Atlanta, Boston, Chicago, Iowa City, Los Angeles, Milwaukee, Portland, San Francisco, Seattle, and Washington, D.C. College students organized many local groups on their campuses (ibid., 325). Meetings were run according to participatory principles, and hierarchy was eschewed as much as possible. Thanks to the courage and hard work of lesbian and gay activists around the country, an impressive amount of organizing was done in a short period of time, confirming the liberationist message about the importance of coalition building and the historical context of the times.

The euphoria and sense of unity that accompanied the birth of the GLF were short-lived, as the post-Stonewall lesbian and gay movements faced the internal conflicts that beset many political and social movements in the late 1960s and early 1970s. There was considerable disagreement within the broader organization over its purpose (should it focus only on gay liberation, or should it be part of a larger political movement for progressive change?), its organizational structure, and the role of women and minorities. Disagreements over the treatment of women led to searing conflicts over sexism within the organization itself. In her memoir, *Tales of the Lavender Menace*, Karla Jay reveals the sexism she faced:

> Despite the push toward a gynandrous center, the sexism of some of the men was—for me, at least—the biggest obstacle toward immediately and completely immersing myself in GLF. A number of the men were more oppressive to women than any heterosexual guy I had known. A few of the men looked at me with such unveiled contempt that I started to give credence to the old adage that some men were gay because they hated or feared women. I'm sure that these guys would have preferred for the women to leave so that the GLF would become an all-men's group, sort of like a political bathhouse, where they could get naked with one another. If we were going to be there, however, a few men thought we might as well make ourselves useful by baking some cookies and making coffee. Some of the other women and I were constantly correcting men who called us "girls." "I'm a woman, not a 'girl.' How would [you] like me to call you 'boy'?" we'd remind them over and over. (1999, 82)

Disagreements over the treatment of women and other issues undermined the overall effectiveness of the GLF, and ultimately led to its destruction. But the lesbian and gay rights movements as a whole did not die out; they merely moved in a more assimilationist direction. As we have already seen, both before and after Stonewall, the movements were always much broader than one group. When the GLF fractured, another less radical organization called the Gay Activists Alliance (GAA) became more prominent in shaping the larger movements' strategies.

Formed by Jim Owles and Marty Robinson in New York City in December 1969, the GAA attempted to focus on the single issue of gay rights, without the issue fragmentation and anarchic organizational style that had characterized the GLF. After initially joining the GLF, Owles and Robinson increasingly became disenchanted with the organization's inability to plan effectively and to temper revolutionary New Left doctrine in an effort to address the daily discrimination faced by lesbians and gays (Adam 1995, 86). They were particularly concerned with the GLF's affiliation with other elements of the political Left, including the Black Panthers and the antiwar movement. To the critics of the GLF, such affiliations "drained energy from the homosexual rights cause," and some of the affiliated groups were also clearly antigay (Hunt 1999, 81).

The GAA membership thought that meaningful reform would occur only if lesbians and gays organized politically and exercised their political muscle to force positive change. Their involvement in electoral politics set the stage for a strategy that has come to dominate the contemporary mainstream lesbian and gay movements. Candidates for election were questioned extensively concerning their views regarding issues of interest to lesbians and gays.

The GAA also embraced direct action in the form of "zaps," that is, direct confrontations in public meetings, on city streets, and in offices. Zaps are carefully orchestrated disruptions of meetings or proceedings by protesters, who often use satirical humor as a way to capture attention (Cruikshank 1992, 77). Such nonviolent civil disobedience captured occasional media attention, disrupted the normal patterns of people's lives, and set the stage for the kind of political organizing associated with the AIDS Coalition to Unleash Power (ACT UP) in the late 1980s (as we will see in Chapter 3). In this way, the GAA's tactics were much closer to the GLF's than the Mattachine Society and Daughters of Bilitis pickets at the White House in the 1960s. Five demands were at the heart of GAA politics:

1. the repeal of New York State's sodomy and solicitation laws;
2. an end to police entrapment of gay men;
3. an end to police harassment of gay bars and an investigation into corruption in the New York State Liquor Authority;
4. a law protecting gays and lesbians against discrimination in employment; and
5. an end to the bonding company practice of denying bonds to gays and lesbians. (By refusing to bond gays and lesbians, bonding companies had the power to exclude them from jobs requiring bonding.) (Hunt 1999, 82)

The early GAA statement "What Is GAA?" stressed the organization's commitment "to a militant but nonviolent civil rights struggle and a membership open to all who shared this approach and objective." Bob

Kohler, a veteran GLF organizer, responded to the more assimilationist GAA approach by calling it "well-mannered conformist shit." On the other hand, Kay Tobin, one of just a handful of women involved in the early years of the GAA's existence, claimed that it was "an exciting place for a range of us who weren't out-and-out revolutionaries" (Loughery 1998, 329). Most acknowledge that the GAA was even less responsive to women and people of color than the GLF had been. GAA members were charged with tokenism when it came to dealing with issues of race and feminism (ibid., 331).

One major accomplishment of the GAA is that it established institutional structures that proved to be more long lasting than those created by the GLF. Indeed, many of these institutional structures have been embraced by an array of lesbian and gay organizations operating at the national level today (see Appendix 3). The GAA ceased formal operations in 1974, soon after its community center suffered a catastrophic fire, but many of the organization's activists founded the National Gay Task Force, which today is the National Gay and Lesbian Task Force (Hunt 1999, 82).

William Eskridge describes the long-term effects of the Stonewall Rebellion: "Literally overnight, the Stonewall riots transformed the *homophile reform movement* of several dozen homosexuals into a *gay liberation movement* populated by thousands of lesbians, gay men, and bisexuals who formed hundreds of organizations demanding radical changes in the way people were treated by the state" (1999, 99; emphasis in the original). The movement introduced four key ideas into the existing homophile movement that remain relevant even now. First, the importance of "coming out" as a crucial personal and political statement is integral to movement politics today. Second, it was thought that a more visible lesbian and gay presence would challenge traditional notions of the family, gender roles, and sexism. Third, Stonewall and its aftermath created a lesbian and gay counterculture (one that included bisexuals and transgender individuals), which helped to establish lesbian and gay identity, thus providing a foundation for the identity-politics strain in the movements today. (This counterculture has been assailed by conservatives, and the progressive Left has taken issue with identity politics.) Finally, the politics of the late 1960s and early 1970s emphasized that the lesbian and gay movements could not be divorced from movements addressing broader economic concerns, gender, and race. A mere rights-based agenda was far too narrow. The principle remains as controversial now as it was when the

GLF introduced it to the existing homophile movement almost thirty years ago. Should the movements embrace a single-issue politics or attempt to build coalitions with other aggrieved groups to foster more progressive social change? This issue continues to tear at the fabric of the movements and is an important question underlying this book as we consider the assimilationist and liberationist perspectives critically.

The 1970s and the Challenge of the Christian Right

Perhaps the greatest policy success of the early 1970s was the 1973–1974 decision of the American Psychiatric Association (APA) to remove homosexuality from its "official Diagnostic and Statistical Manual list of mental disorders." This decision did not come about because a group of doctors suddenly changed their views; it followed an aggressive and sustained campaign by lesbian and gay activists (Loughery 1998, 345). In order to bring about this important policy change, the movements used a combination of insider and outsider strategies with considerable skill and effectiveness. These involved a "louder watchdog presence at psychiatric conferences, behind-the-scenes lobbying, alliances with friendly and influential members of the APA, contact with regional psychiatric societies, the presentation of alternative papers, and a parade of 'healthy homosexuals.'" Most important, activists recognized, in the words of Ronald Gold, "when to scream and when not to. It's an art. It's the art of politics" (ibid., 346). Some ten years later, in the midst of the AIDS crisis, the ability to understand when insider and outsider politics might be most effective proved crucial to the maturing lesbian and gay movements. The "grassroots politics of knowledge" that the movements developed in their struggle with the American Psychiatric Association had consequences for later challenges to the federal government's policies on AIDS research (Escoffier 1980, 139), as we will see in Chapter 3.

But the movements' accomplishments in the arena of psychiatry and in other areas were viewed with increasing concern on the part of those who feared any challenge to the primacy of heterosexuality in all institutions of American society. The Christian Right and other antigay conservatives consistently identified homosexuality as evidence of moral degeneracy in society as a whole. As such, they reacted to movement gains with hostility and a commitment to organizing their own grassroots constituency to undo such victories. During the 1970s, largely as a result of the Christian

Right's effective mobilization, the lesbian and gay movements suffered major setbacks both locally and nationally. Six antigay referenda appeared in 1977 and 1978 alone.

One of the most effective spokespersons for the Christian Right position was Anita Bryant, a celebrity singer and the second runner-up in the 1959 Miss America contest, who helped to galvanize conservative opposition to lesbian and gay rights in 1977 with her "Save Our Children" campaign based in Dade County, Florida. The goal of this campaign was "to convince voters that tolerance of homosexuality threatened society" (Eisenbach 2006, 279). In her first public statement endorsing the Save Our Children campaign, Bryant proclaimed:

> I don't hate homosexuals! But as a mother I must protect my children from their evil influence. Defending the rights of my children and yours. Militant homosexuals want their sexual behavior and preference to be considered respectable and accepted by society. They want to recruit your children and teach them the virtue of becoming a homosexual. . . . I don't hate homosexuals. I love them enough to tell them the truth. . . . [We] must not give them the legal right to destroy the moral fiber of our families and our nation. (ibid., 280)

As an evangelist singer, national promoter of Florida orange juice, and the mother of two children, Bryant was a perfect spokesperson for the Christian Right. Her successful fight to persuade voters to rescind a six-month-old Dade County, Florida, civil rights ordinance garnered considerable national attention in the mainstream press (Alwood 1996, 167). In challenging the Dade County ordinance, Bryant made two arguments that helped her cause. First, she insisted that the new law "discriminates against my children's rights to grow up in a healthy, decent atmosphere" (Loughery 1998, 373). Second, she claimed that God had called her to fight against "preferential legislation" that endorsed a degraded "lifestyle" (ibid., 127). Both of these arguments have been invoked by opponents of lesbian and gay rights over the years, but the latter was particularly important. One activist astutely concluded that "gay rights was in trouble, the day 'special rights' was born" (ibid., 374).

The reactionary climate of the late 1970s was ripe for Bryant's campaign. The Save Our Children organization, which led the Dade County fight, represented a profile of anti–lesbian and gay forces, forces that would galvanize in response to AIDS, the integration of the military, and same-sex marriage, as we will see later in this book. It galvanized conservative religious leaders and politicians; the campaign itself was founded on fundamentalist church networks, and Bryant obtained active support from the National Association of Evangelicals, which represented "more than three million people from 60 denominations" (Adam 1995, 110). The association's television programs, the *PTL Club, 700 Club,* and *The Old-Time Gospel Hour,* afforded Bryant a national platform and raised funds on her behalf. Moral Majority founder Jerry Falwell campaigned against the Dade County ordinance in person, and the direct-mail political lobby Christian Cause extended its organizing efforts into Jewish and Roman Catholic hierarchies. Opposition to the Dade County ordinance arose at the local level as well. For example, Miami's archbishop distributed a pastoral letter to local Roman Catholic churches, exhorting their congregations to vote against lesbian and gay civil rights. The president of the Miami Beach B'nai B'rith and twenty-eight rabbis publicly lent their support to Bryant's cause (ibid.).

The civil rights ordinance resurfaced in 1998, when the Miami–Dade County commissioners voted seven to six to ban discrimination based on sexual orientation. Even the narrow margin of the victory could not detract later from the importance of this victory for the lesbian and gay movements. The 1977 repeal had attracted considerable press attention, and Anita Bryant was now a national figure. She capitalized on her victory by launching an anti-gay-rights campaign throughout the United States. By June 1978 voters in Eugene, Oregon; St. Paul, Minnesota; and Wichita, Kansas, had also rescinded local ordinances that had protected the basic rights of lesbians and gays. Fundamentalist churches, with the financial support of the business community, constituted the foundation of the antigay movement. By 1978, then, the conservative opposition against lesbian and gay rights had solidified and gained momentum. But this did not mean that the opposition was invincible. The lesbian and gay movements proved that they could organize an effective response (Button, Rienzo, and Wald 1997, 69). One of their most successful organizing campaigns came in California in response to the Briggs initiative.

The day after the 1977 Miami vote, California state senator John Briggs, from conservative Orange County, announced his plans to introduce legislation that would prevent lesbians and gays from teaching in California's public schools. When it became obvious that the legislation had little chance of passing, Briggs altered his tactics and organized a campaign to have his proposal placed on the ballot in the form of a statewide initiative (D'Emilio 1992, 89). Within eleven months of Bryant's victory, Briggs filed the half-million signatures that he needed to introduce a voter referendum that would force the removal of lesbian and gay teachers from California's public schools. In May 1978, Briggs had hoped that his teachers' initiative, his support for a second initiative that would expand the use of the death penalty in California, and his public association with Anita Bryant would help make him a strong candidate for governor (Clendinen and Nagourney 1999, 376). Briggs attempted to build on some of the organizing strategies used by Bryant. Although he lacked her connections to the Christian Right, he tried to appeal to the same forces in California, and nationally, with the help of Bryant's contributor list. But Briggs miscalculated severely. In the end, the voters in California overwhelmingly defeated his Proposition 6 by a margin of 58 percent to 42 percent. Lesbian and gay activists worked together in a display of solidarity that overcame gender divides to help defeat the amendment. On the same night, Seattle voters defeated an initiative that would have repealed its gay rights law, by a margin of 63 percent to 37 percent (ibid., 389). As the decade of the 1970s approached its final year, these were two important and highly visible victories for the lesbian and gay rights movements.

The 1970s also witnessed an increase in anti–lesbian and gay violence, as "fag bashings" became more commonplace throughout the United States. Antigay violence attracted considerable public attention in 1978 when Dan White, a member of the San Francisco Board of Supervisors, climbed into an open city hall window and then shot and killed openly gay board member Harvey Milk and Mayor George Moscone, who had supported Milk and lesbian and gay rights more generally. This broader societal hostility that developed in the 1970s helped set the context for how many would react to gay men with the onset of AIDS in the summer of 1981 (and beyond) during conservative president Ronald Reagan's first year in office.

Conclusion

This chapter began by asking how the assimilationist and liberationist strategies have developed over time. In answering this question, we have placed the development of the lesbian and gay movements within their proper historical context. We have seen how tensions between the assimilationist and liberationist strategies have manifested themselves in the pre-Stonewall and post-Stonewall eras. The 1969 Stonewall Rebellion was an important moment in the development of the lesbian and gay movements because mainstream homophile organizations were thrown on the defensive. The rights-based strategy associated with the civil rights, women's, and homophile movements came under increased scrutiny and criticism in light of the Stonewall uprising. What has come to be known as the modern gay liberation movement was born in the face of Stonewall, a movement that was built on some of the same ideas that undergirded the original Mattachine Society almost twenty years earlier. But we cannot refer to the complicated forces that constitute lesbian, gay, bisexual, and transgender organizing as a single movement, given the complicated array of identities involved, as later chapters will make clear.

The lesbian and gay movements achieved a number of victories by the mid-1970s; among the most prominent was the American Psychiatric Association's 1973–1974 decision to remove homosexuality from its Diagnostic and Statistical Manual (DSM) list of mental disorders. This victory, as well as others, was the result of consistent and persistent political organizing. The Christian Right responded to these perceived gains by linking homosexuality with moral degeneracy in society writ large. This theme manifested itself in Anita Bryant's Save Our Children campaign and John Briggs's proposed amendment to prevent lesbian and gay teachers from teaching in California's public schools. The Christian Right's organizing efforts were an augury of the shape of things to come—in the 1980s in response to the onset of HIV/AIDS, in the 1990s in response to military integration, and in the early twenty-first century in response to same-sex marriage.

All of the organizing activity over the past fifty years or so on the part of the lesbian and gay movements and their opponents has had consequences for contemporary politics and policy surrounding sexual-diversity issues today. We examine this argument in the development of HIV/AIDS activism and policy in the next chapter.

3

....

The Conflict Over HIV/AIDS Policy

We will never know how my generation of gay men would have evolved without AIDS.

—Andrew Hollernan

AIDS was divine retribution against the "pederast proletariat."

—Pat Buchanan

The story of the gay response to the AIDS epidemic is about how a community responded to attacks on multiple levels: on the very lives and bodies of those who claimed membership and on its sexual practices, its organizations, and the assumptions around which it was organized.

—Elizabeth A. Armstrong, *Forging Gay Identities: Organizing Sexuality in San Francisco, 1950–1994*

IN WHAT WAYS did the onset of AIDS in the United States during the early 1980s affect the lesbian and gay movements in terms of their organizing and political strategies? How have the movements intersected with the policy process over time as AIDS has developed in America and on a global scale? These are the two questions that are at the core of this chapter. In answering them, we explore the tensions between those activists who embraced an insider assimilationist strategy and those who demanded an outsider liberationist strategy to political and social change, as reflected in the broader movements' responses to AIDS policy. As we explore this tension, we will devote considerable attention to the historical development of AIDS policy and AIDS activism in the United States. It is argued that AIDS changed the landscape of lesbian and gay politics, mobilizing an array of newly politicized activists in the midst of a staggering epidemic that has so far claimed and disrupted millions of lives in America and throughout the world. Direct-action organizations such as ACT UP, the Lesbian Avengers, and Queer Nation grew out of the many policy and political challenges posed by AIDS and demanded a liberationist organizing strategy. Other organizations, such as the Treatment Action Group, did vital AIDS policy work from within the policy process. In examining the development of HIV/AIDS within an appropriate historical context, we will interrogate the intersection between the lesbian and gay movements and the national policy process with particular attention to the presidencies of Ronald Reagan, George H. W. Bush, Bill Clinton, and George W. Bush. This is a particularly opportune time to do so given that the twenty-fifth anniversary of AIDS occurred in June 2006. Numbers provide a sense of the devastating toll of AIDS in the United States. As of 2006, more than 1 million Americans were infected with HIV, the human immunodeficiency virus, and more than 500,000 had died of AIDS, "or autoimmune deficiency syndrome, the weakening of the body's own natural defenses caused by the virus. New infections surged between 2002 and 2003, adding a quarter of a million new cases to the rolls." By 2006, it was clear that the United States had "the most severe HIV epidemic of any developed country" and that anyone was at risk (Hunter 2006, x). But this was particularly true for African Americans, who were becoming HIV positive at a much greater rate than other segments of the population, and for gay men, who were also becoming HIV positive at an alarming rate. The response of the lesbian and gay movements and the federal government needs to be situated within this broad framework of how AIDS policy has developed over time.

Several broad themes are explored. First, it is important to recognize that some of the same lesbian and gay activists who engaged in radical forms of AIDS activism have also run for political offices and have taken seats on government regulatory organizations, such as TAG (Goldstone 2003, 3). In this way, these activists have worked both within and outside of the policy process. Second, in trying to ascertain the response of policymakers at all levels of government, it is equally important to understand that when AIDS was first recognized in the United States, it affected those groups that were the objects of negative perceptions by many Americans and had little political power: sexually active gay men, intravenous drug users, people who suffered from hemophilia, and Haitian immigrants (Siplon 2002, 4). Third, the larger lesbian and gay communities and their straight supporters were able to respond more convincingly to the challenges of HIV/AIDS than other affected groups for an array of reasons, not the least of which was their intensity of political and social organizing that developed out of necessity over time. HIV-positive and -negative lesbians and gay men came together to confront the challenges of AIDS in their communities by creating an array of service organizations, such as the Gay Men's Health Crisis in New York City and the Whitman Walker Institute in Washington, D.C. They played an active role in policy formation and treatment in the face of government indifference (ibid., 8). In doing so, they were aware that public health professionals and government officials could do considerable harm by adopting policies, such as mandatory testing, that were viewed as discriminatory in a highly charged conservative political climate. Fourth, this chapter analyzes the enduring tension between those who argue that we need increased resources for care and treatment and those who claim that we need resources to stop the epidemic. Finally, this chapter explores how the Christian Right and other conservatives have responded to AIDS over time. A major goal is to examine the circumstances under which the assimilationist and liberationist strategies were effective, as well as how the Christian Right responded to these various tactics by using the threat of AIDS as part of its successful fund-raising approach.

AIDS in Historical Context

AIDS first appeared on the scene in the summer of 1981. The *New York Times* reported on July 3 that forty-one gay men were dying from a rare cancer, as well as infectious complications, that stemmed from the depression of the immune system, the cause of which was unexplainable at the time. By 1982 and 1983, the seriousness of the AIDS epidemic "was widely experienced by gay men, not only as a threat to new-found sexual freedoms, but to the broad social and political gains of the community as a whole" (Odets 1995, 121). Many of the initial patients had too many sexual partners in common to be a coincidence. As a result, "sex was quickly isolated as the most likely and perhaps primary means of transmission." The Centers for Disease Control and Prevention (CDC) in Atlanta, the U.S. government agency responsible for tracking the development and incidence of the disease in the United States over time, used existing data regarding male sexual partners to conclude that "repeated exposure to a series of STDs [sexually transmitted diseases] could be leading to the breakdown of the immune system in afflicted individuals" (Bereznai 2006, 225). This information was then used as the foundation for early prevention efforts, and it helped to cement in the public's mind (not to mention in the minds of journalists, politicians, and many in the medical-service delivery process) that AIDS was a "gay disease." Indeed, in the early years the syndrome had two names—"AID for acquired immunodeficiency disease, and GRID for gay-related immunodeficiency" (Engel 2006, 6). All of this had early policy ramifications as well as consequences for those who were stigmatized for being "at risk" for contracting HIV/AIDS. Researchers considered an array of explanations for the cause and dissemination of HIV/AIDS in the early years, but none appeared to be satisfactory (ibid., 7). Within two years, however, on March 3, 1983, the CDC made an official announcement that four groups were particularly vulnerable to AIDS: "homosexual men who had multiple sexual partners, intravenous heroin injectors, Haitians who had immigrated into the United States in recent years, and hemophiliacs" (Siplon 2002, 6). All of these groups reacted to this official CDC announcement in different ways.

By 1984, there was little evidence that AIDS was spreading into the population at large, as fewer than 1,500 people had died from the disease. But the exponential growth pattern within the gay male community suggested an epidemic, one that would not peak anytime soon. With this in mind, gay community advocates demanded that the National Institutes of Health (NIH) devote more funding to basic research. Activist Larry Kramer was particularly vocal when he complained "in late 1983 that the agency was planning to commit only $5 million in funding to AIDS-related projects the following year out of a budget of over $4 billion, despite having already received grant requests for $55 million" (Engel 2006, 21–22). What understandably annoyed Kramer even further is that the NIH had already committed $8 million of its yearly budget to conducting such research, but the money had not yet been spent (ibid., 22).

An array of mainstream politicians also accused the NIH of a laggard response to a growing crisis. Critics pointed out that previous outbreaks of Legionnaires' disease and the swine flu had received immediate attention from the federal government, and they argued that AIDS deserved the same. The National AIDS Vigil Commission, which included prominent political leaders Senators Edward Kennedy (D-MA) and Lowell Weicker (R-CT) and Mayors Dianne Feinstein (D-San Francisco) and Marion Barry (D-Washington, D.C.), marched on Washington, D.C., in an effort to inspire greater federal government attention to AIDS (ibid., 22). But AIDS struck at a terrible political time, one that witnessed the rise of a new fiscal and social conservatism with the election of Ronald Reagan and a more conservative Congress in 1980. In addition, Christian Right fundamentalists had accumulated greater power in American politics and policy. The growth of the Christian Right is epitomized by the rise of the Moral Majority, an organization rooted in religious fundamentalism and committed to grassroots mobilization of its constituency to elect conservative politicians at all levels of government. Galvanized by Reagan's election and the defeat of a number of liberal Democratic senators, the Moral Majority and other Christian Right groups called for the defeat of members of Congress who opposed their conservative moral agenda.

The Reagan/Bush Years

The larger political culture quickly moved right as well. The Christian Right and other antigay conservatives identified homosexuality as evidence of moral degeneracy in society as a whole and AIDS as a punishment for homosexual behavior. The new conservatism engendered hostility toward those with AIDS, who were scapegoated and stigmatized (Koop 1991, 198). It was widely reported as well that Christian Right groups such as the Moral Majority successfully blocked funding for AIDS educational programs and counseling and other services for people with AIDS (PWAs). Pat Buchanan, a former White House aide, expressed a particularly ugly view of homosexuality and its connection to AIDS, when he proclaimed in 1983, "The poor homosexuals. They have declared war on nature and now nature is exacting an awful retribution." Norman Podhoretz, *Commentary* magazine editor, assailed AIDS funding efforts because he perceived that they were "giving social sanction to what can only be described as a brutish degradation." Phyllis Schlafly, executive director of the Eagle Forum, castigated the federal government and AIDS activists for failing to respond properly: "Why are young boys and men not warned that all who engage in homosexual activities can expect to become infected with AIDS? Why is AIDS presented by the media as a homosexuals' civil-rights problem instead of as a public health problem which the government can isolate and treat?" At various points in the epidemic, conservatives called for the quarantining and tattooing of PWAs. For example, *National Review* editor William F. Buckley wrote in March 1986, "Everyone detected with AIDS should be tattooed in the upper forearm, to protect common-needle users, and on the buttocks, to prevent the victimization of other homosexuals" (Engel 2006, 70–71). And Jerry Falwell, the leader of the Moral Majority, was quoted as saying that AIDS "was the judgment of God. . . . You can't fly into the laws of God and God's nature without paying the price" (Clendinen and Nagourney 1999, 488).

It was against this political and cultural backdrop that the Reagan administration's lack of response to AIDS, especially in the early years, must be situated. The rise of the Christian Right and a general climate of conservatism was coupled with the presidential campaign and election of Reagan in 1980. When AIDS was first reported in 1981, Reagan had just assumed office and was pursuing his conservative agenda by slashing social programs and cutting taxes, while at the same time embracing traditional moral values. Reagan did not even mention the acronym *AIDS* publicly until 1987, when he spoke at the Third International AIDS Conference held in Washington, D.C. His administration did little to support medical research, expedite the testing and release of AIDS-related drugs, or promote AIDS education. Reagan's only concrete proposal as of 1987 was to call for widespread, routine testing. The death of his close friend Rock Hudson from AIDS in 1985 had no significant impact on Reagan's policies, although his biographer has said that he was deeply affected personally (Cannon 1991, 814). For Reagan and his advisers, AIDS was not a national problem; instead, it was a series of local problems to be dealt with by states and localities, not the federal government. This stance helped to fragment the limited governmental response early in the AIDS epidemic.

Reagan and his advisers perceived that AIDS presented serious political risks. As a presidential candidate, Reagan had promised to eliminate the role of the federal government in the already limited U.S. welfare state, as well as to embrace social policies that promoted "family values." In the critical 1984–1985 years of the epidemic, Reagan thought of AIDS as if "it was measles and it would go away." Reagan's principal biographer, Lou Cannon, characterizes the president's response as "halting and ineffective" (ibid.). It is not surprising that given his own morally conservative ideology and the strong conservative ethos of almost all of his appointees that the administration had such a poor response to an emerging health crisis, one that affected those who were perceived to be at the margins of American society. For example, in the early 1980s, senior officials from the Department of Health and Human Services maintained publicly for political reasons that they had enough resources to address the AIDS crisis, while behind the scenes they pleaded for additional funding. The administration undercut federal efforts to confront AIDS in a meaningful way by refusing to spend the money Congress allocated for AIDS research (Rimmerman 2002, 88).

Reagan and his close political advisers also successfully prevented his surgeon general, Dr. C. Everett Koop, from discussing AIDS publicly until Reagan's second term. According to a mandate of Congress, the surgeon general's chief responsibility is to promote the health of the American people and to inform the public about the prevention of disease. In the Reagan administration, however, the surgeon general's role was to promote the administration's conservative social agenda, especially prolife and family issues. Thus, at a time when the surgeon general could have played an invaluable role in public health education, Koop was prevented from addressing AIDS publicly. Then, in February 1986, Reagan asked Koop to write a report on the AIDS epidemic. Koop had come to the attention of conservatives in the Reagan administration because of his leading role in the antiabortion movement. Reagan administration officials fully expected Koop to embrace conservative principles in his report on AIDS (ibid.). But as one historian accurately points out, "Koop nonetheless contradicted his conservative views on other subjects to take up the cudgel for a nondiscriminatory approach to the epidemic" (Baldwin 2005, 99).

When the "Surgeon General's Report on Acquired Immune Deficiency Syndrome" was released to the public on October 22, 1986, it was a call for federal action in response to AIDS, and it underscored the importance of a comprehensive AIDS education strategy, beginning in grade school. Koop advocated the widespread distribution of condoms and concluded that mandatory identification of people with HIV or any form of quarantine would be useless in addressing AIDS. As part of Koop's broad federal education strategy, the Public Health Service mailed AIDS information to 107 million American households. Koop's actions brought him into direct conflict with William Bennett, Reagan's secretary of education. Bennett opposed Koop's recommendations and called for compulsory HIV testing of foreigners applying for immigration visas, for marriage license applicants, for all hospital patients, and for prison inmates (Rimmerman 2002, 88–89).

Not surprisingly, the Reagan administration did little to prohibit discrimination against people with HIV/AIDS. The administration placed responsibility for addressing AIDS discrimination issues with the states rather than with the federal government. In the face of federal inaction, some states and localities passed laws that prohibited HIV/AIDS discrimination, but many remained passive in the face of federal government indifference. It took the Supreme Court, in its 1987 *School Board of Nassau County, Fla. v. Arline* decision, to issue a broad ruling that was widely interpreted as protecting those with HIV/AIDS from discrimination in federal executive agencies, in federally assisted programs or activities, or by businesses with federal contracts (ibid., 89).

Reagan did appoint the Presidential Commission on the Human Immunodeficiency Virus Epidemic in the summer of 1987; it was later renamed the Watkins Commission, after its chair, Admiral James D. Watkins. With the appointment of this commission, Reagan was able to placate those who demanded a more consistent and sustained federal response to AIDS. He also answered the concerns of the Christian Right by appointing to the commission few scientists who had participated in AIDS research and few physicians who had actually treated PWAs. In addition, the commission included outspoken opponents of AIDS education (ibid.).

In retrospect, it is clear that the commission was created to deflect attention from the administration's own inept policy response to AIDS. The Watkins Commission's final report did recommend a more sustained federal commitment to address AIDS, but this recommendation was largely ignored by both the Reagan and the Bush administrations. In fact, none of the commissions studying AIDS over the years has recommended a massive federal effort to confront AIDS at all levels of society. How might history view the Reagan approach to AIDS policy? Don Francis, a Centers for Disease Control official, gave one answer in his testimony before a congressional committee on March 16, 1987:

> Much of the HIV/AIDS epidemic was and continues to be preventable. But because of active obstruction of logical policy, active resistance to essential funding, and active interference with scientifically designed programs, the executive branch of this country has caused untold hardship, misery, and expense to the American public. Its effort with AIDS will stand as a huge scar in American history, a shame to our nation and an international disgrace. (Andriote 1999, 143–144)

In what ways did the Bush presidency represent a point of departure from the Reagan administration's AIDS policies? As a sitting vice president, George H. W. Bush had to balance his role as Reagan's adviser with his role as a presidential candidate in the 1988 election. As a candidate, Bush appealed to the Christian Right by endorsing policies that would publicly identify people who were HIV positive and that would require mandatory HIV tests when people applied for marriage licenses. On the campaign trail, Bush argued that HIV testing is more effective than spending money on treatment. After Bush's election in 1988, he continued most of the policies of the Reagan era. Bush did appear, however, to be more sensitive to the magnitude of the AIDS crisis.

The Bush administration continued Reagan's fiscal austerity with respect to AIDS. In addition, Bush embraced mandatory testing to prevent the spread of AIDS. Finally, his administration argued that local officials should design and implement AIDS educational strategies, although federal resources could be used to gather more AIDS information. His surgeon general, Dr. Antonia Novello, generally maintained a low profile on AIDS issues.

It was not until March 30, 1990, almost nine years after AIDS was first identified and more than a year into his presidency, that George Bush gave his first speech on AIDS. He praised his administration's efforts in dealing with the AIDS crisis and asked the country to end discrimination against those infected with HIV. At the same time, Bush refused to eliminate a federal policy that placed restrictions on HIV-positive foreigners who wished to enter the United States. However, he did sign the Ryan White Comprehensive AIDS Resource Emergency (CARE) Act into law in 1990, although he consistently opposed funding this legislation to the level its congressional supporters requested. The legislation was originally designed to provide federal assistance for urban areas that were hardest hit by AIDS; it was later renamed for Ryan White, an Indiana boy who contracted AIDS from a contaminated blood transfusion and whose case received considerable media attention. The legislation was cosponsored by Orrin Hatch (R-UT) and Henry Waxman (D-CA) in the House of Representatives and Edward Kennedy (D-MA) in the Senate. It "provided substantial funds for a variety of purposes, including emergency assistance to the states and health services research." The Title I provision attracted the most attention, as it authorized "hundreds of millions of dollars to the worst-afflicted cities and metropolitan areas in the country. These 13 cities contained over 65 percent of all diagnosed AIDS cases in the country, and were facing dire shortfalls in funds for emergency medical care, public hospitals, private clinics, private hospital reimbursement, and emergency social services for AIDS patients and their families" (Engel 2006, 180). The fact that Congress passed the Ryan White Act and that President Bush signed it into law reflected the slowly changing political climate, the dire lack of funding available to urban areas struggling with the AIDS crisis, and the important organizing work done by the lesbian and gay movements, who fought for consistent and increased funding from all levels of government. Given that AIDS in the United States was first recognized in large urban areas, especially Los Angeles, New York City, and San Francisco, it is not surprising that AIDS activists used the language of "urban disaster" to heighten public attention (Siplon 2002, 94–95). As we will see later in this chapter, disputes have arisen through the years over how resources provided under the Ryan White Act have been used. The debates over spending have accompanied reauthorization of the legislation in 1995–1996, 2000, and 2006.

Even President Bush began to recognize that his administration could not completely ignore the AIDS crisis. Besides signing the Ryan White Act, he called for the passage of antidiscrimination laws to protect those who had HIV/AIDS. In addition, he spoke of the need for greater compassion for those struck by AIDS and their families. And when he appointed Earvin "Magic" Johnson to the National Commission on AIDS (a carry-over from the Reagan years), he received considerable credit, given Johnson's visibility in the world of professional basketball and given the shock of the nation's reaction to the fall 1991 news that he was HIV positive. But AIDS activists, as well as outspoken members of Congress such as Representatives Henry Waxman and Gerry Studds (D-MA), protested the administration's underfinanced and underdeveloped AIDS educational plan, while also deploring its failure to fund key federal AIDS initiatives directed at prevention, research, and treatment (Engel 2006, 189–191).

The chairwoman of the National Commission on AIDS, June Osborn, criticized the president and his cabinet for failing to provide decisive leadership in "leading the national response" (ibid., 191). And Magic Johnson resigned from the AIDS commission in frustration when it became apparent to him (and many others) that he was being exploited for his name and that President Bush had abdicated his own leadership responsibilities in confronting the AIDS crisis in meaningful ways.

Presidents often maintain a low profile with respect to newly identified public health hazards, perceiving them to offer limited political gain and many risks. The response of Presidents Ronald Reagan and George Bush to AIDS fits this pattern. In this case, Reagan and Bush were clearly uncomfortable with a major health problem that targeted those at the margins of American society—gay men and intravenous drug users residing largely in inner cities. Their views of the world simply did not allow for those most despised by society at large to receive their support. Indeed, many of those who assumed power in both administrations embraced political and personal beliefs hostile to gay men and lesbians. The prevailing conservative climate enabled the Reagan and Bush administrations' indifference toward AIDS (Rimmerman 2002, 87).

The Response of the Lesbian/Gay Movements to the Reagan/Bush Years

The lesbian and gay movements endured serious divisions over the treatment of women in the late 1960s and 1970s. Profoundly influenced by the women's movement, lesbian separatists "rejected the gay rights movement as irredeemably misogynist and sexist." Capturing the spirit of the times, Jill Johnston wrote in 1975 that "lesbians are feminists, not homosexuals"

(Gregory 2001, 159). The gap between men and women within the larger movements would continue well into the 1980s, with occasional interruptions, such as when lesbians and gay men joined forces to fight John Briggs's initiative in California in 1978, which would have prevented out lesbian and gay teachers from teaching in the public schools. But when the AIDS crisis produced a tremendous antigay backlash in the 1980s, many lesbians and gay men recognized the importance of putting aside differences in the short term to respond to the heightened bigotry and prejudice that accompanied AIDS. It is no surprise, then, that one leading scholar of the movements would write that "although an AIDS movement and a gay and lesbian movement are conceptually distinct, in practice the boundary proved porous. . . . And AIDS, by arousing from apathy an economically privileged segment of the community, tapped resources that have allowed us to make the transition from a movement of only volunteers to one with an ever-growing number of full-time paid workers" (D'Emilio 2002, 76). Indeed, lesbians and gays who lived in smaller cities and towns in the 1980s established their first organizations with the creation of AIDS service groups; these organizations soon led to opportunities for political organizing. One major reason the lesbian and gay community chose to create their own service organizations is "because it did not want the government and public health professionals to do more, if 'more' meant crafting policies that it feared would be discriminatory and even punitive toward members of the community" (Siplon 2002, 8).

In the face of governmental indifference in the early years, the lesbian and gay movements had to offer their own responses to the emerging crisis. For example, a May 1983 brochure published by AIDS Project/LA offered several preventive measures that individuals could take. They included "eat a nutritionally balanced diet" as well as "reduce your number of sexual partners" (Bereznai 2006, 226). Community organizations that were located in major urban areas, such as AIDS Project/LA, helped fill the void that should have been played by the federal, state, and local governments in responding to AIDS with resources for educational outreach and other social service programs.

The AIDS crisis also politicized an entire generation of lesbian and gay activists. New organizations sprang up in communities throughout the United States, organizations that were created to care for the sick and to organize on behalf of increased attention being devoted to AIDS prevention, treatment, and the drug development process. The issue of how to get those in power at all levels of government to respond to AIDS challenged the lesbian and gay movements in ways that they had never been challenged before. These failures of leadership at all levels of government forced lesbian and gay activists to confront two key dilemmas, articulated so well by Urvashi Vaid: "How were we going to get a response from an administration that did not care about us? And how were we going to motivate and mobilize a community that was largely in the closet and invisible?" (1995, 72–73). The lesbian and gay movements pursued several overlapping strategies in their response to AIDS: the "de-gaying" of AIDS, organizing for heightened visibility of the lesbian and gay movements, separating AIDS-specific reform from structural reform of the overall health care system, and direct action in the form of unconventional politics (ibid., 74). All of these strategies reflected a willingness to embrace both assimilationist and liberationist approaches to political, social, and cultural change, depending on the nature of the political moment and the historical circumstances of the time. But given the reality that people were increasingly getting sick and dying, the lesbian and gay movements were understandably focused on short-term goals, which included getting affordable drugs to those in need and providing AIDS outreach and education to stem the tide of infection. With this in mind, the organizing strategies often associated with the assimilationist perspective dominated the political discourse of the time, though as we will see, groups such as ACT UP, Queer Nation, and the Lesbian Avengers all embraced liberationist strategies along the way.

The De-gaying of AIDS.   In the mid-1980s, AIDS leaders made a crucial decision to publicize the message that "AIDS is not a gay disease." The goal was to gain greater funding and public support and to convey the importance of AIDS prevention to all sectors of the population. The assumption was that the public and politicians would be more receptive if gay men were not the targeted beneficiaries of increased AIDS-related funding. That this strategy had to be used suggests how little progress had been made in combating the prejudice and hatred seemingly woven into the fabric of the larger culture. Thus, for roughly the next eight years, many AIDS groups de-emphasized lesbian and gay participation, denied that they were "gay organizations" per se, "and attempted to appeal to the general public by expunging gay references and sanitizing gay culture" (Rofes 1990, 11). A central goal was to capture the attention of straight society by stressing that heterosexuals—particularly women and children—were at risk of contracting HIV. In this way, AIDS activists embraced an assimilationist strategy, one that allowed nongay public-health officials to lobby on behalf of AIDS-specific issues while avoiding lesbian- and gay-rights concerns (Rimmerman 2002, 97).

Heightened Cultural Visibility.   A second consequence of the AIDS epidemic was to heighten the visibility of the lesbian and gay movements. To the extent that the media helped foster greater cultural change with respect to HIV/AIDS, it served as a means for integrating liberationist ideas into the developing AIDS movement in the United States. Media activism, which had characterized the movement since the 1950s, played an increasingly important role in the AIDS movements of the 1980s and 1990s (Vaid 1995, 79). Well before AIDS, lesbian and gay media were the principal outlets for information pertaining to lesbian, gay, bisexual, and transgender issues. They helped build community, and they were crucial arenas for political debate. The lesbian and gay media remain a vital information source even after the advent of AIDS. For example, in the early years of the epidemic, the *New York Native* provided some of the most forthright, accurate, and courageous reporting on AIDS. Dr. Lawrence Mass, then the paper's medical writer, authored the first news report and first feature article about AIDS, both of which appeared in the *Native* soon after the disease began striking gay men in early 1981. These were the first articles about AIDS to appear in the nonscientific press. Sadly, Mass was threatened with the loss of his job at the New York City Health Department for speaking out publicly about AIDS (Blasius and Phelan 1997, 574). The role of the *New York Native* and other lesbian and gay media sources cannot be ignored, especially given that the mainstream press largely shunned coverage of AIDS in the early years of the epidemic.

In the early years of the crisis, the mainstream press also ignored the grassroots organizations that were committed to education and prevention. For example, in 1982 the Gay Men's Health Crisis (GMHC) was founded by Larry Kramer, Lawrence Mass, and others, including Alvin Friedman-Kien, who had diagnosed the first AIDS cases in New York and served as a faculty member at the New York University Medical Center. GMHC became the first grassroots AIDS service-related organization in the United States. Upon the group's creation, Kramer targeted the mainstream media, hoping they would highlight the organization's

AIDS prevention and educational efforts. But few showed any interest in the story at all. Claiming that this yet-unnamed disease posed too many unanswered questions, they did not wish to contribute to a public panic over something that was still poorly understood (Alwood 1996, 214–215). In ignoring Kramer's request and the request of other concerned activists in major cities throughout the United States, the media abdicated their important reporting and educational responsibilities.

The AIDS memorial-quilt project played a major role as well in raising public awareness of AIDS, yet it caused considerable controversy in the lesbian and gay movements. The October 11, 1987, March on Washington for Lesbian and Gay Rights was the occasion for the Names Project's first display of the AIDS memorial quilt. March participants as well as the general public were reminded by the 1,920 panels, which covered the equivalent of two football fields, that AIDS had already claimed many lives. The timing of the quilt's appearance was deliberate: The 1988 presidential campaign was under way, and the quilt "provided a powerful symbol of the gay community's political struggle for equal rights and of the casualties of the simultaneous struggle for sexual liberation" (Andriote 1999, 365). But much to the consternation of some activists, the opportunities for enhanced public education and greater movement visibility brought by the AIDS quilt did not begin to make up for the assimilationist strategy that undergirded the degaying of AIDS, one that characterized the Names Project's way of representing the disease. One letter writer reported his frustration on visiting the Names Project's AIDS quilt in Washington, D.C.:

> That evening the candlelight march was led by invited parents of people with AIDS as thousands of mostly gay people marched behind them in the silent arc of candles. While this gesture towards parents was certainly admirable and appropriate, it was unforgivable for the project not to show the same level of respect for the partners of people who had died of AIDS. Surely it is not too much to expect an overwhelmingly gay-run organization to strive to recognize gay relationships in a more sensitive manner than society has shown. (Rofes 1990, 12)

Other activists were frustrated by the inability of the Names Project to connect its organizing work to a larger political and cultural strategy, one that was associated with liberationist values and goals. For example, Urvashi Vaid argued that it "didn't do enough to politicize people" (Andriote

1999, 367). And Vaid commented further: "that George Bush, who did so little, could be quoted on the back of the Names Project book reveals the irony of the depoliticization of the AIDS movement" (1995, 78).

In the end, the lesbian and gay movements achieved mixed success in their attempts to achieve heightened visibility around the AIDS issue. The strategy was undermined by tensions over whether the assimilationist or liberationist approach to political, social, and cultural change should prevail.

AIDS-Specific Reform. As we have already seen, AIDS mobilized lesbians and gay men in communities throughout the United States and fostered the creation of new organizations at the national and local levels. The creation of these new organizations raised additional tensions over strategy and goals within the lesbian and gay movements. What should be the relationship between the newly created AIDS service organizations and the broader lesbian and gay movements? Should such organizations critique the prevailing health care system, thus raising linking health care service delivery with economic class, or should they merely focus on providing basic services in a time of crisis? It is certainly understandable why many, faced with scarce resources and a serious public health crisis, embraced a more "pragmatic" response. But this more narrowly focused, assimilationist perspective has understandably been the target of considerable criticism from those who believe in a liberationist approach to political and social change. The primary critique is that AIDS service organizations focused too much on accommodating themselves to the existing health care system rather than linking health care service delivery to class, race, and gender concerns.

The founding and original goals of the Gay Men's Health Crisis and the AIDS Action Council support the liberationist critique. When Larry Kramer and others met in his Greenwich Village apartment in the summer of 1981 to discuss the onset of what eventually came to be known as AIDS, they decided that New York City needed an organization that was "founded by the gay community for the gay community." Over the years, the GMHC has provided counseling, education, and social services in support of those who are sick. Since its creation in 1981, the GMHC has become thoroughly institutionalized. By the late 1990s, the organization had served more than 75,000 clients annually, with a support staff of more than 200 and nearly 7,000 volunteers. Over time, representatives of the GMHC have participated in AIDS-related meetings at all levels of government. Though founded as a local organization, the GMHC has had an important national presence, and it has embraced a quintessential conventional insider approach to political change (Rom 2000, 222). Specifically, the GMHC has largely avoided addressing larger structural inequalities in the health care system. This same approach has characterized the AIDS Action Council.

Founded in 1984, the AIDS Action Council has been a leading national voice on AIDS, representing 3,200 of America's AIDS organizations and the millions of Americans they serve. The organization's mission statement asserts that "AIDS Action is the only organization solely dedicated to responsible federal policy for improved HIV/AIDS care and services, effective HIV prevention and vigorous medical research." A former director of the organization told me that "we realized that there had to be a nongay voice associated with the policy aspects of AIDS, and that is why the AIDS [Action] Council was created" (personal interview, February 19, 1997). In this way, the organization has played an integral role in reinforcing the assimilationist strategy. Like the GMHC, the AIDS Action Council has pursued conventional insider approaches to change. And as a former executive director of the organization acknowledged to me, there was considerable "conflict over short-term responses to AIDS and long-term political and policy planning" (personal interview, February 19, 1997). But it is also easy to understand why the AIDS Action Council pursued a mainstreaming, insider-politics assimilationist strategy. Such a strategy led to tangible political accomplishments, including increased funding for AIDS and major legislation in the form of the Ryan White CARE Act. This same strategy embraced a more narrowly focused political and cultural approach, one that would soon have to make room for unconventional outsider politics with the birth of ACT UP in 1987.

Direct Action and the Rise of Unconventional Politics.   On October 14, 1987, Jesse Helms, a conservative member of the United States Senate (R-NC), responded on the Senate floor to a safe-sex comic book that had been written by the GMHC and distributed in New York City. Helms was outraged by the book, and in protesting its content, he helped to usher in a national debate regarding the most effective ways to halt the spread of HIV. The GMHC had responded to Helms by informing him that the book was not supported by federal government funds. Federal resources were used, instead, for workshops and educational sessions that were created to offer AIDS risk-reduction education. Helms voiced opposition to this workshop program in his Senate floor speech and ultimately concluded that "abstinence only" programs were worthy of federal government support. In support of his claim, he offered a legislative amendment, Amendment 956, which, if passed, would have prevented the CDC from spending any federal government authorized funds to "provide AIDS education, information, or prevention materials and activities that promote, encourage, or condone sexual activity outside a sexually monogamous marriage (including homosexual activities) or the use of intravenous drugs." What is most shocking about this affair is not Helms's rant or his amendment, but the fact that his proposal "drew almost no verbal opposition from his more liberal colleagues in the Senate." At the time, only Senators Lawton Chiles (D-FL) and Senator Lowell Weicker (R-CT) challenged him on the floor. Weicker provided the stronger opposition by arguing that education and research were the only viable weapons in combating AIDS. He claimed that "any sort of an education process that excludes a part of the population, in particular a high-risk population, is not the education effort that the crisis deserves" (Siplon 2002, 67). In the end, Helms's amendment "was modified to only prohibit funding efforts that would seem to be promoting homosexuality" (ibid., 68). But the damage was clearly done, and the incident reveals the power that social conservatives had in the national policy process at the time.

How did AIDS activists respond to such retrograde and pernicious policies and the deepening health crisis? Some responded with fury by embracing unconventional outsider politics in the form of ACT UP. Formed in March 1987 in New York City, the AIDS Coalition to Unleash Power has been responsible "for producing some of the most important advances in AIDS research and some of the most crucial improvements in the lives of people with AIDS" (P. Cohen 1998, 1). The group declared in its founding statement that it is a "diverse, non-partisan group united in anger and committed to direct action to end the AIDS crisis" (Reed 2005, 182). Larry Kramer provided the impetus for the founding of ACT UP with a 1987 speech at the Lesbian and Gay Community Services Center of New York. In this now infamous speech, Kramer challenged the lesbian and gay movements to organize, mobilize, and demand an effective AIDS-policy response. He informed the audience of gay men that two-thirds of them might be dead within five years. In his speech, Kramer asked, "Do we want to start a new organization devoted solely to political action?" Kramer's speech inspired another meeting at the Community Services Center several days later, which more than three hundred people attended. This event essentially signaled the birth of ACT UP. Thereafter, ACT UP/New York routinely drew more than eight hundred people to its weekly meetings. As the organization grew, it remained the largest and most influential of all of the chapters (Rimmerman 2002, 105). By early 1988, active chapters had spread to other cities throughout the country, including Boston, Chicago, Los Angeles, and San Francisco. At the beginning of 1990, ACT UP had spread across the globe, with more than a hundred chapters worldwide (Vaid 1995, 94–95). But as former Rhode Island ACT UP activist Peter F. Cohen makes clear, "ACT UP/New York was originally *the* ACT UP—the first chapter, and historically the largest. Despite the eventual appearance of ACT UP chapters around the country, ACT UP/New York continued to provide leadership for the movement, especially in areas of national concern such as work concerning experimental drugs." In addition, ACT UP/New York received most of the media attention, perhaps because it "organized many of the demonstrations associated with the group as a whole," such as the 1989 "Stop the Church" protest in New York City's St. Patrick's Cathedral (1998, 3). The New York chapter also helped organize highly visible demonstrations in other communities throughout the United States.

ACT UP's original goal was to demand the release of experimental drugs. Underlying ACT UP's political strategy is a commitment to radical democracy and principles of participatory democratic theory. For example, no one member or group of members had the right to speak for ACT UP; this was a right reserved for all members. There were no elected leaders, no appointed spokespeople, and little formal structure to the organization (Rimmerman 2002, 105). ACT UP most often targeted six major institutions: advertising, the arts, the Catholic Church, corporations, government bureaucracies, and the mass media (Reed 2005, 182). Over the years, ACT UP has broadened its original purpose to embrace a number of specific practical goals. It has demanded that the U.S. Food and Drug Administration (FDA) release AIDS drugs in a timely manner by shortening the drug testing and approval process, and it has insisted that private health insurance as well as Medicaid be forced to pay for experimental drug therapies. Ten years into the AIDS crisis, ACT UP understandably questioned why only one drug, the highly toxic azidothymidine (AZT), had been approved for treatment. ACT UP also demanded federally controlled and funded needle-exchange and condom-distribution programs and a serious sex-education program in primary and secondary schools, to be created and monitored by the U.S. Department of Education (Rimmerman 2002, 106–107). One scholar has accurately pointed out that "few social movements are inclined to mix 'moral crusades' with 'practical crusades,'" which ACT UP did successfully (Epstein 1996, 232).

What makes ACT UP such an interesting organization to study is the fact that it has embraced both liberationist and assimilationist approaches to political, social, and cultural change. As one movement scholar has argued, ACT UP "has made self-conscious cultural struggle part of its core work," thus embracing a broad liberationist strategy for change (Reed 2005, 179). But it is also assimilationist to the extent that ACT UP chapters throughout the United States challenged the mainstream policy process to respond to the needs of people with AIDS in the short term. As we have already seen, the group is part of a long tradition of grassroots initiatives in the United States, especially in the form of the African American civil rights movement, which practiced unconventional politics to promote political, social, and cultural change.

What has been the genius of ACT UP? Certainly, it has included its ability to bridge these two approaches by using its creativity, "particularly through use of the visual and performing arts, in challenging the media's packaging of protest and trivialization of movements." It accomplished this goal "most effectively through the use of striking, aesthetically rich images, accompanied by witty, sound-bite-worthy slogans" (ibid., 180). ACT UP embraced slogans such as "Silence=Death" and used political art to convey its message to the public. The organization was adept in securing media attention from the start and, as a result, was able to communicate greater awareness of AIDS issues to the lesbian and gay communities and to the larger society.

The media covered a number of ACT UP demonstrations, including its very first one, held on Wall Street in New York on March 24, 1987 (Rimmerman 2002, 107). The target of this protest action was Burroughs Wellcome, which had charged $10,000 for a one-year supply of its drug AZT. At the time, people were optimistic that AZT was the drug that could finally help those with HIV/AIDS. As one student of AIDS policy points out, "it seemed to be a particularly cruel irony that the long-awaited treatment should be priced out of the reach of many people who sought it" (Siplon 2002, 19). Other high-profile demonstrations included a 1987 protest at New York's Sloan-Kettering Hospital, one that demanded an increase in the number of HIV drugs. In 1988 more than 1,000 ACT UP protesters surrounded the FDA's Rockville, Maryland, headquarters. In 1989, ACT UP activists demonstrated at AIDS hearings held by the U.S. Civil Rights Commission to protest its inept response to AIDS. Also in 1989, ACT UP/New York's "Stop the Church" demonstration disrupted Roman Catholic cardinal John O'Connor's mass in Saint Patrick's Cathedral to protest his opposition to condom distribution. In one action that unavoidably caught the attention of the media, ACT UP members invaded the studio of the *MacNeil/Lehrer NewsHour* on January 22, 1991, chained themselves to Robert MacNeil's desk during a live broadcast, and flashed signs declaring "The AIDS Crisis Is Not Over" (Rimmerman 2002, 108).

Critics both within and outside of the lesbian and gay movements protested some of these actions for being too disruptive and counterproductive. "Stop the Church" and other demonstrations heightened an already existing tension within the movements, between those who favored more traditional assimilationist insider lobbying activities and those who embraced the radical direct action associated with ACT UP. As we have already seen in Chapter 2, these tensions have been prevalent throughout the development of the lesbian and gay movements. One student of social movements offered a perceptive view of ACT UP's approach, a perspective that gives us a deeper understanding of what motivated its creative response to political activism:

> ACT-UP's tacit strategy was to force on public officials, church, and business leaders their most horrific nightmare: exposure by means of actions that signify disrespect. By presenting itself as an "out-of-control" intransigent mélange of queers and misfits, it reveals a capacity to opt out of what is expected of a "responsible" civic organization: to play by the rules. From the perspective of the Establishment's code, to refuse these rules is to engage in the politics of *terror.* (Aronowitz 1996, 131)

By 1992, there were divisions in ACT UP over strategy and tactics and over treatment of women and minorities. The divisions helped to spawn spin-off organizations, organizations such as Queer Nation and the Lesbian Avengers, some members of which had previous connections to ACT UP. Queer Nation appeared in June 1991 with a central goal of radicalizing the broader AIDS movement (and the lesbian and gay movements) by embracing confrontational politics and reclaiming the word *queer*. Perhaps the most controversial tactic promoted by Queer Nation members and supporters was "outing," a strategy designed to publicize and challenge various powerful lesbians and gays who were in positions of importance in American society.

Founded in the fall of 1992, the Lesbian Avengers also embraced unconventional politics as a response to a larger lesbian and gay movement that the six lesbian friends and organizers—Maria Simo, Anne-Christine D'Adesky, Maxine Wolfe, Marie Honan, Ann Maguire, and Sara Schulman—perceived to be dominated by men who refused to address sexism in meaningful ways. The organization has embraced tactics similar to those used by ACT UP in its effort to attract media attention. The Lesbian Avengers has become known for its "Dyke Marches," the first of which was held as a part of the 1993 Gay and Lesbian March on Washington. In addition, it has done important grassroots organizing work in fighting referenda hostile to lesbians, gays, bisexuals, and transgender individuals by organizing in those states where such referenda are on the ballot (Rimmerman 2002, 109).

What distinguishes all of this unconventional political organizing is the determination of the various organizers to reach well beyond their lesbian and gay white male constituencies. The goal was to reach those in power throughout American society and ordinary citizens who organizers perceived could be persuaded that people who have been infected with HIV should not be the targets of discrimination and vitriol. In this way, the organizations mentioned here transcended narrowly focused assimilationist organizing strategies and integrated liberationist ways of thinking into their invaluable work. But the organizations would face more serious challenges with a so-called friend, President William Jefferson Clinton, residing in the White House.

The Clinton/Bush Years

The 1992 election of Bill Clinton promised great opportunities for the lesbian and gay movements, especially after twelve years of conservative Republican rule. Although some AIDS activists were suspicious of Clinton's commitment, the "shriller voices in the AIDS activist community were receding into the background, and a group of leaders were emerging who could mix more easily with the administration" (Levenson 2003,

131–132). After all, Clinton had promised during the campaign that he would appoint an "AIDS czar" who would coordinate AIDS policy from the White House. In addition, he claimed that he would provide more leadership by funding AIDS research and education than his Republican predecessors ever did. And soon after taking office, he requested that Health and Human Services secretary Donna Shalala create an AIDS task force, one that would establish AIDS research and treatment administration priorities. He used the occasion of AIDS Awareness Day to outline his administration's approach to AIDS at Georgetown University (Engel 2006, 234–235). Finally, Clinton excoriated the Bush administration's policy of banning the immigration of HIV-positive foreigners to the United States, thus signaling a more progressive overall policy on those who were HIV positive. At a more symbolic level, he had chosen Bob Hattoy, an openly gay man who had been diagnosed with AIDS, to speak at the summer 1992 Democratic National Convention in New York. Capturing the initial hopes of many AIDS activists, David Kirp wrote in the *Nation* during the summer of 1994, "Clinton at Georgetown, [Kristin] Gebbie on the stump, Shalala rejecting business as usual for AIDS—that kind of official rhetoric matters greatly" (ibid., 234).

It was not mere rhetoric that caught the attention of AIDS activists. From the vantage point of the lesbian and gay movements, Clinton's policy approach to AIDS represented a significant improvement over the policies of Reagan and Bush. Clinton embraced full funding of the Ryan White CARE Act, thus giving further momentum to the importance of maintaining and funding the act over the long term. He created the National Task Force on AIDS Drug Development to examine how new drugs could be released to the market more quickly. Clinton's Department of Justice took action to address discrimination against people who were either HIV positive or diagnosed with AIDS. In June 1993, the Clinton administration announced that rules governing the eligibility of people infected with HIV for disability benefits would be relaxed considerably. Finally, Clinton's 1992 election meant that more federal money was allocated for AIDS research. For example, in fiscal year 1994, funding for AIDS research increased by 18 percent (Foreman 1994, 123).

But it did not take long for lesbian and gay movement activists to be disappointed. As we will see in Chapter 4, Clinton's unwillingness to fight for his campaign promise to overturn the ban on lesbians and gays in the military frustrated many. And AIDS activists and PWAs were soon disappointed as well. Clinton received praise for discussing AIDS more than did his predecessors, but in the end he failed to initiate the kind of comprehensive plan that activists had expected.

His AIDS czar appointments (Kristin Gebbie, Patricia Fleming, and Sandy Thurman) were all deemed to be ineffectual, and soon the idea of the office itself came to be viewed as more symbolic than substantive. His appointment of Dr. Jocelyn Elders, an Arkansas physician and professor of pediatrics, as surgeon general received praise, especially after her outspoken endorsement of sex education and AIDS-prevention outreach. But following Republican victories in the 1994 congressional elections, Clinton forced Elders's resignation when she angered conservatives by appearing to call for the teaching of masturbation to schoolchildren; in fact, Elders had endorsed what were perceived by many as reasonable, comprehensive sex education programs. Her original comments had been badly distorted by conservatives for political reasons, and President Clinton refused to support her, thus further antagonizing lesbian and gay activists (Rimmerman 1998b, 401–402). In June 1995, White House security officers wore blue rubber gloves to check the bags of gay elected officials who were visiting the White House. Soon thereafter, White House spokesman Michael McCurry apologized for "an error of judgment" (Engel 2006, 234).

The issue of needle exchange provided more disappointment for AIDS activists when Clinton failed to endorse a promised needle-exchange program to target injecting drug users. In adopting a cautious middle ground, the administration called for a federally funded study on needle exchange and then concluded that more research was needed before any needle-exchange policy could be proposed. This was particularly disappointing to AIDS activists, who cited studies suggesting that needle exchanges could save lives. In addition, Clinton responded to the demands of social conservatives by eliminating mandatory AIDS educational programs for federal workers, much to the frustration of AIDS activists. The overall Clinton record on HIV/AIDS policy proved to be a mixed one, one that apparently even disappointed him. After he left the White House, he created a foundation on AIDS, the William J. Clinton Foundation, one that would be the focal point of his international policy work as a former president.

Clinton's AIDS policy record allowed newly "elected" president George W. Bush to have room to maneuver between rewarding his Christian Right supporters by focusing on abstinence as a centerpiece of his domestic and foreign HIV/AIDS policies and his 2003 pledge to spend $15 billion to fight global AIDS over a ten-year period. But the prevailing AIDS policy theme of the Bush administration was "abstinence" coupled with efforts to undercut federal funding for "safe sex" education to young Americans. In 2004, the administration established a Web site, aptly named 4parents.gov, which says that it "is a guide to help you and your pre-teen or mid-teen discuss important, yet difficult issues about healthy choices, abstinence, sex and relationships." One analyst claims that "human rights and health groups reviewing the site were so appalled at what they found that 150 organizations asked that the U.S. Department of Health and Human Services . . . immediately take it off the Internet" (Hunter 2006, 59). Esther Kaplan points out in her excellent book on the role of Christian fundamentalists in the George W. Bush White House that none of this should have been a surprise, given Bush's sorry record on HIV/AIDS as governor of Texas from 1994 to 2000. For example, Governor Bush never mentioned AIDS in any public address, despite the reality that "the state's AIDS cases surged to rank fourth in the nation." In addition, his appointment as Texas health commissioner openly opposed condom use because "'it's not what God intended.'" And Bush himself viewed AIDS as such a low item on his policy agenda that "he refused to sign letters of support for AIDS grant applications" (Kaplan 2004, 168).

As a presidential candidate during April 2000, Bush met with prominent gay Republicans in Austin. Carl Schmid, who attended the meeting and worked for the Log Cabin Republicans, said that "Global AIDS wasn't on his agenda and it wasn't on ours" (ibid., 169). A first draft of the 2000 Republican Party platform, which was largely written by Bush campaign officials, failed to even mention AIDS.

Just one month into the new administration, Bush's chief of staff, Andrew Card, announced that the White House office on AIDS would soon be eliminated. In response, protests were vigorous, and the then press secretary, Ari Fleischer, announced that Card's comment was "a mistake," though it soon became clear to AIDS activists that it was a "trial balloon," one meant to signal that AIDS policy would be shunted to the sidelines in the Bush White House. More evidence that the Bush administration was not interested in AIDS policy came in the months that passed before he appointed an AIDS czar, Scott Evertz, and the full year before he appointed his AIDS advisory council members. Scott Hitt, who had served as chairman of the AIDS council under President Clinton, told Esther Kaplan: "I just don't get the sense that this administration is engaged" (ibid., 169).

But in his 2003 State of the Union Address, President Bush surprised many of his critics when he proposed a vigorous global program to fight AIDS. In justifying his plan, he said that "seldom has history offered a greater opportunity to do so much for so many. And to meet a severe and urgent crisis abroad, tonight I propose the Emergency Plan for AIDS Relief—a work of mercy beyond all current international efforts to help the people of Africa." In many ways, his plan was an outgrowth of the "compassionate conservative" philosophy that he first introduced in the 2000 presidential campaign to signal that he was a different kind of conservative when it came to social policy. His pledge would ultimately triple current U.S. funding for global AIDS, "which was already more than double Clinton administration funding" (Behrman 2004, 307). Besides providing huge increases in global AIDS spending, the program's centerpiece is "abstinence only programs" as the primary approach to prevention. Indeed, "the Bush administration has earmarked for abstinence education a third of all the money that it has given for AIDS prevention in the developing world" (Micklethwait and Wooldridge 2004, 149). The program received bipartisan support, as evidenced by Nicholas D. Kristof's September 2006 *New York Times* op-ed essay in which he claimed that "emphasis on testing could be incorporated into the extension of President Bush's fine program against AIDS, which will save some nine million lives and is up for renewal next year. That program, which provided huge increases in spending and will be Mr. Bush's best legacy, should be extended with even more money, while dropping its obsession with abstinence-only programs" (n.p.). But critics such as Esther Kaplan were scathing in their indictment of Bush's global AIDS plan:

> Rather than seek advice from the AIDS researchers, doctors, social workers, advocates, and people living with HIV who had set the AIDS agenda in the past, he would listen to pharmaceutical executives intent on preserving drug profits and to social conservatives whose abhorrence of gay and extramarital sex was matched only by their lack of AIDS expertise. Rather than promote public health solutions, he emphasized "personal responsibility." Rather than condoms, his mantra was abstinence and marriage. In Bush's hands, AIDS was born again—as a conservative issue. (2004, 169–170)

Kaplan and other critics have argued that Bush's focus on global AIDS allows him to avoid addressing the many challenges of the domestic epidemic, which include rising rates of HIV infection among gay men, their partners, and IV drug users, many of whom live in urban America. Bush has done little to recognize the significant increase in HIV infection among African Americans. And the administration has been laggard in supporting full funding for the Ryan White CARE Act, which was targeted by social conservatives in the Republican-controlled House of Representatives during the first six years of the Bush presidency. In the end, his vision of compassionate conservatism is one that ignores the many challenges of funding for HIV/AIDS safe-sex education and policy initiatives at home.[1]

The Response of the Lesbian and Gay Movements to the Clinton/Bush Years

The lesbian and gay movements witnessed an altered political landscape as AIDS entered its second decade in the United States. After twelve years of Republican dominance of the national policy process, Bill Clinton and the Democrats seized control of the White House and Congress. On the night of Clinton's November 3, 1992, victory, I celebrated with hundreds of lesbians and gays and their supporters at the Omni Shoreham Hotel in Washington, D.C. When Clinton mentioned the acronym *AIDS* early in his election-night speech, he inspired the crowd to erupt in a frenzy of excitement and joy. As I turned to survey the scene, I saw a man engulfed in tears, sobbing to his friend, "Maybe I will live after all."

This story captures the hope and anticipation on the part of many (though not all) AIDS activists in response to the changing political landscape. But the policy and human challenges were still there. People were still dying, the drug-approval process was slow and cumbersome, and AIDS organizations were strapped with an array of financial challenges. Against this backdrop, what political organizing strategies made most sense for the lesbian and gay movements in the Clinton era? Should a more narrowly focused assimilationist strategy be used, one that would allow activists possible access to the Clinton White House and supportive members of Congress? Or should the movements embrace a more liberationist strategy, one that would push for comprehensive medical care and demand that policy elites respond in forceful and radical ways to a deepening health crisis?

One of the most interesting organizations to develop in response to these important questions is the Treatment Action Group (TAG). Formed in 1992 by AIDS activists who were committed to a pragmatic assimilationist political strategy emphasizing the treatment of individuals with HIV/AIDS, TAG became a pioneering organization addressing AIDS research and drug-development issues and still exists today. The original founders came out of the disagreements that engulfed ACT UP/New York in the early 1990s. TAG founders embraced both assimilationist and liberationist strategies for political change. Unlike ACT UP, which had a democratic organizational structure, TAG accepted members by invitation only, and membership could be revoked by the board. In addition, TAG members received salaries, and the group accepted a $1 million check from the pharmaceutical company Burroughs Wellcome, the manufacturer of AZT, in the summer of 1992. TAG used this money to finance members' travels to AIDS conferences throughout the world, pay salaries, hire professional lobbyists, and lobby government officials (Rimmerman 2002, 110).

TAG's central goal has been to force the government to release promising AIDS drugs more quickly and to identify possible treatments for opportunistic infections (Burkett 1995, 339–340). It has done so by lobbying for improved clinical drug trials of protease inhibitors and other HIV drugs. In addition, it has called for a more coordinated AIDS research effort at the National Institutes of Health by strengthening the Office of AIDS Research. TAG has been quite effective in lobbying government officials to address its organizational goals in a timely manner. However, considerable criticism was directed toward TAG by some ACT UP members and other activists in the early years of its existence. Because the organization was perceived by some as small, elitist, and undemocratic, it was attacked for not fully representing the interests of the entire AIDS activist movement. These criticisms have largely dissipated in recent years, but they were unfortunate to the extent that they failed to recognize TAG's important contributions in forcing federal government officials to support more aggressive AIDS research. Sociologist Steven Epstein has identified the meaning of these and other conflicts for the larger AIDS movements:

> Gender and racial divisions, as well as debates over internal participatory mechanisms, insider/outsider strategies, and overall priorities and goals, are the kinds of issues that can tear apart any social movement. What particularly complicated the internal battles of the AIDS movement was the additional overlay of the politics of expertise. It was not simply that some people were working on the inside while others were outside—just as important,

those who were on the inside were increasingly mastering specialized forms of knowledge with which their fellow activists on the outside did not come into contact. (1996, 292–293)

These conflicts were compounded by differences of class, gender, race, and education, all of which can divide any social movement, as Epstein suggests.

Despite an array of challenges, from its inception ACT UP has had a considerable impact on AIDS-related public policy. The organization successfully used its nonviolent, direct-action approach to force the FDA to accelerate drug trials for AIDS and to consider ACT UP's "parallel track" proposal. Under this proposal, people with AIDS are given drugs before they complete the time-consuming and bureaucracy-ridden FDA approval process. ACT UP's protests also led Burroughs Wellcome to dramatically reduce the price of AZT. Other pharmaceutical companies have been shamed into cutting the prices of drugs that have demonstrated effectiveness in helping people with AIDS. In addition, ACT UP forced the redefinition of AIDS to include women and to ensure that women with AIDS received disability benefits and were included in drug trials. ACT UP members have established needle-exchange programs, which are now widely credited with helping to reduce the rate of HIV infection among both injecting drug users and their sexual partners (Rimmerman 1992, 111).

By 1996, plagued with internal divisions over tactics and its relationship to the larger AIDS and lesbian and gay movements, and depleted by the deaths of many members, ACT UP still existed but was widely considered moribund. ACT UP suffered as well with the election of Bill Clinton. Without a clear enemy in the White House, ACT UP's efforts were undermined. Nonetheless, the organization's use of direct-action politics demonstrated the effectiveness of unconventional politics in challenging unresponsive policy elites. ACT UP's radicalism has also allowed other lesbian and gay organizations to seem much more moderate in their work on AIDS-related issues. A former executive director of the AIDS Action Council perceives that ACT UP has been quite successful in keeping "mainstream organizations from enjoying their seats at the table too much" and that "multiple political strategies have a tremendous effect" (personal interview, February 19, 1997).

In recent years, the few remaining chapters that exist in major cities, including New York City, San Francisco, and Washington, D.C., have flourished by building creative new alliances, from work with the Rainforest

Action Network to support for Green Party presidential candidate Ralph Nader. In early 2001, ACT UP members in San Francisco protested the thirty-nine pharmaceutical companies that sued the South African government for choosing to produce its own AIDS drugs. The Philadelphia ACT UP chapter has done excellent organizing work on behalf of increasing funding for the Ryan White CARE Act and for supporting President Bush's Emergency Plan for AIDS Relief on a global scale by demanding funding to match rhetoric. As it has broadened its political strategy, some ACT UP chapters have embraced a liberationist social-justice agenda, one that transcends narrowly focused identity politics (Bull 1999, 18–19). The organization marked its twentieth anniversary on March 29, 2007, by marching on Wall Street to demand a single-payer, comprehensive medical care plan. In this and other ways, ACT UP has made an invaluable contribution to saving people's lives in the face of governmental and societal indifference.

In addition to TAG, ACT UP has spawned two other AIDS activist and policy organizations, both of which embrace assimilationist and liberationist strategies in their campaigns on behalf of those with HIV/AIDS. Founded in 1990 as an outgrowth of ACT UP/New York, Housing Works has become a national model for providing housing, health care, and job training, coupled with vigorous advocacy, on behalf of those who are homeless and living with HIV/AIDS in New York City. Throughout its existence, Housing Works, a minority-controlled organization, has "housed and or provided supportive services to well over 15,000 individuals." In addition, "it created New York's first and most successful job training and placement program for homeless people with AIDS and HIV." In the years ahead, the organization promises to "create 1000 units of permanent new housing in New York City that is affordable to persons on public entitlements, persons on fixed incomes, and working persons." And it plans on "establishing a global network of grassroots activists committed to ending the twin epidemics of homelessness and HIV/AIDS" (http://www.housingworks.org, n.p.). In doing so, the organization combines a commitment to political activism with policy results.

A second organization inspired by ACT UP is Health Gap, which does most of its AIDS organizing and policy work in the global arena, fighting for the elimination of "barriers to global access to affordable, life-sustaining medicines for people living with HIV/AIDS as key to comprehensive strategy to confront and ultimately stop the AIDS pandemic." The group's central goal is to challenge "the pharmaceutical industry's excessive profits and expanding patient rights" (http://www.healthgap.org, n.p.). In doing so, it wishes to reform U.S. trade and world trade policies so that affordable medicines are available on a global scale. Health Gap counts as its members U.S.-based AIDS and human rights activists, people living with HIV/AIDS, public health experts, and fair-trade advocates, all of whom embrace assimilationist and liberationist approaches to political action and public policy, with an emphasis on global economic and social justice.

As AIDS approached its twenty-fifth anniversary in the United States in 2006, the complexion of the disease and the public policy challenges had changed significantly. A headline on the front page of the *Washington Blade* captured this new reality: "Experts Debate the 'New' Face of AIDS: Gay Men, African Americans Hardest Hit by the Disease" (Lee 2006a). Many Americans ignored the disease in the 1980s and early 1990s because they perceived it as largely a "gay disease." But by 2006, "many gay Americans seem to have joined their fellow citizens in not paying much attention to HIV/AIDS, thanks to the widespread belief that it is now an African disease." Phill Wilson, founder and chief executive officer of the Black AIDS Institute, claimed in late 2006 that "the whole universe of who is focusing on AIDS is getting smaller, and smaller, and smaller." And this comes at a time when the two groups most affected by HIV/AIDS in the United States are African Americans and gay men, "with both groups accounting for 49 percent of new HIV diagnoses in 2005, according to the Centers for Disease Control and Prevention" (ibid., 22). The challenges facing the AIDS activist movement are to capture larger public attention and the interest of policymakers. How to do that remains to be seen. But it will undoubtedly involve a combination of assimilationist and liberationist political strategies, coupled with insider and outsider politics of the kind that we have seen develop in the AIDS activist movement over time.

Conclusion

This chapter began with two key questions: In what ways did the onset of AIDS in the United States during the early 1980s affect the lesbian and gay movements in terms of their organizing and political strategies? And how have the movements intersected with the policy process over time as AIDS has developed in the United States and on a global scale? In answering these questions, we placed our analysis within its appropriate historical context. And we explored the tensions between those who embraced an insider assimilationist strategy and those who demanded an outsider liberationist strategy to political and social change, as reflected in the broader movements' responses to AIDS policy. The chapter has argued that AIDS changed the landscape of lesbian and gay politics by mobilizing an array of newly politicized activists. The assimilationist and liberationist strategies used by the movements developed out of movement organizing in the 1950s, 1960s, and 1970s, as we saw in the discussion of the rise of the lesbian and gay movements in Chapter 2. We have also seen that the Christian Right furthered its organizing agenda by using the threat of AIDS to mobilize its supporters and to raise money. Over time, the lesbian and gay movements were forced to work with the AIDS activist movement, as the movements eventually became one and the same. But in recent years, the boundaries between the lesbian and gay movements and the AIDS activist movement have grown more rigid, as AIDS has receded from public and policy attention and other issues have become more prominent on the lesbian and gay movements' agenda. We now turn to a discussion of these issues—military integration and same-sex marriage—in Chapters 4 and 5.

4

....

"Don't Ask, Don't Tell": Policy Perspectives on the Military Ban

Experiencing prejudice is shocking, painful, negating, and eye opening. What is subtle and silenced by discreetness can become a battle cry to mobilize action. Never in my wildest imagination had I thought I would end up challenging a military policy. I had spent a lifetime in uniform, believing in democracy, in freedom and justice for all. With four words my world was turned upside down and my belief system challenged. In response to questioning in a topsecret investigation, I said, "I am a lesbian." Those words triggered the military to initiate discharge procedures against me based on military policy barring homosexuals from serving in the military.

> —Colonel Margarethe Cammermeyer, quoted in *Gay Rights, Military Wrongs: Political Perspectives on Lesbians and Gays in the Military,* edited by Craig A. Rimmerman

We all make sacrifices. We all make compromises. I wanted to be a soldier. So I compromised for a while. I sacrificed a part of myself in order to achieve my goals. But had I continued on any longer, my accomplishments would have amounted to a Pyrrhic victory. I wasn't prepared to keep compromising. I left the military in order to save myself. This book is that story, a unique inside look at the U.S. military, where I served as a gay soldier in the Gulf War. . . . *I am* Major Jeffrey McGowan. I lived under just these conditions for twelve years while proudly serving this great country of ours. I now respectfully add my voice to the ever-growing chorus of gay former soldiers who've served well and served proudly under the cloud of a policy that makes the challenge of military an even greater one than it needs to be.

—Major Jeffrey McGowan, *Major Conflict: One Gay Man's Life in the Don't-Ask-Don't-Tell Military*

It is clear that national attitudes toward this issue have evolved considerably in the last decade. This has been led by a new generation of service members who take a more relaxed and tolerant view toward homosexuality.

—Lieutenant General Daniel W. Christman

THE CONTEMPORARY DEBATE over lesbians and gays in the military is informed by the reality that the American military is currently engaged in incursions from Afghanistan to Iraq.[1] Indeed, with the beginning of the war in Afghanistan in 2001, "discharges of openly gay service members have fallen by 40 percent" (Alvarez 2006, n.p.). Those who have been calling for military integration and assimilation have witnessed greater assimilation in recent years due to military expediency. At the same time, however, some 10,000 U.S. service members "have been, at the very least, discharged simply for being gay" since the implementation of the U.S. Armed Forces' "Don't Ask, Don't Tell" policy began in 1994 (Lehmkuhl 2006, xii–xiii). In some ways, the falling number of discharges will be viewed as "progress" by those who embrace the assimilationist perspective. But for those who take a more radical liberationist perspective on U.S. imperialism and military involvement across the globe, permitting lesbians and gays to serve openly in the military means allowing them to support America's quest for global hegemony. This tension between the assimilationist and liberationist perspectives has been present since the debate over integration of the military exploded onto the public policy agenda in 1992–1993.

As we have already seen, a core component of recent social-movement theory is the belief that expanding political opportunities help to determine the overall strength of a social movement. The election of Bill Clinton in 1992 provides a context to evaluate the theoretical claim. After twelve years of conservative Republican dominance of national policy-making, the return of the Democrats to power was greeted with euphoria by many members of the lesbian and gay movements. Indeed, there was tremendous hope and excitement because for the first time a presidential candidate had courted the lesbian and gay vote, had been elected with the support of the community, and now would presumably have to govern with that reality in mind. But as we will see, the debate over the military ban and the subsequent passage of the "Don't Ask, Don't Tell" policy helped to undermine that euphoria and to give the lesbian and gay movements an introduction to the challenges faced by any movement that has so-called friends in power.

This chapter assesses the original circumstances under which the military-ban issue appeared on the policy agenda soon after Clinton was elected. Why did it emerge as an issue early in the first term of the Clinton presidency? What role did the lesbian and gay movements play in forcing the issue onto the agenda? And what role did the Christian Right play? In answering these questions, the analysis interrogates the role of the lesbian and gay movements in interacting with the Clinton administration, Congress, and the Christian Right during the 1993 debate over the military ban. In addition, it explores the implementation of the Don't Ask, Don't Tell compromise since the law was enacted, with an eye toward assessing the policy in light of the lesbian and gay movements' goals and political strategies. In doing so, we examine the arguments for and against allowing openly lesbian and gay members to serve. But in order to fully understand the complexities of this issue, we first turn to an examination of the full historical context for the military ban.

Military Integration in Historical Context

World War I and World War II

To understand the history of homosexuality in the U.S. military, we must first recognize that "the history of homosexuality in the United States armed forces has been a struggle between two intransigent facts—the persistent presence of gays within the military and the equally persistent hostility toward them" (Shilts 1993, 3). It is also true that the place of lesbians and gays within the military has garnered policy attention by the military itself over the past seventy-five years. As one historian accurately points out, "the transition from prosecuting 'sodomists' to separating homosexuals that occurred during World War II, for example, was preceded by psychological and legal research that tried to rationalize the varied practices within the services before the war" (Haggerty 2003, 12).

During World War I, the punishment of homosexual soldiers was codified into law. The 1916 Articles of War specified that assault with the intent to commit sodomy be identified as a felony. This law did not invent sodomy itself as a crime, but revisions to the Articles of War three years later did. Sodomy was identified as a specific felony; the crime was the sexual act itself, whether it was consensual or involved assault. Throughout the 1920s and 1930s, many gay soldiers and sailors were imprisoned, as homosexuality was regarded as a criminal act (Shilts 1993, 15).

World War I also saw acceptance of the idea of "excluding people for having a homosexual orientation, as opposed to punishing only those who committed homosexual acts" (ibid.). A San Francisco psychiatrist, Dr. Albert Abrams, wrote in September 1918 (after San Francisco police discovered a number of soldiers during a raid on a gay club) that "while 'recruiting the elements which make up our invincible army, we cannot ignore what is obvious and which will militate against the combative prowess of our forces in this war. . . . From a military viewpoint, the homosexualist is not only dangerous, but an ineffective fighter. . . . It is imperative that homosexualists be recognized by the military authorities'" (ibid., 253). As we will see later in this chapter, these arguments would be repeated over the years by many who wished to prohibit openly lesbian and gay people from serving in the U.S. armed forces.

But the earliest attempts to regulate homosexuality in the military were inconsistent and sporadic. In 1919, "immoral behaviors" in the Newport, Rhode Island, naval facilities were the subject of an investigation by a chief machinist's mate, Ervin Arnold. This proved to be the first attempt to purge an installation of homosexuals. Arnold launched his own personal investigation of gays in the navy there, gained approval of his plan from his superiors, "and then persuaded seven enlisted men to entrap suspected gays, largely at the local YMCA." Arnold soon expanded his investigation to the point that a number of "presumably" gay soldiers had been caught, were court-martialed for sodomy, and were sentenced to five- to six-year prison terms (ibid., 16). Civilians associated with the navy were also "outed" as part of Arnold's investigation.

During World War II, the move to transform homosexuality from a crime to an illness gained currency. Between 1941 and 1945, the U.S. armed forces mobilized some 16 million soldiers and sailors. The military establishment needed help devising guidelines for eliminating those who might not be fit to serve; it turned to the psychiatry profession, a relatively new field that was legitimated by the role that it played in assisting the military as it issued its first regulations to military psychiatrists pertaining to new recruits. The regulations came with the following notation: "Persons habitually or occasionally engaged in homosexual or other perverse sexual practices are unsuitable for military service." But they did introduce to the military establishment the notion that homosexuals were unfit to serve because they were mentally ill. Indeed, the belief that lesbians and gay men constituted a class of people who had to be excluded from the military became an important part of military policy (Berubé 1990, 33). Final regulations, which remained unchanged for some fifty years, were issued in 1943; they banned homosexuals from all branches of the military (Shilts 1993, 16–17).

The diverse policies of the different services were replaced by the Uniform Code of Military Justice (UCMJ) at the end of World War II. The Uniform Code provided for the following:

> Article 125 of the UCMJ prohibits sodomy, defined as anal or oral penetration, whether consensual or coerced and whether same-sex or opposite-sex, and does not exempt married couples. Under Article 125, the maximum penalty for sodomy with a consenting adult is five years at hard labor, forfeiture of pay and allowances, and dishonorable discharge. Article 134 of the UCMJ, also known as the "General Article," sanctions assault with the intent to commit sodomy, indecent assault, and indecent acts, and prohibits all conduct "to the prejudice of good order and discipline in the armed forces." The maximum penalty is the same for each of these offenses as for sodomy, except in the case of assault with intent, which has a maximum of ten rather than five years confinement. (D'Amico 1996, 6)

Research by several scholars has highlighted the importance of World War II in modern gay history. The work of historian Allan Berubé, published in *Coming Out Under Fire*, is particularly important for pointing out that the wartime experience offered many young lesbians and gay men the opportunity to recognize that they were not alone. They also learned that certain cities allowed them to meet others of their kind and that they could have meaningful lesbian and gay friendships as well. As Berubé points out, "thousands of young lesbians and gay men, many from small towns and rural areas, met large numbers of other homosexuals for the first time on military bases, in nearby bars, or in hotels where service people congregated" (1990, 5). In these ways, the military's mobilization forced soldiers to confront homosexuality in their personal lives.

As the military expanded its antihomosexual policies, it forced many officers and soldiers to come out against their will. Draftees were often forced out as well when they "declared themselves" and received undesirable discharges as a means to escape harassment (ibid., 7). During the

World War II period, the military's "definition of homosexuality was extended to women engaged in same-sex behavior for the first time" (Haggerty 2003, 17). By the end of the war, as antihomosexual practices were vigilantly enforced, many gay men and lesbians were involuntarily discharged and returned to civilian life with a stigma attached, and in some cases lives destroyed. Berubé offers the important argument that when veterans identified their struggles with the government in the broader context of justice and equal rights, they helped to provide ideas that later became cornerstones of the contemporary lesbian and gay movements.

The McCarthy Era and Beyond

During the anticommunist hysteria of the McCarthy era of the 1950s, concern for "national security" was identified as the central reason for keeping gays out of government service, including the military. By the early 1950s, the virulent anticommunist and antihomosexual views associated with McCarthyism pervaded the political and social milieus. Senator Joseph McCarthy and his colleagues claimed that "homosexuals and other sex perverts" threatened to undermine the nation's moral welfare (Benecke and Dodge 1996, 73). Throughout the 1950s and 1960s, individuals were barred from military service for acknowledging a homosexual orientation. For the pre-Stonewall lesbian and gay movements, challenging the military policy became an important goal. For example, the founder of the Washington, D.C., Mattachine Society chapter, Franklin Kameny, had three goals to pursue as a political activist: "to end the Civil Service's ban on gays working for the government, to end discrimination against homosexuals seeking security clearances, and to end the exclusion of gays from the military" (Shilts 1993, 194).

As we saw in Chapter 2, the 1969 Stonewall Rebellion ushered in an array of challenges to discriminatory governmental policies. The military policy became a target of the movement, as reflected in the legal challenge to the policy offered by Leonard Matlovich (Herek 1996, 6). On March 6, 1975, air force technical sergeant Leonard Matlovich hand-delivered a letter to his superior, Captain Daniel Collins, the officer in charge of race-relations instruction at Langley Air Force Base in Hampton, Virginia. The letter was addressed to the secretary of the air force and began in this way: "After some years of uncertainty, I have arrived at the conclusion that my sexual preferences are homosexual as opposed to heterosexual. I have also concluded that my sexual preferences will in no way interfere with my Air Force duties, as my preferences are now open. It is therefore requested that those provisions in AFM-39-12 relating to the discharge of homosexuals be waived in my case." It ended: "In sum, I consider myself to be a homosexual and fully qualified for military service. My almost twelve years of unblemished service supports the position" (Miller 1995, 411). Matlovich's letter signaled the beginning of the contemporary battle to overturn the U.S. military's policy barring lesbians and gays. During the late 1970s, there were a number of challenges to the military ban, including one by Sergeant Perry Watkins, who was stripped of his army clearance and discharged for his homosexuality in 1984. He won a lengthy Supreme Court battle in 1990, as the Court pointed out that the army, realizing he was gay, reenlisted him three times. With the Court's decision, Watkins became the only openly gay man in history who has been permitted to serve in the military by the Supreme Court. The other challenges were largely unsuccessful, but they highlighted the discretion afforded to military commanders who were responsible for implementing existing policy and applied different degrees of rigor and standards in the implementation process.

Matlovich's case had the highest profile in the media. He appeared on the cover of *Time* in uniform six months after his letter was delivered. The caption was "I Am Homosexual." On the inside, there were photos of him recovering from wounds in Da Nang, South Vietnam, and dancing in a gay bar. The prominent coverage that *Time* granted the Matlovich case encouraged Miriam Ben-Shalom to inform her commanding officer that she was a lesbian and inspired Ensign "Copy" Berg to fight his discharge from the navy (ibid., 413).

In November 1975, Matlovich was discharged by the air force, and federal district court judge Gerhard Gesell refused to overturn the air force's decision. But there was legal momentum building in Matlovich's favor. The court of appeals ruled in December 1978 that the discharges of Matlovich and Ensign Berg were illegal. It did not order the reinstatement of either man. It did, however, force Judge Gesell to reexamine the Matlovich case. Gesell's September 1980 decision ordered Matlovich's reinstatement to the air force by December 5 of that year (ibid.).

The air force responded by offering Matlovich a cash settlement in a last-ditch effort to avoid having to take him back in its ranks. Most observers thought that Matlovich would not accept such a settlement. And most realized as well that the air force would appeal Judge Gesell's decision to the United States Supreme Court. But in the end, within days of his reinstatement, Matlovich agreed to drop his case and accept the tax-free $160,000 offered by the air force (ibid., 413–414). Matlovich's courageous battle and the prominent mainstream media coverage it received helped to dramatize the military's pernicious internal policies toward lesbians and gay men.

The military ban remained in place throughout the 1980s, despite occasional sympathetic lower-court decisions. Military regulations were toughened during the Reagan-Bush years. The military revised its policy concerning homosexuality in 1982. A General Accounting Office (GAO) report suggests that the revision was implemented for three central reasons: "(1) to establish uniform procedures concerning homosexuality across the service branches; (2) to clarify the specific actions for which a person could be separated; and (3) to define the extenuating circumstances under which persons found to have engaged in those actions might nevertheless be retained" (Herek 1996, 6). The 1982 policy mandated the following:

> Homosexuality is incompatible with military service. The presence in the military environment of persons who engage in homosexual conduct seriously impairs the accomplishment of the military mission. . . . The presence of such members adversely affects the ability of the Military Services to maintain discipline, good order, and morale; to foster mutual trust and confidence among service members; to ensure the integrity of the system of rank and command; to facilitate assignment and worldwide deployment of service members who frequently must live and work under close conditions affording minimal privacy; to recruit and retain members of the Military Services; to maintain the public acceptability of military service; and to prevent breaches of security. (ibid., 7)

These are arguments that have been advanced by the military at various points over the years, and they were central components of the opposition to overturn the military ban.

That the 1980s were a particularly difficult decade for lesbians and gays in the military is reflected in discharge statistics. Between fiscal years 1980 and 1990, 16,919 men and women were discharged under the separate category of homosexuality. White women, in particular, were targeted. They "were discharged at a disproportionately high rate: 20.2 percent of those discharged for homosexuality were white women, although they constituted only 6.4 percent of personnel." The navy was disproportionately represented, as it accounted for 51 percent of all discharges related to homosexuality, despite the fact that it constituted only 27 percent of the active force during this period. These figures do not even include those lesbians and gay men processed under other categories and involuntarily separated from the military (ibid.).

Advocates for lesbian and gay civil rights embraced overturning the military ban as a priority in the 1980s. Legislation to overturn the ban was introduced by Senator Howard Metzenbaum (D-OH) and Representative Patricia Schroeder (D-CO) in 1992. At that point, there appeared to be mounting opposition to the military policy on the part of many national organizations, as well as colleges and universities that chose to ban military recruiters and Reserve Officers' Training Corps programs from their campuses.

The "Don't Ask, Don't Tell" Debate and Policy

It was in this context that presidential candidate Bill Clinton announced that if he were elected president in the 1992 presidential election, one of his first acts would be to overturn the military ban through executive order. In the fall of 1991, then presidential candidate Bill Clinton was asked by a student at a Harvard University forum whether he would issue an executive order to overturn the ban on lesbians and gays in the military. Clinton responded yes and explained further: "I think people who are gay should be expected to work, and should be given the opportunity to serve the country." He continued to make this pledge as a presidential candidate and then very early in his presidency (Rimmerman 1996c, xix). Clinton's position did not provoke any challenge during the primaries because all of the Democratic contenders, including Jerry Brown, Tom Harkin, Bob Kerry, and Paul Tsongas, had joined him in favoring a change to the policy in response to a question on a questionnaire distributed by the Human Rights Campaign Fund (HRCF). And in May 1992, Clinton gave a "moving and unprecedented" speech to the Los Angeles lesbian and gay community, describing "a vision of America that included gay and lesbian Americans and in which discrimination, particularly the government's own bias-induced policy of keeping homosexuals from serving their country in uniform, would end" (McFeeley 2002, 239).

During the 1992 presidential campaign, President Bush did not make Clinton's promise an issue, and it was certainly not in Clinton's interest to focus attention on it as he tried to woo moderate voters. Why did the Republicans not make it an issue in the campaign? Tim McFeeley, who was executive director of HRCF (now HRC) at the time, offered this explanation: "Why the Republicans, who had to be well aware of Clinton's stand on gays in the military, let it go is unclear, but the probable explanation was to distance Bush from the vitriol and extremism of the 1992 GOP National Convention in Houston, particularly Pat Buchanan's fuming and foaming in his August 13, 1992 address. . . . The assistance that Buchanan provided in the defeat of George Bush in 1992 cannot be overstated" (ibid., 239–240). But the fact that the issue did not come up during the campaign meant that Clinton and his advisers were not ready for the vitriol unleashed by opponents of lifting the ban even before he took office. And the lesbian and gay movements were also unprepared and ill-equipped to provide the considerable organizing effort necessary to support the president's initial effort to overturn the military ban.

The military ban and Clinton's attempt to rescind it raise an array of important questions. Why did such furious and sustained opposition emerge to Clinton's original promise? What are the sources of this opposition? To what extent was Clinton's promise related to changing cultural factors regarding lesbians and gays in the larger society? Why did Congress toughen Clinton's compromise proposal? What are the broader implications of how this issue was resolved for the lesbian and gay movements?

The first major news story in the period between Clinton's election and his inauguration was his announcement that he planned to adhere to his campaign promise and overturn the ban on lesbians and gays through an executive order. At that precise moment, Clinton had no idea that this promise would be an enduring controversy for the first six months of his presidency. After Clinton's inauguration, the controversy reached its zenith as the issue dominated radio call-in programs and newspaper headlines for a week. Congressional offices were flooded with postcards, telegrams, and telephone calls from irate citizens who adamantly opposed the president's suggestion that the military ban be overturned. Some argued that the mobilization of the citizenry against overturning the military ban had been carefully orchestrated by the Christian Right. These religious conservatives gained considerable support when the joint chiefs of staff, led by Chairman Colin Powell, expressed strong opposition to Clinton's promise, and when Sam Nunn, chairman of the Senate Armed Services Committee, expressed public concern. Nunn held much publicized hearings on the issue in the spring of 1993, hearings that those in favor of overturning the ban later characterized as being biased in favor of the military. The hearings themselves produced several dramatic moments, most notably Colonel Fred Peck's outing of his own son Scott. Peck, who at the time was the U.S. Army spokesman in Somalia, testified in favor of the ban because of antigay prejudice in the ranks. He concluded that if his son were in the military hierarchy, "I would be very fearful his life would be in jeopardy from his own troops." Scott Peck later responded to his father by stating, "I have a little more faith in members of the military" (Rimmerman 1996c, 116).

The media's role in defining the context and setting the agenda for the debate was significant. For example, the media captured Colonel Peck's dramatic congressional testimony live, televised it into millions of homes, and gave it considerable coverage on the evening news. The brutal beating and murder of Seaman Allen Schindler after he had identified himself as a gay man and as he prepared for discharge were given coverage by the media as well. In addition, Sam Nunn and several of his colleagues in favor of the ban were given a tour of two navy ships so that they could get a better understanding of the close living quarters experienced by military personnel. He identified for the accompanying C-SPAN camera the closeness of the bunks and shower stalls and asked groups of sailors how they felt about the idea of "open homosexuals" in the armed forces. The press reinforced the most negative stereotypes regarding lesbians and gays by covering this tour extensively. The role of the press, Sam Nunn's ability to dominate the debate with his hearings, and the mobilization of the Christian Right at the grassroots level all had the consequence of forcing the president and his opponents of the ban on the defensive. Opponents of the ban never really recovered from this defensive posture.

Much attention was focused on Clinton's role in the debate, given that it was his attempt to overturn the ban that inspired national attention on the issue. Just what role did Clinton play? When Clinton appeared on a live broadcast of *CBS This Morning* on May 27, 1993, a Virginia minister asked him about the issue of gays in the military. Clinton responded,

"Most Americans believe that the gay lifestyle should not be promoted by the military or anybody else in this country. . . . We are trying to work this out so that our country does not appear to be endorsing a gay lifestyle. . . . I think most Americans will agree when it works out that people are treated properly if they behave properly without the government appearing to endorse a lifestyle" (Bawer 1993, 148–149). With this response, Clinton employed the worst form of language—*lifestyle, endorse, approve, promote*—from the antigay lexicon in his answer. Members of the lesbian and gay community responded quickly. David Mixner, Clinton's longtime friend and a leading openly gay member of the Democratic Party, claimed that he was physically sickened by Clinton's response. Of course, Mixner and others supporting overturning the ban had plenty of good reasons to be disturbed. Clinton had begun to backtrack in public on his promise to overturn the ban through an executive order. One explanation for his actions is that he was trying to distance himself from lesbian and gay groups for political reasons. What better way to do this but to embrace elements of the language of the Christian Right groups that were so feverishly working to uphold the ban (Rimmerman 1996c, 116–117)?

But Clinton's comments also indicate that he was signaling to lesbian and gay groups and their supporters that he would likely compromise on his original promise. There was little surprise, then, when Clinton compromised his original position with his July 1993 "Don't Ask, Don't Tell" proposal. The proposal contained the following elements:

1. The policy bars military recruiters from asking if prospective enlistees are gay or lesbian.
2. Heterosexual conduct is forbidden both on-base and off-base.
3. What constitutes homosexual conduct?
   A. same-sex intercourse
   B. public acknowledgment of homosexuality
   C. attempting a same-sex marriage
   D. same-sex hand-holding or kissing
4. What constitutes permissible activity?
   A. telling a spouse, attorney, or member of the clergy about your homosexuality
   B. associating with openly gay and lesbian people
   C. going to a gay or lesbian bar
   D. marching in a gay pride march in civilian clothes

5. Military personnel found to have engaged in homosexual conduct can be discharged.
6. Military officials can not launch probes merely to discover if an enlistee is gay or lesbian, but if they suspect, based on "articulatable facts," that a person has engaged in prohibited activity, they may investigate to find out if their suspicion is correct.
7. Capricious outing of suspected gays and lesbians by fellow personnel without evidence is forbidden, and any attempt to blackmail a suspected gay or lesbian member of the armed forces is punishable by a dishonorable discharge, a $2,000 fine, and a one-year jail term. (Bull 1993a, 24)

Clinton's proposal was modified by Sam Nunn, whose goal was to toughen it in ways that would make it more punitive toward lesbians and gays in the military. Nunn's efforts were ultimately codified into law by Congress under the rubric of "Don't Ask, Don't Tell, Don't Pursue," thus making it more difficult for opponents of the ban to offer serious structural reforms in the future. Because the previous ban was enforced through an executive order, which could at least be changed through presidential missive, the codification meant that any future changes to Nunn's congressional policy would require congressional consent. Nunn's tough congressional language enabled the specifics of the Clinton plan to take effect while codifying the law into a broad statement of policy, one that rejects the idea of accepting lesbians and gays in the military (see Appendix 2). In addition, the congressional version states that lesbians and gays have no constitutional rights for serving in the armed forces (Rimmerman 1996c, 118). This final element of Nunn's plan is "exactly what President Clinton hoped to challenge in his original determination to overturn the ban through executive order" ("The Legislative Word on Gays" 1993, 2076).

Why did President Clinton support a compromise on this issue? How could he do so, given the clear promise that he stated as a presidential candidate and as the newly elected president of the United States? A number of explanations have been identified by individuals both inside and outside the administration. Clinton's approach to governance has always been rooted in building consensus. This was true when he was governor of Arkansas, and his two-term presidency suggested that he is someone who embraces consensus as a governing methodology rather than adhering to ideology or principle.

In addition, Clinton was obviously motivated by political considerations. His chief advisers—Rahm Emanuel, David Gergen, Bruce Lindsey, Thomas "Mack" McLarty, and George Stephanopoulos—clearly wanted him to put this divisive "no-win" issue behind the new administration. Clinton and his advisers believed that it was important for him to embrace the center of the political spectrum as a proud "new kind of Democrat." It made sense, then, for purely political reasons that Clinton would want to distance himself from an unpopular special interest—lesbians and gays. Clinton certainly did not want to associate himself with Democrats such as Michael Dukakis and Walter Mondale, both of whom had reputations as individuals who could be pushed around by liberal special interests. As one political analyst suggested, "when he made a change in the rules that prohibited homosexuals from serving in the armed forces as one of his first executive orders, Clinton appeared to be taking a stand on the very kind of social issue that had driven so many Democrats away from their party in the first place" (Radosh 1996, 220–221).

It is clear as well that Clinton realized that without a major fight, he did not have the congressional votes needed to uphold his original desire to rescind the ban. This view was reinforced by Representative Barney Frank, when he publicly proposed a compromise plan, much to the consternation of many lesbian and gay activists (Rimmerman 1996c, 118). Under Frank's proposal, which he named "Don't Ask, Don't Tell, Don't Investigate," Pentagon officials would have been forbidden to ask recruits about their sexual orientation. In addition, military personnel also would have been "forbidden to disclose their homosexuality while on duty but would be free to do so during off-duty hours." In providing a rationale for his proposal, Frank argued that it was an improved version of the Clinton-Nunn compromise proposal and said he was worried that Congress was about to codify an even more restrictive proposal into law (Bull 1993b, 25–27). In the end, then, Frank believed that it was better to get something for lesbians and gays in the military rather than nothing at all. President Clinton obviously shared this compromise spirit, and this rationale underlay his entire approach to resolving the broader issue.

By backing away from his original promise, Clinton could also appease and meet the demands of the joint chiefs of staff. Led by Chairman Colin Powell, the joint chiefs were firmly opposed to rescinding the ban. As commander in chief of the armed forces, President Clinton had the authority and power to order the joint chiefs to obey his directives. But in this case,

Clinton chose not to do so. Ultimately, he was convinced that the joint chiefs' perspective deserved more attention in the final policy resolution of the issue than the concerns of lesbian and gay activists. Clinton would not forget either that the 1992 presidential campaign devoted considerable attention to his activities during the Vietnam War. George Bush and the Republicans hammered away at Clinton's opposition to the war and his lack of foreign policy experience. For Clinton, backing off of his support for overturning the ban meant that he could win some much needed support from the military, the group that seemed most threatened by his original campaign promise (Rimmerman 1996c, 119).

Finally, Clinton and his political advisers feared that they were squandering valuable political capital during his honeymoon period over such an emotionally charged issue. From Clinton's vantage point, his first budget plan, health care, and the ratification of the North American Free Trade Agreement were far more important policy initiatives than rescinding the ban. As a result, he did not even lobby members of Congress to overturn the ban because he realized that their support would be needed on policy concerns of much higher priority to his new administration.

How did Clinton defend his own compromise plan? He publicly identified the plan as an "honest compromise" and acknowledged that the plan's specifics were not necessarily identical to his own goals. In the face of intense congressional and military opposition to lifting the ban, Clinton believed that the policy was the closest he could come to fulfilling his campaign promise. One administration official said, "The President believes that it is a solid advance forward in terms of extending rights to gays and lesbians in the military" (ibid., 119).

The Response of the Lesbian and Gay Movements to Clinton's Compromise

Lesbian and gay activists and their supporters did not share the president's optimism. Tom Stoddard, the coordinator of the Campaign for Military Service, a Washington, D.C.–based organization that had been established during the debate to help rally support for overturning the ban, stated, "The President could have lifted up the conscience of the country. Instead, he acceded without a fight to the stereotypes of prejudices he himself had disparaged." Torrie Osborn, at the time the executive director of the National Gay and Lesbian Task Force, argued that the plan is "simply a repackaging of discrimination." And Tim McFeeley, then executive director of the Human Rights Campaign Fund, called the Clinton proposal a "shattering disappointment" (Rimmerman 1996c, 119). McFeeley later argued that "the political loss sustained by Clinton and the gay community was the result of inexperience, bad timing, and a romantic but naïve conviction that the ideal of fairness could trump the politics of fear" (2002, 237). Conservative author and columnist Bruce Bawer assailed the Nunn proposal and Clinton's support for the proposal: "This compromise . . . would essentially write into law the institution of the closet: while heterosexuals would continue to enjoy their right to lead private lives and to discuss those lives freely, gays would be allowed to remain in the armed forces only so long as they didn't mention their homosexuality to anyone or have relationships on or off base" (1993, 117). But it was a *New Republic* editorial that perhaps best captured the fury of those who expected the president to follow through on his original campaign promise: "And the most demeaning assumption about the new provisions is that they single out the deepest moment of emotional intimacy—the private sexual act—as that which is most repugnant. Its assumption about the dignity and humanity of gay people, in and out of the military, in public and in private, is sickening" (ibid., 62). These statements by prominent lesbian and gay activists reflected the larger community's enormous disappointment and frustration after the president issued his compromise.

How the Clinton Administration Might Have Avoided Compromise

To supporters of rescinding the ban, the Clinton administration made a number of very serious strategic mistakes, mistakes that could have been avoided. Some believe that the president should have introduced the executive order as he had promised and then allowed Congress to do what it wished, even if that meant passing legislation that challenged the executive order. By embracing such a strategy, the president would have been given credit for following through with a policy promise rooted in principle (Rimmerman 1996c, 120).

In addition, the administration clearly underestimated the opposition of Congress (most notably Sam Nunn), the joint chiefs of staff, the military, and the Christian Right. The Clinton administration was surprised that Nunn would attempt to embarrass a new president of his own political party, one who generally supported "New Democratic principles."

The administration also failed to establish an honest and open line of communication with lesbian and gay groups. Several officials from an array of lesbian and gay organizations charged that they were deliberately misled about Clinton's intentions regarding overturning the ban from the outset. Apparently during the presidential transition and the first weeks of the Clinton presidency, lesbian and gay groups were told by influential presidential advisers not to lift a finger in terms of organizing grassroots support, because the president would do everything necessary to overturn the ban. In a much-publicized April 1993 White House meeting, just before the March on Washington, President Clinton told lesbian and gay activists in attendance that he would persuade Colin Powell and the joint chiefs of staff to support his plan to rescind the ban.

Yet another serious problem was that during the first several months of the Clinton presidency, no one at the White House was assigned the responsibility of overseeing legislative strategy for overturning the ban. This was the case until David Gergen joined the Clinton White House, at which point George Stephanopoulos was given the responsibility for coordinating the Clinton strategy.

The Clinton administration did little lobbying on Capitol Hill. It is possible that the ban might well have received more congressional support had the president used the powers of his office to enlist that support. But Congress was thrown on the defensive in the face of the administration's emphasis on such an unpopular issue in the early months of the Clinton presidency. Leon Panetta, a former member of the House of Representatives (R-CA) who had been appointed by Clinton as the new director of the Office of Management and Budget, offers this analysis regarding why the Democratically controlled Congress hesitated to give support to the newly elected president: "Once there's some blood in the water, the Hill begins to tighten up a little bit, in terms of 'What's coming next?' and 'Where are we headed?'" (Hamilton 2007, 51).

In retrospect, it is obvious now that the timing of the issue did not work to the president's advantage. His plan to rescind the ban was not a good issue with which to begin his presidency. Panetta, for one, recognizes this as a serious problem: "Anyone with an ounce of experience in Washington knew that you certainly don't want to take on the gays in the military issue as one of the first ones after going into office" (ibid., 47). Some have argued that Clinton would have been much better off raising the issue after his first year in office. At that point, he would have established the credibility of his administration with concrete legislative accomplishments. This might have given him more clout in dealing with Congress.

Finally, it is clear to critics that President Clinton did not perform his important leadership role in educating the public about why he believed that it was necessary to rescind the ban. Many presidential scholars have identified the importance of the president's potential role as an educator. In the words of Leon Wieseltier, "It is not leadership to tell people what they want to hear. It is leadership to tell people what they do not want to hear, and to give them a reason to listen" (1993, 77).

Flaws in the Lesbian and Gay Movements' Political Strategies

In his thoughtful analysis of the military-ban debate, former HRCF director Tim McFeeley identifies three reasons President Clinton lost control of the policy agenda with respect to the military ban. McFeeley points to then Senate Minority Leader Bob Dole, "who saw this issue as one with which he could wound the president and start his own 1996 campaign for the White House" as his first reason. Senator Dole first presented the issue to Congress in the form of an amendment proposal to the Family and Medical Leave Act, "designated S. 1 because it was such a top priority for Democrats, in order to force a vote within the first two weeks of the new administration" (2002, 240–241). A second reason "was the inexperience and ineptitude" of the newly elected president's political team. To support his argument, McFeeley reminds us that "during the weeks leading up to the late-January confrontation with Congress over lifting the gay ban, and even after the controversy erupted, the Clinton staff was not coordinating strategies or sharing information with gay lobbying groups." As McFeeley accurately points out, it was not only the Clinton presidency that made strategic errors in the debate over lesbians and gays in the military. The lesbian and gay movements also made a number of tactical mistakes, mistakes that undermined their attempt to garner greater public support for overturning the ban. The third major reason that Clinton lost control of the policy agenda "was the overconfidence and insufficient grassroots support in the gay community. Despite the incessant warnings of Barney Frank, Pat Schroeder, and others on Capitol Hill, little constituent pressure had been orchestrated with which to support the president's position" (2002, 241). The Campaign for Military Service was largely a Washington, D.C., organizing effort; it failed to generate the kind of grassroots support needed in states whose congressional representatives were wavering in their decisions on whether to rescind the ban. In addition, lesbian and gay rights advocates were never able to marshal the volume of calls and letters from constituents to win over legislators, who were being deluged with calls and mail organized largely by the Christian Right, which supported the ban. Representative Barney Frank received considerable criticism from the lesbian and gay communities for identifying the problems associated with the lesbian and gay organizing efforts. Frank said, "We did a very bad job of mobilizing—getting people to write to members of the House and Senate. We spent a lot of our time and energy on things that are irrelevant to a short-term fight in Congress. People assumed that the March on Washington or demonstrations were a good thing. Those have no effect on members of Congress" (Osborne 1994, 53). Frank's astute observations reveal that he was particularly critical of the March on Washington's organizers' inability to generate a massive congressional lobbying effort on behalf of rescinding the ban.

At the outset of the debate, the mainstream lesbian and gay organizations also put far too much trust in Clinton. Delirious with excitement because a supposed friend had been elected to the White House, the movements largely ignored Clinton's less-than-stellar record on lesbian and gay issues while governor of Arkansas. Historian John D'Emilio captures the challenges facing the lesbian and gay movements well:

> The Clinton administration is going to offer our movement and our community an alternative to outsider status. Will we be ready to accept it? Will we be able to shape our roles as insiders? Will we be able to use the openness of the Clinton presidency to further an agenda for justice? Or will the allure of the system, the perks of power, swallow us up? Can we walk the corridors of power and still retain the animating vision of justice and decency that comes to us from having been cast as outsiders? (2002, 139)

There were some notable exceptions to the prevailing view that the Clinton presidency would lead to tangible public policy gains. Michael Petrelis, a member of the Washington, D.C., chapters of ACT UP and Queer Nation, distributed "Impeach Clinton" buttons the weekend before the

November 1992 presidential election. Unlike many of his counterparts in the mainstream lesbian and gay movements, Petrelis recognized that supposedly having Clinton on his side was simply not enough. From the outset, Petrelis and other more radical members of the movements distrusted Clinton's motives, sincerity, and seriousness of purpose in overturning the ban and addressing HIV/AIDS policy meaningfully. One astute analyst points out that the "enthusiasm for candidate Clinton seemed undeserved given his lackluster support of lesbian and gay issues prior to coming to Washington, and that enthusiasm translated into greater trust and a greater benefit of the doubt than Clinton deserved." This analyst is understandably critical of the response of the lesbian and gay movements' leaders. He cites a letter by then HRCF executive director Tim McFeeley that marked the first time the HRCF had ever endorsed a presidential candidate: "Bill Clinton and Bill Clinton alone, has clearly and unequivocally articulated positive stands on the issues. . . . In the past several months, Bill Clinton has met with lesbian and gay groups and AIDS activists. He has incorporated our agenda and our goals into his own." The letter further explained that Bill Clinton would "use 'whatever means necessary' to eradicate AIDS . . . advocate for the National Lesbian and Gay Civil Rights Law, and who 'with the stroke of a pen' would 'end the exclusion of gays and lesbians from the U.S. military and [would] end discrimination in federal employment based on sexual orientation'" (Lehring 1996, 283). McFeeley's letter was just one of the many encomiums that candidate Clinton reserved from the mainstream lesbian and gay movements, praise and enthusiastic support that he did not deserve.

For those supporting overturning the ban, there were further complications. Some lesbians and gays simply could not garner excitement about the issue. This lack of excitement was due to several factors. Many people thought that the fight had been won by having Clinton as president, especially since he was the one who promised to rescind the ban. The movements had no real experience in dealing with a president who seemingly supported lesbian and gay concerns. In addition, the issue understandably did not seem nearly as important for a community that had been and continues to be ravaged by AIDS. One analyst correctly claims that "it is obvious that allowing lesbians and gays in the military would not have been the issue most people in the gay community would have had at the top of their list of wishes to be granted by a new administration in Washington. Greater funding and awareness for AIDS, or a federal civil rights law for lesbians, gays, and other sexual minorities, were issues that could have potentially generated more excitement at the grassroots level of the lesbian and gay movement" (ibid., 282). Many lesbians and gays cut their political teeth in the antiwar movement of the 1960s and did not want to legitimate participation in the military. Others were frustrated by the narrow assimilationism of the call for overturning the ban and an inability to connect this organizing work to a larger political and social strategy. One historian captured this critique well ten years later when she linked the drive for same-sex marriage and military integration: "The push for gay marriage and military service has replaced the array of political, cultural, and economic issues that galvanized the national groups as they first emerged from a progressive social movement context several decades earlier" (Duggan 2003, 45). We will return to this critique when we interrogate the response of the lesbian and gay movements to same-sex marriage in Chapter 5.

Implementation of the "Don't Ask, Don't Tell" Policy

The initial reports of policy implementation outlined themes that have been present since the policy was first implemented in 1994. One analysis claimed that it "has not made life easier for many gay servicemen and women and in some ways has made it worse." The principal concern in the early stages of implementation is that although the policy may have been designed to enable lesbians and gays to "serve without fear of persecution if they kept their sexual orientation private," it has been carried out by commanders who have misused "the broad new authority granted under the policy to ferret out homosexuals." Eric Schmitt's *New York Times* account also revealed the following: "In addition, while a few gay servicemen and women said they felt the new policy had improved conditions, most of those who were interviewed said it had instead polarized attitudes toward homosexuals and had shifted the burden of proof to the servicemember if accused of engaging in homosexual acts" (1994, A1). These problems were to emerge over and over again in both press accounts and studies undertaken by the Servicemembers Legal Defense Network (SLDN), a Washington, D.C.–based organization founded by Michelle Benecke and C. Dixon Osburn that represents lesbian and gay service members. As the sole national legal aid and watchdog organization for those targeted by the military's new policy on homosexuals, it is the only means currently available to document abuses.

FIGURE 4.1   Total Military Lesbian, Gay, and Bisexual Discharges Under "Don't Ask, Don't Tell"

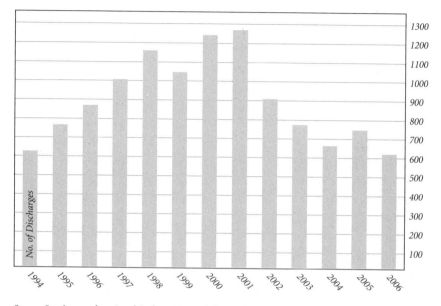

Source: Servicemembers Legal Defense Network (http://www.sldn.org).

One important policy question is "how well has the 'Don't Ask, Don't Tell' policy worked to create a 'zone of privacy' for military members since its enactment?" (D'Amico 2000, 253). The short answer is not well at all. The number of discharges declined steadily since 1982 and reached a low point in 1994, but they began to rise again in 1995 before peaking at their highest point in ten years in 1998 (ibid., 254).

We also know that since 2001 and the beginning of the war in Afghanistan, "'Don't Ask, Don't Tell' discharges have declined by almost half" (see figure 4.1). The SLDN reports that lesbian and gay discharges have dropped during every major military mobilization, including World War II, the Korean War, Vietnam War, Persian Gulf War, and the current war in Iraq. In addition, the SLDN reports that "women account for 30% of 'Don't Ask, Don't Tell' discharges, but comprise only 15% of the military" (http://www.sldn.org, n.p.).

One aspect of the current implementation of the policy that has understandably received considerable attention in the media is the military's decision to discharge fifty-eight Arabic linguists because they are gay. These talented linguists have much to offer the military and the country at large, given American foreign policy interests in the Middle East. The GAO has noted that "nearly 800 dismissed gay or lesbian service members had critical abilities, including 300 with important language skills." The financial cost of replacing these specialized service people is exorbitant. According to the Center for the Study of Sexual Minorities in the Military at the University of California–Santa Barbara, "discharging and replacing them has cost the Pentagon nearly $369 million" ("Army Dismisses Gay Arabic Linguist" 2006, n.p.).

What accounts for all of these developments? Sharon Debbage Alexander, current deputy director for policy at the Servicemembers Legal Defense Network and a former U.S. Army lieutenant, offers these explanations for the current trends:

> I think that many people inside the Pentagon do realize the insanity of discharging anyone—linguist or otherwise—on the sole basis of their sexual orientation. But since the Congressional action in 1993, this is not a Pentagon policy or regulation that Pentagon leaders or the Commander in Chief could just change at their discretion. "Don't Ask, Don't Tell" is a federal statute—10 USC 654, and the Pentagon is bound to enforce it. While many commanders (smartly, in my view) look for ways to avoid enforcing "Don't Ask, Don't Tell" when doing so will hurt their units' abilities to perform their missions, most folks take the law at face value and try to comply with it. And I think that what's happening in practice is also very telling. More military leaders at the operational level are looking the other way when presented with evidence that one of their charges is lesbian, gay, or bisexual.

And why have we seen the significant drop in gay discharges by nearly half when compared to the soaring rates of the late 1990s? Alexander offers a perceptive answer in response to that important policy question:

> It's not because there are fewer gay people serving, nor is it because they're doing a better job staying in the closet—from our legal services case load, we actually see that many more service members are taking a risk and coming out to their colleagues, in most cases with little or no negative consequences. The generation of young officers and enlisted personnel fighting this war by and large doesn't have the same prejudices about gay people that even my generation of officers did. (e-mail to author, June 8, 2007)

In order for the "Don't Ask, Don't Tell" policy to be repealed, Congress must swing into legislative action. Representative Martin Meehan (D-MA) introduced the Military Readiness Enhancement Act in March 2005, which would repeal the military's ban on openly lesbian and gay service personnel. As of November 2006, the bill had 122 cosponsors and Meehan and his supporters hoped to force legislative action on the proposed legislation (Rosenberg 2006, 8).

The Case for the Military Ban

For those who wished to overturn the military ban, they quickly learned during the first several months of the Clinton administration that the opposition to overturning the ban was rooted in a number of deep-seated concerns, concerns that reflect the long-standing hostility toward lesbians and gays in the larger society. Bruce Bawer points out that an individual might be threatened by homosexuality due to several factors. First is utter incomprehension: He or she cannot understand how other human beings could have such feelings and could experience sexual attraction to a member of the same sex. The idea is so foreign as to be threatening, frightening, and repulsive. Male sexual insecurity also helps to explain some men's hostility toward extending gay rights: Those who harbor these concerns fear being the object of desire. Men are used to being in control of their relationships with women and are not used to being the "object of affection" of other men. This fear is reflected in a Michigan airman's statement of what would happen if the ban on lesbians and gays in the military was lifted: "I couldn't sleep at night. I'd be worried that some homosexual is going to sneak over and make a pass at me" (1993, 266).

These concerns underlie some of the more specific arguments offered by those opposed to overturning the ban. It is interesting to note that some of these same arguments were posited by those opposed to Harry Truman's decision to integrate the military racially by executive order in 1948. As one historian's extensive analysis of the comparisons of the debates over race and sexuality in the armed forces shows, those in favor of the ban resisted any meaningful comparisons between race and sexual orientation, despite the fact that there were some clear parallels. For example, Colin Powell, then chairman of the joint chiefs of staff, wrote the following in a letter to Congresswoman Patricia Schroeder: "I can assure you I need no reminders concerning the history of African Americans in the defense of their Nation and the tribulations they faced. I am a part of that history. Skin color is a benign, nonbehavioral characteristic. Sexual orientation is perhaps the most profound of human behavioral characteristics. Comparison of the two is a convenient but invalid argument" (Bianco 1996, 47).

Powell's open opposition to rescinding the military ban had tremendous consequences for the ultimate outcome of the debate. Others certainly shared Powell's views. One scholar wrote that "to lump blacks with homosexuals is an affront to most African Americans" (ibid., 48). As David Ari Bianco suggests, however, few participants in the debate based their conclusions on thoughtful comparisons between the integration of African Americans in the late 1940s and the contemporary debate over lesbians and gays. He concludes that "the arguments used to keep African Americans segregated are so similar to those that barred lesbians and gays in the early 1990s that a gay newspaper, the *Washington Blade*, argued that the history of the military's exclusion of African Americans 'seems to be serving as a blueprint for the military on how to dissuade the government from allowing gays to serve openly in the ranks'" (ibid., 49).

Just what are some of the arguments articulated by proponents of the military ban on lesbians and gays that were also used in the debate to prevent racial integration in the late 1940s? Several of the arguments against lesbians and gays in uniform are informed by the notion that lesbians and gays are inferior to heterosexuals, and as a result would make poor soldiers. One such argument is the belief that gay men have such relentless sexual appetites that they simply cannot be controlled in a military setting. As Bianco points out, "the defenders of the military's ban on lesbians and gays frequently raised the specter of homosexual rapists and pedophiles endangering young soldiers and sailors." Southern conservatives made a similar argument during the racial integration debate of 1948 when they claimed that the higher rate of rape and other crimes attributed to African Americans would endanger the daily functions of the military (ibid., 50).

Another line of argument used to defend the military ban on lesbians and gays was to highlight the higher prevalence of sexually transmitted diseases, specifically AIDS, associated with gay men. The Family Research Council, a conservative organization, made this argument in one of its publications:

The AIDS risk is very real, since two-thirds of all current AIDS cases in-volved the transmission through homosexual activity, according to the Centers for Disease Control. Homosexuals also account for a dispropor-tionate number of cases of sexually transmitted diseases, such as syphilis, gonorrhea, genital warts, hepatitis A, hepatitis B and also diseases associ-ated with anal intercourse, such as the parasites collectively referred to as "gay bowel syndrome." According to the American Medical Association, ho-mosexual youths are 23 times more likely to contract a sexually transmitted disease than are heterosexuals. (ibid., 51)

A similar argument was offered by Kevin Tededo, a cofounder of the conservative group Colorado for Family Values: "There is no question that the homosexual community, particularly males, are [sic] very diseased." During hearings on the military ban, one colonel testified, "At the very least homosexuals would have to be specially identified to ensure their blood not be used as a protection to other soldiers." Similar arguments were once again raised in the racial integration debate of the late 1940s. As Bianco notes, "during World War II the Red Cross—with no scientific jus-tification—maintained racially segregated blood banks at the demand of the armed forces." And former senator Richard Russell highlighted disease rates among African Americans in the quest to keep the military segre-gated (ibid.).

In addition, those opposed to Clinton's campaign promise contended that the presence of lesbians and gays in the armed forces would under-mine the "good order, discipline, and morale of the fighting forces" (Shilts 1993, 17). Norman Schwarzkopf reinforced this point of view in a 1982 sworn deposition in which he "characterized homosexuality as be-ing 'incompatible with military service' because it impaired good order, discipline, and morale." The general said that his twenty-six-year military career led him to conclude that "homosexuals are unsuited for military service" (ibid., 426). Conservative legal scholar Bruce Fein echoed Schwarzkopf's argument and raised the important connection between masculinity and the criteria for being a good soldier as a justification for opposing attempts to integrate lesbians and gays: "The lifeblood of a sol-dier is masculinity, bravery, and gallantry. The battlefield soldier is inspired to risk all by fighting with comrades whose attributes conform to his view of manhood. . . . And it is inarguable that the majority of a fighting force would be psychologically and emotionally deflated by the close presence of homosexuals who evoke effeminate or repugnant but not manly visions" (ibid., 730).

Like Schwarzkopf and Fein, decorated Vietnam veteran David H. Hackworth worried that openly lesbian and gay soldiers would undermine the military's illusion of masculine invincibility: "To survive in a killing field, a warrior has to believe he's invincible, that he's wearing golden armor; that he can buck 1,000 to 1 odds and live. To think that way, he has to be macho. Fairly or unfairly, gays threaten that macho. When it goes, the warrior starts thinking, 'Maybe I won't make it.' And from that moment, the unit goes to hell." The perceived danger of lesbians and gays in the military is so threatening that Hackworth warned: "I cannot think of a better way to destroy the fighting spirit and gut U.S. combat effectiveness." Schwarzkopf's, Hackworth's, and Fein's analyses are important ones because they underscore the importance of how manly visions of masculinity underlie the debate over lesbians and gays in the military. Similar arguments were made during the racial integration debate. Writing in 1948, *New York Times* military editor Hanson W. Baldwin wrote that "one of the surest ways to break down the morale of the army and to destroy its efficiency" is to support racial integration of the military (Bianco 1996, 53).

Supporters of the military ban on lesbians and gays argued, too, that if lesbians and gays were admitted, they would undermine the ability of the military "to recruit and retain members of the armed forces." Ban supporters worried that the United Sates would face "the specter of a depleted military force and weakened recruitment efforts if those who join or remain were forced to associate with people known to be lesbian or gay." Schwarzkopf said, "The impact on the army's public image would also endanger recruitment and retention, by causing potential servicemembers to hesitate to enlist, making parents of potential servicemembers reluctant to recommend or approve the enlistment of their sons and daughters in an organization in which they would be forced to live and work with known homosexuals, and causing members of the army to hesitate to reenlist." Schwarzkopf's views were supported by others in the military hierarchy. A four-star general reported to the *Washington Times*, "It would be a wrenching change. . . . We're not ready for it. Good people will leave the military in droves over this." Similarly, the threat of white desertion was invoked during the debate over racial integration in the late 1940s (Bianco 1996, 55).

The navy defined the rationale for its gay policies by making several arguments. An individual's daily performance of military duties could be hindered by emotional or sexual relationships with other individuals and would interfere with proper hierarchical and command relationships that characterize the military. There was also the concern that homosexual individuals might force their sexual desires on others, resulting in sexual assaults. In the early 1980s, the Pentagon argued that lesbians and gays must be banned in order to "facilitate assignment and worldwide deployment of servicemembers who frequently must live and work under close conditions affording minimal privacy" (Mohr 1993, 92). Furthermore, an internal navy memorandum revealed that "an officer or senior enlisted person who exhibits homosexual tendencies will be unable to maintain the necessary respect and trust from the great majority of naval personnel who detest/abhor homosexuality. This lack of respect and trust would most certainly degrade the officer's ability to successfully perform his duties of supervision and command" (Shilts 1993, 281).

All of the above arguments rely on bigoted and negative stereotypes of lesbians and gays. Indeed, when former head of the joint chiefs of staff Peter Pace said in 2005 that "the U.S. military mission fundamentally rests on the trust among its members and the homosexual lifestyle does not comport with that," he was merely making public his bigotry, which he reinforced in March 2007 when he called homosexual acts "immoral" (Ephron 2007, 34). As Richard Mohr points out, "none of [the arguments] is based on the ability of gay soldiers to fulfill the duties of their stations" (1993, 93). But it is these arguments that served to define the broader context of the debate, arguments that both Clinton and proponents of overturning the ban have had difficulty engaging in, in ways that would shift the grounds of the discussion (Rimmerman 1996c, 114).

The Case Against the Military Ban

Those in favor of lifting the military ban have offered several arguments. Many suggested that the ban itself is rooted in discrimination and prejudice against lesbians and gays, and we should not countenance any discrimination against individuals or groups in our society. In addition, lesbians, gays, and bisexuals have already fought and died on behalf of this country in an array of wars over the years. As a result, they should be afforded the kind of respect and support that their outstanding service to their country has earned. In practice, this means that they should be treated with decency and dignity in their daily lives. By its very nature, the ban is rooted in the most ugly assumptions about the connections between sexuality and military performance—assumptions that are not confirmed by any evidence. Indeed, one early study provided evidence for overturning the ban. In the spring of 1992, the Pentagon commissioned a RAND Corporation study of the military ban. The RAND study concluded that "the ban could be dropped without damaging the 'order, discipline, and individual behavior necessary to maintain cohesion, and performance.'" The report also stated that "many of the problems that opponents of lifting the ban anticipate are exaggerated through education and discipline" (Gallagher 1993, 28). Unfortunately, the Clinton administration chose to delay the timing of the release of the report in a way that diminished its potential impact. News reports circulated that the report was ready for release long before August 1993, when it was finally shared with the public. Indeed, it was released to the press and public at a downtime in Washington, when everyone was on vacation (including the president), so little attention would be focused on it. The release was inspired by a joint congressional letter signed by those in the House and Senate who were committed to overturning the ban, urging the Clinton administration to make the report's findings public (Rimmerman 1996c, 115).

For opponents of the ban, the financial costs of enforcement are exorbitant. Ultimately, these costs are paid by taxpayers. Writing in 1993, Randy Shilts concluded that "the cost of investigations and the dollars spent replacing gay and lesbian personnel easily amount to hundreds of millions of dollars" (4). A June 1992 congressional study revealed that "the ban on homosexuals in the armed forces costs the Pentagon at least $27 million a year" (Bawer 1993, 58). These costs have been corroborated by an array of sources since 1992.

Opponents of the ban also point out that most democracies allow lesbians and gays to serve with dignity in their militaries. More than twenty countries allow gays to serve, including all NATO countries except for Portugal and the United States.[2] Canada's 1992 decision to revoke its military ban caused little or no controversy, and its experience could have been an excellent lesson for the United States. In 2000, Britain was forced to overturn its military ban by the European Court of Human Rights, but as of 2005, the Royal Navy has called on gay rights groups to help recruit gay soldiers, and gay partners have been afforded full benefits (Alvarez 2006, n.p.). Britain, too, could have been a role model for the United States. Unfortunately, we appear to have learned little from Canada's and Britain's successful experiences in eliminating the military ban.

Many opponents of the ban have argued that since the 1993 debate, the U.S. military (and the United States more broadly) has become more open to lesbians and gays serving in the armed forces. For example, former retired army general and chairman of the joint chiefs of staff from 1993 to 1997 John Shalikashvili, argued that "the military has changed, and that gays and lesbians can be accepted by their peers." He bases this claim on a number of meetings that he has had with gay soldiers and marines, some of whom have had combat experience in Iraq. He also spoke to an "openly gay senior sailor who was serving effectively as a member of a nuclear submarine crew." Shalikashvili also points out that this greater openness is mirrored in public opinion, as evidenced by a late 2006 "Zogby poll of more than 500 service members returning from Afghanistan and Iraq, three quarters of whom said they were comfortable interacting with gay people" (2007, n.p.).

Finally, and perhaps most disturbingly, the ban reinforces the horrors of the closet for lesbians and gays in the military. The closet is then sanctioned by the institutional forces of the U.S. government in ways that prevent human beings from living open and fully developed lives. Philosopher Richard Mohr offers an analysis of the horrors of the closet: "The chief problem of the social institution of the closet is not that it promotes hypocrisy, requires lies, sets snares, blames the victim when snared, and causes unhappiness—though it does have all these results. No, the chief problem with the closet is that it treats gays as less than human, less than animal, less even than vegetable—it treats gays as reeking scum, the breath of death" (1993, 114).

The incalculable human costs of the military ban have taken a number of forms, as lives have been ruined and careers destroyed. Despairing women and men occasionally commit suicide in the face of the pressure associated with a purge, and the accompanying rumors that often precede one. This is certainly not surprising, given that military policies have created an atmosphere wherein discrimination, harassment, and violence against lesbians and gays are tolerated and often encouraged. Shilts's analysis of the consequences of the ban provides particularly chilling accounts of how lesbians face significant discrimination and harassment in their daily lives. For this and other reasons, opponents of the military ban argue that it must be overturned.

Conclusion

This chapter has offered a comprehensive overview of the current "Don't Ask, Don't Tell" policy by placing it within its appropriate historical, political, and policy contexts. In doing so, we have explored the tensions between the assimilationist and liberationist perspectives on whether military integration should be a central goal on the lesbian and gay movements' agenda and, if so, how to pursue that goal. We have interrogated the interactions between the movements and the Clinton presidency around this issue with an eye on how the movements interacted with a president who as a candidate promised to overturn the ban but ran into enormous obstacles as he attempted to implement that promise. The mainstream movements moved from being "outsiders" to "insiders" in the policy process as they were granted access to power in ways that they had never experienced before. This increased access did not necessarily lead to concrete policy accomplishments, as the Clinton years suggest. But it did lead to increased conflicts among assimilationists and liberationists over political organizing strategies. These conflicts have increasingly manifested themselves in other contentious policy areas, most notably the politics of same-sex marriage, which we will now explore in Chapter 5.

5

....

Jilted at the Altar:
The Debate Over
Same-Sex Marriage

Many lesbians and gay men have embraced the campaign for marriage rights because they, too, see marriage equality as a fundamental sign of their equality and full citizenship, and because securing the many rights, benefits, protections, and obligations conveyed by marriage would have so many palpable effects on their lives.

—George Chauncey

Equality is a good start, but it is not sufficient. Equality for queers inevitably means equal rights on straight terms, since they are the ones who determine the existing legal framework. We conform—albeit equally—with their screwed-up system. That is not liberation. It is capitulation.

—Peter Tatchell

THE FIGHT over same-sex marriage has become a central issue in the ongoing cultural wars in the United States. Some analysts have argued that gay marriage has replaced abortion as *the* focal issue of cultural conflict. In recent years, we have seen considerable political and organizing activity on all sides of the same-sex-marriage debate. Conservative activists have marched in Washington and throughout the United States, and have flooded the United States Senate with letters, telegrams, and e-mails supporting a constitutional ban limiting marriage to heterosexual couples. Lesbian and gay rights activists have also marched, lobbied, and accessed the legal system to challenge state and local laws that prevent them from marrying. The conflict over same-sex marriage has engulfed all branches and levels of government and has been the focus of many state referenda. The tremendous publicity that the issue has received has also forced presidential and congressional candidates to announce their positions on same-sex marriage during the course of their campaigns. Candidates have chosen to use the subject as a wedge issue in their electoral strategies.

The issue itself is complex. As we will see in this chapter, the debates over same-sex marriage extend back several decades. From the vantage point of many lesbian and gay activists, the right to marry is a logical extension of the assimilationist approach to political and social change. It is viewed as one of an array of issues that are all rights based: decriminalizing same-sex behavior, prohibiting discrimination in employment and housing, and serving openly in the military. All of these political and policy fights share a common goal: to extend the rights, benefits, and privileges that have been and are enjoyed by heterosexual citizens to lesbians, gays, bisexuals, and transgender individuals (Wilcox 2007, ix–x).

As we will see, however, there have been vocal critics of same-sex marriage both within and outside of the lesbian and gay movements. Why has this issue engendered such emotional responses? How has the fight for same-sex marriage affected the goals of the broader lesbian and gay movements? Why has there been disagreement among lesbian and gay activists regarding the desirability of placing marriage on the political organizing and policy agenda? What progress has been made in the fight for same-sex marriage? How has the Christian Right responded with its own organizing efforts? This chapter will address these questions and more. But before we can do so, we must turn our attention to how and when the issue emerged on the policy agenda in the United States.

Same-Sex Marriage in Historical Context

The same-sex marriage debate exploded on the national scene in the early 1990s, despite the fact that lesbians and gay men had been challenging their exclusion from the rights of marriage since the early 1970s. Early legal challenges were pursued without the support of organized lesbian and gay interests, though somewhat surprisingly, "from the earliest days of gay liberation, some activists demanded the right to marry," even as others who identified with the gay liberationist agenda denounced marriage "as a discredited patriarchal institution." Indeed, many liberationists coming out of the 1969 Stonewall Rebellion "rejected everything they associated with heterosexuality, including sex roles, marriage, and the family" (Chauncey 2004, 89). But others claimed that they should have the right to do anything and everything that heterosexuals could do, including holding hands with a partner in public or getting married. Given the repressive context of the times, either of these activities was viewed by many as a radical challenge to straight society. In the end, though, support for marriage was viewed as a minority position within the larger lesbian and gay movements' agenda. As historian George Chauncey points out, lesbian feminist activists were understandably hostile to pursuing marriage rights as a key component of the movements' agenda. To most lesbian feminists, "marriage was an inherently patriarchal institution, which played a central role in structuring the domination of women. As they sought to build a new women's culture shorn of patriarchal influence, many questioned monogamy and worked to construct new kinds of relationships and living patterns" (ibid., 93).

National organizations that were established in the 1970s, including the Gay Rights National Lobby (which later became the Human Rights Campaign), the Lambda Legal Defense and Education Fund, the Lesbian Rights Project, and the National Gay Task Force, and a growing number of local organizations largely ignored the issue, "either because they were critical of marriage, saw it as a hopeless cause, or most commonly, simply had other priorities. Instead of focusing on the rights of same-sex *couples*, gay politics at the time focused on securing the rights of *individuals* against discrimination in employment and on building *community* institutions and a collective culture" (ibid., 94).

Lone couples who filed legal challenges did so within this broad movement context and without the support of experienced legal advocates (Pinello 2006, 23). In May 1970, Jack Baker and J. Michael McConnell became the first gay couple to apply for a marriage license. Their marriage license application was denied by the Hennepin County, Minnesota, clerk, and in *Baker v. Nelson* (1971), the Minnesota Supreme Court ruled that "the men had no federal due process or equal protection rights to marry. The first marriage case involving a lesbian couple arose in Kentucky and met a similarly unsuccessful fate" in the 1973 decision *Jones v. Hallahan* (ibid., 22).

Over the course of the next two decades there were "at least four more failed attempts to seek judicial recognition of same-sex marriage (*Singer v. Hara* 1974; *Adams v. Howerton* 1980; *DeSanto v. Barnsley* 1984; and *Dean v. District of Columbia* 1992)." These developments prompted Yale law professor William Eskridge to conclude that "legal agitation for gay marriage in the 1970s [and 1980s and 1990s] was a complete flop" (ibid., 22). But a number of important factors came to the fore by the early 1990s that allowed same-sex marriage to emerge as an issue for national debate. Chauncey identifies those developments well: "The stage for the national marriage debate was set by the changing character of marriage, the changing circumstances of gay life, and the changing place of gay people in American society. . . . But it was the vision of a few key legal strategists and the decisions of a few state courts that took the issue to the next level" (2004, 123).

One of the most important developments in the lesbian and gay movements' organizing strategy was the emphasis on family issues by the early 1990s. These family issues included parenting by same-sex couples, partnership recognition, spousal benefits in the workplace, gay-supportive public school policies, and policies to support lesbian, gay, bisexual, and transgender youth. There were several factors that contributed to the changing historical circumstances that had consequences for the larger lesbian and gay movements and for the human beings that were the basis for the movements. One key development was the case of Sharon Kowalski.

Historian John D'Emilio provides a good overview of the importance of the Kowalski case for the lesbian movement:

> In 1983 Kowalski was involved in an automobile accident that left her ability to communicate seriously impaired. The courts awarded guardianship to Kowalski's father rather than to her partner, Karen Thompson, who for years was denied access to Kowalski. Across the United States, lesbian communities hosted forums, organized fundraisers, and worked to raise public awareness about the case. After an eight-year battle the courts eventually made Thompson the legal guardian, but in the meantime "Free Sharon Kowalski" became a rallying cry among lesbians concerned about the lack of legal recognition for their relationships. (2007, 49)

The Kowalski case received considerable coverage in the gay press, heightening attention to the broader policy issues involved. Some gay-pride marches opened with an empty wheelchair as a way to dramatize the injustices associated with the Kowalski case (Chauncey 2004, 113).

The AIDS crisis that emerged in the 1980s also inspired a call for full legal recognition of gay marriage by some movement activists. The reality of AIDS "suddenly forced tens of thousands of committed gay couples to deal with powerful institutions—hospitals, funeral homes, state agencies—that did not recognize their commitments. Even if AIDS patients were on their deathbeds, their life-partners were often excluded from visiting because they were not officially 'spouses' or next of kin" (Eisenbach 2006, 307). What made matters even worse is that hospitals were under no obligation to inform partners or loved ones about the medical-care process. This situation was devastating; those personally enveloped in these untenable circumstances and their supporters in the larger lesbian and gay movements looked for meaningful policy change in the form of same-sex marriage.

Another important factor contributing to the emphasis on family issues and the attention to same-sex marriage was the lesbian and gay baby boom. More people were choosing to become parents, thus challenging traditional notions of "family." The process varied considerably, as babies were "conceived through the cooperation of gay men with the procreative desires of lesbian friends to the use of sperm banks, adoption agencies, surrogacy, and sex among friends" (D'Emilio 2007, 50). These developments all meant that children and families became a more visible face of the lesbian and gay movements, thus challenging traditional notions of heteronormativity while at the same time reinforcing the assimilationist approach to political, social, and cultural change. In the end, the Kowalski case, the AIDS crisis, and the lesbian and gay baby boom all helped to catapult same-sex marriage onto the movements' policy agenda by the late 1980s and early 1990s.

The 1990s witnessed legal developments that had profound consequences for the same-sex marriage debate, consequences that still reverberate today. Indeed, the campaign for same-sex marriage has depended on the courts for much of the success that it has achieved. The broad assimilationist legal-rights strategy adopted by the lesbian and gay movements in the 1980s and early 1990s received judicial legitimacy with the Supreme Court of Hawaii's decision in *Baehr v. Lewin*.

Baehr v. Lewin

In 1991, three couples who were all residents of Hawaii challenged the state's marriage law by filing a declaratory judgment stating that the law was unconstitutional because it "denied same-sex couples the same marriage rights as different-sex couples." They based their claims on the privacy and equal-protection clauses of the Hawaii Constitution. The Hawaii Supreme Court's 1993 decision rejected the privacy argument but responded more positively to the equal-protection argument. It found nothing in the state constitution that prevented lesbian and gay marriage, and it concluded that denying same-sex couples access to the benefits and rights associated with marriage is a form of sex discrimination (Dolkart 1998, 316–317). With this decision, the Hawaii Supreme Court "challenged volumes of existing legal doctrine" (O'Connor and Yanus 2007, 294). It appeared that same-sex marriage might be headed toward approval in Hawaii and the United States writ large.

But the Supreme Court of Hawaii remanded the case to the state trial court, affording Hawaii the opportunity to present evidence at trial to justify the marriage statute. Prior to the trial, the Hawaii state legislature responded to the *Baehr* decision by passing a bill that "defined marriage in Hawaii as the union of a man and a woman. This bill also called for the establishment of a Commission on Sexual Orientation and the Law, which was to investigate and issue a report describing the legal and economic benefits of marriage and stating whether public policy reasons existed to extend these benefits to same-sex couples" (ibid., 300). The new trial was held during the summer of 1996, and because it found that "the state had failed to prove a compelling interest in denying same-sex couples the right to marry," the trial court ruled the state's marriage law unconstitutional. The decision itself "was stayed pending appeal" (Dolkart 1998, 316–317). The case returned to the Hawaii Supreme Court, which on December 9, 1999, issued a ruling of fewer than five hundred words stating, in essence, that the State of Hawaii can bar lesbian and gay couples from obtaining marriage licenses. It also ruled that a 1998 initiative passed by voters legitimated a previous statute that restricted licenses to one man and one woman. The court also, however, opened the door to the possibility that same-sex couples could still be eligible for "the same benefits of marriage—even without the license" (Keen 1999, 1).

Shortly after the 1993 *Baehr* decision, there was a well-organized conservative backlash, which served as an augury of the shape of things to come over the next fifteen years. For example, the Hawaii legislature passed legislation forbidding same-sex marriage, thus codifying the heterosexual character of marriage. Later, after the trial judge's 1996 decision, the Hawaii state legislature also proposed a constitutional amendment that "would permit the legislature to restrict marriage to opposite-sex couples." This amendment, which appeared on the ballot during the November 1998 elections, was accepted by Hawaii voters, thus dealing same-sex-marriage advocates a serious blow (Dolkart 1998, 317).

As part of this broader backlash, conservative groups created strategies designed to be implemented prior to the judicial resolution of the *Baehr* case. David L. Chambers accurately points out that "they provided conservative legislators in every state with draft legislation that would direct their state's courts and other agencies to refuse to recognize a marriage between two persons of the same sex conducted in another state" (2000, 294). Why did promoting this legislation prove to be such an effective strategy? It was because the legislation itself served as an important wedge issue by rallying conservatives and dividing liberal legislators from their lesbian and gay constituents. The conservative Right has used this strategy with great success in recent years with respect to same-sex marriage. Chambers offers a compelling explanation for its effectiveness in 1996. His analysis is relevant for understanding how the same-sex-marriage issue is played out today:

Many Democratic state legislators across the country either themselves believed that marriage should be limited to one man and one woman, or at least believed that they could not vote against the far right's bill because of the views of most of their heterosexual constituents. So, just as the far right had hoped, many otherwise liberal legislators voted for the bills and infuriated gay and lesbian voters. Gay groups, local and national, were forced to devote huge amounts of effort in nearly every state to persuade legislators to reject the bills. (ibid., 276)

From 1993 to 2003, forty-eight of the fifty states "introduced laws that limited legal recognition of marriage to opposite-sex couples." In Alaska (1998), Hawaii (1998), California (2000), Nebraska (2000), and Nevada (2000 and 2002), citizens used a direct democracy process to "codify same-sex marriage bans in statutory or constitutional law" (Lofton and Haider-Markel 2007, 314).

The 1996 Defense of Marriage Act

The conservative backlash also manifested itself in national-level politics during the 1996 campaign. Same-sex marriage became a major issue in the 1996 presidential campaign when conservative activists and politicians organized a rally condemning the practice three days prior to the Iowa caucuses. Three of the announced Republican presidential candidates attended, addressed the rally, and "signed a pledge to 'defend' heterosexual marriage against the threat posed by three lesbian and gay couples in Hawaii who had sued the state for the right to marry" (Cahill 2004, 81). This pledge, the Marriage Protection Resolution, had been introduced by a coalition of eight conservative religious groups (Rimmerman 2002, 75). The *Los Angeles Times* observed in April 1996 that "homosexual marriage has abruptly emerged as an emotional flashpoint in the debate about America's social mores" (Cahill 2004, 81). It was no surprise, then, that Republican presidential nominee Bob Dole introduced the federal Defense of Marriage Act (DOMA) in the Senate, though it was surprising to some that President Clinton ultimately signed it into law on September 21, 1996. The Senate had voted 85-14 in September 1996 in favor of the act, which the House had passed by a vote of 342-67 that summer. Congressional hearings about the legislation had turned ugly, as Congress members and witnesses warned that if men were allowed to marry other men, "they would soon be permitted to marry children and other animals" (Chambers 2000, 295). Others worried that same-sex marriage would lead to the collapse of Western civilization. The official Republican Party position was a conservative one: "let the people of each state decide whether or not to allow homosexuals to marry in their state. If a state decides to permit such unions, so be it" (Whitman 2005, 97). Proposed by Republicans with the enthusiastic support of their Christian Right supporters, the legislation was timed perfectly to coincide with the 1996 election season. The law was designed to accomplish two goals: "(1) prevent states from being forced by the Full Faith and Credit Clause to recognize same-sex marriages validly celebrated in other states, and (2) define marriages for federal purposes as the union of one man and one woman" (Strasser 1997, 127). What the law meant in practice is that gay couples, once the couples can actually legally be married, would be excluded "from all federal protections, responsibilities, and benefits that ordinarily accompany any other marriage in America" (Wolfson 2004, 42).

What prompted Clinton to sign the Defense of Marriage Act into law? He was clearly worried that the same-sex-marriage issue could achieve heightened saliency as a potential wedge issue during the 1996 general election. Having endured the unpleasantness of the debate about gays in the military during the first six months of his presidency, he wanted to avoid a similar controversy about marriage. With this in mind, he signed it into law after midnight, eschewing the Rose Garden ceremony that often accompanies White House bill signings. Understandably, Clinton received strong criticism from some members of the lesbian and gay movements when he did so. Whereas he had reversed his position regarding the military ban, he at least was consistent with regard to lesbian and gay marriage: He had announced his opposition in the 1992 campaign. But those who were most critical of the president argued that DOMA was both unnecessary and highly discriminatory and that Clinton was forced to sign the law in order to avoid attacks by the Christian Right during the 1996 presidential campaign. Indeed, the Dole campaign had run a radio ad that criticized Clinton for supporting an end to the military ban. The Clinton forces responded by releasing their own ad celebrating the president's signing of DOMA. This ad was run on Christian radio stations across the country, despite the fact that the president criticized the authors of the act for attempting to inject such a difficult issue into presidential politics during an election year.

Lesbian and gay rights groups protested the radio ad loudly. In response, the Clinton campaign pulled the ad after two days (Rimmerman 2002, 76). Ever the politician, Clinton recognized the potency of same-sex marriage as a potential wedge issue during the 1996 campaign. In stopping the ad, he helped remind other candidates of how they might balance their desire for electoral victory with the interests of their lesbian and gay supporters.

Could the lesbian and gay movements have done more to force the Clinton administration to support same-sex marriage? Note that it was not a crucial issue for many movement members at that time. Those who think it should be a key goal—individuals such as Jonathan Rauch, Andrew Sullivan, and Bruce Bawer—generally represent the movement's more moderate to conservative element. But as we know from the military debate discussed in Chapter 4, the movements cannot control when specific issues will come to the fore. And in many ways, the issue of same-sex marriage could not have come up at a worse time. The Republicans now controlled both houses of Congress, it was a presidential election year, and the movements simply did not have the time, skills, or resources to mount an effective organizing and educational campaign for an issue that appeared to be unpopular with the American public—certainly not a campaign equal to challenging the Christian Right's vast organizational resources. Indeed, the Republicans were searching for a wedge issue when they introduced the Defense of Marriage Act on May 8, 1996. Rich Tafel, then executive director of the Log Cabin Republicans, supported several of these points when he said, "Marriage is so visceral, such a negative in the polls. My experience in debating this issue is that if I have an hour or two hours, I can win, but if I have five minutes, I can't. This is all being done in five minutes" (Gallagher 1996, 21). As a campaign issue, opposition to same-sex marriage served several purposes. It was an opportunity for some politicians to reach out to both the center and the Right, given the larger public's apparent lack of support for the issue. And it forced Clinton to tackle a difficult issue at a time when he did not want to relive the military fiasco of several years before. Clinton had no choice, then, but to alienate some members of his voting base.

How might Clinton have handled the situation differently? He could have forbidden his campaign team to broadcast a radio ad supporting

DOMA on Christian radio. That the campaign ran such an ad suggests how badly Clinton and his campaign advisers wanted to straddle all sides of the issue. He might also have vetoed DOMA while expressing his own opposition to same-sex marriage, arguing that such legislation was being used as a political weapon, without the kind of lengthy public education and discussion that the issue deserved. We should not be surprised that Clinton did not follow the latter strategy, given his previous record with regard to the military ban. For him to take a bold and creative position, one rooted in educational leadership, would have been out of step with his political character.

But fortunately for advocates of same-sex marriage, the issue moved out of the national arena and back to the states with the historic December 1999 decision by Vermont's chief justice, Jeffrey Amestoy, that Vermont's legislature must grant lesbian and gay couples the "common benefits and protections" that heterosexuals receive. Not surprisingly, a conservative backlash soon emerged against the decision. Vermont legislators who supported the civil union legislation were targeted for defeat by Christian Right organizers, and some lost their reelection bids in 2000. Conservative forces throughout the United States immediately moved to preempt attempts to recognize same-sex marriages in their own states. The publicity surrounding the *Baehr* case appears to have done much more for opponents of lesbian and gay marriage than for its proponents. Further, the marriage issue vaulted to the forefront of the movements' agenda without a full and frank discussion of what this rights-based strategy would mean for the movements' organizing and educational efforts and for the direction of both short-term and long-term political and cultural change. Same-sex marriage would not manifest itself in the national political scene again until the June 16, 2003, U.S. Supreme Court decision in *Lawrence v. Texas*, a ruling that political scientist H. N. Hirsch has called "a stunning federal Supreme Court decision" (2005, ix).

The Implications of Lawrence v. Texas for the Same-Sex Marriage Debate

One analyst has argued persuasively that "the single most serious barrier to recognizing the right to marry was a 1986 Supreme Court decision, *Bowers v. Hardwick*, which upheld state laws criminalizing consensual sodomy" (Sullivan 2004, 106). This is why same-sex marriage proponents (and opponents) viewed *Lawrence v. Texas*, which overturned *Bowers*, as a landmark decision in advancing the interests of the lesbian and gay movements. With the *Lawrence* decision the Court struck down the sodomy laws of thirteen states, laws that ban "private, consensual sexual intimacy" (Cahill 2004, 2), and it "extended the right to privacy—which includes the right to make decisions about one's intimate life—to lesbians and gay men" (Chauncey 2004, 1). In essence, the Court admitted that it had made a grave mistake when it ruled in *Bowers* that states could regulate sodomy. Writing for the six-to-three majority, Justice Anthony Kennedy celebrated "the liberty" of gay people to form relationships, "whether or not [they are] entitled to formal recognition in the law," and condemned the Bowers decision for "demeaning the lives of homosexual persons" (ibid., 1). But Kennedy also cautioned that the decision does not apply to marriage per se by noting that the legal case opposing the Texas sodomy law "does not involve whether the government must give formal recognition to any relationship homosexual persons seek to enter." And Justice Sandra Day O'Connor argued in her concurrence that the "'traditional institution of marriage' was not an issue" (Cahill 2004, 3).

But Justice Antonin Scalia (joined by Chief Justice William Rehnquist) warned of the dangers to the institution of marriage that might result from the *Lawrence* decision: "Today's opinion dismantles the structure of constitutional law that has permitted a distinction to be made between heterosexual and homosexual unions, insofar as formal recognition in marriage is concerned" (ibid.). Scalia's concerns were seconded by conservative politicians and activists in ways that contributed to a shift in coverage by the mainstream news media, some of which suggested that the Court's decision would ultimately lead to the legalization of same-sex marriage.

Lesbian and gay movement activists also reacted in ways that provided support for Scalia's claim. For example, Lambda Legal Defense Fund attorney Ruth Harlow, who served as the lead attorney in *Lawrence*, argued, "The ruling makes it much harder for society to continue banning gay marriages." And Patricia Logue, cocounsel in *Lawrence* and also a Lambda attorney, claimed, "I think it's inevitable now. In what time frame, we don't know" (ibid.). Judicial scholar David Garrow perhaps put it best when he said, "There's no getting around the fact that this changes the political and legal landscape forever" (Bull 2003, 36).

The *Lawrence* decision elicited responses from national politicians as well. At a press conference in late July 2003, President Bush endorsed a federal definition of marriage that defined marriage as being between a man and a woman. He also faced increasing pressure to endorse an amendment to the U.S. Constitution enshrining that definition. Some Republican Party leaders, including Senate Majority Leader Bill Frist (R-TN), went public with their concerns almost immediately. Frist endorsed sodomy laws on the June 29, 2003, episode of ABC's *This Week*: "'I have this fear' that the ruling could create an environment in which 'criminal activity within the home would in some way be condoned . . . whether it's prostitution or illegal commercial drug activity'" (ibid., 38). Frist then endorsed a constitutional amendment that would ban same-sex marriage. "I very much feel that marriage is a sacrament, and that sacrament should extend and can extend to that legal entity of a union between—what is traditionally in our Western values has been defined—as between a man and a woman" (Crea 2003, 1). And he had the continued and enthusiastic support of Senator Rick Santorum (R-PA), who claimed that "the greatest near-term consequence of the *Lawrence v. Texas* anti-sodomy ruling could be the legalization of homosexual marriage" (Cahill 2004, 3). Of course, Santorum's support was no surprise, given his April 2003 warning that if the Supreme Court legitimated the right to gay sex "within your home, then you have the right to bigamy, you have the right to polygamy, you have the right to incest, you have the right to adultery. You have the right to anything" (Hertzberg 2003, 33).

The constitutional amendment that Frist endorsed had been introduced in the House of Representatives by Marilyn Musgrave (R-CO) and five other sponsors on May 23, 2003. Drafted by the Alliance for Marriage, the amendment defines marriage as the union of a man and a woman. Musgrave and her cosponsors later introduced a slightly different version on March 22, 2004, one that would not "bar same-sex civil unions allowed by state law." The goal of the revised amendment was to "broaden support for the initiative and blunt the appeal of alternatives that could leave the definition of marriage up to individual states." Some supporters of the gay marriage ban also had worried that the original amendment went too far and would frighten more moderate voters by nullifying the nation's domestic partner laws and Vermont's civil unions law as well as ban same-sex marriage. The revised amendment therefore stated: "Marriage in the United States shall consist only of the union of a man and a woman. Neither this Constitution, nor the constitution of any state, shall be construed to require that marriage or the legal incidents thereof be conferred upon any union other than the union of a man and woman" (Hulse 2004, n.p.). Musgrave justified the introduction of her original amendment (Senator Wayne Allard, a Colorado Republican, introduced a companion measure in the Senate) by asking: "If we are going to be redefining marriage, who should decide: unelected judges, or the people and their elected representatives?" (Perine and Dlouhy 2004, 84). It was no surprise that Musgrave, serving her first term in Congress at the time, would lead the charge against same-sex marriage, given that she had organized a successful drive to abolish it as a Colorado state representative prior to her arrival in the House of Representatives. In this way, she linked her state-level experience with her new career on the national stage.

In order for Musgrave's constitutional amendment to be codified into law, it would need a two-thirds supermajority in the House and the Senate. If Musgrave and her supporters in both chambers could garner that much support for it, it would then go to the states, where thirty-eight of the fifty state legislatures (three-fourths of the states) would have to vote to ratify it before it could become law. Assuming that all of these challenging constitutional hurdles were overcome, Musgrave's amendment would replace the 1996 Defense of Marriage Act and protect the ban on same-sex marriages from all legal challenges (ibid., 85).

How did President Bush react to the possibility of such an amendment? In late June 2003 Bush's spokesperson, Ari Fleischer, claimed that the president had never discussed the idea of a constitutional amendment with Frist. Instead, Fleischer said that "the president is proud to support the Defense of Marriage Act. We have a law on the books right now that was signed by President Clinton, that passed with massive, overwhelming bipartisan majorities in 1996. And the president supports that legislation and that's where he stands now" (Crea 2003, 14).

But the president's position was an evolving one because he and his advisers perceived political opportunities in making same-sex marriage an electoral issue. Bush served notice that he recognized the power of same-sex marriage as a wedge issue when he proclaimed October 12–18, 2003, "Marriage Protection Week." In doing so, Bush signaled his support "for the proposed Federal Marriage Amendment, which would amend the U.S. Constitution to ban same-sex marriage and government recognition of civil unions or domestic partnerships" ("Declaration of Intolerance" 2003, 15). In introducing his proclamation, Bush underscored the importance of traditional marriage for children:

Research has shown that, on average, children raised in households headed by married parents fare better than children who grow up in other family structures. Through education and counseling programs, faith-based, community, and government organizations promote healthy marriages and a better quality of life for children. By supporting responsible child-rearing and strong families, my Administration is seeking to ensure that every child can grow up in a safe and loving home. (Office of the Press Secretary 2003, n.p.)

His statement also highlights the importance of his faith-based approach to social policy and its connections to traditional family structures.

The response to Bush's proclamation from the Log Cabin Republicans was swift and severe. Executive director Patrick Guerriero recognized the political rationale for Bush's approach to same-sex marriage almost a full year before the 2004 elections: "Early polls indicate that opposition to same-sex marriage could become a wedge issue." Guerriero also recognized that Bush's approach would lead to a "civil war in the Republican party. We are very disappointed to see Bush catering to the extraordinary hypocrisy of the antimarriage groups, which call themselves pro-family and then go around encouraging discrimination against gay and lesbian families" ("Declaration of Intolerance" 2003, 15). He later argued that "using the Constitution as a campaign tool and using gay families as a political wedge sets a new low for shameful campaigning" (Guerriero 2004, n.p.). And Mark Mead, the political director of the organization, warned that "a federal marriage amendment has the potential to ignite a culture war. As conservative Republicans, we know what can happen when you ignite a cultural war" (Perine and Dlouhy 2004, 84).

The Austin Twelve, the group of handpicked gay Republicans who had met with George W. Bush in Texas during the 2000 presidential campaign, also reacted with consternation to the president's handling of the marriage issue. Once viewed as the base of Bush's support among gays, the group became increasingly critical of Bush's support of the federal marriage amendment. Rebecca Maestri, the only lesbian in the original group and president of the Northern Virginia Log Cabin Republicans chapter, said that "the Bush campaign people were principally concerned with getting elected [in 2000]. I do feel we were Bushwhacked." David Catania, a District of Columbia councilman and an outspoken critic of the president's position regarding same-sex marriage, announced his support for John Kerry in the 2004 election. John Hutch, another member of the Austin

Twelve and president of a direct marketing firm, claimed that "there's nothing that Bush can possibly do right now to regain the support of gays and lesbians. He would have to publicly go on television, repudiate his position on the amendment and acknowledge that he was wrong to get involved in the process. And he would probably have to go further than that. I just don't see it happening" (Crea 2004, n.p.). The responses of the Log Cabin Republicans and some Austin Twelve members are reminders of how presidents often disappoint their most fervent supporters. To be sure, as we have already seen, Bill Clinton's lesbian and gay supporters reacted similarly to his betrayal with regard to the military and same-sex-marriage bans after he had campaigned fervently for their votes in the 1992 and 1996 campaigns.

The Massachusetts Supreme Court's 2003 Decision

With the Massachusetts Supreme Judicial Court ruling in *Goodridge v. Department of Public Health* (November 17, 2003), the same-sex marriage issue was catapulted further onto the national stage. Politicians in both parties were forced to respond to the court's ruling that "the ban on marriage licenses to gay couples violated the Commonwealth's guarantee of equal protection of the laws." The court ruled in 2004 that "no separate-but-equal institution of 'civil unions' would suffice to meet constitutional requirements" (Sullivan 2004, xvii). Richard Land, president of the Southern Baptist Ethics and Religious Commission, offered an opening salvo in the debate that followed the court's initial decision, and his view represents the Christian Right's perspective well: "The Federal Marriage Amendment is the only way to adequately deal with this judicial assault on the sanctity of marriage being defined as God intended it, the union of one man and one woman" (Foust 2003, n.p.).

It was only a matter of time before Bush announced his support for the Musgrave amendment. He did so on February 24, 2004, after highlighting the issue in his State of the Union Address. Bush declared that "the union of a man and woman is the most enduring human institution" (Sokolove 2004, 1). Why did Bush announce his endorsement at this time? It is clear that he was not eager to take such a step, but the possibility of using marriage as a winning edge issue during his reelection campaign proved to be too attractive. Once the Massachusetts Supreme Judicial Court legalized same-sex marriage in that state and San Francisco mayor Gavin Newsom began the process of granting marriage licenses to lesbian and gay couples,[1] then Bush and his advisers perceived that his endorsement of the amendment was part of a winning electoral strategy. In addition, others have argued that "with social conservatives up in arms, Bush had little alternative to backing the amendment" (Micklethwait and Wooldridge 2004, 149). Of course, it should come as no surprise, given his administration's overall record on lesbian and gay rights during Bush's first term.

Nor did it come as a surprise when Bush endorsed a constitutional ban on same-sex marriage on the eve of a Senate vote on the amendment in early June 2006, well into his second term in office. The bill's Senate sponsor, Colorado Republican Wayne Allard, introduced the measure with the support of the White House and the Christian Right. They perceived that this measure could help rally the conservative base in the November 2006 midterm elections, when Democrats stood to make large gains in light of the setbacks associated with the war in Iraq and rising energy prices. It is especially noteworthy that Bush highlighted his support for the amendment with a news conference in the White House Rose Garden on Monday, June 5, the day before the vote. In the end, the Republicans suffered a stinging debate in the Senate on the vote held to decide whether to have an up-and-down vote on the amendment itself (the 49-48 vote fell well short of the 60 votes needed).

Bush's attempt to distance himself from the Log Cabin Republicans and the Republican Unity Coalition revealed how far he would go to avoid antagonizing his Christian Right supporters, whose votes he had desperately needed to win the 2000 election and whose votes he perceived he would need if he were to win in 2004 and keep congressional Republicans in power in 2006. The president was also undoubtedly aware that the Christian Right had caused his father considerable difficulty during his one-term presidency when they perceived him as compromising too much on conservative principles. George W. Bush clearly did not want to repeat the political mistakes made by his father. Slightly more than 70 percent of self-identified lesbian and gay voters (more than 2.8 million Americans) cast their ballots for Al Gore in the 2000 election, while Bush received the votes of more than 11 million religious conservatives (Rimmerman 2002, 163). These figures indicate that Bush owed his conservative base his loyalty, given their strong support for him in such a close election and their role in his victory over John Kerry in 2004. One political scientist captured well the challenges confronting Bush following his 2000 election "victory":

"Gay rights is a no-win situation for Bush. If he aligns with the antigay right wing, the media will accuse him of bigotry. If he doesn't, he'll get attacked by conservatives" (Bull 2001, 26). Bush and some congressional Republicans also recognized that support for a constitutional amendment could turn off potential swing voters who might view the Republican Party as too intolerant. In addition, Republican strategists were well aware that President Bush secured 25 percent of the lesbian and gay vote in the 2000 election, support that both he and Republican Congress members needed in future elections. During a December 2003 interview on ABC, Bush was asked whether he supported a constitutional amendment that would abolish same-sex marriage. His response reveals his attempt to balance competing interests: "If necessary, I will support a constitutional amendment which would honor marriage between a man and a woman, codify that . . . the position of this administration is that, you know, whatever legal arrangements people want to make, they're allowed to make, so long as it's embraced by the state" (Perine and Dlouhy 2004, 85). But despite these various political concerns, soon after the *Lawrence* decision was handed down, Bush and his advisers recognized the utility of using same-sex marriage as a divisive political issue.

The Massachusetts Supreme Judicial Court decision provided more support for conservatives, who believed that the Republican Party should use same-sex marriage as a wedge issue. Indeed, a little more than a month before the November 2004 elections, social conservatives in Congress recognized the potential of using the same-sex marriage issue to mobilize their political base. House leaders brought the revised Musgrave amendment to the floor on September 30, 2004, bypassing the Judiciary Committee and its chairman, F. James Sensenbrenner (R-WI). Sensenbrenner opposes same-sex marriage but has also voiced serious concerns about amending the United States Constitution, thus revealing an important split among social conservatives. In justifying the procedural maneuver, House Majority Leader Tom DeLay (R-TX) claimed that "this debate will spill over into the elections, I think, and rightly so." And Marilyn Musgrave used the latest procedural debate as an opportunity to bash the court system, which, she claimed, had stymied the will of the people: "The trajectory of the courts' decisions is unmistakable" (Perine 2004, 2322). Both DeLay and Musgrave helped President Bush's cause by highlighting the saliency of the same-sex-marriage issue in a volatile election year and making the case against the practice with a stridency that the president could not emulate. He was hampered by Dick Cheney's announcement in August 2004 that he did not support the president's determination to amend the U.S. Constitution, presumably out of consideration for his lesbian daughter, Mary.

Bush's attempts to appease the Christian Right help explain his discomfort with addressing lesbian and gay civil rights issues during his first term. Since assuming the presidency, Bush had done little to support issues that were of broad interest to the lesbian and gay movements. If anything, he was openly hostile, as reflected in some of his appointments, such as that of former senator John Ashcroft (R-MO) as attorney general during his first term. As a member of the United States Senate, Ashcroft consistently voted in support of the Christian Right's positions when lesbian and gay issues came up for consideration. Bush's appointment of former Colorado attorney general Gale Norton also did little to comfort the movements, as Norton was a vigorous defender of Colorado's Amendment 2, which would have eliminated all lesbian and gay rights laws in the state. Indeed, by the end of his first term, Bush had no real policy achievements that lesbians and gays could justifiably celebrate. Therefore, his support for a constitutional amendment was merely an extension of his overall approach to gay rights issues since assuming office. His support also represented a point of departure from his first presidential campaign in 2000, when he indicated that he "did not believe in punitive action against gays" and refused to support a constitutional amendment against same-sex marriage (Wald and Glover 2007, 123).

The Implications of the Marriage Debate for the Lesbian and Gay Movements

As we have already seen, the campaign for same-sex marriage has been rooted in litigation, and it has now garnered the support of most major national lesbian and gay organizations, including the Lambda Legal Defense and Education Fund, the National Gay and Lesbian Task Force, and the Human Rights Campaign. Its status as one of the leading issues of the late 1990s and early twenty-first century is evidenced by Lambda's Evan Wolfson's contention that, in the wake of the Hawaii Supreme Court's *Baehr* decision, there should be no "intra-community debate over whether to seek marriage. The ship has sailed" (Warner 1999, 83). For strategic reasons, Wolfson believes that the lesbian and gay movements should present a united front in support of same-sex marriage if homophobic Christian Right initiatives are to be defeated.

The results of the 2004 election, which saw the reelection of George W. Bush, the election of a more conservative Congress, the passage of eleven state ballot initiatives banning same-sex marriage, and election-day polls indicating that 22 percent of voters focused more on "moral values" than on other factors (Keen 2004, 20), did not bode well for those supporting same-sex marriage and lesbian, gay, bisexual, and transgender issues more broadly. In the wake of the election, movement leaders held discussions about future strategy and whether more moderate goals and strategies should be pursued in light of the grim election results. The Human Rights Campaign, the country's largest lesbian and gay advocacy group, accepted the resignation of Cheryl Jacques as its executive director, appointed to its board the first nongay cochair, and publicly announced a more moderate political and electoral strategy, one that would focus less on "legalizing same-sex marriages and more on strengthening personal relationships" (Broder 2004, A1).

But the reality is that same-sex marriage will now be a part of the national political debate about lesbian, gay, bisexual, and transgender rights for the foreseeable future. And the movements must fashion a political and educational organizing strategy that recognizes and accepts this reality. It is a reality that plays to the strength of the Christian Right's grassroots organizing efforts, because same-sex marriage is the kind of hot-button social issue that can mobilize voters to support conservative candidates and conservative ballot initiatives, as the 2004 and 2006 election results indicate. Two experts on the Christian Right have argued persuasively that it has done an excellent job in building a grassroots network to fight same-sex marriage: "The efforts to build a diverse coalition—in terms of race and religion—underscore the political sophistication of the religious activists who oppose gay marriage. . . . And for the battle over gay marriage, the coalition of opponents has been broad indeed" (Campbell and Robinson 2007, 146). Since the legalization of same-sex marriage in Massachusetts in 2003, twenty states have adopted a constitutional amendment that preserves traditional marriage. In the 2006 midterm elections, only Arizona rejected such a constitutional amendment that would have defined "marriage as a one-man, one-woman institution. The measure also would have forbid civil unions and domestic partnerships" (Crary 2006, n.p.).

FIGURE 5.1   The State of the States

States Allowing Same-Sex Marriage	Massachusetts
States Allowing Civil Unions	New Jersey Vermont
States with Laws Banning Discrimination *Based on Sexual Orientation*	California Colorado Connecticut Hawaii Illinois Iowa Maine Maryland Massachusetts Minnesota Nevada New Hampshire New Jersey New Mexico New York Oregon Rhode Island Vermont Washington Wisconsin

	Note: The District of Columbia also
	    bans laws that discriminate on the
	    basis of sexual orientation.

Source: Lambda Legal (http://www.lambdalegal.org/news/quick-facts/quick-facts.html).

Although the Arizona results were reason for celebration on the part of those who support same-sex marriage, the overall view from the states is a sobering one (see figure 5.1), despite the Massachusetts legislature's June 2007 overwhelming 151-45 vote that defeated an effort to place same-sex marriage before voters in a statewide referendum ("The World at a Glance" 2007, 7). John D'Emilio offers this dismal assessment of where things stand for those who support same-sex marriage: "Simply put, the marriage campaign has been a disaster. It is far better to assess the damage and learn from it, better to figure out if a course correction can be made, than to proceed down the current road blissfully in denial, claiming that night is day, stop means go, and defeats are victories" (2007, 45). D'Emilio believes that reliance on a judicial strategy has been a "catastrophe" because it has helped to foster "new legislation and state constitutional provisions" that have undermined the entire same-sex-marriage campaign (ibid., 61).

The Case for Same-Sex Marriage

Those who argue for same-sex marriage often invoke a practical argument. For example, the late gay political activist Thomas B. Stoddard pointed out that "the legal status of marriage rewards the two individuals who travel to the altar (or its secular equivalent) with substantial economic and practical advantages." What are these advantages? By filing a joint tax return, married couples can reduce their tax liabilities. In addition, "they are entitled to special government benefits, such as those given surviving spouses and dependents through the Social Security program." Even when there is no will, they can inherit from one another. Furthermore, "they are immune from subpoenas" that require testimony against the other spouse. Any foreigner who marries an American citizen gives that foreigner "a right to residency in the United States" (1989, 754).

And there are advantages that accrue to married couples through custom as well. Health insurance is a major issue for everyone in a country that provides health care as a privilege or benefit rather than as a right. Many employers offer health care to their employees and to their spouses, but few employers "include a partner who is not married to an employee, whether of the same sex or not" (ibid.). Stoddard offered this astute summary of the legal realities facing same-sex couples:

> In short, the law generally presumes in favor of every marital relationship, and acts to preserve and foster it, and to enhance the rights of the individuals who enter into it. It is usually possible, with enough money and the right advice, to replicate some of the benefits conferred by the legal status of marriage through the use of documents like wills and power of attorney forms, but that protection will inevitably, under current circumstances, be incomplete. (ibid., 755)

But the reality is that for those who do not have the resources to hire quality legal advisors, the legal avenue for redress is unavailable.

A second set of arguments emanate from the exalted place that marriage occupies in our entire social structure. Marriage transcends what is sanctioned by law because it is at the core of what Americans mean by "family." Marriage in every state but Massachusetts is conceptualized to suggest that "two men or two women are incapable of achieving such an exalted domestic state." Lesbian and gay relationships are viewed, then, as "somehow less significant, less valuable" (ibid., 756). Furthermore, the U.S. government "cannot legitimately pass laws discriminating against lesbian and gay citizens—denying them the civil right to marry or treating their relationships differently than those of heterosexuals" (Snyder 2006, 11). As a result, gays and lesbians must fight for full equality.

One same-sex-marriage advocate offers an argument steeped in democratic theory: "The fundamental principles of American democracy not only allow, but also require the legalization of same-sex marriage" (ibid., 2). How can people identify themselves as supporters of democracy but discriminate against a minority group?

> Lesbian and gay Americans are citizens, just like heterosexuals, and must be treated equally before the law. While many people may view the traditional heterosexual family as the most desirable family form, there is no evidence that it does a better job of producing democratic citizens. And even if there were, lesbian and gay citizens would still have the right to form families and raise children, just like anyone else. (ibid., 11)

The underlying argument here is that for democracy to be alive and vibrant, to even exist, it requires equality among all citizens, including lesbians, gays, bisexuals, and transgender individuals. Marriage "has come to be regarded as a fundamental civil right and a powerful symbol of full equality and citizenship" (Chauncey 2004, 165). As a result, the opportunity to marry must be extended to all citizens.

A fourth set of arguments derives from the nature of "marriage as a symbol of personal commitment and as a means of gaining recognition for that commitment from others." The argument here is that domestic partnerships and civil unions are far too limiting, even though they had once appeared to be a huge advance (see figure 5.2). Why did some rush to get married as soon as they were legally permitted to do so? One woman

FIGURE 5.2   Ways to Recognize Same-Sex Relationships: A Comparison

Marriage	Domestic Partnership	Civil Union
Federal Law Federal protections conferred by 1,049 federal laws and policies, such as Social Security, federal taxation, family and medical leave, and immigration policy.	*Federal Law* No federal protections.	*Federal Law* No federal rights, responsibilities, or protections.
Region Available Available in all states, unless couple is the same sex.	*Region Available* Available in a range of states and cities, as well as in the context of some private and public employment. Provisions vary widely.	*Region Available* Available only in New Jersey and Vermont and only to same-sex couples.
Benefits Provided The broadest array of federal and state benefits, including Social Security benefits, the right to inherit from a partner without a will, the right to take family leave under federal law, the right to file federal taxes jointly, the right to sponsor a partner for immigration, and many others.	*Benefits Provided* Benefits range from health care alone, provided by some public and private employers, to a broader array of state benefits, such as in California.	*Benefits Provided* Provides a separate form of equality at the level of state policy, except for eligibility for health insurance through private employers.

Source: Adapted from Cahill 2003, p. 7.

said: "First and foremost, I love this woman and she loves me." Marriage is "the best sign of a commitment that you can make" (ibid., 142).

The profound psychological benefits of marriage are offered as key justifications by other proponents. Andrew Sullivan, for one, has argued passionately that the right to marry is "the mark of ultimate human respect." If we deny human beings the right to marry, then we cause "the deepest psychological and political wound imaginable." With this in mind, Sullivan believes that allowing lesbians and gays to marry would afford "the highest form of social approval imaginable" and provide "the deepest means for the liberation of homosexuals" (Robinson 2005, 63). And he connects his advocacy for same-sex marriage to the larger lesbian and gay movements' political program: "If nothing else were done at all, and gay marriage were legalized, ninety percent of the political work necessary to achieve gay and lesbian equality would have been achieved. It is ultimately the only reform that truly matters" (ibid., 62).

The positive impact of same-sex marriage on "the self perception and psychological well being" of lesbian and gay children is also an argument made by some proponents (ibid.). Sullivan thinks that with the legalization of same-sex marriage, children would have important role models as they contemplate relationships as adults. But the key is for society to place its imprimatur of acceptance on same-sex relationships, an acceptance that would infuse the larger culture.

Sullivan makes another important argument in his fervent case for marriage. He claims that same-sex marriage will lead to a reduction of promiscuity in the lesbian and especially gay male community. This promiscuity undermines stable and healthy relationships and contributes significantly to the AIDS epidemic.

Finally, some argue that same-sex marriage would not only be good for lesbians and gays, but it would also be positive for American society as a whole—good for lesbians and gays, for heterosexuals, and for the broader institution of marriage. Jonathan Rauch is the foremost advocate of this position, and he justifies his argument in this way:

> Far from opening the door to all sorts of scary redefinitions of marriage, from polygamy to incest to who knows what, same-sex marriage is the surest way to shut that door. Far from decoupling marriage from its core mission, same-sex marriage clarifies and strengthens that mission. Far from hastening the social decline of marriage, same-sex marriage shores up the

key values and commitments on which couples and families and society depend. Far from dividing America and weakening communities, same-sex marriage, if properly implemented, can make the country both better unified and truer to its ideals. (2004, 5–6)

To Rauch, then, the fight for same-sex marriage is a stabilizing rather than destabilizing force because it would normalize all marriages. But this argument and the other arguments outlined above are vehemently rejected by those who are opposed to same-sex marriage.

The Case Against Same-Sex Marriage

The arguments against same-sex marriage can be divided into two broad categories: those most often offered by the Christian Right and its supporters and those articulated by members of the lesbian and gay movements who argue that same-sex marriage is too accommodating and assimilationist and as a result should not be a central focus of the movements' policy and political agenda. Why did same-sex marriage provoke such virulent responses by the Christian Right? A persuasive explanation is that the most outspoken opponents to same-sex marriage are those who have been fighting against greater equality for lesbians, gays, bisexuals, and transgender individuals for many years. They are the people who have steadfastly "opposed gay rights ordinances, the right of gay couples to adopt children, and the appearance of gay characters in the media" (Chauncey 2004, 145).

A consistent argument offered by the Christian Right in its opposition to same-sex marriage is that children raised by lesbian or gay parents will be injured or abused in some way. Focus on the Family, a leading Christian Right organization, states that "same-sex parenting situations make it impossible for a child to live with both biological parents, thus increasing their risk of abuse" (Cahill 2007, 161). It was no surprise, then, that in response to the Massachusetts *Goodridge* decision Focus on the Family bought a full-page advertisement in the January 23, 2004, *Boston Globe* that stated: "'Same-sex marriage advocates and the Massachusetts Supreme Court are asking our state and nation to enter a massive, untested social experiment with coming generations of children. We must ask one simple question: Is the same-sex 'family' good for children?" (ibid., 162). This line of argument is not surprising, given the Christian

Right's fixation over time on the negative consequences of homosexuality for children in the classroom, children in families, and children in society at large. They have consistently argued that "American democracy requires the traditional heterosexual family (two *heterosexual, married* parents) in order to function properly (Snyder 2006, 10; emphasis in the original). In making this argument, the Christian Right ignores a "large body of social science research that confirms that children raised by gay or lesbian parents are not disadvantaged relative to their peers." For example, an array of child advocacy organizations, including the American Psychological Association, the American Academy of Pediatrics, and the National Association of Social Workers, all "recognize that gay and lesbian parents are just as good as heterosexual parents and that children thrive in gay- and lesbian-headed families" (Cahill 2007, 162).

The Christian Right and its supporters have defended traditional marriage ferociously because they perceive that the issue has "special symbolic significance for the opponents of gay rights." They worry about any challenge to the institution of marriage and see same-sex marriage as "the ultimate sign of gay equality and the final blow to their traditional idea of marriage, which had been buffeted by thirty years of change" (Chauncey 2004, 145). And they are well aware that American acceptance of lesbians and gays has grown over time.

Antigay groups have also embraced the argument that "homosexuality is a choice" and that people can choose heterosexuality if they wish to do so and try hard enough. This has long been an argument of the Christian Right, which has supported reparative therapy, the process whereby people can be "cured" of their same-sex desires through therapy and support, and serves as the basis for the "ex-gay movement." This movement was founded in 1973 when the "Love in Action" ministry was created. A coalition of Christian Right groups paid for full-page advertisements in major U.S. newspapers in 1998. These advertisements claimed that lesbians and gays could be "cured" through religious conversion (Cahill 2007, 171). Such assumptions have informed the Christian Right's campaign against same-sex marriage. For example, the Massachusetts Coalition for Marriage has justified its opposition to sexual-orientation nondiscrimination laws by stating on its Web site that "we do not believe that a person's sexual behavior is comparable to other protected categories such as race or sex—characteristics that are inborn, involuntary, immutable, innocuous and/or in the Constitution." The

Christian Right has also used the "homosexuality as choice" claim to fight against programs that would create safe spaces in schools for kids who are grappling with sexual-orientation issues as well as nondiscrimination laws. In doing so, they believe that rewarding "bad choices by granting 'special protections' or 'special rights' based on sexual behavior" is poor public policy (ibid., 172).

The claim that "gay rights are special rights" goes back to Anita Bryant's Miami–Dade County, Florida, campaign in the 1970s. It has been a fundamental tenet in the Christian Right's organizing efforts against same-sex marriage and other policy areas, including discussion of homosexuality in schools, sexual-orientation nondiscrimination laws, and domestic-partner recognition. Over time, the Christian Right has portrayed gay rights as "special rights" that would threaten "the civil rights of 'legitimate minorities,' that is, African Americans and other people of color" (ibid.). President Bush has used this language as well, most notably during the second presidential debate in October 2000. In response to the question of whether "gays and lesbians should have the same rights as other Americans," Bush said, "Yes. I don't think they ought to have special rights. But I think they ought to have the same rights." Bush was asked to clarify his use of the term *special rights,* and he said, "Well, it'd be if they're given special protective status" (ibid., 173). These claims pivot on faulty rationale because, legally, there are no "special rights" in the United States.

The Christian Right has also argued that if sodomy laws are struck down and same-sex marriage is permitted, we would see many instances of bestiality, incest, pedophilia, and polygamy, all of which the Christian Right has long associated with homosexuality. Indeed, groups opposed to same-sex marriage often argue that "those seeking to legalize marriage for same-sex couples are also seeking the legalization of marriages among three or more people" (ibid., 176). Of course, no group advocating for same-sex marriage has argued for recognizing marriages between more than two people.

The second broad set of arguments against same-sex marriage emanates from activists within the lesbian and gay movements. For example, the most vocal critics of same-sex marriage within the movements argue from a feminist perspective that all marriage reinforces patriarchy and for that reason alone should be rejected. Paula Ettlebrick has articulated this position well: "Steeped in a patriarchal system that looks to ownership, property, and dominance of men over women as its basis, the institution of marriage long has been the focus of radical feminist revulsion. Marriage defines certain relationships as more valid than all others" (1997, 757). She develops her important critique even more fully in ways that cut to the heart of the dilemma underlying this book. For Ettlebrick and other critics of the assimilationist approach, "marriage will not liberate us as lesbians and gay men. In fact, it will constrain us, make us more invisible, force our assimilation into the mainstream, and undermine the goals of gay liberation" (ibid., 758). Furthermore, she claims that the push for marriage undermines all other possible relationships that people might have with one another.

> By looking to our sameness and deemphasizing our differences, we don't even place ourselves in a position of power that would allow us to transform marriage from an institution that emphasizes property and state regulation of relationships to an institution which recognizes one of many types of valid and respected relationships. Until the constitution is interpreted to respect and encourage differences, pursuing the legalization of same-sex marriage would be leading our movement into a trap; we would be demanding access to the very institution which, in its current form, would undermine *our* movement to recognize many different kinds of relationships. We would be perpetuating the elevation of married relationships and of "couples" in general, and further eclipsing other relationships of choice. (ibid., 759)

Michael Warner extends Ettlebrick's analysis by offering a scathing critique of marriage based on two arguments: First, it reinforces the worst elements of heteronormativity by "normalizing" the lesbian and gay movements; and second, by embracing same-sex marriage, lesbian and gay movements are endorsing the real economic privileges associated with marriage as an institution in the United States, such as health care coverage, inheritance rights, Social Security survivors' benefits, and tax breaks. Warner joins other critics in criticizing those national organizations that have "accepted the mainstreaming project and, in particular, the elevation of the marriage issue as the movement's leading goal" (1999, 46).

Like Warner, other critics worry about the primacy of marriage on the movements' political organizing and policy agenda. John D'Emilio, for example, raises this important question as a possible response to the movements' focus on marriage in recent years: "What about *urgent* issues like

AIDS prevention, homophobic violence, and the safety of queer youth, issues that legitimately might be termed matters of life and death?" (2007, 41). Chapter 6 will explore these tensions over same-sex marriage when we discuss the movements' future organizing strategies and attempt to navigate possible common ground between those who call for a liberationist approach to political, social, and policy change and those who believe that the assimilationist perspective is more realistic and pragmatic.

Conclusion

This chapter began with several key questions: How has the fight for same-sex marriage affected the goals of the broader lesbian and gay movements? How has the Christian Right responded with its own organizing efforts? And what progress has been made in the fight for same-sex marriage? In answering these questions, we have placed the battle over same-sex marriage in its proper historical context. We have seen the role that the courts have played in advancing the cause of same-sex marriage over time, most notably in the *Baehr v. Lewin, Lawrence v. Texas,* and *Goodridge v. Department of Public Health* decisions. But we have also seen how all of these decisions have galvanized the Christian Right and other opponents of same-sex marriage.

Where do things stand now? One group of analysts believes that the term *marriage* is a major obstacle for many Americans: "They are torn between a desire to treat gay men and lesbians with equality and respect, on one hand, and core beliefs that marriage is a sacred institution designed by God, on the other. This suggests that it would be more profitable for gay and lesbian rights activists to focus first on building additional support for civil unions" (Wilcox et al. 2007, 239). The public supports civil unions in many states. But virtually all surveys reveal that the vast majority of Americans are opposed to same-sex marriage, though the young are opposed to same-sex marriage by a much smaller margin, which bodes well for the future.

We have also seen in this chapter that the Christian Right will use a full arsenal of resources and political tactics to undermine the promarriage forces at the grassroots level. And this undoubtedly will have an impact on American politics, as most politicians, certainly at the national level, will find the issue of same-sex marriage a difficult one to navigate. There is little evidence that Democrats have the political courage to support same-sex marriage in the foreseeable future, and the Republicans are largely hopeless on this issue (and other policy issues that we have discussed in this book).

But the other reality is that the issue does not enjoy the kind of fervent support among the larger lesbian and gay movements that is necessary to mount a sustained strategy for fighting the forces against same-sex marriage. Much of the conflict within the movements derives from the larger tension underlying this book regarding assimilationist and liberationist approaches to political and policy change. This tension grows out of the messy nature of social movements themselves, as we have seen. In this book's final chapter, we will explore possible ways that we might ameliorate this tension as we consider the movements' futures.

6

···

The Movements' Futures

Every successful social movement eventually moves from the
unthinkable to the impossible to the inevitable.

—Laura Liswood, founder of Women World Leaders, quoted in
"If I Bend This Far I Will Break? Public Opinion About
Same-Sex Marriage," by Clyde Wilcox, Paul R. Brewer,
Shauna Shames, and Celinda Lake

In Laramie, Wyoming, on the night of October 6, 1998, a twenty-one-year-old gay University of Wyoming senior stopped in downtown Laramie for a drink at the Fireside Bar. One day later, that same student was found by a mountain biker "lashed to a fence on the outskirts of town, beaten, pistol-whipped, unconscious, and barely breathing" (Loffreda 2000, ix). The young man never regained consciousness and died five days later, on October 12. His name was Matthew Shepard. His murder, funeral, and the subsequent trials of his killers—Russell Henderson and Aaron McKinney—received international attention. His killers, also from Laramie, were in their early twenties, like the young man whom they had brutally murdered.

Why did his murder happen? One explanation offered in the aftermath of the murder is that Matthew made a pass at his killers in a space that had become known as a "hospitable" place for lesbians and gays to gather, to share a drink, and to find the kind of community and solace that bars have often provided in the face of a hostile world. But another more important explanation is it occurred because we live in a country where we do not provide the young with appropriate education at all levels regarding the importance of respecting and understanding racial, gender, and sexual-orientation differences. As one of my colleagues said to me in the wake of the murder, "This underscores the crucial importance of education." Had Russell Henderson and Aaron McKinney been given the opportunity to confront their anxieties regarding their own sexualities and their views of those who fall outside the "heterosexual norm" in an educational setting many years before, perhaps the murder would not have happened. And had we had national hate-crimes legislation on the books that applied to bias crimes related to the victim's sexual orientation, perhaps the crime might not have occurred, and even if it had, we would have had a clear policy regarding how to punish the perpetrators.[1] But as we have seen in this book, we also live in a country where people who are lesbian, gay, bisexual, and transgender are reviled and targeted by many. For example, soon after Matthew Shepard's death, Fred Phelps, a defrocked minister from Kansas and creator of the Internet site GODHatesFags.com, "faxed reporters images of the signs he and his followers intended to carry at the funeral: 'Fag Matt in Hell,' 'God Hates Fags,' 'No Tears for Queers'" (ibid., 18). The media's coverage of Phelps's attacks publicized his hatred and vitriol, thus giving them more attention than they deserved. Not to be outdone, in the wake of the September 11 attacks, the late Rev. Jerry Falwell, founder of the Moral Majority, said on the Rev. Pat Robertson's *700 Club* television show, "I really believe that the pagans and the abortionists, and the feminists, and the gays and the lesbians who are actually trying to make that an alternative lifestyle, the ACLU, People for the American Way, all of them who have tried to secularize America, I point the finger in their face and say 'you helped this happen'" (Duggan 2003, 43). His remarks were publicized and denounced by many, though once again the media saw fit to highlight them at a particularly difficult time for the country and the world. The revulsion expressed by Phelps and Falwell is reflected in the public debates that we have had about sex education, HIV/AIDS, military integration, and same-sex marriage (to name just a few of the most contentious issues) and in our laws. We are a country that forbids openly lesbian and gay people to get married, to serve in the military, to teach in our schools in many places, and, in most states, to adopt children as well.[2] It is no surprise, then, that the laws that we have crafted as a nation reflect a country that is and has been retrograde in its ability to have open, honest, mature, and dignified discussions of many of the issues underlying this book.

In light of these realities, what political organizing strategy is the most viable for addressing the policy issues discussed here? To what extent can we imagine a strategy that combines the best of what the assimilationist and liberationist perspectives have to offer? How much progress have we made in advancing the various issues of importance to the larger lesbian and gay movements? And why is educational curricular reform needed to help prevent the kind of vicious hate crimes that have been and are perpetrated against lesbians, gays, bisexuals, and transgender people? Before we can answer these questions, we must first review the strengths and weaknesses of the assimilationist and liberationist strategies in light of the analysis presented throughout this book. In doing so, we recognize that it is important for the members of any social movement to reflect critically upon strategies, tactics, accomplishments, and failures.

The Assimilationist and Liberationist Strategies Revisited

As we have already seen, much of the work of the contemporary national and lesbian and gay organizations has relied on an insider assimilationist strategy, one that strives for access to those in power and is rooted in an interest-group and legislative-lobbying approach to change. The strategy is largely based on civil rights, legal reform, legitimation, political access, and visibility. It is an approach that works within the political and economic framework that is associated with our classical liberal ideology. And it highlights the importance of allowing lesbians, gays, and bisexuals (but rarely those who are transgender) to have access to power and to have a seat at the table. This strategy often emphasizes national-level policymaking as opposed to organizing at the grassroots level, though in recent years the mainstream lesbian and gay movements have increasingly recognized the importance of organizing and educating at the local level.

The assimilationist approach recognizes that the American political system and the policy process growing out of that system are characterized by slow, gradual, incremental change. One way of thinking of political, policy, and cultural change is to think of it in terms of cycles of change. Incremental change means "creeping along" the path to reform, whereas more radical change means "leaping" toward more radical goals. The period of "creeping" is often associated with "strategic incoherence" on the part of social movements (D'Emilio 2000, 50). Assimilationists are typically more patient with creeping toward long-term movement goals, whereas liberationists are more likely to try to force more radical and ambitious structural challenges to the system at large. The lesbian and gay movements have witnessed cycles of creeping change and cycles of leaping change throughout their history. There have been three key moments of "leaping change" throughout the development of the lesbian and gay movements. The first leap forward occurred in the 1950s with the founding of the Mattachine Society and the Daughters of Bilitis, organizations that engaged in acts of courage and resistance, especially given the context of the times. By the time of the 1969 Stonewall Riot, another great leaping moment, the rights-based strategy called for by the Mattachine Society and the Daughters of Bilitis seemed too assimilationist in the face of greater liberationist calls for change. The third major leap forward was framed "by the 1987 March on Washington and the debate over the military exclusion policy in 1993. Like gay liberation of the Stonewall era, activists in these years frequently used militant direct action tactics. But unlike the two earlier periods of leaping ahead, this one witnessed movement and community organizations sinking secure roots in every region of the country" (ibid., 43). We are now clearly in a period of creeping political, social, and policy change. What evidence is there to support this claim?

For one, lesbians, gay men, bisexuals, and transgender individuals "are outnumbered and despised" by many. Political scientist Kenneth Sherrill has argued that "their quest for political power is disadvantaged by barriers to the formation of political community as well as by lack of access to significant power resources. The relative political powerlessness of gay people stands in contradistinction to their depiction by advocates of 'traditional values' as a powerful movement advancing a 'gay agenda' in American politics." Indeed, "the attention paid to the occasional electoral victories of openly lesbian and gay candidates distorts the reality that fewer than one tenth of 1% of all elected officials in the United States are openly lesbian, gay, or bisexual" (1996, 469). Sherrill's analysis was written in 1996, but it is still relevant today. How can we expect creeping (or leaping) political and policy change when the larger political process is most often associated with the values and assumptions underlying heteronormativity? Is it no surprise, then, that the lack of formal political power within the American policy process has yielded disappointing policy outcomes at all levels of government?

The quest for equal rights is at the core of the contemporary lesbian and gay rights movements' strategy. As we have seen throughout this book, this rights-based approach has dominated mainstream-movement thinking from the early years of the homophile movement to today's debates over the military-service ban and same-sex marriage. Over time, this rights-based strategy has pivoted on the state's relationship to lesbians and gay men. Lesbians and gay men have fought for the right to live their personal lives as fully and freely as possible from negative state intervention. At the same time, they have asked the state to intervene more positively to protect their ability to meet basic daily needs.

How have these issues manifested themselves politically? The movements have organized to abolish laws that restrict the right of individuals to engage in private, consensual sexual relations. In addition, they have fought against discrimination in employment, housing, and public accommodation and for equal legal protection. This claim of equal legal rights has led to the further demand that lesbians and gays should be entitled to have their intimate relationships recognized in the form of same-sex marriage. And they have organized to serve openly in the U.S. military. These demands, if transformed by the state into rights, would enable lesbians and gays to enjoy the same privileges that are currently the province of heterosexuals. Finally, in light of the AIDS crisis, the movements have demanded that the state provide lesbians and gays with "distributive justice" in their right to pursue their sexual health, free from stigma and discrimination. These are the central elements of the rights-based assimilationist strategy, which have largely been unquestioned and unchallenged by the contemporary lesbian and gay movements.

How has this approach worked in the policy arenas that we have discussed in this book? Same-sex marriage is the issue that has dwarfed nearly all others on the lesbian and gay movements' policy agenda in recent years. For a positive interpretation of the progress made in the fight for same-sex marriage and how that progress connects to larger movements' accomplishments, political scientist David Rayside claims:

> The United States is an unusual case, in part because of the extraordinary range of legal and political outcomes across states and localities. It is also unusual in several characteristics that impede the march to equity. But it is not as exceptional as is widely believed. A great majority of Americans now believe in extending recognition to lesbian and gay couples, if only a minority favor marriage. Most large corporations extend their family benefits coverage to the same-sex partners of employees. A steadily growing number of U.S. states and municipalities extend some form of recognition to such partners of their own employees. Openly lesbian and gay characters make regular appearances on American television dramas, even if their portrayals have limitations. In everyday life, sexual diversity is as visible in American society as in any. And across a wide range of regions and localities in the United States, countless lesbians, gays, bisexuals, and the transgendered are asserting their right to be visible. (2007, 361)

Rayside's positive assessment is important to consider when we remember how the Christian Right has mobilized and organized successfully to fight same-sex marriage at the state and national levels in recent years. Indeed, John D'Emilio is certainly right to remind us that the legal-rights strategy pursued by the lesbian and gay movements on this issue has largely been a failure thus far. D'Emilio claims that "the battle to win marriage equality through the courts has done something that no other campaign or issue in our movement has done: it has created a vast body of *new* anti-gay law" (2006, 10). Given this failure, should same-sex marriage occupy such an exalted position on the movements' organizing agenda? That is the question that should generate considerable discussion among the movements' activists.

Likewise, the progress in overturning the ban on lesbians and gays in the military has also been stymied, despite the outstanding efforts of the Servicemembers Legal Defense Network. The campaign has faced stiff opposition in light of the "Don't Ask, Don't Tell" policy passed by Congress and signed into law by a so-called friend, Bill Clinton. It will now take congressional action and the support of a president to overturn the ban, which will be an uphill battle in these conservative times, though the need for more personnel to fight on behalf of imperialistic U.S. foreign policy may finally provide an opening to overturn the ban, largely due to practical considerations. Integration of the military has also been an important hallmark of the assimilationist rights-based strategy.

In the area of HIV/AIDS policy, we have seen attention shift in recent years. With President Bush's global plan to fight AIDS, attention given to the many policy challenges growing out of the domestic HIV/AIDS crisis has diminished. These challenges include funding for community-based and local AIDS initiatives, recruiting committed and qualified people to the AIDS service-delivery communities at the local level given the paucity of resources available to pay them proper wages, and a sense that with the advent of protease inhibitors, the AIDS crisis is not as immediate, as people are living longer, "healthier," and more productive lives with HIV. Considering all of these factors, coupled with a more conservative Congress and a president who believes in "compassionate conservatism" only insofar as it extends to the global AIDS crisis, we can see why adequate funding for the Ryan White CARE Act has been in dispute in recent years. And as we have seen, the primacy of same-sex marriage on the movements' policy agenda has displaced the urgency of fighting for a thoughtful and well-funded HIV/AIDS policy at the national level, one that would provide adequate resources to communities, health care service-delivery professionals, and community organizations battling the AIDS crisis on a daily basis.

But if the rights-based assimilationist strategy has provided us with the "virtual equality" that Urvashi Vaid and other liberationists deride, then why might the movements want to embrace a more fully developed liberationist strategy and policy agenda? And what would such a strategy and agenda look like in practice? One scholar-activist offers an insightful overview of the challenges facing those who embrace a liberationist approach:

> Queer radicals today face a dilemma. Should we try to steer the mainstream GLBT [gay, lesbian, bisexual, transgender] movement in a more progressive direction or work with other progressive activists in groups that are not queer-focused? Can—and should—a movement focused on gay and lesbian identity expand to encompass a full range of progressive causes? And how can a movement organized around sexual identity embrace the intersecting identities of gay men and lesbians (and bisexuals? and transgendered people?) who are also women, people of color, disabled, youth, or working class? (Highleyman 2002, 110)

These theoretical and practical considerations challenge the larger lesbian and gay movements in compelling ways, and as we have seen in this book, they have been the source of considerable disagreement and tension among the movements over time. These are questions that the Gay Liberation Front was forced to confront coming out of Stonewall in the early 1970s. Activist-scholar Michael Bronski provides an excellent rationale for the importance of embracing a broader coalition-based, progressive organizing strategy:

> We need to reassess what kind of a movement we want it to be. Will it be a movement that continues arguing, with diminishing success, for the rights of its own people—and even at that, only for those who want to formalize a relationship? Or will we argue for a broader vision of justice and fairness that includes all Americans? If the movement does not choose the latter course, we risk becoming not just irrelevant, but a political stumbling block to progressive social change in general. (2006, 18)

Bronski's vision will require the movements to develop a broad coalition-building strategy, which is no easy task, especially given the disagreements among lesbians, gays, bisexuals, and transgender individuals over what the movements' central issues should be and how they should be addressed. It is to that coalition-building strategy that we now turn.

Coalition Politics

If our goal is to move beyond a narrow rights-based assimilationist strategy, one that is often focused on identity politics, we have two possible options. The first is what Urvashi Vaid calls "the coalition-around-an-issue strategy," which involves working with people who share interests around the same issues. The second option is much more ambitious because it requires people to create a "common movement." The "coalition-around-an-issue strategy" could lead to the recognition of common ground, which is the precursor to a common movement, whereby individuals come together to talk about issues of interest and strategies for working toward common goals that have been identified through participatory democratic processes. Vaid poses three important questions that should be asked by organizers at the outset of any campaign or political project: "How does this issue affect different populations within the gay and lesbian community? Can we build coalitions within the non-gay community around this issue? How can we educate the different segments of our community on the direct way this project or campaign affects them?" (1995, 303).

Beyond these questions, the movements need to identify the kinds of issues that will foster the building of short- and long-term alliances that are rooted in a radical democratic politics. Coalitions have surely been the catalyst behind virtually all of the movements' legislative victories, including the Americans with Disabilities Act, the Hate Crimes Statistics Act, the Ryan White CARE Act, the local laws that lesbian and gay activists have passed working with other community members, and the antigay referenda that have been defeated throughout the United States (Vaid 1997, 7).

The importance of coalition building certainly has not been lost on those who are concerned with national-level policymaking. Tom Sheridan, a former high-ranking official at the AIDS Action Council, explains its importance: "Coalition politics is effective because it's the hardest to get people to do. The Hill really respects its speaker because they figure that if you can get up here with a coalition that big and that diverse and have everyone agreeing on something, you must have hit something" (Andriote 1999, 230). A central goal of radical democratic politics is to build permanent coalitions around political strategies and concrete public policies that cut across race, class, and gender divides, coalitions that will be ready to respond to the Christian Right's distortions in all political arenas. The goal is to organize around issues that provide "a comprehensive system of social and economic protections for all families and household groupings" (Bronski 2006, 19). What issues might inspire individuals to work together to build a common movement?

Comprehensive Medical Care

"Comprehensive medical care will never happen in the United States. As a result, we need to be much more pragmatic about how we approach health care" (personal interview, February 5, 1997). That is the view of one member of the national movement's elite class. The pragmatism to which this person refers characterized the Clinton White House's health care–reform efforts in the administration's first term. When Bill Clinton took office in January 1993, some 39 million Americans lacked adequate medical insurance. As I write this in the summer of 2007, that number has ballooned to 46 million, with many more Americans close to the edge of financial disaster due to escalating health care costs. It is in the interest of the lesbian and gay movements to support major health care–policy reform that moves toward comprehensive medical care in light of HIV/AIDS and the exorbitant costs of the medicines that people depend on in order to survive.

How might we pay for comprehensive health care? Coalitions of citizens' groups can challenge the federal government to reduce spending for costly and unneeded weapons systems and to cut spending on the reckless war in Iraq. These moneys could then be used to develop a comprehensive national health insurance program over time. This will not be easy, given the realities of the well-entrenched military-industrial complex. Such a plan would likely also require a substantial, progressive tax increase that would place the financial burden on those who can best afford it, no easy task given the power of wealthy entrenched interests in the American policy process. We also need to finance further research and support for women's health issues, including breast, cervical, and ovarian cancers.

Comprehensive Government Responses to HIV/AIDS, Especially Resources for Education, Prevention, and Treatment

As we saw in Chapter 3, AIDS has had devastating consequences for many communities in the United States, not to mention countries throughout the world. With this in mind, we need support for a new AIDS movement, one that recognizes that AIDS is a global problem and also takes into account the specific needs of lesbians, gay men, African Americans, poor people, and others who are marginalized in American society.

This new AIDS movement requires a society that refuses to stigmatize sex, but instead provides accessible information about safer sex practices. We need a new AIDS movement that organizes on behalf of legalizing and financing the distribution of clean needles in inner cities throughout the United States. If these public policy goals are to be achieved, they will need the support of coalitions of diverse individuals committed to humane AIDS policies. But they will also need the support of the mainstream lesbian and gay movements, which appear to have lost interest in AIDS in recent years, as same-sex marriage has dominated their agenda. ACT UP/Philadelphia provides us with a model of how community-based organizing can link funding for programs in the United States with funding for programs on a global scale. The following appears on the organization's Web site, as an announcement for a political rally to take place on November 29, 2006, one that featured the following policy demands:

- $2.6 billion for the Ryan White CARE Act, the life-line for people living with AIDS in the U.S. The Care Act has been largely flat-funded since President Bush came into office, even as the number of HIV infections has continued to climb.
- $8 billion to train, retain and sustain enough healthcare workers in Africa to achieve universal access. Without significant new investments in the health workforce in Africa, current investments such as the President's Emergency Plan for AIDS Relief will not succeed. (http://www.critpath.org/actup, n.p.)

ACT UP/Philadelphia has been on the cutting edge of linking community-based organizing with global concerns. Its work is an excellent model for organizations at all levels associated with the American policy process.

In addition, the movements need to support those community institutions that were created in the midst of the epidemic's major infection wave in the 1980s. We need to continue to do the following: distribute information about HIV/AIDS prevention; organize to challenge discrimination; pressure federal, state, and local governments around AIDS-related issues; and provide the changing social services and support systems that become necessary as people who are HIV positive live longer, thanks to their access to new medical advances. As we build coalitions with others (outside the lesbian and gay movements) around HIV/AIDS, we must work to ensure that more people have access to the information and drugs associated with these medical advances. This is challenging but crucial work, especially since some younger gays coming of age perceive that AIDS is not nearly the threat that it was during the 1980s and 1990s, given the development of drugs that have allowed some to live "normal" lives.

Support for Lesbian and Gay Youth Issues

One of the most serious issues facing the lesbian and gay movements is the problem of teen suicide. One Canadian study "claims to provide the most compelling proof to date of a link between homosexuality and youth suicide, concluding that gay and bisexual males are nearly 14 times more at risk than their heterosexual contemporaries of making a serious attempt on their own lives" (King 1996, 41). Lesbian, gay, bisexual, and transgender youth are often subjected to considerable harassment in school. A significant number report having been physically assaulted as well.[3] There is a connection between the harassment faced by lesbian and gay youth in their schools and suicide. Once again, these issues need a committed coalition of groups to come together to discuss how to protect and promote the well-being of all our youth, but certainly that of lesbian, gay, bisexual, and transgender youth, who, although they are particularly at risk, are often ignored in social policy. One organization that has done tremendous outreach work in this area is the Gay, Lesbian, and Straight Education Network. GLSEN's goal is to make America's schools safe for all youth. They have focused on four major fronts: (1) a fight for new laws that would extend equal protection to all students regardless of sexual orientation; (2) efforts to change the attitudes of all those who influence daily life in schools—"from public policy leaders in Washington, DC to state superintendents to local school board members"; (3) providing materials that can help train teachers about lesbian, gay, bisexual, and transgender issues in ways that help stop harassment and violence; and (4) organizing for change by strengthening grassroots activism (*GLSEN Fundraising and Information Newsletter* 2000, 3). GLSEN's national organization is located in New York City; it has eighty-five chapters nationwide.

A number of other organizations already represent the interests of lesbian, gay, bisexual, and transgender youth. At the national level, there is the National Youth Advocacy Coalition (NYAC), which was formally established in 1994. It attempts to educate members of Congress and other decisionmakers on youth-related issues. NYAC also pushes other organizations to "develop the capacity to represent the concerns of gay, lesbian, bisexual, and transgendered people." All too often the national organizations discussed in this book largely ignore youth. Since its creation in 1994, NYAC has worked on a number of youth-related issues: supporting student groups in high school and even on some college campuses, supporting students who have been harassed in schools, fighting against federal funding cuts in programs that benefit youth, working on suicide issues in the context of mental health services, addressing youth substance abuse, supporting youth-related HIV education and treatment programs, and addressing youth homelessness (personal interview with NYAC staff member, March 4, 1997).

All of these important issues deserve a much higher profile in the contemporary lesbian and gay movements. Though hundreds of local and regional organizations exist at the grassroots level to provide social and educational services to lesbian and gay youth, many lack the resources to provide services at the level they are needed. In addition, in many small towns and rural communities throughout the United States, these crucial resources are nonexistent. This set of issues poses a unique opportunity for the lesbian and gay movements to build coalitions with others around the importance of providing basic services and support for all of our youth. It also opens the door to discussions about what can be done in the schools, where young people spend so much time in the formative years of their lives.

Education for Understanding of and Respect for Difference

Given that schools have long been regarded as having important responsibilities for the moral development of youth, it is no surprise that the Christian Right has organized in communities throughout the United States to prevent the discussion of sexual orientation in school curricula. These efforts have been generally effective, thus reinforcing the antilesbian and antigay climate that exists in virtually all American educational institutions. Lesbian, gay, bisexual, and transgender students are the targets of daily verbal harassment, and some are physically abused as well. Educational institutions reinforce the larger society's heterosexism by tolerating antigay jokes and harassment and by promoting heterosexual coupling (Button, Rienzo, and Wald 1997, 139). As we have already seen, suicides and the threat of suicide are serious problems for adolescents who are struggling with how society treats their homosexuality.

In the 1990s, schools became an arena for the politics of lesbian and gay rights, as activists targeted school boards in an effort to persuade them to adopt curricula that promote nonjudgmental discussions of homosexuality and safe-sex education within the context of AIDS. One educator, Karen Harbeck, believes that when homosexuality and education come together for public discussion, they provoke "one of the most publicly volatile and personally threatening debates in our national history" (ibid., 148). The volatile 1992 debate over New York City's "Children of the Rainbow" multicultural curriculum provides plenty of evidence to support this claim. New York City emerged as a battleground between the Christian Right and the lesbian and gay grassroots movements when Joseph Fernandez, then chancellor of the city's school system, attempted to implement his Children of the Rainbow program. This curriculum was the "first-grade portion of the multicultural Rainbow Curriculum, which dealt with, among other issues, gay and lesbian families" (Bronski 1998, 133). Sexual orientation occupied a minor, but important, part of the entire plan; the curriculum was rooted in the assumption that the potential for homosexuality exists in students. Children of the Rainbow articulated this assumption in the following way: "Teachers of first graders have an opportunity to give children a healthy sense of identity at an early age. Classes should include references to lesbians and gays in curricular areas and should avoid exclusionary practices by presuming a person's sexual orientation, reinforcing stereotypes, or speaking of lesbians and gays as 'they' or 'other.'" Two related books chosen for classroom use were *Heather Has Two Mommies* and *Daddy's Roommate*. Children of the Rainbow and the broader multicultural Rainbow Curriculum received the support of former mayor David Dinkins in addition to Chancellor Fernandez.

The Christian Right responded to this curricular initiative with disdain and aggressive political organizing. New York's Roman Catholic Archdiocese and a coalition of right-wing community groups organized against the curriculum when it was still being developed and considered for adoption. The conservative Family Defense Council distributed a flyer that said, "We will not accept two people of the same sex engaged in sex practices as 'family.'. . . In the fourth grade the Chancellor would demonstrate to pupils how to use condoms. . . . He would teach our kids that sodomy is acceptable but virginity is something weird" (ibid.). Ultimately, Fernandez lost his job as a result of the controversy generated by the Rainbow Curriculum, giving the Christian and antigay Right a major victory.

The highly visible curriculum battle in New York City is just one of many battles that have occurred in communities across the country with respect to teaching about issues relating to homosexuality and difference. The Christian Right is well ahead of the movements in challenging education-for-difference efforts in many communities throughout the United States. Local school boards in some communities have been stacked with candidates supported by the Christian Right, making them morally and culturally conservative. This is the reality that the movements must face if they hope to reach out and build coalitions with others who have been the targets of hate and discrimination. The importance of education cannot be overestimated. In institutions where difficult issues are supposed to be examined with understanding and respect for difference, lesbian and gay teachers often remain closeted for fear of harassment, ridicule, and, even more seriously, loss of job. To the extent that the Christian and antigay Right continues to create a context for these sorts of attitudes, it challenges the fundamental tenets of the lesbian and gay liberation movements that are at the core of this book. Although winning the passage of assimilationist civil rights, antidiscrimination, or hate-crime laws may provide some tangible benefits for lesbians and gays, these measures will not challenge prejudices and fears that are deeply rooted. Properly trained and committed educators at all levels of education are in the best position to do so.

Hate-Crimes Legislation

The brutal murder of Matthew Shepard prompted a national debate over the merits of federal hate-crimes legislation called the Hate Crimes Prevention Act, which would afford federal agencies jurisdiction over bias incidents. Shepard's death and the murder of Billy Jack Gaither, who in February 1999 was beaten to death and whose body was burned in Sylacauga, Alabama, galvanized the lesbian and gay movements and their straight allies around federal hate-crimes legislation, but the reality is that hundreds of lesbians, gays, bisexuals, and transgender people (as well as people suspected of falling into these categories) have been the targets of bias-related crimes over the years, often with little response from the police, government officials, schoolteachers, principals, and community leaders.

A number of natural coalitions can be built around hate-related violence, such as lesbians and gays with battered women and civil rights groups. To the extent that these groups fail to work together and instead organize themselves according to their separate identities, there will be no long-lasting coalition to address the sources of hate crimes. Hate-crimes legislation at the federal, state, and local levels is an important symbolic gesture, but most forms of the legislation address the issue *after* a crime has been committed. What is desperately needed is a long-term coalition to explore how the sources of hate crimes can be targeted before they occur. Many of these conversations are already occurring in communities throughout the United States, but the problem also needs the formal involvement of educators. Their research-based insights into the roots of bias crimes can help communities devise appropriate responses, and they can also push for curricular innovations in schools that emphasize respect for and understanding of diversity.

The Employment Non-Discrimination Act (ENDA)

The vast majority of lesbians and gay men can be fired for their sexual orientations, despite the fact that more than ten states and many cities now outlaw job discrimination. There is a need for federal legislation, such as ENDA, that bans discrimination in employment based on sexual orientation. Support and publicity for this legislation serve an important symbolic purpose as well, because they highlight the reality that employment discrimination exists. Despite the fact that the legislation was defeated by the U.S. Senate in 1996 by the narrowest of margins, ENDA will probably not pass in the short term unless a decidedly more liberal Congress is elected with a Democrat in the White House. President George W. Bush has consistently opposed ENDA because he believes, erroneously, that it provides "special treatment."

This is an issue where lesbians and gays can build an effective coalition with other civil rights groups, while recognizing that how the issue is framed will determine the American public's support. Gregory B. Lewis and Marc A. Rogers have studied both demographic and attitudinal sources of support for lesbian and gay employment rights. They conclude:

Americans support the concept of equal rights more than they favor laws to enforce them, especially when they are asked to expand legal coverage rather than just to support existing laws. If the debate over gay employment protections can be framed as simply preventing employment discrimination, gay rights supporters should garner majority support, but opponents have frequently been able to reframe the issue around morality or to focus attention on the occupations where public distrust is greatest, especially elementary school teachers. Defusing fears of gay teachers will be a key issue in winning employment protections for gay and lesbian people in all occupations. (1999, 130)

These findings suggest that passage of ENDA will require a broad-based coalition of civil rights activists to come together to educate the public about the importance of this legislation and to rally support around a basic civil rights issue. In the meantime, the lesbian and gay movements will need to work with coalitions of civil rights supporters at the state and local levels in order to combat job discrimination based on sexual orientation.

Barriers to Building Coalitions

Perhaps the most important barrier to building coalitions is that a narrow assimilationist rights-based organizing strategy is supported by the political, cultural, and economic ethos of American society, as enshrined in the Bill of Rights and the Constitution, which uphold the importance of protecting *individual* rights. We are socialized to think in terms of protecting the individual's right to life, liberty, and happiness—often defined in ways that emphasize the acquisition of private wealth. An identity politics that embraces narrow civil rights goals, such as same-sex marriage or overturning the ban on lesbians and gays in the military, reinforces the primacy of the individual. And in fact, there are practical advantages to a narrowly circumscribed identity-based organizing strategy, as writer and activist Suzanne Pharr suggests. These include "'clarity of focus in tactics and strategies, self-examination and education apart from the dominant culture' and the 'development of solidarity and group bonding. Creating organizations based on identity allows us to have visibility and collective power, to advance concerns that otherwise would never be recognized because of our marginalization within the dominant society'" (Vaid 1995, 286). Pharr's analysis goes a long way toward explaining why narrow identity politics will continue to dominate the mainstream lesbian and gay movements' strategic thinking, despite the setbacks of the Clinton and Bush eras.

The other major barrier is one that we have seen repeatedly throughout this book, that is, the lesbian and gay movements are highly fragmented across identities and subject to conflicting and multiple cross-pressures. Given this reality, how can they build a coherent agenda, one that reflects agreement on a political and cultural strategy? And if the movements cannot agree on a coherent agenda, how can we expect them to build the coalitions needed to address the issues we have discussed? As Kenneth Sherrill points out, "to the degree that there is any agenda in the United States, it is for equality and freedom from discrimination and violence. A more sophisticated agenda would require a level of collective identity among gay people not found anywhere in the world" (1996, 473).

And what does all of this mean for the central dilemma of this book—the tensions between the assimilationist and liberationist approaches to political and social change—that has characterized the lesbian and gay movements over the years? One clear answer is it means that the movements should pursue a dual organizing strategy, one that builds on the best of the assimilationist perspective, but one that also always considers the possibilities for more radical, liberationist, structural, social, and policy change. We have seen in our discussion of the three major policy areas of this book—HIV/AIDS, the military ban, and same-sex marriage—that the assimilationist strategy has much to offer the movements, but in and of itself, it is far too limiting. We have also seen in this book that any social movement needs a variety of political organizing strategies that can be applied at different points and times at all levels in response to the Christian Right and at all levels of the political system. This chapter began with a quotation from Laura Liswood, the founder of Women World Leaders: "Every successful social movement eventually moves from the unthinkable to the impossible to the inevitable" (Wilcox et al. 2007, 241). There are moments in any social movement's history when it seems as if very little progress can be achieved toward larger goals. The 1990s and the early twenty-first century have provided plenty of evidence to support the claim that the larger lesbian and gay movements, working with others, have much work to do to make progress on the issues that we have discussed in this book, so that the unthinkable and impossible can be turned into the inevitable. And to ensure that this happens, we rely on the courage and resistance of ordinary people who come together out of shared necessity and commitment across sexual-orientation, gender, race, and class divides. This is not easy work, but it is the necessary and messy work of social movements. And it is work that awaits, inspires, and challenges us all.

Conclusion

This chapter began with this key question: What political organizing strategy is the most viable for addressing the policy issues discussed in this book? The answer is we need to build on the best of what the assimilationist and liberationist strategies have to offer. The assimilationist strategy, in and of itself, is far too limiting. And in the words of the late civil rights activist Bayard Rustin, those who embrace radical, outsider, unconventional, liberationist politics must eventually recognize the importance of moving "from protest to politics" (D'Emilio 2002, 5). All social movements recognize over time the importance of building coalitions with others across issues of common interest that will help bridge sexual-orientation, gender, race, and class divides. We have discussed the barriers to doing so throughout this book, but these barriers are not insurmountable. Indeed, much of the hope for the future resides in the attitudes and values of young people today, many of whom have indicated to pollsters and in classrooms across the country that those who are lesbian, gay, bisexual, and transgender deserve to live in a world free from prejudice, discrimination, and harassment, and deserve, at a bare minimum, the rights afforded to those in the heterosexual majority. What we must ultimately do is reconceptualize what it is to be an American, challenge what Audre Lorde has called the American norm: someone who is "white, thin, male, young, heterosexual, christian, and financially secure." It is important to do so because "this mythical American norm" is socially constructed and is the locus of considerable power and privilege in American society (1984, 116). No single political strategy can begin to accomplish this goal; multiple strategies for political, social, cultural, and economic transformation are at the core of this radical democratic conception of politics. As we approach our task, we are challenging what it means to be a citizen in the United States and a citizen of the world. This book has been written with these goals in mind.

Appendix 1: AIDS Timeline

1981

- Doctors in New York and California begin to notice immune system disorders in otherwise healthy gay men.
- On June 5, the CDC reports the first case of the illness that will come to be called AIDS.
- Number of known AIDS deaths in the United States during 1981: 234.

1982

- The CDC links the new disease to blood. The name "gay-related immune deficiency" (GRID) is replaced with "acquired immunodeficiency syndrome" (AIDS). The disease is linked to four risk factors: male homosexuality, intravenous drug use, Haitian origin, and hemophilia A.
- Gay Men's Health Crisis, the first community AIDS service provider in the United States, established in New York City.
- First AIDS case reported in Africa.

1983

- The CDC warns blood banks of the risk of infection through transfusion; the first AIDS discrimination trial is held in the United States.
- People living with AIDS, as they want to be called instead of "AIDS sufferers" or "AIDS victims," take over plenary stage at U.S. conference and issue statement on the rights of PWAs referred to as the Denver Principles.
- National Association of People with AIDS formed.

1984

- Virus isolated by Luc Montagnier of the Pasteur Institute and Robert Gallo of the National Cancer Institute determined to be cause of AIDS; later named the human immunodeficiency virus (HIV).
- The secretary of health and human services announces that "a vaccine will be ready for testing within two years."
- San Francisco officials order gay bathhouses shut down; major public controversies over bathhouses rage in New York and other cities.

1985

- First International AIDS Conference held in Atlanta.
- Rock Hudson announces he has AIDS.
- Ryan White, fourteen, is barred from attending public school in Indiana because he is HIV positive.
- First HIV test licensed by the U.S. Food and Drug Administration.

1986

- President Ronald Reagan uses the acronym *AIDS* in public for the first time.
- Surgeon General C. Everett Koop calls for AIDS education of children of all ages and for widespread use of condoms.
- Ricky Ray, a nine-year-old hemophiliac with HIV, is barred from Florida school, and his family's home is burned by arsonists in the following year. Ray died in 1991.
- Fifth anniversary of AIDS. Cumulative known AIDS deaths: 16,301.

1987

- ACT UP—the AIDS Coalition to Unleash Power—founded after a speech by Larry Kramer at the Lesbian and Gay Community Services Center in New York.
- Azidothymidine (AZT) is approved to fight AIDS itself.
- The United States adds HIV as a "dangerous contagious disease" to its immigration exclusion list.
- Pianist and performer Liberace dies of AIDS.
- AIDS memorial quilt founded.

1988

- First World AIDS Day held on December 1.
- ACT UP members demonstrate at FDA offices in Washington, D.C., over slow process for drug approval.

1989

- The CDC issues guidelines for preventing Pneumocystis carinii pneumonia, a major cause of death for people with AIDS.
- Choreographer Alvin Ailey dies of AIDS.
- Gay artist Robert Mapplethorpe dies of AIDS.

1990

- Ryan White dies from AIDS at age eighteen. The Ryan White Comprehensive AIDS Resources Emergency (CARE) Act of 1990 is approved by Congress, providing federal funds for community services.
- President George H. W. Bush signs the Americans with Disabilities Act, which in part prohibits discrimination against people with HIV.
- Artist Keith Haring dies of AIDS.
- Fashion designer Halston dies of AIDS.

1991

- NBA superstar Magic Johnson announces that he has tested positive for HIV and will retire from professional basketball.
- Red ribbon introduced as the international symbol of AIDS awareness at the Tony Awards by Broadway Cares/Equity Fights AIDS and Visual AIDS.
- Freddie Mercury, lead singer of the rock band Queen, dies of AIDS.
- Housing Opportunities for People with AIDS Act of 1991 enacted by the U.S. Congress, to provide housing assistance to people living with AIDS through grants to states and local communities.

1992

- The International Olympic Committee rules that athletes with HIV can compete. First clinical trial of multiple drug therapy is held.
- AIDS becomes number-one cause of death for U.S. men ages twenty-five to forty-two.
- HIV-positive speakers Mary Fisher and Bob Hattoy address the Republican and Democratic National Conventions, respectively.
- Tennis star Arthur Ashe announces he has AIDS.
- *Brady Bunch* star Robert Reed dies of AIDS.

1993

- Arthur Ashe dies from AIDS.
- President Clinton establishes White House Office on National AIDS Policy, commonly known as the office of the "AIDS czar."
- *Angels in America,* a play about AIDS by Tony Kushner, wins the Tony Award and Pulitzer Prize.
- Ballet dancer Rudolf Nureyev dies of AIDS.

1994

- AIDS becomes leading cause of death for all Americans ages twenty-five to forty-four; remains so through 1995.
- Elizabeth Glaser, cofounder of the Pediatric AIDS Foundation, dies of AIDS.
- Pedro Zamora, an HIV-positive gay man, appears in the cast of MTV's popular show *The Real World*. Zamora dies later that year at twenty-two.
- Randy Shilts, author of *And the Band Played On*, dies of AIDS at age forty-two.

1995

- First protease inhibitor, saquinavir, approved in record time by the FDA, ushering in new era of highly active antiretroviral therapy (HAART).
- First guidelines for the prevention of opportunistic infections in persons infected with HIV issued by the CDC.
- First National HIV Testing Day created by the National Association of People with AIDS.
- Olympic Gold Medal diver Greg Louganis announces that he is living with HIV.
- Rap star Easy E (Eric Wright) dies of AIDS.

1996

- At Eleventh AIDS Conference in Vancouver, new protease inhibitors and combination therapies bring renewed optimism.
- The FDA approves viral-load test, a new test that measures the level of HIV in the body.
- The number of new AIDS cases diagnosed in the United States declines for first time in the history of the epidemic, though experience varies by sex, race, and ethnicity.
- HIV is no longer leading cause of death for all Americans ages twenty-five to forty-four; remains leading cause of death of African Americans in this age group.

1997

- AIDS-related deaths in the United States decline by more than 40 percent compared to the prior year, largely due to HAART.
- President Clinton announces goal of finding an effective vaccine in ten years.

1998

- Minority AIDS Initiative created in United States after African American leaders declare a "state of emergency" and Congressional Black Caucus Foundation calls on the Department of Health and Human Services to do the same.
- The U.S. Department of Health and Human Services issues the first national guidelines for the use of antiretroviral therapy in adults.
- First large-scale human trials (Phase III) for an HIV vaccine begin.
- The U.S. Supreme Court rules in *Bragdon v. Abbot* that the Americans with Disabilities Act covers those in earlier stages of HIV disease, not just AIDS.

1999

- Study finds that numbers of new HIV infections are rising among gay men.

2000

- At the Thirteenth AIDS Conference in Durban, South Africa, 5,000 doctors and scientists sign the "Durban Declaration," stating that HIV causes AIDS, in response to South African president Thabo Mbeki's statements to the contrary.
- The CDC reports that, among men who have sex with men in the United States, African American and Latino HIV cases exceed those among whites.

2001

- The United Nations General Assembly convenes first-ever special session on AIDS.
- First National Black HIV/AIDS Awareness Day in the United States.
- The World Trade Organization, meeting in Doha, Qatar, announces the "DOHA Agreement" to allow developing countries to buy or manufacture generic medications to meet public health crises.

2002

- HIV is leading cause of death worldwide among those ages fifteen to fifty-nine.
- UNAIDS reports that women constitute about half of all adults living with HIV and AIDS worldwide.
- FDA approval of OraQuick Rapid HIV-1 Antibody Test, the first rapid test to use finger prick.
- Cumulative AIDS deaths in United States through 2002: 501,669.

2003

- President Bush announces PEPFAR, the President's Emergency Plan for AIDS Relief, during the State of the Union Address; PEPFAR is a five-year, $15 billion initiative to address HIV/AIDS, tuberculosis, and malaria, primarily in hard-hit countries.
- First National Latino AIDS Awareness Day in the United States.

2004

- Leaders of the Group of Eight nations call for creation of the "Global HIV Vaccine Enterprise," a consortium to accelerate research efforts to find an HIV vaccine.
- OraQuick Rapid HIV-1 Antibody Test approved by the FDA for use with oral fluid.

2005

- First National Asian and Pacific Islander HIV/AIDS Awareness Day in the United States.
- In a historic and unprecedented joint news conference, the World Health Organization, UNAIDS, the U.S. government, and the Global Fund to Fight AIDS, Tuberculosis, and Malaria announce results of joint efforts to increase the availability of antiretroviral drugs in developing countries.

2006

- Twenty-fifth anniversary of the outbreak of AIDS.

Source: Lee 2006b.

Appendix 2: The "Don't Ask, Don't Tell" Law

107 STAT 1671, PUBLIC LAW 103-160—November 30, 1993
SUBTITLE G—OTHER MATTERS
SEC. 571. POLICY CONCERNING HOMOSEXUALITY IN THE ARMED FORCES.

(a) CODIFICATION.—(1) Chapter 37 of title 10, United States Code, is amended by adding at the end the following new section:

"Sec. 654. Policy concerning homosexuality in the armed forces

"(a) FINDINGS.—Congress makes the following findings:

"(1) Section 8 of article I of the Constitution of the United States commits exclusively to the Congress the powers to raise and support armies, provide and maintain a navy, and make rules for the government and regulation of the land and naval forces.

"(2) There is no constitutional right to serve in the armed forces.

"(3) Pursuant to the powers conferred by section 8 of article I of the Constitution of the United States, it lies within the discretion of the Congress to establish qualifications for and conditions of service in the armed forces.

"(4) The primary purpose of the armed forces is to prepare for and to prevail in combat should the need arise.

"(5) The conduct of military operations requires members of the armed forces to make extraordinary sacrifices, including the ultimate sacrifice, in order to provide for the common defense.

"(6) Success in combat requires military units that are characterized by high morale, good order and discipline, and unit cohesion.

"(7) One of the most critical elements in combat capability is unit cohesion, that is, the bonds of trust among individual service members that make the combat effectiveness of a military unit greater than the sum of the combat effectiveness of the individual unit members.

"(8) Military life is fundamentally different from civilian life in that

"(A) the extraordinary responsibilities of the armed forces, the unique conditions of military service, and the critical role of unit cohesion, require that the military community, while subject to civilian control, exist as a specialized society; and

"(B) the military society is characterized by its own laws, rules, customs, and traditions, including numerous restrictions on personal behavior, that would be acceptable in civilian society.

"(9) The standards of conduct for members of the armed forces regulate a member's life for 24 hours each day beginning at the moment the member enters military status and not ending until that person is discharged or separated from the armed forces.

"(10) Those standards of conduct, including the Uniform Code of Military Justice, apply to a member of the armed forces at all times that the member has a military status, whether the member is on base or off base, and whether the member is on duty or off duty.

"(11) The pervasive application of the standards of conduct is necessary because members of the armed forces must be ready at all times for worldwide deployment to a combat environment.

"(12) The worldwide deployment of United States military forces, the international responsibilities of the United States, and the potential for involvement of the armed forces in actual combat routinely make it necessary for members of the armed forces involuntarily to accept living conditions and working conditions that are often Spartan, primitive, and characterized by forced intimacy with little or no privacy.

"(13) The prohibition against homosexual conduct is a longstanding element of military law that continues to be necessary in the unique circumstances of military service.

"(14) The armed forces must maintain personnel policies that exclude persons whose presence in the armed forces would create an unacceptable risk to the armed forces' high standards of morale, good order and discipline, and unit cohesion that are the essence of military capability.

"(15) The presence in the armed forces of persons who demonstrate a propensity or intent to engage in homosexual acts would create an unacceptable risk to the high standards of morale, good order and discipline, and unit cohesion that are the essence of military capability.

"(b) POLICY.—A member of the armed forces shall be separated from the armed forces under regulations prescribed by the Secretary of Defense if one or more of the following findings is made and approved in accordance with procedures set forth in such regulations:

"(1) That the member has engaged in, attempted to engage in, or solicited another to engage in a homosexual act or acts unless there are further findings, made and approved in accordance with procedures set forth in such regulations, that the member has demonstrated that—

"(A) such conduct is a departure from the member's usual and customary behavior;

"(B) such conduct, under all the circumstances, is unlikely to recur;

"(C) such conduct was not accomplished by use of force, coercion, or intimidation;

"(D) under the particular circumstances of the case, the member's continued presence in the armed forces is consistent with the interests of the armed forces in proper discipline, good order, and morale; and

"(E) the member does not have a propensity or intent to engage in homosexual acts.

"(2) That the member has stated that he or she is a homosexual or bisexual, or words to that effect, unless there is a further finding, made and approved in accordance with procedures set forth in the regulations, that the member has demonstrated that he or she is not a person who engages in, attempts to engage in, has a propensity to engage in, or intends to engage in homosexual acts.

"(3) That the member has married or attempted to marry a person known to be of the same biological sex.

"(c) ENTRY STANDARDS AND DOCUMENTS.—(1) The Secretary of Defense shall ensure that the standards for enlistment and appointment of members of the armed forces reflect the policies set forth in subsection (b).

"(2) The documents used to effectuate the enlistment or appointment of a person as a member of the armed forces shall set forth the provisions of subsection (b).

"(d) REQUIRED BRIEFINGS.—The briefings that members of the armed forces receive upon entry into the armed forces and periodically thereafter under section 937 of this title (article 137 of the Uniform Code of Military Justice) shall include a detailed explanation of the applicable laws and regulations governing sexual conduct by members of the armed forces, including the policies prescribed under subsection (b).

"(e) RULE OF CONSTRUCTION.—Nothing in subsection (b) shall be construed to require that a member of the armed forces be processed for separation from the armed forces when a determination is made in accordance with regulations prescribed by the Secretary of Defense that—

"(1) the member engaged in conduct or made statements for the purpose of avoiding or terminating military service; and

"(2) separation of the member would not be in the best interest of the armed forces."

"(f) DEFINITIONS.—In this section:

"(1) The term 'homosexual' means a person, regardless of sex, who engages in, attempts to engage in, has a propensity to engage in, or intends to engage in homosexual acts, and includes the terms 'gay' and 'lesbian.'

"(2) The term 'bisexual' means a person who engages in, attempts to engage in, has a propensity to engage in, or intends to engage in homosexual and heterosexual acts.

"(3) The term 'homosexual act' means—

"(A) any bodily contact, actively undertaken or passively permitted, between members of the same sex for the purpose of satisfying sexual desires; and

"(B) any bodily contact which a reasonable person would understand to demonstrate a propensity or intent to engage in an act described in subparagraph (A)."

(2) The table of sections at the beginning of each chapter is amended by adding at the end the following:

"664. Policy concerning homosexuality in the armed forces."

(b) REGULATIONS.—Not later than 90 days after the date of enactment of this Act, the Secretary of Defense shall revise Department of Defense regulations, and issue such new regulations as may be necessary to implement section 654 of title 10, United States Code, as added by subsection (a).

(c) SAVINGS PROVISION.—Nothing in this section or section 654 of title 10, United States Code, as added by subsection (a), may be construed to invalidate any inquiry, investigation, administrative action or proceeding, court-martial, or judicial proceeding conducted before the effective date of regulations issued by the Secretary of Defense to implement such section 654.

(d) SENSE OF CONGRESS.—It is the sense of Congress that—

(1) the suspension of questioning concerning homosexuality as a part of the processing of individuals for accession in the Armed Forces under the interim policy of January 29, 1993, should be continued, but the Secretary of Defense may reinstate that questioning with such questions or such revised questions as he considers appropriate if the Secretary determines that it is necessary to do so in order to effectuate the policy set forth in section 654 of title 10, United States Code, as added by subsection (a); and

(2) the Secretary of Defense should consider issuing guidance governing the circumstances under which members of the Armed Forces questioned about homosexuality for administrative purposes should be afforded warnings similar to the warnings under section 831 (b) of title 10, United States Code (article 31 [b] of the Uniform Code of Military Justice).

Source: Belkin and Bateman 2003, 177–181.

Appendix 3: Lesbian, Gay, Bisexual, Transgender, and Christian Right Organizations

Lesbian, Gay, Bisexual, and Transgender Organizations

ACT UP
http://www.critpath.org/actup

AIDS Action
202-530-8030
http://www.aidsaction.org

Astraea Lesbian Foundation for Justice
212-529-8021
http://www.astraea.org

Basic Rights Oregon
503-222-6151
http://www.basicrights.org

Bisexual Resource Center
617-424-9595
http://www.biresource.org

Children of Lesbians and Gays Everywhere
415-861-5437
http://www.colage.org

Family Pride
202-331-5015
http://www.familypride.org

Freedom to Marry
http://www.freedomtomarry.org

Gay, Lesbian, and Straight
Education Network
212-727-0135
http://www.glsen.org

Gay and Lesbian Alliance
Against Discrimination
http://www.glaad.org

Gay and Lesbian Medical Association
415-255-4547
http://www.glma.org

Gay Asian Pacific Support Network
213-368-6488
http://www.gapsn.org

Gay Men's Health Crisis
212-367-1000
http://www.gmhc.org

GenderPAC
202-462-6610
http://www.gpac.org

Human Rights Campaign
202-628-4160
http://www.hrc.org

Immigration Equality
http://www.immigrationequality.org

International Lesbian and
Gay Organization
http://www.ilga.org

Lambda Legal Defense and
Education Fund
212-809-8585
http://www.lambdalegal.org

Log Cabin Republicans
202-347-5306
http://www.logcabin.org

National Association of Lesbian,
Gay, Bisexual, and Transgender
Community Centers
202-639-6325
http://www.lgbtcenters.org

National Association of People with AIDS
202-898-0414
http://www.napwa.org

National Black Justice Coalition
http://www.nbjcoalition.org

National Center for Lesbian Rights
415-392-6257
http://www.nclrights.org

National Center for Transgender Equality
202-903-0112
http://www.nctequality.org

National Gay and Lesbian Task Force
202-332-6483
http://www.ngltf.org

National Minority AIDS Council
202-483-6622
http://www.nmac.org

National Stonewall Democrats
202-625-1362
http://www.stonewalldemocrats.org

National Transgender Advocacy Coalition
http://www.ntac.org

National Youth Advocacy Coalition
800-541-6922
http://www.nyacyouth.org

Parents, Families, and Friends of Lesbians
and Gays
202-467-8180
http://www.pflag.org

People for the American Way
202-467-4999
http://www.pfaw.org

Servicemembers Legal Defense Network
202-328-3244
http://www.sldn.org

Soulforce
http://www.soulforce.org

Straight Spouse Network
510-595-1005
http://www.straightspouse.org

Universal Fellowship of Metropolitan
Community Churches
310-360-8640
http://www.mcchurch.org

Christian Right Organizations

Alliance Defense Fund
800-TELL-ADF
http://www.alliancedefensefund.org

American Center for
Law and Justice
http://www.aclj.org

American Family Association
http://www.afa.net

Christian Broadcasting Network—Pat Robertson's *700 Club*
757-226-7000
http://www.cbn.com

Christian Coalition of America
202-479-6900
http://www.cc.org

Concerned Women for America
202-488-7000
http://www.cwfa.org

Eagle Forum
618-462-5415
http://www.eagleforum.org

Family Research Council
http://www.frc.org

Focus on the Family
800-232-6459
http://www.family.org

Moral Majority
http://www.moralmajority.com

Traditional Values Coalition
202-547-8570
http://www.traditionalvalues.org

Discussion Questions

Chapter 2

1. How have the assimilationist and liberationist strategies developed over time? In answering this question, be sure to discuss the specific tensions that have emerged between the two perspectives, as well as the ways that the two perspectives have worked well together.
2. In what specific ways was there political organizing by the lesbian and gay movements prior to the Stonewall Rebellion of June 1969?
3. In what specific ways did the homophile movement provide a foundation for contemporary lesbian and gay movements' political organizing?
4. What connections can be made between the African American civil rights movement and the lesbian and gay movements?
5. What was the impact of the 1969 Stonewall Rebellion for the larger lesbian and gay movements?
6. Discuss the specific ways in which the Gay Liberation Front reflected a liberationist approach to political, social, and policy change.
7. Discuss the specific ways in which the Gay Activists Alliance reflected an assimilationist approach to political, social, and policy change.
8. In what ways did the Christian Right emerge as a formidable opponent to the lesbian and gay movements during the 1970s?

Chapter 3

1. In what ways did the onset of AIDS in the United States during the early 1980s affect the lesbian and gay movements in terms of their political organizing strategies?
2. How have the lesbian and gay movements intersected with the policy process over time as AIDS has developed in the United States and throughout the world?
3. What direct-action organizations grew out of the HIV/AIDS movements, and in what specific ways did they reinforce the liberationist approach to political and policy change?
4. What role has ACT UP played over time in the AIDS political and policy debates? To what extent has its role been an effective one? Be sure to define what you mean by "effective" as you answer this question.

5. Why has HIV/AIDS receded in importance on the lesbian and gay movements' political organizing agenda?

6. How has the Christian Right intersected with the AIDS policy arena over time?

7. Discuss and evaluate how various presidents (Reagan, Bush, Clinton, and Bush) have responded to HIV/AIDS in the United States and on a global scale. What do you perceive to be the strengths and weaknesses of each of their policy responses?

8. In what specific ways is the Ryan White CARE Act an important policy initiative in response to HIV/AIDS? Why do you think that there continue to be debates over fully funding the legislation when it is up for renewal?

9. In what ways have the boundaries between the lesbian and gay movements and the AIDS activist movement grown more rigid as AIDS has receded from public and policy attention and other issues have become more prominent on the lesbian and gay movements' agenda?

10. In what specific ways does the HIV/AIDS policy area reflect the underlying dilemma of this book—the tension between the assimilationist and liberationist approaches to political and policy change?

Chapter 4

1. In what specific ways does the debate over lesbians and gays in the military reflect the underlying dilemma of this book—the tension between the assimilationist and liberationist approaches to political and policy change?

2. Why did the lesbian and gay movements perceive that the Clinton presidency offered them political opportunities?

3. Discuss the treatment of lesbians and gays in the military over time.

4. Why did the military ban emerge on the national policy agenda in late 1992 and 1993?

5. Could President Bill Clinton have avoided the "Don't Ask, Don't Tell" compromise? If so, how?

6. What might the lesbian and gay movements have done differently in 1993 as the military ban emerged on the national policymaking agenda?

7. What are the broader implications of how the military ban issue has been resolved for the larger lesbian and gay movements?

8. How has the Christian Right responded to the military ban debate over time?

9. What are the most persuasive arguments in the case for the military ban? What are the most persuasive arguments in the case against the military ban?

10. What comparisons can be drawn between the integration of African Americans in the military during the 1940s and the contemporary debate over the military ban?

Chapter 5

1. How, why, and when did same-sex marriage emerge on the national policy agenda?

2. How, why, and when did same-sex marriage emerge on the lesbian and gay movements' policy agenda?

3. Why do you think that same-sex marriage has emerged as a wedge issue in political campaigns? To what extent do you think that it is an effective wedge issue? In answering this question, be sure to define what you mean by "effective."

4. What role have the courts played in the debate over same-sex marriage? What role do you think that they should play?

5. How has the Christian Right responded to the same-sex marriage debate? Do you believe that their response has been effective? In answering this question, be sure to identify your criteria for "effective."

6. Why do you think President Clinton signed the Defense of Marriage Act in September 1996?

7. In what ways has the United States Supreme Court's 2003 *Lawrence v. Texas* decision impinged upon the same-sex marriage debate?

8. What are the most persuasive arguments for same-sex marriage? What are the least-persuasive arguments?

9. In what ways does same-sex marriage reflect an assimilationist approach to political and policy change? In what ways does it reflect the liberationist approach?

Chapter 6

1. Discuss the implications of the analysis presented here regarding the assimilationist and liberationist approaches to political and policy change for social-movement theory.

2. Can the tensions between the assimilationist and liberationist perspectives be resolved over time? If so, how? If not, why not? To what extent are these tensions a healthy part of any social movement?

3. In what specific policy areas do you think the lesbian and gay movements have made progress over time? In answering this question, be sure to define what you mean by "progress."

4. What are the sources of the possible lesbian and gay movements' progress in the future? What are the barriers? How might the barriers be overcome?

5. Do you believe it is possible for the lesbian and gay movements to embrace the assimilationist and liberationist approaches at the same time? If so, how? If not, why not?

6. Construct a political organizing strategy for the lesbian and gay movements. In doing so, be sure to identity what political strategies you would use and why, and identify what policy issues you would emphasize (and which ones you would de-emphasize) and why. Be sure to discuss the role that you think conventional insider, work-within-the-system political organizing strategies would play. Discuss as well the role that you think unconventional outsider organizing strategies would play.

7. Is there a way to build political coalitions across identities within the lesbian and gay movements? If so, how? If not, why not? And is there a way to build political coalitions between the lesbian and gay movements and other social movements? If so, how? If not, why not?

Glossary

ACT UP, the commonly used acronym for the AIDS Coalition to Unleash Power, is a grassroots AIDS organization associated with nonviolent civil disobedience. In the late 1980s and early 1990s, ACT UP became the standard-bearer for protest against governmental and societal indifference to the AIDS epidemic. The group is part of a long tradition of grassroots organizations in American politics, especially those of the African American civil rights movement, which were committed to political and social change through the practice of unconventional politics. ACT UP was founded in March 1987 by playwright and AIDS activist Larry Kramer.

The **Campaign for Military Service** is an organization created by prominent gay Democrats, including David Mixner, David Geffen, and Barry Diller, all of whom had ties to President Bill Clinton. The goal was to counteract the Christian Right's organizing efforts against President Clinton's attempt to overturn the military ban. The founders believed that the lesbian and gay movements needed to do much more in the way of grassroots organizing, and this organization was created with that goal in mind.

The **Christian Right** is a political alliance of evangelical Protestants and conservative Roman Catholics who argue against any form of equality for gay people. Antigay activism is central to their political organizing strategy, though they have also been on the forefront in the antiabortion movement as well. In addition, the Christian Right opposes teaching evolution in schools, affirmative action, and women in combat. The Christian Right opposed funding for HIV/AIDS education initiatives and the distribution of condoms in the 1980s, and since the mid-1990s, it has organized against same-sex marriage. Some of the most important Christian Right groups include Concerned Women for America, Focus on the Family, the Family Research Council, and the Traditional Values Coalition. The Christian Right has been particularly effective in using grassroots organizing over the years.

Classical liberalism is the underlying ideology in the United States, one that promotes such values as individualism, equality of opportunity, liberty and freedom, the rule of law, and limited government. The constitutional framers, influenced by eighteenth-century theorists John Locke and Adam Smith, embraced classical liberal principles from the outset.

Compassionate conservatism is a governing philosophy introduced by George W. Bush prior to the 2000 presidential election. Bush has used compassionate conservatism as his chief governing and campaign philosophy with respect to education, poverty, and global AIDS policy. It is rooted in the notion that government at all levels of society can help fellow citizens who are in need, but there must also be the required accompanying responsibility on the part of the individual and social service agencies and demonstrated results.

The **Daughters of Bilitis** was the first lesbian organization in the United States. Founded in San Francisco in September 1955, the group's name came from Pierre Louys's *Song of Bilitis*, a book of poetry that had been written by a man. Two of its founders—Del Martin and Phyllis Lyon—chose the name because they perceived it would be safe during the repressive environment of the 1950s. The organization was originally formed as a social and discussion group, and it eventually published the *Ladder*, a monthly magazine that first appeared in 1956, with Barbara Gittings as its first editor.

The **Defense of Marriage Act** was introduced by Senator Bob Dole (R-KS) in 1996, and President Bill Clinton signed it into law on September 21, 1996. The law defined marriage as the union of one man and one woman and also prevented states from being forced to recognize same-sex marriages that were viewed as valid in other states.

The **degaying of AIDS** refers to the period of the mid-1980s when AIDS activists made a crucial decision to publicize the message that "AIDS is not a gay disease." The goal was to gain greater funding and public support, and to convey the importance of AIDS prevention to all sectors of the population. The assumption was that the public and politicians would be more receptive if gay men were not the targeted beneficiaries of increased AIDS-related funding.

Distributive justice is a form of justice based on normative principles concerning what is the just allocation of rewards and goods in a society. Egalitarianism is at the core of this approach to the distribution of resources.

Domestic partnerships are composed of individuals of the same or opposite sex, who often live in committed relationships together but are not joined together in a traditional civil union or marriage.

Executive orders are presidential directives that become law. Congress allows presidents to issue executive orders to lessen its overwhelming legislative load, thus contributing to the president's legislative power.

The **ex-gay movement** refers to religious-based organizations and groups that purport to represent mental health interests. The movement claims that it can change the sexual orientations of those who identify as lesbian, gay, bisexual, or transgender by using a combination of strategies: Bible study, religious commitment, repentance, and reparative therapy. Organizations associated with the ex-gay movement include Exodus International, Love in Action, and Parents and Friends of Ex-Gays.

Focus on the Family is a Christian Right organization, headed by fundamentalist James Dobson, that has been on the forefront of antigay activity in the United States. It has engaged in aggressive education and grassroots campaigns to thwart the contemporary lesbian and gay movements' organizing efforts.

The **Gay Activists Alliance** was founded by former GLF members Jim Owles and Marty Robinson in New York City in December 1969. The GAA attempted to focus on the single issue of gay rights while avoiding issue fragmentation and anarchic organization. The GAA eschewed more radical liberationist change and instead embraced a more assimilationist approach to organizing. The GAA membership thought that meaningful reform would occur only if lesbians and gays organized politically for clearly defined demands (the repeal of New York State's sodomy and solicitation laws, an end to police entrapment of gay men, and employment discrimination protection) and exercised their political muscle to force positive legislative change.

The **Gay Liberation Front** was formed by gay and lesbian activists in the wake of the Stonewall Riots of late June 1969. Unabashedly celebrating liberationist approaches to change, the GLF drew on the principles and rhetoric of the more radical strands of the student, women's, and civil rights movements of the 1960s. Its goal was to dismantle and rebuild existing institutions—heterosexual marriage, the family, and relationships at all levels of society—according to liberationist principles.

Heteronormativity refers to the prevailing heterosexual standards by which people are judged and expected to conform in terms of their identities and as they interact with the world.

The **homophile movement** is the name given to the broad movement that emerged in the early 1950s. In its early stages, it embraced liberationist principles through the Mattachine Society. But by the 1960s, the homophile movement embraced more mainstream assimilationist goals. Mainstream homophile organizations were thrown on the defensive in the wake of the Stonewall Rebellion, as a new style of political organizing and leadership was demanded by newly energized lesbian and gay activists, many of whom were veterans of the various social and political movements of the 1960s.

Insider political strategies work within the formal channels of the U.S. political system (voting and interest-group politics) to effect policy change. This approach to political organizing is often associated with assimilationist political strategies.

Lawrence v. Texas is a 2003 Supreme Court decision that overturned the 1996 *Bowers v. Hardwick* ruling permitting states to regulate sodomy. Writing for the 6-3 majority, Justice Anthony Kennedy celebrated the freedom of gay people to come together and to form relationships. The decision is viewed as a landmark decision because it essentially ruled state sodomy laws unconstitutional. In a bitter dissent, Justice Antonin Scalia (joined by Chief Justice William Rehnquist) warned of the dangers to the institution of marriage that might result from the *Lawrence* decision.

The **Lesbian Avengers** was founded in the fall of 1992 by six lesbian friends, most of whom had been active in AIDS, feminist, and other forms of progressive politics. They came together to create this new organization because they believed that more lesbians needed to engage in direct street action on their own terms, and they were frustrated with the unwillingness of gay men to address sexism in meaningful ways. Like ACT UP, they embraced unconventional politics in an effort to secure media attention.

The **Mattachine Society** was an organization founded in Los Angeles in 1951 and a key element of the early homophile movement's liberationist strategies. Based on an idea by Harry Hay, then working at the Los Angeles People's Education Center as a music teacher, the Mattachine Society was founded by Hay and several of his colleagues. Hay and his coorganizers built the Mattachine Society based on communist principles of organizing and social change, a model that would soon lead to considerable controversy within the organization. In 1953, the organizational structure and militant ideology of the Mattachine Society were challenged by rank-and-file organization members who favored a more assimilationist approach. The organization published the magazine *One* soon after its founding. The name *Mattachine* was first used by medieval masked singers. Hay and his cofounders used this name to suggest that homosexuals were also invisible.

The **military-industrial complex** is a term that was first used by President Dwight Eisenhower in his farewell address. It refers to the enormous political and economic power that is associated with the military and industry that work together under capitalism.

The **Mississippi Freedom Summer** was the summer of 1964, when 1,000 college student volunteers, many from prominent northern white families, went to Mississippi in an organized effort to highlight white violence against blacks. Civil rights activists, including Robert Moses, believed that attacks on white college students would receive national attention and more likely prompt federal action than the continuing and long-standing beatings of African Americans in Mississippi and elsewhere in the South.

Outsider political strategies are political organizing strategies that are often referred to as unconventional politics. They require participants to go outside the formal channels of the U.S. political system and policy process to embrace the politics of protest, direct action, and mass involvement.

Patriarchy refers to the societal dominance of men over women in all political, social, and economic institutions.

Pluralist democracy is a model of democracy that has, as its central tenet, the view that power is not concentrated in the hands of any one element in society; it is widely distributed among a host of competing groups. This broad distribution of power means that the political system is open and responsive to a wide array of competing claims.

Protease inhibitors were developed in the mid-1990s and are a class of anti-HIV drugs. They are often used in combination with other anti-HIV drugs, usually three or more. The drugs work together as combination therapy to block the replication of HIV in a person's blood.

Queer Nation was a short-lived radical lesbian and gay organization. It appeared in June 1991 with a goal of radicalizing the broader AIDS movement by reclaiming the word *queer* and embracing confrontational politics. "Queer" politics rejected the politics of assimilation and the labels "lesbian" and "gay."

The **regaying of AIDS** is a movement that began in 1992. At its core, the regaying of AIDS requires that gay men and lesbians play a much larger role in rethinking and restructuring community-based organizations' responses to AIDS. Those who support the regaying of AIDS argue that gay and bisexual men are far more at risk of HIV than anyone else and that public policy needs to reflect this reality.

Reparative therapy is a controversial therapeutic technique, one that is closely associated with the ex-gay movement. It is also often referred to as conversion therapy or reorientation therapy. The goal is to change the sexual orientations of people who identify as lesbian, gay, bisexual, or transgender to heterosexual.

Social movements are movements that have the following characteristics: an ideology, multiple leaders, group consciousness, and social group identity. In addition, they are decentralized and made up of an array of organizations. Finally, social movements typically represent those at the margins of American society, as defined by class, race, gender, or sexual orientation.

The **Stonewall Rebellion** of 1969 helped to usher in what is regarded as the contemporary lesbian and gay rights movements, though it is important to recognize that there were considerable political organizing and individual and group acts of courage for many years before in the United States and around the world. The Stonewall Rebellion (or Stonewall Riots) occurred at the Stonewall Inn in Greenwich Village, New York, over a period of several days beginning on the evening of June 27, 1969. When police raided the bar, many of the patrons decided to fight back, culminating in violent clashes between New York City police officers, patrons, and others in the area who were angered by the police action. By the time order was finally restored, the incident had received national and international media attention.

The **Treatment Action Group** is an organization that grew out of ACT UP/New York and was founded in 1992 by activists committed to a political strategy emphasizing the treatment of individuals with HIV/AIDS. Unlike ACT UP, which had a democratic organizational structure, TAG accepted members by invitation only, and membership could be revoked by the board. In addition, TAG members received salaries, and the group accepted a $1 million check from the pharmaceutical company Burroughs Wellcome, the manufacturer of AZT, in the summer of 1992. TAG used this money to finance members' travels to AIDS conferences throughout the world, pay salaries, hire professional lobbyists, and lobby government officials.

Unconventional politics is a form of politics that requires participants to go outside the formal channels of the U.S. political system (voting and interest-group politics) and embrace the politics of protest and mass involvement. Unconventional politics was employed with great success by the civil rights movement and has been used in contemporary American politics by groups across the ideological spectrum, including Earth First! ACT UP, Operation Rescue, and the militias.

Virtual equality is a concept coined by political activist Urvashi Vaid, former director of the National Gay and Lesbian Task Force, who argued that the assimilationist perspective should be rejected because it is far too accommodationist and too likely to be co-opted by more conservative elements in the lesbian and gay movements and society writ large. She worried that the lesbian and gay movements are more likely to accept the illusion of equality with straight people rather than to fight for true equality that would require a more liberationist political organizing strategy.

Wedge issues are highly salient issues, those that rally a candidate's supporters and divide his or her political opponents. Same-sex marriage has been used as a wedge issue in political campaigns at all levels of the political process.

Notes

Chapter 1

1. As this book will make clear, the so-called lesbian and gay movements are composed of a diversity of groups and individuals, and in them we see the convergence of a wide range of identities, including bisexuals and transgender individuals. Judging it inappropriate to collapse this rich diversity into a unitary discussion, I will refer to the lesbian and gay *movements* in the plural throughout this book. I place *lesbian* first in acknowledgment of the reality that women continue to occupy a position of structural inequality in the larger society.

Chapter 3

1. On May 30, 2007, President Bush requested that Congress double the funding of his U.S. global AIDS program to "30 billion over five years, which sets goals of helping support AIDS treatment of 2.5 million people" (Donnelly 2007, A15). This announcement was made at a White House Rose Garden ceremony and was part of the president's plan to secure at least one lasting, meaningful policy accomplishment as part of his legacy.

Chapter 4

1. From *St. James Press Gay and Lesbian Almanac* 1st edition by Schlager, Neil (Editor). 1998. Reprinted with permission of Gale, a division of Thomson Learning: http://www.thomsonrights.com. Fax (800) 730-2215.

2. Countries that allow out lesbians and gays to serve are: Australia, Austria, the Bahamas, Belgium, Britain, Canada, the Czech Republic, Estonia, Finland, France, Germany, Israel, Italy, Lithuania, the Netherlands, New Zealand, Norway, Slovenia, South Africa, Spain, and Sweden (Servicemembers Legal Defense Network 2005, 1).

Chapter 5

1. On February 10, 2004, San Francisco mayor Gavin Newsom mandated that the San Francisco County clerk must "provide marriage licenses on a nondiscriminatory basis, without regard to gender or sexual orientation" (Snyder 2006, 1). In doing so, he called "the ability of lesbian and gay couples to marry a 'fundamental right.'" He argued that his commitment to upholding the "California state constitution required him to overrule a state

law prohibiting same-sex marriage because it violates the constitutional principle of legal equality." But on August 12, 2004, the California Supreme Court ruled that the mayor's decision was unconstitutional because it "had violated the principle of 'separation of powers'" (ibid., 1–2).

Chapter 6

1. The federal government does not prosecute any hate crimes that are "based on sexual orientation," though it "does collect data on them and provides specific training to local law enforcement." As of July 2007, nineteen states failed to include sexual orientation as part of their hate-crimes legislation. Some members of Congress are understandably concerned about this patchwork of laws throughout the United States. On March 20, 2007, "Reps. John Conyers (D-Mich.) and Mark Kirk (R-Ill.) introduced the Local Law Enforcement Hate Crimes Prevention Act (H.R. 1592)," and Senators Gordon Smith (R-OR) and Ted Kennedy (D-MA) introduced a companion bill on April 12, 2007. If passed, the act would add "'actual or perceived . . . sexual orientation, gender, gender identity or disability,' to the list of conditions that trigger federal support to investigate and prosecute" (Ireland 2007, 19).

2. As of July 2007, ten states and the District of Columbia permitted lesbian and gay "partners to adopt children as couples instead of restricting parental rights to one partner" (Padgett 2007, 51). These states are California, Colorado, Connecticut, Illinois, Indiana, Massachusetts, New Jersey, New York, Pennsylvania, and Vermont.

3. The Gay, Lesbian, and Straight Education Network (GLSEN) has collected survey data regarding the lesbian and gay experience in schools. These data provide empirical evidence to support the claim that lesbian and gay students (and those suspected of being so) face hostile environments in many of the nation's schools. The following data were gathered by GLSEN:

- 97 percent of students in public high schools in Massachusetts reported regularly hearing homophobic remarks from their peers in a 1993 report of the Massachusetts Governor's Commission on Gay and Lesbian Youth;
- 53 percent of the students reported hearing antigay remarks made by school staff;
- 46 percent of gay, lesbian, and bisexual students reported in a 1997 Massachusetts Youth Risk Behavior Study they attempted suicide in the past year compared to 9 percent of their peers;
- 22 percent were in a fight that resulted in receiving medical attention compared to 3 percent of their peers;
- gay students are three times as likely to have been threatened with a weapon at school than their peers during the previous twelve months, according to Youth Risk Behavior surveys done in Massachusetts and Vermont;
- 28 percent of gay youths drop out of high school altogether, according to a U.S. Department of Health and Human Services study. (Bronski 1999, 16)

References

Adam, Barry D. 1995. *The Rise of a Gay and Lesbian Movement*. Rev. ed. New York: Twayne Publishers.

Allyn, David. 2000. *Make Love, Not War: The Sexual Revolution, an Unfettered History*. New York: Little, Brown.

Alvarez, Lizette. 2006. "Gay Groups Renew Drive Against 'Don't Ask, Don't Tell.'" September 14. http://www.nytimes.com/2006/109/14/us/14.gay.html.

Alwood, Edward. 1996. *Straight News: Gays, Lesbians, and the News Media*. New York: Columbia University Press.

Andriote, John-Manuel. 1999. *Victory Deferred: How AIDS Changed Gay Life in* America. Chicago: University of Chicago Press.

"The Armchair Activist." 2006. *Advocate*, October 10, 34.

Armstrong, Elizabeth A. 2002. *Forging Gay Identities: Organizing Sexuality in San Francisco, 1950–1994*. Chicago: University of Chicago Press.

"Army Dismisses Gay Arabic Linguist." 2006. July 27. http://www.nytimes.com/aponline/us/AP-Gays-Military.html.

Aronowitz, Stanley. 1996. *The Death and Rebirth of American Radicalism*. New York: Routledge.

Baer, Denise L., and David A. Bositis. 1993. *Politics and Linkage in a Democratic Society*. Upper Saddle River, N.J.: Pearson Educaction, Inc.

Bailey, Robert W. 1999. *Gay Politics, Urban Politics: Identity and Economics in the Urban Setting*. New York: Columbia University Press.

Baldwin, Peter. 2005. *Disease and Democracy: The Industrialized World Faces AIDS*. Berkeley and Los Angeles: University of California Press.

Bawer, Bruce. 1993. *Place at the Table: The Gay Individual in American Society*. New York: Poseidon Press.

Behrman, Greg. 2004. *The Invisible People: How the U.S. Has Slept Through the Global Epidemic, the Greatest Humanitarian Catastrophe of Our Time*. New York: Free Press.

Belkin, Aaron, and Geoffrey Bateman, eds. 2003. *Don't Ask, Don't Tell: Debating the Gay Ban in the Military*. Boulder: Lynne Rienner Publishers.

Benecke, Michelle M., and Kristin S. Dodge. 1996. "Military Women: Casualties of the Armed Forces' War on Lesbians and Gay Men." In *Gay Rights, Military Wrongs: Political Perspectives on Lesbians and Gays in the Military*, edited by Craig A. Rimmerman. New York: Garland Publishing.

Bereznai, Steven. 2006. *Gay and Single . . . Forever?* New York: Marlowe.

Berubé, Allan. 1990. *Coming Out Under Fire*. New York: Free Press.

Bianco, David Ari. 1996. "Echoes of Prejudice: The Debates Over Race and Sexuality in the Armed Forces." In *Gay Rights, Military Wrongs: Political Perspectives on Lesbians and Gays in the Military*, edited by Craig A. Rimmerman. New York: Garland Publishing.

Blasius, Mark, and Shane Phelan, eds. 1997. *We Are Everywhere: A Historical Sourcebook of Gay and Lesbian Politics*. New York: Routledge.

Broder, John M. 2004. "Groups Debate Slower Strategy and Gay Rights." *New York Times*, December 9, A1.

Bronski, Michael. 1998. *The Pleasure Principle: Sex, Backlash, and the Struggle for Gay Freedom*. New York: St. Martin's Press.

_____. 1999. "Littleton, Movies, and Gay KIDS." *Z Magazine*, July–August, 12–16.

_____. 2006. "Is the Gay Rights Movement Doomed to Fail?" *Z Magazine*, July–August, 18–20.

Bull, Chris. 1993a. "Broken Promise." *Advocate*, August 27, 24.

_____. 1993b. "No Frankness." *Advocate*, June 29, 24–27.

_____. 1999. "Still Angry After All These Years." *Advocate*, June 19, 18–19.

_____. 2001. "Uncharted Waters." *Advocate*, January 30, 24–26.

_____. 2003. "Justice Served." *Advocate*, August 19, 36.

Burkett, Elinor. 1995. *The Gravest Show on Earth: America in the Age of AIDS*. Boston: Houghton Mifflin.

Button, James, Barbara Rienzo, and Kenneth D. Wald. 1997. *Private Lives, Public Conflicts: Battles Over Gay Rights in American Communities*. Washington, D.C.: Congressional Quarterly Press.

Cahill, Sean. 2003. "Public Policy Issues Affecting Gay, Lesbian, Bisexual, and Transgender People: Envisioning a GLBT-Inclusive Introductory American Political Science Textbook." Prepared for Delivery at the 2003 Annual Meeting of the American Political Science Association, August 28–31.

_____. 2004. *Same-Sex Marriage in the United States: Focus on the Facts*. New York: Lexington.

_____. 2007. "The Anti–Gay Marriage Movement." In *The Politics of Same-Sex Marriage*, edited by Craig A. Rimmerman and Clyde Wilcox. Chicago: University of Chicago Press.

Campbell, David C., and Carin Robinson. 2007. "Religious Conservatives for and Against Gay Marriage: The Culture War Wages On." In *The Politics of Same-Sex Marriage*, edited by Craig A. Rimmerman and Clyde Wilcox. Chicago: University of Chicago Press.

Cannon, Lou. 1991. *President Reagan: The Role of a Lifetime*. New York: Simon and Schuster.

Carter, David. 2004. *Stonewall: The Riots That Sparked the Revolution*. New York: St. Martin's Press.

Chambers, David L. 2000. "Couples: Marriage, Civil Union, and Domestic Partnership." In *Creating Change: Sexuality, Public Policy, and Civil Rights*, edited by John D'Emilio, William B. Turner, and Urvashi Vaid. New York: St. Martin's Press.

Chauncey, George. 1994. *Gay New York*. New York: Basic Books.

_____. 2004. *Why Marriage? The History Shaping Today's Debate Over Gay Equality*. New York: Basic Books.

Clendinen, Dudley, and Adam Nagourney. 1999. *Out for Good: The Struggle to Build a Gay Rights Movement in America*. New York: Simon and Schuster.

Cohen, Cathy J. 1999. *The Boundaries of Blackness: AIDS and the Breakdown of Black Politics*. Chicago: University of Chicago Press.

Cohen, Peter F. 1998. *Love and Anger: Essays on AIDS, Activism, and Politics*. New York: Harrington Park Press.

Crary, David. 2006. "Gay Marriage Ban Rejected in Arizona." http://news.yahoo.com/s/ap/20061108/ap_on_el_st_/o/eln_ballot_measures.

Crea, Joe. 2003. "Frist Supports Gay Marriage Ban." *Washington Blade*, July 4. http://www.washblade.com.

———. 2004. "'Austin 12' Divided on Bush: One Feels Bush-Whacked." *Washington Blade*, September 17. http://www.washblade.com.

Cruikshank, Margaret. 1992. *The Gay and Lesbian Movement*. New York: Routledge.

D'Amico, Francine. 1996. "Race-ing and Gendering the Military Closet." In *Gay Rights, Military Wrongs: Political Perspectives on Lesbians and Gays in the Military*, edited by Craig A. Rimmerman. New York: Garland Publishing.

———. 2000. "Sex/uality and Military Service." In *The Politics of Gay Rights*, edited by Craig A. Rimmerman, Kenneth D. Wald, and Clyde Wilcox. Chicago: University of Chicago Press.

"Declaration of Intolerance." 2003. *Advocate*, February 27, 15.

D'Emilio, John. 1983. *Sexual Politics, Sexual Communities: The Making of a Homosexual Minority in the United States, 1940–1970*. Chicago: University of Chicago Press.

———. 1992. *Making Trouble: Essays on Gay History, Policies, and the University*. New York: Routledge.

———. 2000. "Cycles of Change, Questions of Strategy: The Gay and Lesbian Movement After Fifty Years." In *The Politics of Gay Rights*, edited by Craig A. Rimmerman and Clyde Wilcox. Chicago: University of Chicago Press.

———. 2002. *The World Turned: Essays on Gay History, Politics, and Culture*. Durham: Duke University Press.

———. 2006. "The Marriage Fight Is Setting Us Back." *Gay and Lesbian Review,* November-December, 10–11.

———. 2007. "Will the Courts Set Us Free? Reflections on the Campaign for Same-Sex Marriage." In *The Politics of Same-Sex Marriage*, edited by Craig A. Rimmerman and Clyde Wilcox. Chicago: University of Chicago Press.

D'Emilio, John D., William B. Turner, and Urvashi Vaid, eds. 2000. *Creating Change: Sexuality, Public Policy, and Civil Rights*. New York: St. Martin's Press.

Dolkart, Jane. 1998. "Law." In *St. James Press Gay and Lesbian Almanac*, edited by Neil Schlager. Detroit: St. James Press.

Donnelly, John. 2007. "With AIDS Funding Proposal, Bush Looks to His Legacy." *Boston Globe*, May 31, A15.

Duggan, Lisa. 2003. *The Twilight of Equality? Neoliberalism, Cultural Politics, and the Attack on Democracy*. Boston: Beacon Press.

Edsall, Nicholas. 2003. *Toward Stonewall: Homosexuals and Society in the Modern Western World*. Charlottesville: University Press of Virginia.

Eisenbach, David. 2006. *Gay Power: An American Revolution*. New York: Carroll and Graf.

Engel, Jonathan. 2006. *The Epidemic: A Global History of AIDS*. New York: HarperCollins.

Ephron, Dan. 2007. "General Comment." *Newsweek*, March 26, 34.

Epstein, Steven. 1996. *Impure Science: AIDS, Activism, and the Politics of Knowledge*. Berkeley and Los Angeles: University of California Press.

Escoffier, Jeffrey. 1980. *American Home: Community and Perversity*. Berkeley and Los Angeles: University of California Press.

Eskridge, William. 1999. *Gaylaw: Challenging the Apartheid of the Closet*. Cambridge: Harvard University Press.

Ettlebrick, Paula. 1997. "Since When Is Marriage a Path to Liberation?" In *We Are Everywhere: A Historical Sourcebook of Gay and Lesbian Politics*, edited by Mark Blasius and Shane Phelan. New York: Routledge.

Faderman, Lillian, and Stuart Timmons. 2006. *Gay LA: A History of Sexual Outlaws, Power Politics, and Lipstick Lesbians*. New York: Basic Books.

Foreman, Christopher. 1994. *Plagues, Products, and Politics: Emergent Public Health Hazards and National Policymaking*. Washington, D.C.: Brookings Institution.

Foust, Michael. 2003. "Ruling Highlights Need for Marriage Amendment, Leaders Say." November 18. http://www.sbcbaptistpress.org/bpnews.asap?Id=7117.

Gallagher, John. 1993. "Terrible Timing." *Advocate*, October 5, 28.

———. 1996. "Speak Now." *Advocate*, November 11, 21.

GLSEN Fundraising and Information Newsletter. 2000. New York: Gay, Lesbian, and Straight Education Network.

Goldstone, Jack A. 2003. Introduction to *States, Parties, and Social Movements*, edited by Jack A. Goldstone. Cambridge: Cambridge University Press.

Gregory, Nancy. 2001. "The Gay and Lesbian Movement in the United States." In *Doing Democracy: The MAP Model for Organizing Social Movements*, edited by Bill Moyer, Joann McAllister, Mary Lou Finley, and Steven Soifer. British Columbia: New Society Publishers.

Guerriero, Patrick. 2004. "Gay Republicans Not for Bush." *Washington Blade*, October 8. http://www.washblade.com.

Haggerty, Timothy. 2003. "History Repeating Itself: A Historical Overview of Gay Men and Lesbians in the Military Before 'Don't Ask, Don't Tell.'" In *Don't Ask, Don't Tell: Debating the Gay Ban in the Military*, edited by Aaron Belkin and Geoffrey Bateman. Boulder: Lynne Rienner Publishers.

Hamilton, Nigel. 2007. *Bill Clinton: Masking the Presidency*. New York: Public Affairs.

Herek, Gregory M. 1996. "Social Science, Sexual Orientation, and Military Personnel Policy." In *Out in Force: Sexual Orientation and the Military*, edited by Gregory M. Herek, Jared B. Jobe, and Ralph M. Carney. Chicago: University of Chicago Press.

Hertzberg, Hendrick. 2003. "Comment: Dog Bites Man." *New Yorker*, May 5, 33.

Hertzog, Mark. 1996. *The Lavender Vote: Lesbians, Gay Men, and Bisexuals in American Electoral Politics*. New York: New York University Press.

Highleyman, Liz. 2002. "Radical Queers or Queer Radicals? Queer Activism and the Global Justice Movement." In *From ACT UP to the WTO: Urban Protest and Community*

Building in the Era of Globalization, edited by Benjamin Shepard and Ronald Hayduk. New York: Verso.

Hirsch, H. N. 2005. Introduction to *The Future of Gay Rights in America*, edited by H. N. Hirsch. New York: Routledge.

Hulse, Carl. 2004. "Backers Revise Amendment on Marriage." http://www.nytimes.com/2004/03/23/politics/23AMEN.html.

Hunt, Ronald J. 1999. *Historical Dictionary of the Gay Liberation Movement: Gay Men and the Quest for Social Justice*. Lanham, Md.: Scarecrow Press.

Hunter, Susan. 2006. *AIDS in America*. New York: Palgrave Macmillan.

Ireland, John. 2007. "Defining Hate in the United States." *In These Times*, May, 18–19.

Jay, Karla. 1999. *Tales of the Lavender Menace*. New York: Basic Books.

Johnson, David K. 2004. *The Lavender Scare: The Cold War Persecution of Gays and Lesbians in the Federal Government*. Chicago: University of Chicago Press.

Kaiser, Charles. 1997. *The Gay Metropolis, 1940–1996*. New York: Houghton Mifflin.

Kaplan, Esther. 2004. *With God on Their Side: How Christian Fundamentalists Trampled Science, Policy, and Democracy in George W. Bush's White House*. New York: New Press.

Keen, Lisa. 1999. "Vermont's 'Step Forward.'" *Washington Blade*, December 24, 1. http://www.washblade.com.

———. 2004. "Did 'Moral Values' Tip the Scale?" *Bay Windows*, November 11.

King, Mike. 1996. "Suicide Watch." *Advocate*, November 12, 41–44.

Koop, C. Everett. 1991. *Koop: The Memoirs of America's Family Doctor*. New York: Random House.

Kristof, Nicholas D. 2006. "The Deep Roots of AIDS." http://select.nytimes.com/2006/0919/opinion/19kistof.html.

Lee, Ryan. 2006a. "Experts Debate the 'New' Face of AIDS: Gay Men, African Americans Hardest Hit by Disease." *Washington Blade*, December 1. 1, 22. http://www.washblade.com.

———. 2006b. "25 Years of AIDS." *Washington Blade*, June 2. http://www.washblade.com.

"The Legislative Word on Gays." 1993. *Congressional Quarterly Weekly Report*, July 31, 2076.

Lehmkuhl, Reichen. 2006. *Here's What We'll Say: Growing Up, Coming Out, and the U.S. Air Force Academy*. New York: Carroll and Graf.

Lehring, Gary. 1996. "Constructing the 'Other' Soldier: Gay Identity's Military Threat." In *Gay Rights, Military Wrongs: Political Perspectives on Lesbians and Gays in the Military*, edited by Craig A. Rimmerman. New York: Garland Publishing.

Levenson, Jacob. 2003. *The Secret Epidemic: The Story of AIDS and Black America*. New York: Pantheon.

Lewis, Gregory B., and Marc A. Rogers. 1999. "Does the Public Support Equal Rights for Gays and Lesbians?" In *Gays and Lesbians in the Democratic Process*, edited by Ellen D. B. Riggle and Barry L. Tadlock. New York: Columbia University Press.

Lewis, John, and Michael D'Orso. 1998. *Walking with the Wind: A Memoir of the Civil Rights Movement*. New York: Simon and Schuster.

Loffreda, Beth. 2000. *Losing Matt Shepard: Life and Politics in the Aftermath of Anti-Gay Murder*. New York: Columbia University Press.

Lofton, Katie, and Donald P. Haider-Markel. 2007. "The Politics of Same-Sex Marriage Versus the Politics of Gay Civil Rights." In *The Politics of Same-Sex Marriage,* edited by Craig A. Rimmerman and Clyde Wilcox. Chicago: University of Chicago Press.

Lorde, Audre. 1984. *Sister Outsider: Essays and Speeches.* Freedom, Calif.: Crossing Press.

Loughery, John. 1998. *The Other Side of Silence: Men's Lives and Gay Identities: A Twentieth Century History.* New York: Henry Holt.

McFeeley, Tim. 2002. "Getting It Straight: A Review of the 'Gays in the Military' Debate." In *Creating Change: Sexuality, Public Policy, and Civil Rights*, edited by John D'Emilio, William B. Turner, and Urvashi Vaid. New York: St. Martin's Press.

McGowan, Jeffrey. 2005. *Major Conflict: One Gay Man's Life in the Don't-Ask-Don't-Tell Military.* New York: Broadway Books.

Micklethwait, John, and Adrian Wooldridge. 2004. *The Right Nation: Conservative Power in America.* New York: Penguin Press.

Miller, Neil. 1995. *Out of the Past: Gay and Lesbian History from 1869 to the Present.* New York: Vintage Books.

Mohr, Richard. 1993. *A More Perfect Union: Why Straight America Must Stand Up for Gay Rights.* Boston: Beacon Press.

Moyer, Bill, Joann McAllister, Mary Lou Finley, and Steven Soifer. 2001. *Doing Democracy: The MAP Model for Organizing Social Movements.* British Columbia: New Society Publishers.

O'Connor, Karen, and Alixandra B. Yanus. 2007. "'Til Death—or the Supreme Court—Do Us Part: Litigating Gay Marriage." In *The Politics of Same-Sex Marriage*, edited by Craig A. Rimmerman and Clyde Wilcox. Chicago: University of Chicago Press.

Odets, Walt. 1995. *In the Shadow of the Epidemic: Being HIV-Negative in the Age of AIDS.* Durham: Duke University Press.

Office of the Press Secretary. 2003. "Marriage Protection Week, 2003." http://www.whitehouse.gov/news/releases/2003/10/120031003-12.html.

Osborne, Duncan. 1994. "Military." *Advocate*, January 25, 53.

Padgett, Tim. 2007. "Gay Friendly Values." *Time*, July 16, 51–52.

Perine, Keith. 2004. "House Conservatives Seek Voters' Attention with Action on Gay Marriage Amendment." *CQ Weekly*, October 2.

Perine, Keith, and Jennifer A. Dlouhy. 2004. "Parties Worry About Political Risk in Stands on Gay Marriage." *CQ Weekly*, January 10.

Phelan, Shane. 2001. *Sexual Strangers: Gays, Lesbians, and Dilemmas of Citizenship.* Philadelphia: Temple University Press.

Pinello, Daniel R. 2006. *America's Struggle for Same-Sex Marriage.* New York: Cambridge University Press.

Radosh, Ronald. 1996. *Divided They Fell: The Demise of the Democratic Party, 1964–1996.* New York: Free Press.

Rauch, Jonathan. 2004. *Gay Marriage: Why It Is Good for Gays, Good for Straights, and Good for America.* New York: Times Books.

Rayside, David. 2007. "The United States in Comparative Context." In *The Politics of Same-Sex Marriage*, edited by Craig A. Rimmerman and Clyde Wilcox. Chicago: University of Chicago Press.

Reed, T. V. 2005. *The Art of Protest: Culture and Activism from the Civil Rights Movement to the Streets of Seattle*. Minneapolis: University of Minnesota Press.

Riggle, Ellen D. B., and Barry L. Tadlock, eds. *Gays and Lesbians in the Democratic Process*. New York: Columbia University Press.

Rimmerman, Craig A., ed. 1996a. *Gay Rights, Military Wrongs: Political Perspectives on Lesbians and Gays in the Military*. New York: Garland Publishers.

———. 1996b. Introduction to *Gay Rights, Military Wrongs: Political Perspectives on Lesbians and Gays in the Military*, edited by Craig A. Rimmerman. New York: Garland Publishing.

———. 1996c. "Promise Unfulfilled: Clinton's Failure to Overturn the Military Ban on Lesbians and Gays." In *Gay Rights, Military Wrongs: Political Perspectives on Lesbians and Gays in the Military*, edited by Craig A. Rimmerman. New York: Garland Publishing.

———. 1998a. "Military." In *St. James Press Gay and Lesbian Almanac*, edited by Neil Schlager. Detroit: St. James Press.

———. 1998b. "U.S. Presidency." In *Encyclopedia of AIDS*, edited by Raymond A. Smith. Chicago: Fitzroy Dearborn.

———. 2000. "A 'Friend' in the White House? Reflections on the Clinton Presidency." In *Creating Change: Sexuality, Public Policy, and Civil Rights*, edited by John D'Emilio, William B. Turner, and Urvashi Vaid. New York: St. Martin's Press.

———. 2002. *From Identity to Politics: The Lesbian and Gay Movements in the United States*. Philadelphia: Temple University Press.

———. 2007. "The Presidency, Congress, and Same-Sex Marriage." In *The Politics of Same-Sex Marriage*, edited by Craig A. Rimmerman and Clyde Wilcox. Chicago: University of Chicago Press.

Rimmerman, Craig A., Kenneth D. Wald, and Clyde Wilcox, eds. 2000. *The Politics of Gay Rights*. Chicago: University of Chicago Press.

Rimmerman, Craig A., and Clyde Wilcox, eds. 2007. *The Politics of Same-Sex Marriage*. Chicago: University of Chicago Press.

Robinson, Paul. 2005. *Queer Wars: The New Gay Right and Its Critics*. Chicago: University of Chicago Press.

Rofes, Eric. 1990. "Gay Lib vs. AIDS: Averting Civil War." *Outlook*, no. 8 (Spring).

Rom, Mark Carl. 2000. "Gays and AIDS: Democratizing Disease?" In *The Politics of Gay Rights*, edited by Craig A. Rimmerman. Chicago: University of Chicago Press.

Rosenberg, Debra. 2006. "A Renewed War over 'Don't Ask, Don't Tell.'" *Newsweek*, November 27, 8.

Schlager, Neil, ed. 1998. *St. James Press Gay and Lesbian Almanac*. Detroit: St. James Press.

Schmitt, Eric. 1994. "Gay Troops Say the Revised Policy Is Often Misused." *New York Times*, May 9, A1.

Scott, James. 1990. *Domination and the Arts of Resistance: Hidden Transcripts*. New Haven: Yale University Press.

Seidman, Steven. 2002. *Beyond the Closet: The Transformation of Gay and Lesbian Life*. New York: Routledge.

Servicemembers Legal Defense Network. 2005. *Fact Sheet*, August 30, 1. http://www.sldn.org.

Shalikashvili, John M. 2007. "Second Thoughts on Gays in the Military."
   http://www.nytimes.com/2007/01/02/opinion/02/shalikashvili.html.

Shepard, Benjamin, and Ronald Hayduk, eds. 2002. *From ACT UP to the WTO: Urban Protest and Community Building in the Era of Globalization*. London: Verso.

Sherrill, Kenneth. 1996. "The Political Power of Lesbians, Gays, and Bisexuals." *PS: Political Science and Politics* 29, no. 3 (September): 469–473.

Shilts, Randy. 1993. *Conduct Unbecoming: Gays and Lesbians in the U.S. Military*. New York: St. Martin's Press.

Siplon, Patricia. 2002. *AIDS and the Policy Struggle in the United States*. Washington, D.C.: Georgetown University Press.

Snyder, R. Claire. 2006. *Gay Marriage and Democracy: Equality for All*. Boulder: Rowman and Littlefield.

Sokolove, Michael. 2004. "Can This Marriage Be Saved?" *New York Times Magazine*. http://www.nytimes.com/2004/04/IImagazine.

Stoppard, Thomas B. 1989. "Why Gay People Should Seek the Right to Marry." In *We Are Everywhere: A Historical Sourcebook of Gay and Lesbian Politics*, edited by Mark Blasius and Shane Phelan. New York: Routledge.

Strasser, Mark. 1997. *Legally Wed: Same-Sex Marriage and the Constitution*. Ithaca: Cornell University Press.

Sullivan, Andrew. 2004. *Virtually Normal: An Argument About Homosexuality*. New York: Alfred A. Knopf.

Tarrow, Sidney. 1994. *Power in Movement: Social Movements, Collective Action, and Politics*. Cambridge: Cambridge University Press.

Teal, Donn. 1995. *The Gay Mandates*. New York: St. Martin's Press.

Vaid, Urvashi. 1995. *Virtual Equality: The Mainstreaming of Gay and Lesbian Liberation*. New York: Anchor Books.

_____. 1997. "Coalition as Goal, Not Process." *Gay Community News* 22, no. 4 (Spring): 6–9.

Wald, Kenneth D. 2000. "The Context of Gay Politics." In *The Politics of Gay Rights*, edited by Craig A. Rimmerman, Kenneth D. Wald, and Clyde Wilcox. Chicago: University of Chicago Press.

Wald, Kenneth D., and Graham B. Glover. 2007. "Theological Perspectives on Gay Unions: The Uneasy Marriage of Religion and Politics." In *The Politics of Same-Sex Marriage*, edited by Craig A. Rimmerman and Clyde Wilcox. Chicago: University of Chicago Press.

Warner, Michael. 1999. *The Trouble with Normal: Sex, Politics, and the Ethics of Queer Life*. New York: Free Press.

Whitman, Christine Todd. 2005. *It's My Party Too: The Battle for the Heart of the GOP and the Future of America*. New York: Penguin Press.

Wieseltier, Leon. 1993. "Covenant and Burling." *New Republic*, February 1, 77.

Wilcox, Clyde. 2007. Preface to *The Politics of Same-Sex Marriage*, edited by Craig A. Rimmerman and Clyde Wilcox. Chicago: University of Chicago Press.

Wilcox, Clyde, Paul R. Brewer, Shauna Shames, and Celinda Lake. 2007. "If I Bend This Far I Will Break? Public Opinion About Same-Sex Marriage." In *The Politics of Same-*

Sex Marriage, edited by Craig A. Rimmerman and Clyde Wilcox. Chicago: University of Chicago Press.

Wolfson, Evan. 2004. *Why Marriage Matters: American Equality and Gay People's Right to Marry*. New York: Simon and Schuster.

"The World at a Glance." 2007. *Week*, June 29, 7.

Index

Abrams, Albert: on World War I/
    homosexuality, 69
Abstinence only programs, 49, 56, 57
Accommodationist strategy, 17, 135
ACLU, September 11th and, 132
Acquired immunodeficiency syndrome. *See*
    AIDS
ACT UP. *See* AIDS Coalition to Unleash Power
Activism, 13, 19, 21, 29, 49, 53, 59
    assimilationist strategy and, 45
    attention for, 8
    development of, 33
    "let us in" approach to, 5
    media, 45
    radical, 16, 34, 52
ADA. *See* Americans with Disabilities Act
Adams, Barry, 13
Adams v. Howerton (1980), 101
Adoption, same-sex, 174n2
Adoption agencies, access to, 102
African Americans
    AIDS and, 62
    HIV and, 34, 58
    homosexuals and, 91
    military and, 89–90
    segregation and, 90, 91
AIDS
    African Americans and, 62
    awareness for, 85, 150, 151, 153, 154
    challenges of, 34
    Christian Right and, 29, 34, 35, 63
    as civil-rights problem, 37
    deaths from, 33, 36, 149, 150, 152, 154
    debate over, 10

degaying of, 9, 44–45, 168
as gay disease, 35, 62
historical context of, 33, 35–63
homelessness and, 61
as judgment of God, 37
naming, 4, 149
number of cases of, 152
onset of, 28, 33, 62
regaying of, 9, 170
research on, 38, 39, 54, 59
responding to, 27, 31, 34, 36, 37, 38, 39,
    40, 139–141
spread of, 35, 36
twenty-fifth anniversary of, 33, 62, 154
U.S. funding for, 57
vulnerability to, 35–36, 62
women and, 153
AIDS Action Council, 47, 48, 60, 138, 159
AIDS Awareness Day, 54
AIDS Coalition to Unleash Power (ACT
    UP), 159, 167
    AIDS crisis and, 8, 33, 49
    Catholic Church and, 50
    Clinton and, 84
    demonstrations by, 51–52, 60, 150
    drug trials and, 60
    Health Gap and, 61
    internal divisions in, 60
    media and, 50, 53
    organization of, 23, 48, 50
    political strategy of, 50
    Ryan White CARE Act and, 61
    strategy/tactics of, 44, 52, 61
    TAG and, 59

Who's Your Mama, Are You Catholic,
And Can You Make A Roux?

A Family Album
Cookbook

Marcelle Bienvenu

Times Of Acadiana Press, Inc.
Lafayette, Louisiana
1991

Designed by Margaret Madere Design
Edited by Susan Cole Doré
Manufactured in the United States of America
ISBN 0-9631637-0-1

Times of Acadiana Press, Inc.
201 Jefferson Street
P.O. Drawer 3528
Lafayette, Louisiana 70502

Table of Contents

I was born and raised in St. Martinville, Louisiana, in the heart of Acadiana. When I was growing up, I innocently believed that I lived in a romantic Eden. The town was the setting for Longfellow's poem "Evangeline" which tells of the deportation of French peasants from their beloved Acadie (Nova Scotia) and of their search for a new home. It is also the story of the star-crossed lovers Evangeline and Gabriel. As a child I played at the feet of the statue of Evangeline at the rear of the St. Martin de Tours Catholic Church in the center of town.

St. Martinville, once known as *Poste des Attakapas* because it was a French and Indian trading post, later became known as *Le Petit Paris,* for it was there that many French aristocrats came to settle after the French Revolution. There were visitors from New Orleans who came every year for fashionable balls, operas, and long hours of formal dining and dancing. The little town developed a unique culture, with food an integral part.

So it was in this atmosphere that I grew up. My father's father, Lazaire Bienvenu, was a pioneer in the newspaper business, establishing St. Martin Parish's oldest newspaper with his brother Albert. It was then called the *Weekly Messenger*. Now in its third generation and called the *Teche News*, it continues as the official journal of the parish. Pop Lazaire and his wife Leoncia Tertrou (whose family had been in the hotel business) had twelve children. Their home was a mecca for much cooking and eating. The old stove never got cold.

My mother's father, Antoine Broussard, was an overseer for several large sugarcane plantations. Their family of six children and the workers on the plantations required hearty food from dawn until dusk.

I can't remember a day that tables were not filled with tureens of gumbo or stew, platters of baked chicken or variously prepared seafood, bowls of garden vegetables, and baskets of French bread and biscuits. There were pitchers of milk heavy with cream, jars of fig preserves, and crocks of pickled meats.

Many noon meals were taken at Pop Lazaire's house. Back then time allowed businessmen to go home for lunch. Weekends found us in the country participating in boucheries or carrying pails of food to the workers in the fields.

I walked through my childhood believing everyone enjoyed the pleasure of preparing and consuming jambalaya, crawfish bisque, and stewed okra. Children and adults all participated in the tasks of cooking. Aunt Grace, with her kitchen helpers Yola and *La Vielle* ("the Old One"), showed me how to bake biscuits and cornbread that were so light they could have floated on air. Papa, who with his eleven siblings assisted in Leoncia's kitchen, patiently showed me how to make a roux. Mama, who grew up on the plantations, was the source for information on canning and preserving fresh produce. We were not aware that we were assimilating any special kind of cuisine. We only knew that our food was good. Food and its preparation were at the very center of our lives.

Not only was I surrounded by good cooks and good food, but I was also enchanted by the family newspaper. When I was six years old, I hand-folded the newspaper on press day. Later I learned to proofread hot type coming off the linotype. I was my father's shadow around the plant, watching him and Pop Lazaire as they sat on old rockers at their desks discussing what news was to be included in the paper. After I became an adult, I had careers in both the newspaper business and the food business.

I operated my own restaurant, worked for the Brennan family of New Orleans, and wrote for the New Orleans *Times-Picayune*.

I offer this collection of recipes—some traditional and some new—because I want to share with others the dear memories and delicious food that are the natural result of a lifetime of good times spent with family and friends.

To my father who showed me how to see the brighter side of life,
and to my mother who taught me the pleasure of cooking.

Acknowledgments

I must, first of all, thank my many aunts and uncles, the countless cousins, and of course my brothers Henri Clay and Bruce, my sister Edna, and their families for giving me all the memories that are at the heart of this collection of recipes and stories.

I will be forever indebted to my many friends who constantly urged me to do this book, and a special thanks to Ella Brennan, who gave me the courage to put it all together. Without the patience, support, and incredible talent of Susan Doré, my editor, I would have thrown out the skillet a long time ago.

And thanks to Steve May, Richard Baudouin, and Odie Terry, three very special gentlemen who have held my hand, dried my tears, and listened endlessly to my ideas.

Last but not least, I thank my husband Rock for giving me the time and space (figuratively and literally) to complete THE BOOK and for being so patient and loving.

Spring

S*pring arrives quickly in south Louisiana. One day the landscape along the highways and country roads is pale and lonely. Limp strands of Spanish moss hang on barren tree limbs. Then suddenly, in early March, the purple, pink, and lavender of Japanese magnolias and redbud trees burst into the leafless countryside. With the last cold front behind them, men and women don straw hats and garde-soleils (sunbonnets) and begin to work the soil for spring gardens. Soon it will be time to put in Creole tomato plants, eggplant, bell pepper, corn, and squash. The glory of nature and the renewal of life are celebrated with a unique combination of reverence and gaiety during springtime in Louisiana.*

Easter Bonnets, Painted Eggs, And A Feast

I love Easter time!

The countryside is alive with color—the lavish hues of azaleas mingle with bright white bridal wreath—and yards and pastures alike are lush dark-green carpets.

Everyone is frantically getting Easter outfits together. Girls deck straw bonnets with ribbons and flowers, while boys dig out their white linens. Our family goes through its own special rites of spring.

For years now, the weekends leading up to Easter find us all at the camp, cleaning and sprucing, planting and planning for the long Easter weekend. The Bienvenu clan gathers at the camp on Good Friday. Early in the day we pile into a pickup truck or van and go for a ride on the levee between Catahoula and Henderson. It seems that everyone has taken a holiday. Hundreds of families gather along the waterways to picnic, fish, or put out crawfish nets. Children sit in patches of clover and amuse themselves by making flower necklaces. We pick up a few sacks of live crawfish and go to three o'clock church services. Then we head back to the camp for a crawfish boil. As we are just about finishing up the crawfish, the ladies of Catahoula come by to drop off SWEET DOUGH PIES.

There is a wonderful custom in Catahoula. For many days prior to Good Friday, the ladies of the town make sweet dough pies or *tarte a la bouillie*, and then on Good Friday, all the families gather to eat them. Miss Tootie Guirard, a local historian and storyteller, says they know they're just supposed to have one meal on Good Friday, so they make it a good long one. They eat practically all day long!

TARTE A LA BOUILLIE (SWEET DOUGH PIES)

Makes 4 9-inch pies

3/4 cup shortening
1 cup sugar
1/2 cup milk
2 eggs
1 teaspoon vanilla
4 cups all-purpose flour
4 teaspoons baking powder

Cream shortening and sugar. In a small bowl, mix together the milk, eggs, and vanilla. Mix well. Add to the shortening and sugar; blend all together. Combine flour and baking powder. In a large mixing bowl, alternate blending the liquid mixture with the dry ingredients. Continue to alternate adding the mixtures. The dough should come away from the sides of the bowl. Divide dough into 4 equal parts and roll out on a floured board. Place dough in 4 9-inch pans, crimp edges, and add filling. Bake at 350 degrees for 30 minutes or until golden brown.

The Catahoula ladies do not usually put tops on the large pies, but any extra dough can be used to make a lattice top for each pie. If you're making pies on a hot and humid day, it is wise to refrigerate the dough for an hour or two so that it will be easier to work with.

You can also use the dough to make small turnovers. Simply roll the dough into smaller circles, add filling, fold over, and bake. The dough can also be used to make sugar cookies. Roll out the dough a bit thicker and cut with a cookie cutter. Place on cookie sheets and bake at 350 degrees until golden brown.

BLACKBERRY FILLING

Wash berries and drain well. Pick them over and remove any stems. For every quart of berries, use 1-1/2 or 2 cups sugar (depends on how sweet you like it) and 1/4 cup water. Mix sugar and water in a large pot and bring to a boil. Add berries and allow to cook for 20-30 minutes until the mixture is thick. Stir to prevent sticking.

CUSTARD FILLING

One 12-ounce can evaporated milk
12 ounces of water in which 1/2 cup of cornstarch has been dissolved
1 cup sugar (or more if you like sweet filling)
2 eggs
1 teaspoon vanilla

Combine all ingredients in a saucepan. Slowly bring liquid to a gentle boil and stir until custard thickens. Cool and spoon onto sweet dough crusts. To make coconut filling, add 1 cup of shredded coconut to the custard when it is cooling.

Friends and relatives join us every year for our Easter celebration. Sometimes we have a baked ham and barbecued chicken, but more likely it's lamb with all the trimmings. Whatever the fare, the important thing is that we are all together sharing the bounty.

The following recipe is not a traditional family dish, but rather a new twist on one. A friend of mine who would rather be a chef than the attorney he is shared this with me. His hobby is cooking, and he is always improving on a dish. I personally don't think he needs to do anything to this one.

I don't know about anybody else, but I associate food memories with people. For instance, every time I make a sandwich I think of my friend Judy. Meat pies bring my old Aunt Belle to mind. Caviar and Dom Perignon conjure up great memories of a couple who used to invite me over for this treat on cold Sunday afternoons after the football games. And whenever Mama fixes stuffed onions, I think of her old friend from Boston who thought these were a mouthful of heaven.

Every once in a while the stuffed onions show up on a holiday table, and are great when served with the Easter lamb. They take a little time to prepare, but they're worth it.

HALLMAN'S LEG OF LAMB WITH SPINACH AND FETA CHEESE

Serves 8-10

1 boneless leg of lamb, about 5-6 pounds
3 pounds fresh spinach
1/4 cup virgin olive oil
1 teaspoon garlic powder
1 teaspoon salt
1 teaspoon sugar
1 cup French bread crumbs
fresh ground black pepper to taste
2 teaspoons Dijon mustard
One 5-ounce package feta cheese

Stuffing:

Clean spinach and chop coarsely in a food processor or by hand. Remove to a mixing bowl and add olive oil, garlic powder, salt, sugar, bread crumbs, black pepper, and Dijon mustard. Mix thoroughly.

Either debone the leg of lamb or have your butcher do it for you. Be sure the outer membrane is removed. Butterfly the leg by slitting it open so that it lies flat on a cutting board, skin side down. Make horizontal cuts the length of the leg, about 2 inches apart, being careful not to cut all the way through. Pat the inner surface of the meat with olive oil and some Dijon mustard. Sprinkle with fresh ground black pepper to taste. Crumble the feta cheese and press evenly over the entire inner surface and into the slits in the lamb. Then pat and press the spinach stuffing mixture evenly onto the lamb. Roll the lamb back into shape and tie it up with string about every 2 inches. When completely secured, pat the roll with a little more olive oil and Dijon mustard. Season with 2 tablespoons of rosemary and a handful of bread crumbs. Insert a meat thermometer into the thickest part of the roast. Cook in a smoker or covered grill, or in a 350-degree oven, until the thermometer reaches 125-130 degrees for medium rare. Remove and let rest for 30 minutes before slicing and serving. This can be refrigerated overnight and served cold on a buffet.

STUFFED ONIONS

Serves 6-8

6-8 medium yellow onions
4 tablespoons butter
1 large tomato, peeled, seeded, and chopped
1/2 cup finely chopped fresh mushrooms
2 garlic pods, minced
1 pound lean ground beef, or sausage of any kind—removed from the casing—or chopped raw shrimp
1/4-1/2 cup unseasoned bread crumbs
1 egg, beaten
2 tablespoons chopped parsley
1/4 teaspoon basil
1/4 teaspoon marjoram
salt and pepper to taste
freshly grated Parmesan cheese
1 cup chicken broth

Peel the onions. Cut off a slice from the top and bottom of each onion. With a spoon, scoop out the center of each onion, leaving a thick shell. Reserve the extra pieces of onion. Place the onions in a large, deep pot and cover with water. Bring to a gentle boil and cook for several minutes or until they become slightly tender. Carefully remove from water and allow to drain.

Chop the reserved pieces of onion. Sauté the chopped onions in 2 tablespoons of butter in a large skillet or heavy saucepan. Add the chopped tomato, mushrooms, and garlic; cook for 5 minutes. Add the ground beef, sausage, or shrimp and cook for another 10 minutes, stirring gently. Remove from heat and stir in the bread crumbs and beaten egg. Mixture should become thick. Add seasonings. Melt the remaining 2 tablespoons of butter and pour into a baking dish. Stuff each onion with filling and arrange in the baking dish; sprinkle with Parmesan cheese. Pour in the chicken broth. Place dish in 350-degree oven; after 30 minutes raise temperature to 400 degrees and bake for 10 minutes. The onion tops should brown a bit. To serve, baste with pan juices.

My Aunt Lois makes a vegetable casserole that's pretty good and perfect for serving to a large Easter Sunday crowd.

LOIS' VEGETABLE CASSEROLE

Serves 15

2 1-pound cans green beans
2 15-ounce cans green or white asparagus
2 14-ounce cans artichoke hearts (packed in water)
1 2-ounce jar sliced pimiento
1 4-ounce can sliced mushrooms
1/2 cup fried crumbled bacon
1/2 cup melted margarine
juice of 1/2 lemon
garlic juice to taste
salt and black pepper to taste
2 8-ounce cans sliced water chestnuts

Drain all vegetables. In a large baking dish, gently toss all ingredients, except water chestnuts, with seasonings. Top with water chestnuts and bake for 30 minutes at 350 degrees.

If there are some picky children around for the meal, consider serving scalloped potatoes or *petit pois* simmered with lots of butter. Forgo the green salad and make a festive fruit salad.

Use your imagination. Any and all fresh fruit combined with freshly grated coconut makes a delicious and refreshing salad. Add a little powdered sugar and whipped cream to make it really luscious. Top with fresh mint from the garden.

Once Lent is over and we are into Eastertide, it's like being released from bindings. With winter behind me, I look forward to outdoor activity and all the food treats that go with it. Spring is crawfish season! There will be crawfishing trips, followed by crawfish boils and crawfish cooked a hundred different ways. Ah, what good times we have.

There is a story that Acadians tell about how the crawfish came to live in south Louisiana. Before the Acadians were exiled from their beloved Acadie (now known as Nova Scotia) in the 1750s, they were accustomed to eating lobster which they caught in the cold waters of the North Atlantic. When the Acadians began the journey in search of a safe haven, their travels took many of them along the eastern seaboard, and eventually they arrived in Louisiana where there were other Frenchmen who allowed the Acadians to carve themselves a sanctuary in the marshes along the Gulf of Mexico.

The lobsters followed their friends (so the story goes), but the long and arduous journey caused the crustacean to become smaller and smaller until it became the size it is today. The crawfish, like the hearty Acadian, adapted to its new home, and soon there were thousands and thousands of these delicious crustaceans for all to enjoy.

Up until thirty years ago, the tasty mudbugs were known only to the natives along the Louisiana and Texas Gulf coast. In 1959, the small town of Breaux Bridge in St. Martin Parish decided to honor its crawfish friend, and since then, there has been a yearly festival held every spring. There's dancing in the streets (called a *fais do do*), parades, crawfish eating and cooking contests and yes, even crawfish races. The people of Breaux Bridge are a tireless and innovative group, and because of their loyalty and faith in the crawfish, the whole world now knows about the little lobster-like delicacies.

Through the years, cooks and chefs have discovered just how versatile the crawfish can be. You can boil them, stew them, stuff them, fry them, bake them, and combine them with other seafood to create innovative new dishes.

Back before crawfish was king, local fishermen brought the crawfish from the swampy waters primarily for consumption by their own families. If there was more than enough for even the largest Acadian family, the fishermen peddled the crawfish to friends and neighbors.

Once crawfish were recognized for their sweet tasty meat, the world clamored for them. To meet the demand, crawfish farming has developed into a science. Crawfish peeling and processing plants have sprung up all along the coast. There are now crawfish ponds dotting the prairies and swamps from Lake Charles to Grand Isle. Before all of the technical innovations came about, crawfish were caught in the swamps from April through June; now they are harvested at crawfish farms from January to July.

One of my favorite ways to enjoy crawfish is in "stew-fay." It's a cross between a stew and an *etouffée*. The crawfish meat is so delicate and sweet I don't want to dress it up too much. My rule is to keep it simple and above all, do not over cook the crawfish.

CRAWFISH STEW-FAY

Serves 8

2 pounds crawfish tails
8 tablespoons butter
2 onions, coarsely chopped
1 large sweet green pepper, coarsely chopped
1 stalk celery, finely chopped
1 tablespoon cornstarch
1 cup water
1/3 cup finely chopped green onions
1/4 cup finely chopped parsley
salt and cayenne pepper to taste

In a heavy pot, slowly melt the butter. Add the onions, sweet green pepper, and celery; cook until transparent. Add the crawfish tails and cook for 10 to 15 minutes, or until they begin to throw off a little liquid. Stir occasionally. Dissolve the cornstarch in a cup of tap water. Add the cornstarch/water mixture to the crawfish and simmer for 20 minutes or until the gravy thickens a bit. Add salt and cayenne pepper. Don't be stingy with the spices. Stew-fay should have a little bite to it. Serve immediately over steamed rice. Garnish with a sprinkling of green onions and parsley.

Once I have my first taste of the season's crawfish, it is difficult to resist eating more. I do try to pace myself so I won't have too much all at one time.

I watch the advertising signs at roadside stands and at the seafood market, and just when I think the price is getting right, I take the plunge and have a crawfish boil. It must be understood that each person in south Louisiana has his very own way of boiling, so there are no hard and fast rules about how it should be done. Some cooks add tons of salt, cayenne pepper, and other spices. Others are not so heavy-handed with seasonings. It's perfectly acceptable to throw in whole onions, new potatoes, corn-on-the-cob, smoked sausage, and even whole fresh artichokes into the boiling pot. These are wonderful accoutrements to eat along with crawfish.

I also recommend that the boiling be done outdoors in large boiling pots over butane burners. If you do it indoors, you run the risk of having live crawfish escaping from sacks and running around the kitchen. Plus, there'll be a mess to clean up if the pot boils over. Anyway, it's practically a sacred ritual to spread old newspapers out on a large picnic table in the yard and let everyone gather around to peel and eat at their own pace. Here is one way to boil crawfish.

BOILED CRAWFISH

Serves 4

20 pounds live crawfish (allow 5 pounds per person)
5 gallons water
One 26-ounce box salt
6 heaping tablespoons cayenne pepper
4 lemons, halved
10 bay leaves
6 medium whole onions
12 new potatoes (leave skins on)
6 ears shucked corn
1/4 cup olive oil (optional, but it makes peeling easier)

If the crawfish appear to be a little muddy, rinse them well with cool water in a large tub, changing the water several times until it runs clear. Put 5 gallons of water in a 10-gallon boiling pot. Add all ingredients except for the crawfish. Bring water to a rolling boil, then add live crawfish. Cover and allow water to return to a boil. Cook for 8-10 minutes. Drain and serve on trays or on that big newspaper-covered outdoor table. The corn and potatoes absorb the seasonings and are delicious.

When crawfish are plentiful, you can bet there's a pot of something made with them on just about every stove in south Louisiana. Crawfish pies, bisques, stews, and jambalaya are traditional favorites, but innovative cooks and chefs have created many different recipes. I was once served a martini with, what else, a marinated crawfish tail instead of an olive. I keep waiting for someone to serve me crawfish ice cream—God forbid!

When time is short, a quick way to make a delicious crawfish jambalaya is in an electric rice cooker. A tossed green salad, hot French bread, and something cold to drink make a great meal.

CRAWFISH JAMBALAYA

Serves 6-8

One 10-1/2-ounce can beef consomme
1 medium onion, chopped
1 medium sweet green pepper, chopped
1 seeded pickled jalapeño pepper, minced
One 4-ounce can sliced mushrooms, drained
8 tablespoons melted butter or margarine
1 pound peeled crawfish tails
2-1/2 cups raw rice
1/2 teaspoon salt
1/4 teaspoon cayenne pepper

Place all ingredients in an 8-10 cup rice cooker. Do not add water. Turn on cook cycle. When cycle is over, keep on warm cycle for at least 30 minutes. Do not attempt to cook in a smaller rice cooker or to double the recipe when using an 8-10 cup rice cooker.

There are times when friends shove me out of the kitchen and cook for me. Now that's what I call a real treat. There are also times when friends challenge me with a recipe they claim is better than mine. I always allow them to cook their recipe for me because that gives me the opportunity to sit back and learn something new. Such was the case when my husband Rock came home one evening with a bag of groceries under his arm and offered to cook supper. His only clue as to what was in store was that it was going to be something with crawfish. He ordered me out of the kitchen saying this was a secret recipe passed on to him by his father. His challenge to me was to determine the secret ingredient.

I could hear him chopping and stirring as I contented myself with swinging in my hammock, watching the late afternoon clouds brewing into one of those Louisiana thunderstorms. I was a bit mystified when I noticed Rock wrapping up the garbage and depositing it in the outdoor garbage bin. When I asked him what all that was about, he explained that he was getting rid of the evidence.

While the crawfish bubbled on the stove, I was allowed to come in for a whiff. It smelled like an *etouffée*, and it had a rich color. In fact, it had a gravy that looked better than Mama's. I couldn't wait to taste it. Finally, I was invited to the table which had been grandly set with my best china and crystal. Rock stood over me, rubbing his hands as I took my first bite. Ah, it was delicious! "Well," Rock asked anxiously, "What do you think?"

I admitted it was quite good, and although it didn't taste exactly like a traditional *etouffée*, which is usually made with extra fat, it certainly had a rich, full taste. He was pleased with himself when I admitted that I couldn't detect the secret ingredient.

The next day when my garbage was being picked up, I ran out to investigate what Rock had deposited in the garbage. Ah ha! I found the evidence.

LASSERRE'S MAGIC CRAWFISH

Serves 6-8

1 pound peeled crawfish tails
6 tablespoons butter
2 medium onions, chopped
2 garlic cloves, minced
1/2 sweet green pepper, chopped
1 rib celery, chopped
One 10-3/4-ounce can cream of shrimp soup (the secret ingredient)
1/2 cup water
1/4 cup dry white wine or dry sherry
salt, cayenne pepper, and hot sauce to taste
minced green onions for garnish

In a heavy black iron pot, melt the butter and sauté the onion, garlic, sweet green pepper, and celery until wilted. Add the crawfish tails and cook for 10 minutes. Add the soup, water, and wine or sherry; stir and simmer for 30 minutes. Add the seasonings and simmer another 10 minutes. Serve over steamed rice or your favorite pasta and garnish with minced green onions.

If there is any left over crawfish mixture, mix together with cooked rice or bread crumbs to make a stiff dressing and stuff into sweet green peppers. Bake at 350 degrees for 20 minutes.

The kitchens of Acadiana are the heartbeat of its unique cuisine. The parlors or living rooms of Acadian homes are seldom used. I often wonder why we have them. They are probably used only for special occasions, and even rarely for those. The only way Mama is able to shoo family or guests out of the kitchen is to turn off the lights and close the door. And even then, sooner or later, we find ourselves back at the kitchen table or hanging around the stove.

An old friend of mine says much the same about her mother's kitchen. We have spent many hours in Marie Angelle's kitchen. I do not remember a single time I went there to visit that a pot was not simmering on the stove. Mrs. Angelle, if not busy stirring a pot or chopping up vegetables, sat in a rocking chair near her stove and shared endless cups of coffee with us, listening to the news and gossip of our lives. Bustling around us, checking the pots or refilling our cups was 'Tite Fille, Mrs. Angelle's faithful kitchen helper and companion.

When I called my friend Tina, Mrs. Angelle's daughter, to come for a visit one April, she declined emphatically. "Impossible, Marcelle. We're just getting started on making a batch of Mama's famous crawfish bisque. The crawfish are beautiful, and the whole family says it's time for their first share of the season."

My mouth was watering, and I was hoping against hope they would either invite me to come help or at least tell me they would keep some for me. In my heart, though, I knew the family came first, and before the season was over I too would have a couple of quarts of bisque for my very own.

Having been around several times when the making of crawfish bisque took the better part of the day, I allowed my spirit to be with the Angelles as they worked diligently at their task.

For instance, I knew they had gone and hand-selected the crawfish from their supplier, for you must have just the right size to make bisque. Then the heads and tails have to be perfectly cleaned and readied. The vegetables have to be chopped just so, and then begins the arduous task of stuffing, stirring, and cooking.

Although I wouldn't have the bisque made by the magical hands of Mrs. Angelle, Tina did give me the recipe, and I can vouch you will never have better— maybe different, since each cook has his or her own version, but definitely not more delicious, in my opinion.

CRAWFISH BISQUE

Serves 10-12

To stuff the heads:
150 crawfish heads, cleaned
1 pound crawfish tails
8-10 slices of stale bread, soaked in water and squeezed dry
3 medium onions, minced
4 stalks celery, minced
4 medium sweet green peppers, minced
1/2 cup vegetable oil or butter
5 cloves garlic, minced

Combine minced vegetables and sauté well in oil or butter. Grind crawfish tails and bread in a meat grinder or food processor. Set aside.

1/2 cup vegetable oil or butter
2 tablespoons salt
2 tablespoons black and red pepper, combined
5 cloves garlic, minced
1/2 pound crawfish tails
1 cup plain bread crumbs
1 cup seasoned bread crumbs

In a large pot, combine the sautéed vegetables, ground crawfish tails, and bread. In the cooking oil or butter, stir in salt, black and red peppers, garlic, and the 1/2 pound of crawfish tails. Cook for 5 to 8 minutes. Remove from heat.

Allow the stuffing to come to room temperature, then stuff the crawfish heads with the mixture, packing tightly. Combine the bread crumbs and roll the stuffed heads in the bread crumb mixture. Place in a baking pan and bake for 15-20 minutes at 375 degrees.

To make the bisque:
1/2 cup vegetable oil or butter
2-1/2 pounds crawfish tails
2 tablespoons salt
1 tablespoon cayenne pepper (This amount makes for a spicy dish; amend according to taste.)
2 tablespoons paprika
1-1/2 cups hot water
Crawfish fat, if available (Some stores will give you a small packet of fat per pound of crawfish.)
4 tablespoons roux
4 medium onions, chopped
4 sweet green peppers, chopped
4 stalks celery, chopped
1/2 cup vegetable oil
6-8 cups of water

Heat 1/2 cup of oil in a large, heavy pot. Sauté tails with seasonings for 3 minutes. Mix hot water, the crawfish fat, and roux together and add to pot.

Cook for 2 minutes. In a separate pot, sauté the onions, green peppers, and celery in oil and add to the sautéed tails in the large pot. Add 3-4 cups of water and cook for 2 minutes. Add 3-4 cups more water and cook for 15 minutes on a slow fire.

2 tablespoons chopped green onions
2 tablespoons chopped parsley

To the simmering pot of crawfish bisque, add the stuffed heads, green onions, and parsley; cook for 5-10 more minutes. Serve over rice.

From The Basin To The Bay

When the snow begins to melt up north, the waters of the Mississippi River and its tributaries often rise to dangerously high levels. Held in check by intricate levee systems, it's not uncommon to see huge vessels prowling along the river above sea level. Most of south Louisiana is below sea level, so no one pays much attention to the situation.

The gradual influx of fresh water into the rivers, streams, and bayous creates ideal fishing conditions. Many early mornings find fishermen armed with simple bamboo poles trying their luck along the banks of the nearest bayou.

Bass anglers with more sophisticated equipment head out to numerous lakes. Deep sea sportsmen make their way into the bays and the Gulf of Mexico seeking the big ones. Shrimpers and crabbers begin hauling in their catch, and the waterways are alive with vessels heading in and out of ports. It is time for fish-fries, shrimp boils, and outdoor suppers featuring seafood culled from the rich waters of the Atchafalaya Basin and Vermilion Bay.

When I was a child, late afternoon was my favorite time to bicycle around the neighborhood checking out who was having what for supper. Mama's only instruction was to be back by sundown because that was when our supper was served. If I was lucky, I would be invited by neighbors to sample whatever was coming off the grill, simmering in their pots, or being spread out on backyard tables. I sometimes ate three suppers before I arrived home for Mama's evening meal. The fresh evening air kept my gastric juices flowing!

Even after growing up and moving to New Orleans, I continued the habit of scouting the neighborhood, checking out what other people were eating for supper. I made friends with local seafood shop owners asking them to call me when fresh seafood arrived.

One spring afternoon, walking home from the streetcar stop, I spotted a family in their backyard frying up a batch of catfish. I quickened my pace and dashed into the nearest seafood market. I must have appeared to have a pack of wild dogs on my heels as I rushed in the door and ran to the counter. The shopkeeper looked at me anxiously.

"What do you need today?"

"Catfish!" I shouted back.

After we checked out several big cats, he happily skinned and filleted my pick. I tucked the package under my arm and headed home. I had enough for a small feast. I hoped my neighbors hadn't eaten supper yet.

I found a few willing friends who generously offered to bring the trimmings—potato salad and hush puppies. I agreed to make a batch of homemade mayonnaise for the salad and tartar sauce.

The fist task at hand was to prepare the fish for frying. I had a large deep black iron pot—perfect! Let's see now. Does Mama fry her catfish in corn meal or cracker meal? Do I pass the fillets in an egg wash before dredging them in meal? It appeared that I would have to reach out and touch someone. No answer at Mama's. I dialed Aunt Lois. She gave me directions.

FRIED CATFISH

Serves 4

2 pounds catfish fillets, cut into 2-inch square pieces
2 teaspoons salt
1 tablespoon yellow mustard
1 tablespoon Creole mustard
a few good shots hot sauce

juice of 1/2 lemon
4 cups yellow corn meal
3 tablespoons flour
Vegetable oil for frying

Season fish with salt, rubbing it in well. Blend the mustards, hot sauce, and lemon juice; spread the mixture all over the fish. Let it sit a while to soak up the marinade. Pour 4 fingers of vegetable oil into a deep, heavy frying pot. Mama always said the fish must have enough oil to float in. Heat the oil to 350 degrees.

Put yellow cornmeal and flour into a large paper bag. Add the fish fillets and shake the bag to coat the catfish well. Put 2 or 3 pieces of fish into the hot oil at one time. Fry until the fish floats to the top. Drain on paper towels.

My friend Matt says the best thing about fried catfish is the tartar sauce he makes to go with it.

MATT'S TARTAR SAUCE

1 cup homemade mayonnaise (recipe follows)
1 large pod garlic, mashed
1 large sweet pickle, minced
5 dashes of Tabasco®
3 good shots of Worcestershire sauce
1 teaspoon grated onion

Mix all ingredients together and chill before serving.

HOMEMADE MAYONNAISE

1 hard-boiled egg yolk
1 raw egg yolk
2/3 cup vegetable oil
1 teaspoon vinegar
1/2 teaspoon sugar
1/2 teaspoon salt
1/4 teaspoon black pepper

In a small mixing bowl, combine the egg yolks and mix well, leaving no lumps. Slowly add the oil, about a tablespoon at a time, and whip with a wire whisk each time you add the oil. When you have 1/4 cup oil left, add the sugar, salt, and vinegar; whip well. Add the remaining oil and whip again. While you're at it, you might as well make a double batch—some for the tartar sauce and the rest for potato salad.

When I lived at Oak Alley Plantation, upriver from New Orleans, I always opted to cross the Mississippi by ferry boat. One Saturday evening, I had a few minutes to kill before the next ferry, so I decided to cruise around the riverside villages near the ferry landing. I spied a seafood market and went in to browse. There was a wonderful aroma of boiled crawfish, and my mouth began to water. A glass-fronted cooler displayed beautiful fresh shrimp and containers of lump crabmeat. I also spotted bags of "gumbo crabs," so called because they are perfect for simmering in a stew or gumbo.

I hesitated to buy anything since I wasn't expecting company, and it seemed a waste to cook such delicacies just for me. But my time was running short. I heard the ferry blowing, announcing departure from the other side of the river. Oh, what the heck! I grabbed a bag of six gumbo crabs and a pound of large shrimp. I made it just in time to board the ferry.

As I floated to the other side, I gave some thought to what I was going to do with my purchases. Nothing else would do but to make a crab and shrimp stew, the kind that's thick and full of flavor. On the way to my cottage, I stopped and invited a neighbor and his girlfriend to join me the next afternoon for an early Sunday dinner.

I was just beginning to make the roux when my neighbor called and informed me that a few friends had dropped by unexpectedly and wondered if it was O.K. to bring them along. No problem. I could stretch my stew. Imagine my chagrin when they arrived and I realized there would be a total of seven at my dinner table! I would just have to do what Mama does when assorted hungry nieces and nephews drop by with friends. I would have to add a little more stock, cook more rice, and make a bigger salad. Luckily I had a two-loaf bag of French bread.

As everyone gathered in my tiny kitchen, my mind was racing. I didn't even have seven matching dinner plates. I did remember having eight small soup bowls shaped like fish. As I dug around the cabinet looking for them, I managed to break one. That left seven. Perfect.

Just when I was about to begin serving, everyone decided to crowd around the stove to have a taste test. I hated to tell them that if everyone had a spoonful, servings would be small. Oh, what the heck! Everyone oohed and aahed during dinner, and that helped to relieve my anxieties.

CRAB AND SHRIMP STEW

Serves 6

6 medium-sized crabs
1 pound large shrimp, peeled and deveined. Reserve heads and shells
1 pound lump crabmeat
4 tablespoons vegetable oil
4 tablespoons flour
1 large onion, chopped
2 stalks celery, chopped
1 sweet green pepper, chopped
5 cups seafood stock (recipe follows)
2 pinches ground thyme
2 bay leaves
salt and cayenne pepper to taste (be generous)
1/2 cup chopped green onions
2 tablespoons finely chopped parsley

If you're using live crabs, you'll have to to scald them. Bring 8 cups of water to a boil in a large pot. Add the crabs and scald for 3 minutes. Remove the crabs from the water and allow to cool. Pry off the top shell of the crabs and remove the legs. With a small spoon, remove the rich yellow fat and reserve.

Remove the gills and inedible parts. Return the crab shells and legs to the pot of boiling water along with the shrimp heads and shells. Reduce heat and simmer while you make the roux.

Slowly make a roux with the oil and the flour. When dark brown, add the onions, celery, and sweet green pepper. Sauté until vegetables are wilted. Meanwhile, strain the stock and measure 5 cups. Slowly add the stock to the roux, stirring and blending. Simmer for 45 minutes. Add the crabs, lump crabmeat, and shrimp along with the seasonings and reserved fat. Cook for 15 minutes. Add chopped green onions and serve immediately over rice in soup bowls. Garnish with minced parsley.

From the time I was a toddler until I was well into my teens, I learned all there was to know about the blue hard-shell crabs caught in both freshwater lakes and saltwater bays of south Louisiana. But it wasn't until Papa deemed me old enough to accompany him on a business trip to New Orleans that I was introduced to the true delicacy known as soft-shell crab. The term soft-shell refers not to a kind of crab, but to a specific point in a crab's life cycle.

Crabs periodically outgrow their shells and live for few hours in a soft-shell state before the new shell begins to harden. It is at this point that they must be removed from their water environment for immediate consumption.

It's a time-consuming and arduous task for the workers who must check the submerged boxes holding the crabs several times a day, waiting for just the moment the crabs begin to molt.

Soft-shell crabs are an epicure's delight and have always been a popular item in the famous and not so famous restaurants of the Crescent City.

Papa chose a waterfront restaurant on Lake Pontchartrain to christen my taste buds with what he said was a secret passion of his. Without even perusing the menu, he gave the waitress the order.

"Fried soft-shell crabs for the young lady and myself," he boomed. "And make sure they're done just right!"

Sailboats glided past our seaside perch while Papa and I waited for our order. He explained that I would be able to eat the entire crab. No peeling or messing with hard shells. I was a bit apprehensive, but having trusted Papa all my life, I figured this was no time to have misgivings.

Our platters arrived, piled high with two golden fried soft-shell crabs, French fries, and hot buttered French bread. I watched Papa snap off a huge claw encrusted in a crunchy batter and pop it into his mouth. A look of ecstasy appeared on his face. That was all the encouragement I needed. I dug in. Oh, what fun it was not to have to do battle with the hard crab shell. No pieces of shell to spit out. And the flavor! I savored the legs, then tore into the body where the lump crabmeat and rich fat was held together by the light batter. I dared not dip the chunks into my little cup of tartar sauce lest I lose the taste of the sweet lake crab.

I had a new and dear respect for Papa. Throughout the rest of his life, whenever he and I shared a meal of soft-shell crabs, we exchanged secret winks and remembered that wonderful meal on the lakefront.

When I had my own restaurant near Lafayette, one of my chefs, Bryan Richard, created a dish using soft-shell crabs that became a fast favorite of our clientele.

STUFFED SOFT-SHELL CRABS AND JAMBALAYA

Serves 6

To stuff the crabs:
6 fresh jumbo soft-shell crabs (uncooked)
1 bunch green onions, finely chopped
1 clove garlic, minced
1 pound lump crabmeat
1 pound small shrimp, peeled and finely chopped
1/2 cup dry white wine
1 tablespoon each of salt, cayenne pepper, and white pepper
3 cups stale bread crumbs
8 ounces fresh mushrooms, finely chopped
3 egg yolks
One 3-ounce jar diced pimientos
Flour for dredging
2 cups buttermilk
4 eggs, beaten
3 cups crackermeal
1/2 gallon peanut oil

Remove the apron and lungs from each crab, then lift the shoulders and remove gills. Leave the top flaps on.

Sauté green onions, garlic, crabmeat, and shrimp in white wine. Add salt, cayenne pepper, white pepper, and bread crumbs. Add mushrooms and stir in egg yolks and pimiento. Mix gently. Allow to come to room temperature, then chill stuffing for at least 1 hour or until firm.

Carefully lift the shoulders on each crab and gently stuff the cavity with the mixture. Press the shoulders down to hold in the stuffing. Be careful not to break off any of the legs of the crab. Lay crabs on a heavy baking sheet; sprinkle with salt and cayenne pepper. Dredge them in flour, seasoned with a little salt, cayenne pepper, and white pepper, then gently dip the crabs in a wash made of buttermilk and the beaten eggs. Dredge each crab in crackermeal, breading each leg individually with the meal.

In a deep pot, heat the peanut oil to 350 degrees. To fry the crabs, hold by the body, allowing the legs to dip into the hot oil for a few seconds before dropping the whole crab into the oil. This will make the legs stand up rather than lie flat. Crabs will float to the surface when cooked.

Jambalaya:
3 tablespoons shortening
2 tablespoons all-purpose flour
1-1/2 cups chopped onions
1/2 cup chopped sweet green pepper
1 cup chopped celery
1 clove garlic, minced
One 1-pound can whole tomatoes
3/4 cup tomato sauce
2 cups raw rice
1 teaspoon salt
1-1/4 teaspoons cayenne pepper
2-1/2 cups water
1 pound raw, peeled, and deveined shrimp

Heat shortening. Add flour and stir over medium heat until golden brown. Add onions, green pepper, celery, and garlic. Cook slowly in roux until vegetables are transparent, stirring often. Add whole tomatoes and tomato sauce and cook until an oil film rises to the top. Stir in raw rice, salt, cayenne pepper, and water. Cover and cook over a low heat until rice is tender. Add more water if mixture becomes dry.

Serve the crabs, legs up, over a bed of jambalaya. Ladle a tablespoon of CREOLLAISE SAUCE over the crabs. Garnish with a wedge of lemon and fried parsley.

CREOLLAISE SAUCE

2 cups bearnaise sauce
2 tablespoons Creole mustard

Mix well.

Oh, if Papa could see me now!

Before the spring shrimp season gets into full swing, I like to test the waters, so to speak. I call a friend who has a small fishing camp near the mouth of the Mississippi River and suggest an excursion. Just the two of us go down late in the afternoon and prepare for an early morning adventure.

All we need to pack is a small ice chest, the fixings for a cold breakfast, a throw net, and bathing suits. The kitchen at the camp is equipped with a small butane stove and a collection of iron pots. If we're lucky we'll catch our supper. On our way down, we pick up some vegetables from roadside stands. We're on an adventure!

The plan is to rise with the sun and be on the wharf for our first cup of coffee. Who's going to cast the net first? We flip a coin. He wins. I stand aside as he spins the net gracefully into the water that at this time of morning is the same color as the sky. The spinning net looks like a giant spider web as it sinks into the gray-blue water. He adroitly pulls the rope in his hand and quickly drags the net in.

What treasures will it hold? I stand at the edge of the pier, my toes curled around the rough, weathered cypress boards. The net is hauled up onto the wharf. In its folds we count six-seven-eight shrimp, a small crab, and a couple of large minnows. I pick out the shrimp, still kicking, and carefully put them into our small pail containing a bit of crushed ice. Everything else goes back to the sea.

My turn now with the net. I'm not as adept as my companion, but I manage to set the net spinning into the cool blue depths. I yank the cord and pull the net in. Ah, ah! Another eight or ten large, sweet shrimp. A few more castings bring in enough for our late afternoon meal.

Now we can wile away the day. We set out a small crab trap in hopes of catching a few to go with our meal later in the day. With ham sandwiches and soft drinks packed in the small ice chest, we tie a small dingy on a tether rope, jump in, and spend the day on the water.

With a large umbrella to protect us from the sun and armed with a small radio, we are perfectly content. We discuss how we plan to prepare the catch. We doze off and on, pointing out now and then the egrets and seagulls soaring above us. No one comes our way throughout the day, and we feel secluded from the outside world of hot afternoon traffic and ringing telephones. Is this the little bit of heaven we all dream about?

Before we know it, the sun is moving into the western sky. It's time to check the crab trap, take a quick shower under the watering hose that hangs from a post on the pier, change into shorts and T-shirts, and prepare supper before heading back to the city.

Let's see—we have a couple dozen shrimp, six medium-sized crabs, a couple of red-ripe tomatoes, one Vidalia onion, and a loaf of French bread we brought from the city. On the pantry shelf in the camp I find a can of small potatoes, a can of sliced beets, and a surprise—a can of hearts of palm.

We pull out the collection of iron pots and choose our weapons. He's to take care of the shrimp and crabs. I will try to be innovative with the potatoes, beets, and hearts of palm.

POT CRABS AND SHRIMP

Serves 6

2 dozen shrimp
6 medium-sized crabs
2 cups water
1 teaspoon salt
1 teaspoon cayenne pepper
2 tablespoons butter
1 small onion, chopped
2 ripe tomatoes, peeled, seeded, and chopped
1 cup seafood stock

Peel the shrimp, reserving shells and heads. Scald the crabs, allow to cool, and then pick out the crabmeat. Reserve the shells. Place shrimp and crab shells in a small saucepan with 2 cups of water seasoned with salt and cayenne pepper. Simmer for about 30 minutes. Strain the stock.

In a large skillet, melt 2 tablespoons of butter and quickly sauté the onion and tomatoes. Add the shrimp and crabmeat, stir for a few minutes and then add the seafood stock. Simmer for 10 minutes.

While my friend cooked the seafood, I drained the canned potatoes, dredged them in some flour seasoned with a little salt, black pepper, and a pinch of nutmeg. I deep-fried them to a golden brown.

The beets and hearts of palm were sliced, chilled, drizzled with vinegar, and garnished with sprigs of fresh parsley I found near the back door steps.

We loaded all of the food onto a large cutting board and set it out on the wharf where we dined *al fresco*. We sopped up every drop with chunks of French bread.

Oh dear, do we really have to go home?

There comes a point in late spring when I feel it in my bones—the need to head out toward the open waters of Vermilion Bay. I want to smell the salty sea air and see the horizon, uninterrupted by land or trees.

I believe that feeling comes from listening to Mama and Papa talk as summer neared, and they too yearned to get away to the camp at Cypremort Point. Situated on the northeastern edge of Vermilion Bay, practically dead center on the Louisiana Gulf coast, the Point is often referred to as the "Cajun Riviera."

At the Cypremort Point of my childhood, camps were strung out along the water, each with its own covered piers and many with names such as "Camp Sip-More." The camps were simple, with screened porches wrapped around the fronts and painted bright red and yellow with green roofs and trim.

Mama loaded up all of us kids, along with boxes of towels and sheets, a portable washing machine and bags of food, stopped in New Iberia to pick up Aunt Eva and her daughter Candy, and headed south. Louisa was the last stop before we got on the only road to the Point. At the general store we were allowed to buy Popsicles to keep us contented for the final stretch. More times than not, we had to wait as the bridge over the Intracoastal Canal opened for the long barges to pass beneath. With Popsicles melting in our hands we would visit with the other families waiting in line at the bridge.

Finally we would be on our way. The last few miles were treacherous. This was before air-conditioned cars, so we had a choice to make. Keep the windows down in hopes of getting a breath of air and choke on the dust kicked up along the shell road, or roll up the windows and die of suffocation. We compromised. Roll up the windows for a few minutes, then roll them down for very brief periods.

We looked like a tribe of wild Indians when we arrived. Along with hands made red and sticky by the Popsicles, our faces were coated with white dust streaked with perspiration, and we had great mosquito bites all over our bodies. But who cared? We were in paradise!

After we unloaded the car, we would drag the crab nets out of storage and quickly bait them with chicken necks. After all, Mama and Aunt Eva said we had to hurry and catch our supper. They knew how to get us out of their hair while they transformed the camp into our home away from home.

In a matter of hours we caught several dozen crabs, despite losing one of the younger children off the end of the pier and getting splinters in our rear ends.

While we hacked away at our boiled crabs, Mama and Aunt Eva would sip on their cold beers and peel the biggest crabs so that we could have crab chops the next day. I can't tell you which meal we liked best. You can decide after you try these.

CRAB CHOPS

Serves 6

3 green onions, minced
3 tablespoons butter or margarine
2 tablespoons flour
1 cup milk
1 pound crabmeat
20 saltine crackers, crumbled
1 egg, beaten
1/2 teaspoon salt
1/4 teaspoon cayenne pepper
2 dashes Tabasco®
Crackermeal or bread crumbs for dredging
Butter and vegetable oil for frying
Boiled crab claws for garnish (optional)

Sauté onions in butter or margarine. Alternate adding flour and milk, stirring constantly to make a medium-thick white sauce. Remove from heat and add crabmeat, cracker crumbs, egg, salt, and cayenne pepper. Gently mix together and set aside to cool thoroughly. Shape into 6 patties and dredge in cracker meal or bread crumbs. Put about 1/2 inch of equal parts vegetable oil and butter in a skillet and fry patties on both sides until they are golden brown.

At Cypremort Point we ate crab chops on paper plates as we sat on the pier. Every person had his own garnish. My sister doused hers with ketchup. I daintily spread mine with tartar sauce. My brother sandwiched his between two chunks of French bread spread with mustard. We all agreed they went well with shoestring potatoes. Ah, the good old days.

Spring Al Fresco

When the first warm spring breezes ripple through the trees, I find myself making any excuse to be out in the open air. Since I love this time of year, I roam the countryside, either on foot or by car, looking for the first signs of blackberries, checking crawfish ponds, and watching for the purple thistles that grow in abundance in fallow fields and pastures, or in open ditches in rural areas.

The purple thistles, called *chardrons* by the natives, are delightful to eat. Although I had seen them all of my life, it wasn't until a few years ago that I learned from a friend that parts of them are edible.

Having lived all her life near Bayou Bouef and Lake des Allemands, she had a great knowledge of the land. She knew which swamp mushrooms are edible, when it was time to harvest *graine à voler* (an edible seed from certain water chinquapins), and of course, she knew all about *chardrons*.

She brought the thistles to me in a large brown paper bag and proceeded to tell me how to handle these gigantic purplish-green thistle bushes.

"First of all," she explained, "If it doesn't have a large prickly head on it, it's not ready to pick. It MUST have a big head."

I nodded and promised I wouldn't dare pick one if it didn't have a big head.

"Be sure to wear boots that go up to your knees and arm yourself with a big knife," she continued.

I had a great picture of myself stalking a pasture wearing big rubber boots while wielding a big knife.

"With the long knife, cut the *chardron* down at the base near the ground. Let it fall away from you and carefully pick it up with your fingers. Use gloves if you must. Then, with a knife, scrape off the stickers and chop off the head at the top. Put the stalk in a brown paper bag. Plastic bags won't do."

I didn't dare ask why. I rather like brown paper bags anyway. They have more character than plastic.

What she then pulled out of the paper bag was the *chardron* up to that point.

"Now with a sharp knife, scrape off the strings, much like you do with celery."

What she held up to show me was a cone-shaped stalk, light green in color, that looked like an odd piece of celery.

She went on.

"Trim off both ends and chop into half-inch pieces. Put the pieces in a colander and rinse with cold water. Drain. Place the pieces in a bowl and season with vinegar, salt, and black pepper."

With the bowl before me, I chomped away. The *chardrons* were crunchy and had the taste of celery, cucumber, and hearts of palm. I managed to salvage some to take home for supper. They would be perfect with some French bread and a chicken liver pâté made the night before.

CHICKEN LIVER PATE

1/4 cup chopped onion
4 tablespoons butter
1-1/2 pounds chicken livers
2 hard-boiled egg yolks
4 tablespoons softened butter
1/2 cup heavy cream
1/3 cup Cognac
1/4 teaspoon nutmeg
salt and black pepper to taste

Sauté the onions in 4 tablespoons butter until transparent. Add the chicken livers and cook just until the pink disappears. Purée the mixture in a blender or food processor. Put the egg yolks through a sieve and add to the chicken liver mixture, together with the 4 tablespoons of softened butter, heavy cream, Cognac, nutmeg, salt, and pepper.

Blend together until smooth, You may also add a handful of chopped chives or green onions for a little extra taste and color. Chill the pâté before serving with toast points or crackers.

Those warm, velvet evenings of spring make me pull back the curtains, throw open all the French doors opening onto the patio, and take deep breaths of jasmine-scented night air.

The evenings are perfect for *al fresco* dining. Quick, simple dishes are in order. One of my favorites is from Commander's Palace in New Orleans. The dish can be elegantly prepared "tableside," but can also be done in a skillet on the stove. It's easy, delicious, and versatile.

SINGING SHRIMP

Serves 2

6-8 large shrimp per person, peeled and deveined
8 tablespoons butter or margarine
1/2 cup chopped green onions
1 teaspoon minced garlic
1/2 cup sliced fresh mushrooms
1 ounce brandy
Several dashes of Worcestershire sauce
salt and cayenne pepper to taste

Melt butter in skillet, then add green onions, garlic, and mushrooms; sauté for a few minutes. Add shrimp and cook slowly until shrimp turn pink. Add brandy, Worcestershire sauce and seasonings; cook for a few more minutes, stirring gently. Serve over toast points, in pastry shells, or with pasta of your choice.

For a variation on the above recipe, add 1/2 cup chopped tomatoes with the brandy and other ingredients. Season with a little sweet basil to give the dish another dimension.

Any way you serve this dish, eating outside will make it all taste just a little bit better. Serve this dessert after the shrimp.

STRAWBERRY (OR RASPBERRY) ROMANOFF

Serves 2

2 cups French vanilla ice cream
1 cup fresh strawberries or raspberries, chopped
1 tablespoon sugar
3 ounces Grand Marnier
1/2 cup whipping cream

Place everything in a blender; blend until smooth. Serve in large wine glasses. It's also good served over cubed pound cake placed in a small bowl. Garnish with a sprig of fresh mint.

When spring is in the air, so is the heady smoke of outdoor barbecues. Late in the afternoon, when the humid heat begins to subside, people are either in their back yards, on patios, or even on small French Quarter balconies, lighting up the barbecue pit. Some families opt for tree-shaded parks. But wherever one goes, the aroma of sizzling hamburgers, steaks, ribs, and chicken fills the air.

When I lived in New Orleans (the third time around), all I had for outdoors at my apartment was a patio the size of a postage stamp. But it was fenced in, and I made it quite lush with potted palms, small flower beds filled with blossoming plants, and a small selection of herbs and pepper bushes.

On many evenings my neighbors witnessed smoke spewing forth from my barbecue pit. I often feared for my upstairs neighbors. I'm sure they kept a fire extinguisher close at hand when they heard me on the patio.

One of my favorite things to barbecue is a good hamburger. I like mine big and juicy; I guess everybody does. I don't think I've ever heard anyone

say they like a small, dry one.

I also like my hamburger with bits of onion and bell pepper mixed into the ground beef. Others prefer a large thick slice of raw onion shoved between the burger and the bun. That's a bit too heavy for my taste.

The primary criterion, though, is that the hamburger is grilled over an open flame, rather than fried in a skillet or broiled in the oven. And I like mine medium-rare. I like to see a little blood ooze out when I bite into it.

I'm not much on shredded lettuce, and I don't particularly care for sliced tomato, unless it's a Creole tomato, fresh from the garden. And cheese? Well, I've been known to put a couple of slices of American or Swiss on my burger, but what I like best is a big chunk of Blue cheese spread over the burger just as it comes off the grill. I'm not picky about mustard and mayonnaise, but if I have homemade mayonnaise flavored with a little garlic, I'll choose that over the commercial kind.

But the crowning touch is the bun. I like it hot, but not toasted, and it has to be big enough to cover the burger. I don't like a hamburger on an onion roll or French bread, even less on regular old white sliced bread. It has to be a real hamburger bun.

MARCELLE'S BIG AND JUICY HAMBURGERS

Makes 6 hamburgers

2 pounds lean ground beef
2 tablespoons minced onions
2 tablespoons minced sweet green pepper
1 tablespoon soy sauce
1/2 teaspoon cayenne pepper
1/4 teaspoon garlic powder
1 tablespoon Worcestershire sauce
1 tablespoon olive oil

Mix all ingredients together except Worcestershire sauce and olive oil. Let stand in the refrigerator, covered, for at least 1 hour. Shape meat into thick patties. Place on a platter and dribble with Worcestershire sauce and olive oil. Let the patties come to room temperature before grilling. Cook until desired degree of doneness, turning only once.

Warm Buns:

In a large heavy skillet, melt 1 tablespoon of margarine or butter per bun.

Add a few dashes of Worcestershire sauce and place both halves of the bun, inside down, in the skillet and heat quickly over medium fire. Place burgers on the bun and add your favorite condiments.

At another time of my life I lived at Oak Alley Plantation, a wondrous place, quiet and serene. My cottage was nestled in a spot surrounded by an old wooden fence draped with honeysuckle and shaded by ancient crepe myrtle and live oaks.

Friends from New Orleans often wound their way along the River Road to Oak Alley to get away from it all. One such evening, we huddled around a fire we built in the yard, listening to a portable radio and sipping red wine. Someone came up with the idea of having a camp-out in the clearing near my cottage.

There were to be certain rules for the camp-out. No electrical equipment would be allowed, and we'd have to cook our own supper on an open fire.

On the appointed day, we were there early setting up tents and cots. Ice chests held food and beverages. By late afternoon, the barbecue pits were being readied. And needless to say, there was a lot of tasting of one another's dishes. But we were all in agreement: The best of the lot was the pork and beans prepared by an old friend, Jet Smith.

JET'S MEAN BEANS

Serves 10

1 pound sliced bacon
2 large onions, thinly sliced
2 pods garlic, minced
juice of two lemons
Four 16-ounce cans of good quality pork and beans
2 cups dark brown sugar
1/2 cup barbecue sauce
salt and pepper to taste

In a large black iron pot, fry the bacon until slightly crisp. Add the onions and garlic; cook until transparent. Add the lemon juice; stir for a minute or two. Then add the pork and beans, brown sugar, and barbecue sauce. Season to taste. Simmer on the stove, stirring occasionally, or bake in the oven at 250 degrees for 1-1/2 hours or until as Jet says, the onions are well smothered in the beans. He also suggests that you cook them the day before serving and let them stand in the refrigerator overnight. Reheat to serve.

Another friend from Texas cooked the best ribs that night.

COUNTRY RIBS

Serves 6-8

4 pounds country-style pork ribs
1 teaspoon garlic powder
1/2 teaspoon hot sauce
1/3 cup soy sauce
1/2 teaspoon black pepper
1/2 cup catsup
1 tablespoon yellow mustard
1 tablespoon cane syrup or honey
1 tablespoon bourbon

Place ribs in a pan. Make the marinade/basting sauce by combining all remaining ingredients. Pour over the ribs. Let stand at room temperature for at least two hours. Grill the ribs over slow coals, about six inches above the fire. Baste with sauce and turn ribs every 15 minutes. Continue basting. Grill until juices run clear.

Some of my favorite side dishes for barbecues are new potatoes, boiled and tossed with butter and fresh parsley, or corn-on-the-cob, dripping with butter. And my all-time favorite dessert is a good lemon pie.

LEMON PIE

Makes one 9-inch pie

1-1/3 cups sugar
6 tablespoons cornstarch
dash of salt
1-1/4 cups boiling water
3 eggs, separated (Set aside whites for use later.)
1/3 cup lemon juice
2 teaspoons grated lemon rind
2 tablespoons margarine
1 baked 9-inch pie shell

Combine sugar, cornstarch, and salt in saucepan; gradually add water. Bring to a boil, stirring constantly. Cook one minute or until mixture becomes clear and thickened. Stir small amount of hot mixture into beaten egg yolks and return to hot mixture. Cook over medium heat for about three minutes, stirring constantly. Stir in lemon juice, margarine, and lemon rind. Pour into pie shell.

(Recipe continues on next page.)

Topping:
One 7-ounce jar marshmallow creme
dash of salt
3 egg whites

Beat egg whites and salt until soft peaks form. Gradually add marshmallow creme, beating until stiff peaks form. Spread over filling, sealing to the edge of the crust. Bake at 350 degrees for 12-15 minutes or until lightly browned. Cool and serve.

It was one of those perfect spring days. There was a light breeze blowing off the river. Wild clover covered the levee, and the fragrance of sweet olive trees filled the air. I decided it was a day to play hookey from work. Two or three hours away from the office might be just what I needed to clear my overloaded brain.

As I pulled out the picnic hamper I knew tuna fish sandwiches were out. I wanted a gourmet picnic lunch. Fortunately, I had stopped the day before at a roadside vegetable and fruit truck and picked up fresh produce. And the night before I had experimented with an idea given to me by a reader, so I had six cold garlic-stuffed meatballs I could use to make poorboy sandwiches. I was on a roll! Since I felt like I was going on a mini-vacation, I packed my basket with linen napkins, china, and crystal. I threw in several magazines I hadn't had time to read.

All I needed now was a convertible so I could feel the sun on my face. But alas, I had to settle for an old army jeep, which turned out to be great. I could ride up and down the levee in search of the perfect picnic hideaway.

I found a small grove of cypress trees, turned on a portable radio, and spread out my goodies. There wasn't a soul around. Ah, sweet solitude.

GARLIC MEATBALLS FOR POORBOYS

Makes 2 large poorboy sandwiches

1/2 pound ground chuck
1/4 pound ground veal
1/4 pound lean ground pork
6 large garlic pods, split in half
1/2 teaspoon salt
1/4 teaspoon cayenne pepper
1/4 teaspoon black pepper
1 tablespoon Worcestershire sauce
1/4 teaspoon oregano leaves
3 tablespoons cooking oil
1/2 cup water or beef broth

Mix together all ingredients except garlic pods in a large mixing bowl. Shape the meat mixture into six large meatballs. Carefully poke the split garlic pods, two to each meatball, into the center of the balls. In a large skillet, heat the cooking oil and brown the meatballs on all sides. Then add 1/2 cup of warm water or beef broth, cover and let simmer for 15 to 20 minutes or until juices run clear from the meatballs. Allow to cool. Split the meatballs in half and make a poorboy, dressed to your taste, on French bread.

I had crisp munchies to go with my splendid poorboy.

MARINATED GREEN BEANS AND CHERRY TOMATOES

Serves 4

1 pound fresh green beans
8 cups water
1 teaspoon salt
8 cherry tomatoes
olive oil
tarragon vinegar
Dijon mustard
1 yellow onion, sliced
salt and black pepper

Bring water to a boil in a large saucepan. Add salt and green beans. Boil for 5-10 minutes or until beans are *al dente*. Drain in a colander and toss with a few ice cubes to cool down the beans. Toss together with the cherry tomatoes, olive oil, vinegar, mustard, sliced onion, salt, and black pepper to taste.

To complete my picnic lunch, I filled a thermos with cold tea and added a few crushed mint leaves and fresh-squeezed lemon juice to taste. To satisfy my sweet tooth, I rolled some strawberries in brown sugar and sour cream.

It's amazing what a couple of hours in the fresh air and Louisiana sunshine can do for your state of mind.

Lazy, Crazy May

By the middle of May, the foliage is so dense along the highways, yard fences, and bayou banks, it is like a heavy curtain enclosing the countryside.

Just a few weeks before, you could spot a neighbor working in his garden.

Now, you can barely see him as he hoes, weeds, and mulches. Not so long ago, I could watch my neighbor sitting on his back porch mending his fishing nets.

Today, I would have to fight my way through a tangle of vines and bushes with a machete if I wanted to watch him at his work.

Ligustrums blossom with thick sweet flowers that attract hordes of bees and bring on sneezing attacks. Magnolia trees with their shiny dark leaves and glorious blossoms are at their peak. People work fanatically in their yards trying to keep lawns mowed, bedding plants watered, and hedges trimmed.

Late afternoon showers send the leaves of the banana trees reaching for the sky. June is fast approaching, and children are getting restless in classrooms all over the state. Everyone wants to head for the nearest swimming hole. Summer is creeping in.

Mama says the month of May makes her crazy. There is Mother's Day, followed by First Communions, graduations, and pre-nuptial parties for June brides. She is tired of her linen dresses even before the slew of weddings begin. We try to get her in an improved state of mind and plan a big celebration for Mother's Day. It's always our hope that if she can make it through that, she'll manage the rest.

All the children and grandchildren plan for days. Once we decided to arrive with all the trimmings and simply take over her house and yard. Since my sister Edna and her brood live next door to Mama, Sis bore the brunt of the work. But the rest of us thought it quite appropriate because Mama adores Edna's husband, who is fondly referred to by Mama as "Poor Al." We've never figured out why Mama calls him that because we believe that while he's not rich, he's the only one in our family who has a pool in his back yard. He also has a great sense of humor and doesn't appear to let anything bother him, despite the presence of four lively children who are always into everything. We still laugh about the time one of his sons drove a brand new riding lawn mower into the deep end of the swimming pool and all Poor Al did was shake his head and chuckle for hours.

Anyway, Poor Al takes good care of Mama—he trims her hedges, mows the yard, fixes fences, and runs endless errands for her. And he always volunteers to cook for Mother's Day.

Poor Al prepares the main course, while the rest of us take care of all the other dishes. For many years, he barbecued everything from chicken to ribs, but lately his thing is to fry whole turkeys. Yep, the whole thing, not pieces.

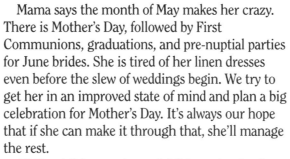

POOR AL'S FRIED TURKEY

For a crowd

Two 10-12-pound fresh turkeys
1 large yellow onion, minced
8-10 cloves of garlic, peeled
1/2 cup chopped peppers; your choice of green, jalapeño, or banana, or a combination of all three
3 tablespoons salt
3 tablespoons cayenne pepper

Clean turkeys well; rinse with cool water. Leave the skin flap at the neck on. In a small mixing bowl, combine the minced onion, whole garlic, peppers, and 1-1/2 tablespoons each of salt and cayenne pepper. With a sharp boning knife, make slits in the breasts and upper thighs and stuff this seasoning mixture into the slits with your fingers. Pack it in well. Season the outside of the turkeys with the remaining salt and pepper, rubbing well. Place the turkeys in large plastic bags and refrigerate overnight.

Before you begin frying, you must do a little preparation. Al strongly recommends that you do not cook the turkeys in your kitchen. You will need a butane burner and a very large, deep, heavy pot with a cover.

Spread newspaper or thick cardboard beneath the burner to protect the area from grease splatters. Have on hand two large paper bags and arm yourself with two long-handled forks, the kind used for barbecuing. I also suggest having barbecue mittens or large insulated pot holders.

Ready? Here we go.

Pour enough vegetable oil (lard is better if you can get it, and peanut oil is also acceptable) to fill the pot 3/4 full. The oil must be at 350 degrees before adding the turkey. Grab the turkey by the neck flap and gently submerge it into the hot oil. Be careful—the hot grease may overflow and splatter. Cover the pot. Turn the turkey every 5-10 minutes, using the long-handled forks. It will take 45 minutes to 1 hour to cook a turkey. When the legs begin to spread open, the turkey is done. Remove it from the grease and put it inside of a large brown paper bag; close tightly with a piece of twine or wire twist. Let the turkey stand for 15-20 minutes before removing from the bag. Carve as usual.

I have another great turkey recipe I must share. My first encounter with my Aunt Git Broussard's famous baked turkey was at a family gathering held after a funeral. I was hesitant about serving myself some although everyone raved and raved about it. But Aunt Git was serving some equally famous rice dressing, so I spread the dressing over a couple of turkey slices. As luck would have it, I was left with a slice of turkey with no dressing left to accompany it. Oh well—I decided to eat the plain turkey. It was juicy, well-seasoned, and absolutely delicious. I hounded Aunt Git for the rest of the afternoon until we made a date for her to show me her secret. I couldn't wait.

I picked up a turkey and, armed with paper and pencil, met her in her kitchen for the demonstration.

The directions may seem complicated, so read the recipe carefully and have the turkey and ingredients ready at hand.

AUNT GIT'S TURKEY

You can use any size turkey. Remove the neck, gizzards, and livers from the cavity. Rinse the turkey both inside and out and pat dry with clean dish towels; place on a large tray or cutting board. Aunt Git says it's best if the turkey is not thoroughly defrosted, as it will make it easier to do what we are about to do.

1 or 2 sticks margarine (depending on size of turkey)
1 onion, coarsely chopped
1 sweet green pepper, coarsely chopped
3-5 cloves garlic, sliced (again, amount depends on size of turkey)
6-10 Cajun Chef Brand "sport peppers" (small green hot peppers packed in vinegar)
2 tablespoons vinegar from the pepper bottle
salt
cayenne pepper

Cut margarine into tablespoon slices. Place in a small bowl and season generously with salt and cayenne pepper. Place seasoned margarine in the freezer for several hours.

Place the onions, sweet green pepper, garlic, sport peppers, and vinegar in a small bowl and sprinkle lightly with more salt and cayenne pepper. Allow this to marinate together for a couple of hours.

In a third small bowl, combine 2 tablespoons salt and 1 tablespoon cayenne pepper, more if using a large turkey.

What you are going to do is season the turkey with all of the above ingredients without breaking the outside skin. You need to use a narrow 6-inch boning knife, and a spoon with a thin rounded handle is also useful. Be prepared to use your hands; you may want to wear a pair of surgical gloves if your hands are irritated by pepper.

Have all of the ingredients ready with the turkey on a tray or large cutting board. Go into the turkey's cavity and make a slit in the breast meat on either side of the center breast bone. Do not cut through the skin. Spoon in some of the salt and pepper mixture, and then, with your fingers, stuff in the onion, green pepper, garlic, and sport pepper mixture. Insert 2 or 3 of the frozen margarine slices into the slits. If you have a large turkey, you will be able to make two slits on each side of the main breast bone.

With the turkey lying breast side up with the legs facing you, gently pull the drumstick forward to expose the inner thigh. Pull the skin away from the meat. Make a slit following the bone line from the top of the leg. Use your finger to make a path and repeat the stuffing procedure described above. Where the skin has been loosened on the inner thigh, spoon in the salt and cayenne mixture. Repeat the procedure on the other leg.

Now, turn the turkey breast side up with the neck opening facing you. Lift the skin flap and make a slit down the wing from the shoulder, again following the bone line. Repeat the stuffing process on both wings.

Season the outside of the turkey with the salt and cayenne pepper you mixed up in the third small bowl. Any leftover seasonings, vegetable mixture, and frozen margarine pieces may be placed in the cavity. Secure the wings by folding the lower half back over the top of the wing. Tie the legs together with twine. Place the turkey in a roasting pan, preferably granite. Do not put oil in the pan.

Preheat oven to 400 degrees. Put the turkey in the oven and cook for 15 to 20 minutes just to get the browning process going. Lower the oven temperature to 350 degrees and cover with the roaster lid.

Baking times:

8-9 pounds: 2-2-1/2 hours

12 pounds: 3-3-1/2 hours

18-20 pounds: 4-4-1/2 hours

Baste often with pan drippings. Do not over cook; the meat will dry out if you do.

It may sound like alot of work and struggling, but the reward is great. After you carve the turkey, return the meat to pan drippings and allow it to soak for a few minutes. Any leftover meat may be used to make an incredible gumbo. Add drippings to the gumbo pot. Delicious!

I really have digressed. I was telling about our Mother's Day celebration. Poor Al fries the turkeys, and everybody else provides the rest of the meal. I usually prepare a dish given to me by an old friend, Henry L. Mayer Jr., who is known for his culinary expertise.

HENRY'S FIELD PEA CASSEROLE

Serves 6

3 cups cooked field peas
2 large tomatoes, sliced
3 large white onions, sliced
3 large sweet green peppers, sliced
1/2 cup Parmesan cheese
6 slices bacon
salt and black pepper to taste

In a casserole dish layer field peas, tomatoes, sweet green peppers, and white onions. Repeat until all ingredients are used. Season with salt and pepper on each layer. Sprinkle cheese and place bacon on top of casserole. Bake covered at 400 degrees for 1 hour. Remove cover and place under broiler for a few minutes until bacon becomes slightly crisp.

Homemade ice cream is a must for Mother's Day.

NICK'S HOMEMADE ICE CREAM

Two 14-ounce cans sweetened condensed milk
16 ounces sour cream
Two 12-ounce cans evaporated milk
3/4 cup sugar
1 tablespoon vanilla
whole milk

Mix all above ingredients, then add milk to fill line on ice cream freezer container. Two cups of chopped fresh fruit may be added. Freeze ice cream according to machine instructions.

If you prefer an ice cream that is more custard-like, here is Mama's recipe.

CUSTARD ICE CREAM

6 whole eggs
4 cups milk
1 cup sugar
1 tablespoon vanilla
2 cups chopped fresh fruit

In a large saucepan, combine the eggs, milk, sugar, and vanilla and cook slowly, stirring constantly, until the mixture thickens. Allow to cool. Add fruit. Pour into ice cream freezer container and freeze according to machine instructions.

On the last day of school, the moment report cards are handed out and reviewed by parents, my sister Edna loads her van with her brood and several of their friends and heads for the camp at Catahoula Lake. She figures they deserve a couple of days of running around in the fresh air, doing whatever they please. One year she invited me to join them so she would have another adult to keep her company. I must have had a screw loose, because I agreed to meet her at the lake by noon on the appointed day. Children of all ages were everywhere—playing volleyball, jumping off the wharf, playing hide-and-seek in the woods, fishing, and eating everything put before them. It was late into the night when they finally settled into their sleeping bags. My sister and I had some peace and quiet. I was afraid to think what the next day would bring.

Fortunately I was up before everyone. I carefully stepped over sleeping bodies and made my way to the kitchen where I made a pot of coffee. I fixed myself a tray and headed down to the wharf with a fishing pole hooked under my arm. There was a mist over the water as I made myself a nest on the old wooden bench. I felt like I was the only one in the world, and I was going to make the best of it.

I had nearly an hour to clear the cobwebs from my mind before being discovered. A gaggle of children soon joined me on the wharf. My sister yelled at me to be sure everyone had on life-preservers. A five-year-old insisted he needed my fishing pole and two rambunctious teenagers managed to knock my coffee tray into the water. So much for peace and serenity. After a couple of days, I was looking forward to some time with adult company.

When I got home I called an old friend who is an ace at cooking steaks. In a short time he was at my door with steaks in hand, along with a basket of fresh strawberries. I had put together a corn pudding and green salad, so I left the kitchen and told him to have at it.

Be forewarned. If you are a purist about steak, you're not going to like this recipe, because we're going to "goop it up" with lots of seasonings.

Get a fire going in the pit while you're getting the steaks ready. Select the steak of your choice. My friend, James, swears that a Porterhouse is best.

Me, I prefer a ribeye. Whatever you choose, be sure the steaks are thick and of good quality.

JAMES' STEAK

Serves 2

2 steaks of your choice
4 cloves garlic, minced
12 tablespoons butter
2 teaspoons lemon juice
2 teaspoons Worcestershire sauce
2 teaspoons Italian salad dressing
1 teaspoon garlic salt
1/4 teaspoon ground oregano
1/2 teaspoon basil
1 teaspoon black pepper

Melt 4 tablespoons butter in a saucepan. Allow the butter to get hot enough to sauté the minced garlic. When the garlic just begins to brown, remove from heat. Be careful not to let the garlic burn, or you'll have a bitter taste. Add the rest of the butter to the pan and return to a low fire. The aroma of the garlic butter will get your gastric juices flowing. At this point, all I want to do is dab a chunk of bread into the butter sauce and forget about the steaks. Fight temptation and continue. Let the garlic butter simmer a bit, whisking constantly. When foam begins to rise to the top, add the lemon juice, Italian salad dressing, and Worcestershire sauce and continue to whisk. Blend well for a couple of minutes, then remove from fire.

Rub the steaks well with the garlic salt, black pepper, oregano, and basil leaves. Coals should be turning gray and should not be too hot. Brush the steaks liberally with some of the sauce and place them on the grill. Continue basting with the sauce until steaks are cooked to desired doneness. Any leftover sauce can be tossed with pasta or poured over French bread.

We ate like savages. After his departure and while I was cleaning up the kitchen, I realized we had forgotten about the strawberries. I sprinkled them with powdered sugar and munched on them while I sat on the dark porch. I wondered what the children were doing at the camp. The quiet was welcome.

Just before the long hot summer is at hand, I'm always eager to enjoy the sights, sounds, and smells of the swamps and marshes that constitute the lower half of my native state.

Skimming along in a boat down a bayou or canal leading to the Gulf, I can always tell when we're getting close to the coast because I catch a whiff of the salty sea air. Above the whine of the boat engine, I can hear the shrill calls of the birds as they swoop down to pluck shrimp or tiny fish from the water. Turtles, large and small, sun themselves on stumps and exposed roots along the route. After a good rain, resurrection fern flutters in the breeze.

It's a good time for a fishing trip. Early one morning I met a companion at a prearranged site. While he put the boat in the water, I scanned the shore for blue herons and ibis. Nothing moved. Perhaps it was too early.

Once we were in motion and the sun began to rise, we spotted movement. We communicated by pointing as we observed birds, a fish jumping at the bow of the boat, and the beady eyes of an alligator in the distance. The water was like glass as the sun rose to warm our faces. We had no real destination in mind, but had brought along an assortment of rods and reels just in case we decided to fish.

When we entered the Gulf it was almost anticlimactic. We chose to keep close to the shore, stopping here and there, casting our lines, waving to fellow fishermen as they sped out to the open water. It was a lazy day. No deadlines, no responsibilities, no nothing.

By the end of the day, our ice chest held nothing more than a couple of leftover sandwiches and cold drinks. We weren't disappointed. We had enjoyed ourselves.

When we returned to the boat launch area, a fellow inquired about our luck, and when we showed him the empty ice chest, he offered us some of his catch—several speckled trout. Heading home, my friend and I discussed various methods of

paration. Should we fry them or broil them in
tter? Then in unison we shouted, "roulades!" We
uldn't wait to get home.

There's nothing like fresh fish cooked the same
day it was plucked out of the Gulf. Ah, let the
summer steam on in!

ROUT ROULADES

ves 6

**6-8-ounce fillets of trout or redfish (or any firm
)**
e of one lemon
blespoons butter
reen onions, finely chopped
love garlic, minced
pound fresh mushrooms, chopped
ound shrimp or lump crabmeat
aspoon basil leaves

:k pepper
enne pepper
pint half-and-half
/2 cups chicken broth
up bread crumbs

Pound fillets a bit to make them lie flat. Sprinkle with
on juice; set aside. Sauté next 4 ingredients in butter
il soft. Add shrimp or crabmeat, basil, salt, black
per, and cayenne. Add half-and-half and 1 cup chicken
th and simmer 5 minutes. Thicken mixture with
ad crumbs so that it sticks together. Place a
espoon of the mixture on top of the fish fillet and roll
like a jelly roll. You may have to use a toothpick to
d the roll together. Place the roulades in a baking pan
h 1/2 cup chicken stock and dots of butter. Bake for
25 minutes at 350 degrees until the fish flakes easily
h a fork. Top with CREOLLAISE SAUCE (p. 17).

Summer

It's hot in Louisiana in the summertime. When June slips in after Memorial Day, the air is still and humid. Late afternoon thunder showers rumble in from the Gulf of Mexico, making life bearable for an hour or two before dusk. Summer is a time for cold food—deviled eggs, potato salad, cold fried chicken, homemade ice cream, watermelon, and giant snowballs. Ladies dress in crisp white cotton, gentlemen wear seersucker, and children live in swimming pools.

The Mystique of the Camp

Life moves more slowly in Louisiana than it does in the rest of the country. People come home earlier from work, or does it just seem so because the days are longer? Entertaining is less formal, and the days are planned not by the clock but rather by the position of the sun.

Cooking is best done early in the day or late in the afternoon. Food comes from home gardens and neighboring waterways rather than from supermarkets.

Families take long vacations at beach cottages in nearby Mississippi, Alabama, or Florida. Often they opt for weekend jaunts to the family camp.

For as long as I can remember, my family has had a summer camp at Catahoula Lake. Folklore has it that the lake, situated just outside the Atchafalaya Basin levee system, was created by an earthquake. Supposedly, the quake ripped open a huge cavern about 500 feet wide, two miles long, and more than 100 feet deep.

Cata-oula is an Indian word meaning "Lake of Sacrifice." Indians held the belief that the lake, which produces fine fresh fish and sweetmeat crabs, swallowed up an entire Indian village when the earth gave way. They also believed that the waters had magical powers, and they often came to bathe and make pilgrimages, asking the gods to keep them safe and protect them from evil spirits.

My father, an old Boy Scout leader known for his colorful campfire stories, chose a site for our first family camp in a clearing surrounded by centuries-old oaks, some of which leaned gracefully over the calm water. Muscadine vines clung to willows and swamp maple, and the hated poison ivy and sweet-smelling honeysuckle intertwined, forming a jungle-like wall around the clearing.

There Papa set up several army-issue tents with the inevitable mosquito nets and cots. A main tent, which was simply a large tarpaulin stretched over several big limbs of a huge live oak, served as the kitchen, or canteen, as he liked to call it. It was the heart of the camp, and it was here we gathered in the early morning for cups of dark, rich, hand-dripped coffee and crusty biscuits Papa managed to cook in a black iron pot over an open fire.

Large metal tubs filled with blocks of ice wrapped in sacks kept soft drinks, beer, lemonade, and milk cool. We filled metal lined boxes, the forerunner of what we now know as ice chests, with our daily catch from the lake—catfish, bream, *sac-a-lait* (white crappie), and huge blue point freshwater crabs.

The campfire never went out. It was fed regularly by Papa, for besides fishing, cooking was his next love. There were always large black cast iron pots of bubbling *courtbouillon* and his own version of *bouillabaisse*. Late in the afternoon, large skillets were dragged out to fry fish, and if we were lucky, a pot of crabs steamed and hissed on the fire.

Today, our camp is situated on a lovely spot, with moss-draped oaks, cypress, and tupelos. It's now a compound comprised of several permanent buildings. Gone are the tents, mosquito nets, and makeshift outdoor kitchen. There are a couple of wharves to dock the fishing and ski boats. And *Mon Dieu*, air-conditioning and telephones. Shame on us! But we still have a campfire site, and much of our cooking is still done outdoors.

The "season" for the camp begins Easter weekend and ends soon after Labor Day. Virtually every weekend in between these holidays the campsite is alive with family and friends. It has always been a place for each of us to find solace from a stressful world. It is here we can commune with nature, throw a fishing line baited with worms or crickets into the water, find a tree trunk to lean against to read a book, or watch the sun set through the dripping moss trailing from the limbs of the splendid oaks.

Like Scarlett in *Gone With the Wind* I need only to pick up a handful of the dark earth to gain strength to face the world.

I remember a summer weekend when I was working at Oak Alley Plantation on the Great River Road, and I had writer's block. I had decided not to join the family for that weekend because I was trying to make a deadline for my food column which appears in *The Times-Picayune* in New Orleans.

It was the typical block—not one word would come forth from my mind, other than the name of the column and my own name. I tried a leisurely walk around the plantation grounds. Certainly inspiration would come forth. But alas, after turning on and off my dilapidated typewriter so many times, I broke the switch. I tried using the office computer and managed to bungle *it* up. I resorted to a legal pad and several No. 2 pencils and ended up chewing off the erasers in a matter of minutes.

That was it! I felt that my days as a columnist were numbered. I had a lump in my throat and a pounding headache beginning at the nape of my neck. I thought of all the people who would be disappointed in me. My Mama wouldn't have my column to show off to her friends, and my baby brother Bruce wouldn't have a desk blotter on Thursday. I hung my head and wept. I needed my Mama. I knew she and the rest of the family were at

the camp, so I packed up a couple of pairs of shorts, some T-shirts, and my yellow flip-flops, grabbed my box of tapes and headed down the River Road toward the interstate. In a couple of hours, I was at the Henderson exit. I decided to ride along the levee to the camp.

It was late afternoon, and fishermen were pulling their boats out of the water. Guys were leaning against pickup trucks with cans of cold beer clenched tightly in their hands. With faces glowing from sunburn, they were telling of the day on the water. I could hear bits and pieces of conversation, in half French and half English. In the distance I saw a water skier taking his last lap down the borrow pit before the sun went down.

I had visions of what the group was doing at the camp. Sitting around the campfire, they were contemplating supper. Was it to be fried catfish, or perhaps a crab stew? I couldn't wait as I turned off

the levee and followed the dirt road that led to the camp. When I pulled up and blew the horn to announce my arrival, little kids ran to greet me. Mama ran to get a drink for me and Bruce gave up his seat on the swing for me. I was home.

When things quieted down, I turned to Mama.

"What's for supper? I need some inspiration for my food column."

She smiled and answered, "Liver and grits."

I went into shock. You don't eat liver and grits at the camp. No fish, no seafood gumbo? I can't even stand the smell of liver cooking. The group was adamant. They had taken a poll and liver and grits had won hands down.

I thought they had all gone mad, but by the time I had watched Mama cook supper and had enjoyed it myself, I was sold on the idea.

LIVER AND GRITS

Serves 6

4 tablespoons cold bacon drippings
3 pounds calf's liver, membrane removed
salt and cayenne pepper to taste
2 large yellow onions, thinly sliced
grits, cooked according to package directions (Don't use instant grits.)

In a large black iron skillet, spread the cold bacon drippings on the bottom of the pan. Season the liver with a little salt and cayenne pepper. Add the liver to the cold drippings, then turn on the fire to medium high. When liver begins to brown, turn a couple of times and add a little water and the sliced onions. Cook until the onions wilt. Do not overcook. Pour the onions, gravy, and liver over hot grits.

With this Mama served an old family favorite.

POTATO CROQUETTES

Serves 6

3-4 pounds red potatoes
1 yellow onion, finely chopped
1 small sweet green pepper, finely chopped
3 whole eggs, beaten
salt and black pepper to taste
several dashes of Tabasco®
flour for dredging
2-1/2 cups bacon drippings or peanut oil

Boil potatoes, let cool and peel. In a large bowl mash the potatoes, leaving some lumps. Add the chopped onion, green pepper, seasonings, and beaten eggs. With your hands, shape the potato mixture into balls, about 2 inches in diameter or, if you prefer, shape into 3-inch pancakes. Dredge the balls or pancakes in flour and drop them into hot oil. Fry until golden brown. Drain on paper towels.

After supper the children went in search of gowns and pajamas, and we grown-ups sat by the lake listening to the *cigales* (locusts) and talking about what tomorrow would bring. I knew that I could go back to Oak Alley and do my column, and that gave me a great sense of well-being.

Like the Indians who performed their pilgrimages and thought the lake to be magical, we too felt the mystical powers of Catahoula. Because we've spent such a great part of our lives there, we have developed some rituals of our own.

Every year when it's time to close down the camp, we throw a party. It's our way of saying farewell until next spring.

The cycle of the ritual actually begins in spring when we come armed with rakes, mowers, work gloves, and wheel-barrows to get the place ship-shape for the season. The buildings are washed down, and the wharves are repaired. Mama, Aunt Lois, and Cousin Cooney are wild with paint. With whatever colors they can find, they paint everything from swings to benches, flower pots, and tables. One year everything had a polka-dot theme. Because they had little cans of lots of leftover assorted colors, they splashed away. By Easter Sunday the place looked like a colored egg fantasy.

Bedding plants are put in, and bird feeders are filled. Buttercups and other wild flowers bloom along the levee, and the first tiny green leaves of the cypress trees poke through. The fish are jumping, and boats are taken down from their winter sheds and slipped into the water.

By Good Friday the place is in its glory.

With our work done, some of us head for the levee for a couple of hours of crawfishing. If we have no luck, we go in search of a commercial fisherman who has. Two sacks of live crawfish, about forty or so pounds, will be our evening repast. After the afternoon church services, huge pots are filled with crawfish generously seasoned with salt, cayenne pepper, and lemons. Sometimes new potatoes and whole onions are pitched in for good measure.

When spring gives way to summer and school lets out, the camp looks like a disturbed ant hill. In the morning, the first person up makes a big pot of coffee. Slowly, like the sun rising, adults and children find their way to the stove and the cups of black liquid that will get the blood flowing. Still in robes and gowns, they sit on folding chairs and benches near the edge of the lake, sipping the hot brew and waiting for someone to make breakfast.

By midday, children are water skiing, teenagers are floating on inner tubes, and adults are at their favorite fishing spots.

But come late September, it's time to close down for the cold months, and so, time for our party.

Mama, Aunt Lois, and Cooney have put away their paint brushes and now wield cooking utensils. They issue invitations, plan the menu, and cook and cook.

The day before the party finds them running around arranging flowers, icing down cold drinks, and making pitchers of spicy Bloody Marys. Sometimes we have grillades and grits, or baked egg pies; one year we had a seafood brunch. Mama served this contemporary Louisiana crowd-pleaser.

CRABMEAT AND SHRIMP FETTUCINI

Serves 12

3 sticks butter
3 medium onions, chopped
3 stalks celery, chopped
2 sweet green peppers, chopped
1/2-3/4 cups flour
4 tablespoons chopped parsley
1-1/2 pounds shrimp
1-1/2 pounds lump crabmeat (or crawfish can be substituted)
2-3 cups half-and-half
1 pound Velveeta cheese, cubed
2 tablespoons chopped jalapeño peppers
3 cloves garlic, minced
1 pound fettucini, cooked and drained
1 cup grated Parmesan cheese

Melt butter in a heavy, large saucepan. Sauté vegetables until transparent. Add flour and stir for 15 minutes, blending well. Add parsley and seafood and cook for 20 minutes, stirring gently. Add half-and-half, cheese, jalapeño peppers, garlic, and mix. Season with salt and cayenne pepper to taste; simmer for 15 minutes more. Add fettucini and toss gently. Pour into a 3-quart buttered casserole and sprinkle with Parmesan cheese. Bake at 350 degrees until bubbly. Serve with lots of French bread and a fruit compote of seasonal fresh fruit dribbled with dark rum and topped with fresh mint leaves.

One year as I bade everyone *au revoir* I took one last glance around the campground. People had pulled chairs close to the bank of the lake and were taking in the glories of the setting sun. That memory and others of past summers made my trip back to the city an easy one.

I remembered one year when I was unable to attend the "close down the camp" party because the date fell on the same weekend that I planned a house party of my own.

When I informed Mama of my previous engagement, she was so disappointed she called several times.

"I can't believe you're not going to be with us. We have a fabulous menu planned—chicken pies, spinach casserole, and Cousin Cooney's special bread." She tempted me and then tried the old guilt trip.

But I too had what I thought to be a no slouch menu—chicken *fricassée*, potato salad with homemade mayonnaise, lima beans that make you cry they're so good, and creamy bread pudding with whiskey sauce.

She telephoned again.

"We're putting balloons and palmetto leaves everywhere!"

I shot back, "I have hundreds of little white paper bags with candles plus large torches to light up the yard."

I didn't want to rub it in, but I planned to serve mint juleps at dusk under the alley of twenty-eight oak trees that lead up to the main house at Oak Alley Plantation.

Her final call was to suggest that we all come after my party and watch the sunset with them. Exasperated, I told her that sounded divine, but a two-hour drive was out of the question. Amen.

I bid her goodbye once again and told her I would be there in spirit if not in body. As I hung up the phone, I heard my guests arriving.

I hurriedly showed them to their respective cottages and told them to meet back at the Big House. There we watched the sky turn pink and purple, listened to the sounds of the traffic on the Mississippi River, sipped our mint juleps from silver goblets, and exchanged ghost stories as the sun slipped down behind the levee. When goose bumps and mosquitoes began to take their toll, we headed for my cottage where the yard was dancing with shadows from the torches. The aroma of the *fricassée* bubbling in the pot greeted us. French bread was coming out of the oven, and the smell of whiskey sauce wafted out over the deck.

CHICKEN FRICASSEE

Serves 8

2-1/2 pound hen, cut into frying pieces
2/3 cup cooking oil
1/2 cup flour
2 large onions, chopped
1 sweet green pepper, chopped
salt, black pepper, and cayenne pepper
2 quarts chicken stock or warm water
1/4 cup chopped parsley
1/4 cup chopped green onions

Season the chicken pieces with salt, black pepper, and cayenne pepper. In a large black iron or stainless steel pot, make a roux with flour and oil. Cook roux until dark brown. Add chicken pieces and coat well with roux. Add onions and green peppers and cook for 10 minutes. Add chicken broth or water and cook over medium low fire for at least 2 hours. Add more broth or water if it becomes too thick. Check seasonings. A few minutes before serving, add parsley and green onions. Serve in soup bowls with steamed rice.

WET POTATO SALAD

I like potato salad made with lots of mayonnaise, preferably homemade. Mama was always heavy-handed with her homemade mayonnaise so one of my cousins dubbed it "wet potato salad."

Boil red potatoes and eggs. Peel both and chop coarsely. I'm a purist, but you can add chopped celery, onions, etc. To make the mayonnaise:

1 hard-boiled egg yolk
1 raw egg yolk
1 cup cooking oil
1 tablespoon vinegar or lemon juice
a pinch of sugar
salt to taste

In a mixing bowl, blend the egg yolks together. Slowly add the cooking oil, about a tablespoon at a time, and beat well with a fork or wire whisk. Add the vinegar or lemon juice, sugar, salt to taste and if you wish, a couple of dashes of Tabasco.® Blend well. Chill for an hour or so before adding to potato salad.

RHENA'S BREAD PUDDING

Serves 6-8

1 quart milk
about 1/2 loaf of stale French bread,
broken into small pieces
4 egg yolks, beaten
1/2 cup sugar
2 teaspoons vanilla

Soak milk and bread for about 1 hour. Then, with a fork, mash the bread well in the milk so that there are no lumpy pieces. Beat eggs, sugar, and vanilla in a separate bowl, then add to bread and milk mixture. Pour into a baking pan and place pan in another larger pan half filled with water. Place in a 300-degree oven and bake for 1 to 1-1/2 hours until pudding firms up. Remove from oven and top with meringue.

MERINGUE

8 egg whites
8 tablespoons sugar

Beat egg whites and sugar until meringue is thick and forms stiff peaks. Spread over the baked pudding and return to oven. Increase the temperature to 425 degrees and allow meringue to brown. Watch carefully.

WHISKEY SAUCE

1/2 stick butter
1/2 cup sugar
4 egg yolks, beaten
1/4 cup bourbon, rum, or brandy

In a double boiler, melt butter over low heat, then add sugar gradually, beating with a fork or wire whisk. Do not allow mixture to become too hot. Add beaten eggs in a stream, whisking constantly. Remove from heat and add your choice of liquor. Spoon over bread pudding and serve immediately.

After my guests had been served and satisfied and began drifting back to their cabins, I thought of Mama and the group at the camp.

I pictured them watching the sunset, listening to bull frogs croaking and the distant sound of an engine whining as a lone fisherman made his way through The Forks, a nearby fishing spot. The blazing fire was turning to glowing embers and an empty black iron pot was probably dangling from a contraption fashioned by Papa.

Papa mastered the art of cooking over a wood fire. And it is indeed an art. There are no little knobs to turn to "simmer" or "medium." One has to be able to move the pot to that part of the fire that has a low or high flame. Papa had set up a metal swinging arm which he could rotate around the fire to the desired heat area. He cooked everything from fried chicken and biscuits to *bouillabaisse* and *courtbouillon* over a wood fire.

The next two recipes are camp favorites.

Bouillabaisse and *courtbouillon* both have more or less the same ingredients, but the difference is in how they are put together. These are not dishes that can be pulled together in a minute, so plan to make these when you have a leisurely day. The *bouillabaisse* of south Louisiana is somewhat different from the classic dish served in France. Thackeray complimented the Acadian-Creole version in this tribute: "In New Orleans you can eat a *bouillabaisse*, the like of which was never eaten in Marseilles or Paris."

In New Orleans, and in the land of the Acadians, everyone has his own version of this delectable dish. Each is different, yet each is superb.

AUNT LOIS' BOUILLABAISSE

Serves 8

2-1/2 pounds fish (freshwater or
saltwater fish can be used)
1 pound of shrimp, peeled and deveined
3 large onions, coarsely chopped
2 sweet green peppers, coarsely chopped
2 stalks celery, coarsely chopped
3 cloves garlic, minced
Two 1-pound cans whole tomatoes, undrained and
broken into chunks
1/2 cup vegetable oil
1/4 cup dry white wine
salt
cayenne pepper
2 whole bay leaves

If you're going to use freshwater fish, clean and dehead them but keep them whole. Make 2 to 3 slits on each side. If using large saltwater fish, clean and cut them into either 2-inch steaks or fillets. Season the fish generously with salt and cayenne pepper, rubbing the seasonings into the flesh of the fish with your hands. In a large, deep, heavy pot, slowly heat the oil, then beginning with the fish, layer the ingredients, i.e., onions, green pepper, celery, tomatoes, then fish, then again the vegetables until all are used. Pour in the wine. Add the shrimp, garlic, and bay leaves. Cover and cook over a low fire for 1 to 1-1/2 hours. Restrain yourself from peeking in the pot. Play a game of *bourrée* (a Cajun card game) or otherwise entertain your guests.

Serve the *bouillabaisse* in deep bowls over steamed rice. Be sure to have plenty of hot French bread to "sop up" the juice.

CATAHOULA COURTBOUILLON

Serves 8

As with the *bouillabaisse*, there are as many recipes as there are Acadians and Creoles. Papa's version is a thick soup, much like a chowder, and can be made with either fresh or saltwater fish. If using the smaller freshwater fish, keep them whole; large saltwater fish can be cut into fillets or steaks.

Living Is Easy

Early on summer mornings, before the sun gets too high, I like to play in the kitchen, preparing sussies for the day. One never knows when a picnic may be inspired or an invitation to supper issued. And it's always nice to have goodies stashed around for impromptu excursions to the camp.

2-1/2 pounds fish
2/3 cup flour
2/3 cup cooking oil
2 medium onions, chopped
1 sweet green pepper, chopped
2 stalks celery, chopped
3 cloves garlic, minced (optional)
One 1-pound can whole tomatoes,
undrained and chopped
1 can Rotel tomatoes (tomatoes packed with peppers)
1 quart fish stock or water
1 tablespoon salt
1 teaspoon cayenne pepper
1 bunch green onions, tops only, chopped
1/4 cup finely chopped fresh parsley

In a large heavy pot, make a dark brown roux with flour and oil. Add onions, green pepper, celery, and garlic; cook for 5 minutes. Add both cans of tomatoes and cook slowly over a low fire. Now, here's the secret to making a good *courtbouillon*—let it cook until the oil forms a thin layer, like paper, over the top of the mixture. You will have to stir occasionally, but after a half hour or so, the oil will rise to the top. Add warmed fish stock or water and seasonings and let cook for 1 hour, stirring occasionally. Add the fish and cook for 15-20 minutes. Right before serving, add onion tops and parsley. Check seasonings and make any necessary adjustments. I usually put a bottle of Tabasco® on the table for those who wish to make it hotter. Serve in deep bowls with rice and of course, French bread.

You may not have the night sounds of the swamp around you, but close your eyes for a minute and make believe. Imagine the sounds of fish jumping in the water, of crickets chirping in the night, and the crackling of a wood fire as it burns down. There—now take a piece of crunchy French bread and dip it into your bowl—that first bite makes you feel like you're at the camp.

SPINACH BREAD

1/4 cup butter or margarine
3 eggs
1 cup flour
1 teaspoon salt
1 teaspoon baking powder
1 cup milk
1 teaspoon dill
4 cups chopped fresh spinach
1 pound grated Monterrey Jack cheese

Melt butter or margarine in a 9-1/2 x 13 x 2-inch baking pan in a 375-degree oven. In a separate bowl, beat the eggs and add flour, salt, baking powder, milk, and dill. Mix well and add the spinach and 3/4 pound cheese.

Spread the mixture in the buttered baking pan. Sprinkle the top of the mixture with the remaining 1/4 pound cheese. Bake for 30 minutes at 375 degrees. Cool and cut into small squares. Great with a meal or as *hors d'oeuvres*. It can be frozen and reheated for later use.

FIG CRUNCH PIE

Makes one 9-inch pie

Crust:
1 cup flour
2 tablespoons sugar
1/4 teaspoon salt
1/3 cup softened butter
1/4 cup finely chopped pecans or walnuts

Combine the flour, sugar, and salt. Add softened butter and with a pastry blender or fork, combine until pastry is coarse. Add the chopped pecans or walnuts and mix again. Press dough into a 9-inch pie pan and bake at 350 degrees for 20 minutes or until barely golden.

Filling:
2 cups orange-pineapple juice
10 dried figs, cut in half
1/2 cup dark brown sugar
2 tablespoons cornstarch

In a saucepan, heat the orange-pineapple juice and dried figs. In a separate bowl combine the dark brown sugar and cornstarch. Add to juice and figs. Cook several minutes, stirring constantly. Pour mixture into baked pie shell and serve plain or topped with chilled whipped cream.

Depending on the weather, blackberries can be picked from late April to early June. I love them so much, I call my sister regularly to get picking reports. When she reports they are at their peak, we make plans to go berry picking.

Edna organizes our foray into the blackberry patches she's had under surveillance. Her children hold paper bags, small pails, and are armed with long sticks. The long sticks are for poking around the underbrush to scare away snakes, and they are also handy for holding back the thorny blackberry trailers so one can reach the big berries nestled in hard to reach places.

We all head in different directions. Within a few minutes, everyone is squealing in delight. I rarely fill my pail since I tend to pop every other one into my mouth. One for the pail; one for my mouth. I don't care if they're a bit dusty. My philosophy is that if I were to be poisoned, let it be with a mouthful of juicy berries.

Before long I was far from the crowd and my attention was focused on a patch of bushes laden with so many berries I picked three and four at a time. I was on my knees bending down near a barbed-wire fence when I felt a breath of warm air on the back of my neck. I froze. I slowly looked up and came face to face with a cow that had wandered over to investigate what was going on near her pasture. Relieved, I bent down to resume my picking and found myself staring into the beady eyes of a snake! So much for that. I ran in the opposite direction to join my group where the activity hopefully kept snakes at a distance.

When our containers were full, we walked home along the side of the road. Everyone had an idea of what to do with our pickings. We could make dumplings, or maybe a cheesecake topped with blackberries. Or maybe some pies or a cobbler. We discussed the choices as we rinsed the berries in Edna's large outdoor sink. What about blackberry ice cream?

BLACKBERRY ICE CREAM

Sauce:
2 quarts fresh blackberries (Rinse the berries in cool water and pat dry with a towel.)
2 cups sugar

Place berries and sugar in a saucepan and cook slowly over medium heat. Don't add any water, because the berries release lots of juice. Cook long enough for them to soften and create a syrup. Let cool, then strain the mixture through a sieve.

Ice Cream:
6 whole eggs, beaten
4 cups milk

1 cup sugar
1 tablespoon vanilla
1 teaspoon cornstarch

In a mixing bowl, combine the eggs with milk. Add sugar, vanilla, and cornstarch; mix well. Transfer mixture to a saucepan and cook slowly until it thickens enough to coat a wooden spoon. Do not allow to come to a boil. Add one cup of the berry sauce and freeze in an ice cream freezer according to freezer directions.

When serving, you can add a couple of drops of *crème de cassis* liqueur to each serving.

If you prefer a cobbler, this is an easy one that is quickly gobbled up. Or, you can be completely decadent and make both the ice cream and the cobbler and top the cobbler with the ice cream.

BLACKBERRY COBBLER

3 cups rinsed blackberries
2 cups sugar
1 cup flour
1 egg
1/4 pound melted butter
1 teaspoon vanilla
1 teaspoon baking soda
1 teaspoon baking powder
1 teaspoon salt

Place rinsed berries in a 9 x 13 glass baking dish. Sprinkle with 1 cup sugar. In a separate bowl, mix together with flour, 1 cup sugar, 1 egg, melted butter, vanilla, baking soda, baking powder, and salt. Pour this mixture over the berries and bake at 350 degrees until the pastry sets and turns golden brown.

One of my all-time summer treats is to spend a weekend with friends at a woodsy hideaway near Poplarville, Mississippi. It's fun to get away from bayou land and spend a couple of days in piney woods thick with wild magnolias and dogwood. The cottage is like a cool island amid the towering trees. The Wolf River that runs along the property is perfect for wading, canoeing, and tubing.

We take leisurely hikes and visit the blueberry farm nearby where we can pick our own. Some curl up in canvas chairs and read the hours away. Others take turns on the old hammock strung between two giant pines. We hide all the clocks and let the stress drain away.

One thing we all do is eat well, but with a minimum amount of trouble. Everyone pitches in. Someone brings pies for desserts, others bring fresh fruit and croissants.

One Friday, upon our arrival, we put on a pot of shrimp and ham jambalaya and let it simmer while we settled in.

On Saturday, we packed sandwiches and spent the day on the sand and gravel beach by the river. That evening, we enjoyed grilled fresh tuna, brought in from the city, along with baked onions and Creole tomatoes.

GRILLED TUNA

Serves 10

5 pounds fresh tuna,
trimmed and cut into 1-inch steaks
salt and fresh ground black pepper
3 tablespoons olive oil
2 tablespoons fresh lime juice

Season the tuna with salt, pepper, olive oil, and lime juice. Let stand for an hour. Grill the steaks on a fairly hot barbecue grill until the fish flakes easily. Serve with a wedge of lime.

BAKED ONIONS

Serves 10

10 medium onions (regular yellow onions will do, but if you can get your hands on some Vidalia onions, they're even better)
10 tablespoons olive oil
1 teaspoon chopped garlic
4 tablespoons pureed green onions
1 teaspoon cayenne pepper
4 tablespoons water
black pepper
salt
vinegar

Cut off the ends of the onions so that they will sit flat on a baking pan. Leave skins on. Lightly brush the baking pan with some of the olive oil and place the onions in the pan. Bake at 300 degrees for 1 hour. Turn onions with a spatula and continue baking for 30 minutes. Onions should turn slightly brown, but not burned. Transfer onions to a shallow serving dish. Remove the skins and any dried out rings. Mix remaining olive oil with garlic, pureed green onions, cayenne pepper, and 4 tablespoons water. Spoon over the onions. Then sprinkle with salt and black pepper and a teaspoon or two of white vinegar. Serve at room temperature.

Sliced Creole tomatoes, slightly chilled, made the meal a true feast.

After dinner, we retired to the screen porch with slices of blueberry pie to enjoy the night sounds.

On Sunday afternoon my friends each found a comfortable lounge chair and thumbed through a stack of assorted magazines and newspapers, occasionally making comments on their reading. I was content in the kitchen, julienning red and green peppers, yellow squash, and eggplant. I had also come across a pound of shrimp and a pound of pasta. I was humming and tapping my feet to the sounds of Glenn Miller's big band when one of my hosts joined me in the kitchen. He busied himself making garlic bread and a dessert that looked absolutely devastating.

As dusk fell, a thunderstorm rolled in with gusty wind and flashes of lightning. We sat down to dinner in our glass-enclosed room lit only by many candles.

PASTA WITH GARDEN VEGETABLES AND SHRIMP

Serves 4-6

4 tablespoons butter
4 tablespoons olive oil
1 sweet green pepper, julienned
1 sweet red pepper, julienned
1 medium yellow summer squash, julienned
1 medium eggplant, peeled and julienned
1 bunch green onions, finely chopped
1 pound shrimp, peeled and deveined
salt, freshly ground black pepper, garlic powder, and basil to taste
green hot sauce to taste
1 pound angel hair pasta, cooked and drained
Romano cheese

In a large skillet heat butter and oil. Add all vegetables and shrimp and stir fry quickly until shrimp turn pink. Add seasonings to taste. Toss with cooked pasta and cheese. Serve immediately with hot garlic bread.

As the thunderstorm turned into a misty drizzle, we devoured dessert—thin slices of rum cake layered with blueberries that had been cooked in orange liqueur and port wine, topped with freshly whipped cream.

The blueberries we ate came from the Pearl River Blueberry Farm near Poplarville. Since most summer trips to Wolf River result in me bringing home lots of hand-picked berries from the farm, I asked owners Angie and Cas Larrieu to share their collection of blueberry recipes with me. One of Angie's favorites is one she calls JAR BREAD. It's cooked in jars, an idea which intrigued me.

JAR BREAD

Makes 8 jars of bread

2/3 cup shortening

2-2/3 cups sugar

4 eggs

2/3 cup water

3-1/3 cups flour

1/2 teaspoon baking powder

2 teaspoons baking soda

1-1/2 teaspoons salt

1 teaspoon cinnamon

1 teaspoon ground cloves

2/3 cups chopped nuts

2 cups blueberries

Cream together shortening and sugar. Beat eggs and water into the mixture. Set aside.

In a separate bowl, sift together the flour, baking powder, baking soda, salt, cinnamon, and ground cloves.

Add dry ingredients to the creamed mixture and mix well. Add chopped nuts and blueberries. Mix gently.

Spray 8 wide-mouthed pint canning jars with cooking spray. Fill the jars half-full; place on a cookie sheet. Bake at 350 degrees for 45 minutes. Allow to cool slightly. Seal tightly with sterilized lids. INCREDIBLE.

Angie notes that you can substitute the blueberries with the same amount of figs, pumpkin, carrots, or zucchini. She also said that you can cut off the top of cotton socks, dampen them slightly, and slip them over the jars before baking. This off-beat method helps to keep the bread moist.

Summer has always been a time for an excursion out-of-state, and the Mississippi Gulf Coast is close enough for south Louisianians. I've always been a fan of the area.

At age seven, along with Mama and Papa and siblings, a Mississippi beach was the first sand beach my little Cajun toes had ever touched. Until that time I knew only the squishy muddy bottoms of Bayou Teche. We went back every year until I was twelve when we graduated to the Pensacola, Florida, beach where I was indeed overwhelmed with the crashing waves and bright blue water of the Gulf.

Every summer during high school, my best friend Cathy and I journeyed with her mother for a week-long stay in Biloxi. We always stayed at a gracious old hotel, complete with a huge veranda where the older guests sat on rocking chairs and visited the day away. Cathy and I were allowed to spend the day on the beach where airmen from nearby Keesler Air Force Base entertained us for hours. Cathy's mother asked only that we return to the hotel before sundown, dress, and be with her for dinner. After our meal we were allowed to return to the beach for moonlight strolls with our airmen. From a perch on the seawall, we watched youngsters armed with kerosene lanterns and spears fishing for flounder. I recounted the story of how I did the same thing with my brothers summers before and accidently speared my own foot, thinking it was a small flounder.

One summer I joined my sister and her family for a few days of fun in the sun on the same coast. As I rolled through Waveland and Bay St. Louis, then headed for the highway that would take me past Henderson Point, Long Beach, Gulfport, and Biloxi, the passing landscape reminded me of both the rednecked earthiness of Bonnie and Clyde and the romantic elegance of the Great Gatsby.

When I pulled into the driveway at the rented cottage, I was greeted by my frazzled sister who quickly told me it was my turn to take the children

to the beach. She and her husband were headed for a sand-free pool.

With five children in tow, all shod with flip-flops, we dashed across busy Highway 90. The two-year-old informed us he loved the "snow"—actually the sand. Never having seen sand or snow, he was enthralled. Oh, well. The fifteen-year-old nephew wanted to know where all the women were. The twelve and thirteen-year-old girls oiled themselves down and settled in on their beach towels to watch the boys. The eight-year-old amused himself by making a sandcastle. By late afternoon everyone was ready for a shower except for the baby who wanted to stay and play in the snow.

By sunset, we were back on the beach armed with lanterns, spears, and a small ice chest. It was floundering time.

As luck would have it, the older children managed to spear several fish. And I was appointed keeper of the catch and had to promise to cook them for supper the following night.

STUFFED FLOUNDER

Serves 4

4 medium-size flounder, cleaned and gutted

1 cup chopped onion

1/2 cup finely chopped green onions

1 stick (8 tablespoons) butter

1 cup seasoned bread crumbs

1-1/2 cups boiled shrimp, finely chopped

1-1/2 cups crabmeat

2 tablespoons chopped parsley

1 egg, beaten

several dashes of Tabasco®

1 teaspoon salt

1 teaspoon cayenne pepper

4 lemon wedges

In a heavy saucepan, sauté onions in butter until transparent. Add the bread crumbs, shrimp, crabmeat, parsley, egg, and mix gently. Add the seasonings and remove from heat. Cut each flounder down the center, from tail to head, on the dark side of the fish.

Carefully slit each fish crosswise. With a sharp pointed knife loosen the meat from the bone to form a pocket. Lightly season the inside of the pocket with salt and cayenne pepper. Stuff the pocket with the seafood mixture. Drizzle a little butter and lemon juice over the stuffed fish. Place the fish in a shallow pan with about 1/4 cup water and broil until fish flakes easily with a fork. To prevent fish from becoming dry, baste with pan drippings. Garnish with lemon wedges.

Make it a simple meal and serve boiled new potatoes drenched with butter and topped with fresh chopped parsley. Ice cold watermelon is great for dessert.

When we were children, fried seafood was a staple of summer suppers. More often than not, Papa opted to travel the few miles to the camp at Catahoula Lake and cook out in the open over a hot wood fire in one of his many well-seasoned black iron pots.

Small whole skinned catfish was the family favorite, fried to perfection, and easy to consume because it has few bones. Sometimes Mama also brought along a couple of pounds of shrimp and a carton of freshly shucked oysters for added treats. There was always either French fried potatoes or potato salad, and maybe some crunchy cole slaw tossed with raisins and mayonnaise.

Papa made a big production out of getting his cook station organized. He had to have several brown paper bags, a couple for shaking the seafood in the cornmeal or flour and a couple on which to drain the fried food.

As we all huddled around his fire, sitting on folding canvas stools, he explained how the oil had to be heated to just the right temperature. Mama, forever at his elbow, was instructed on seasoning everything to his taste.

We all love to tell the story about how we asked Papa when he knew the fire was hot enough, and he explained that Mama would stick her finger in the hot oil, and if she said it was hot enough, it was time to begin frying. Of course, as far as we know, she never actually did this, but I wouldn't have been surprised since she usually went along with all of Papa's shenanigans.

But despite watching many fish, shrimp, and oyster fryings, I never seem to succeed in this art. My oysters come out like rocks, and my fish are usually soggy. When I have an *envie* for fried seafood, I usually take myself to seafood restaurants specializing in these dishes, or at least make sure Mama or Aunt Lois is around to assist me in my kitchen or at the camp.

Not very long ago, I was confronted with a challenge. I had been given several pounds of fresh catfish fillets, some shrimp and some oysters, the last of the season. I decided it was time that I master the art of frying, so I talked to some of the best in the business.

My first encounter was with Bryan Bourque at Black's, the famous oyster house in Abbeville. Besides having wonderful cold, salty oysters on the half shell, Bryan serves some of the best fried seafood to pass my mouth.

While sitting in his tiny office watching the crowds come in for lunch, he gave me his secrets.

BLACK'S FRIED SEAFOOD

Fish

Always season the fish one day in advance of cooking. Season well with black, cayenne and white peppers, salt, and Louisiana Hot Sauce (his choice in hot sauces). He fries his fish only in a black iron pot in Lou-Ana Cottonseed oil heated to 375 degrees. He dredges the fish in Aunt Jemima fine white cornmeal right before frying. When the fish pops up to the surface, drain and serve immediately.

Shrimp

Season peeled and butterflied shrimp with black pepper and salt. Then pass in a batter made with eggs, milk (2 egg yolks, 2/3 cup milk) and seasoned with a little salt and pepper, then dredge in all-purpose flour, shake off excess batter and flour and deep fry in 375-degree cottonseed oil. Drain on paper towels, and serve immediately.

Oysters

Bourque drains them well before coating them in Aunt Jemima fine white cornmeal seasoned with salt and pepper. He did mention that some of his customers ask that the oysters be coated in flour rather than cornmeal, and he accommodates these requests.

My next call was to Don's Seafood and Steak House in downtown Lafayette. Randy Hamilton, the kitchen manager, parted with their secrets.

DON'S FRIED SEAFOOD

Fish

Season fish and fine corn meal with salt and cayenne pepper (he referred to the corn meal as cream meal since it's fine like flour) and fry at 350 degrees in peanut oil. Drain and serve immediately.

Shrimp

Dredge peeled and butterflied shrimp in flour, then in an egg and milk bath, then in a mixture (half and half) of bread crumbs and cracker meal seasoned with salt and pepper. Fry in 300-degree Lou-Ana cottonseed oil. Seems like the Lou-Ana oil is preferred because it's a local product and works well.

Oysters

Don's uses the same procedure as for fish.

My next inquiry was at Poorboy's Riverside Inn restaurant, a Lafayette legend now located near Broussard. Curtis Chaisson gave me his tips.

POORBOY'S RIVERSIDE FRIED SEAFOOD

Fish

Season fish with salt and cayenne pepper, then pass through an egg and water wash that is also seasoned with salt and pepper, then dredge in flour and breadcrumbs.

Shrimp

The shrimp are seasoned, then go through the egg and water wash, then dredged in flour before frying.

Oysters

Oysters should be well drained, then dredged in cornmeal, or in flour and bread crumbs. Curtis says their customers specify which they prefer. They use peanut oil and fry at 350 degrees for all their fried food.

General frying tips include:

1. Be sure oil is clean and at the desired temperature.
2. Do not fry in large batches; cook a few pieces at a time to prevent oil from dropping below the correct temperature.
3. Use enough oil to completely submerge the seafood.
4. Bread and/or batter the fish, oysters, or shrimp right before frying; otherwise, items will become gummy and hard.
5. Drain and serve fried foods immediately after cooking.

Aunt Lois and Mama put a couple of pods of peeled garlic in their pot of oil. They claim this prevents the oil from burning and keeps the oil clean while frying. Aunt Lois uses shortening and lately has begun adding a little of the butter-flavored shortening to her oil because she says it makes the fish, shrimp, and oysters come out a beautiful golden color.

Now that you know the secrets, you might want to experiment to see which method you prefer. With my new-found knowledge, I made a dish called Shrimp Benedict. You can also do it with oysters when they're in season. It's prepared like Eggs Benedict, but instead of eggs, fried seafood is used. Cut an English muffin in half, butter, and toast it. Then put broiled Canadian bacon or ham on the muffin slices, pile on the fried shrimp or oysters and top with hollandaise sauce. You might try adding a little Creole mustard to the hollandaise sauce for added zip.

Another popular vacation spot for us is Destin, Florida. Every year, I join a group of college buddies (all ladies) and head for the Emerald Coast. There, for a week, we sit on the beach, comb the shops, read until we're cross-eyed, and talk ourselves into a stupor. Our cottage reminds me of dorm life.

Bathing suits of every shape and size dangle from shower heads, door knobs, and deck railings. Makeup, suntan lotion, and magic formulas cover every inch of bathroom counter tops. Books on all subjects are piled on sofas, chairs, and beds.

We talk in whispers late into the night catching up on each other's lives. We do everything at our own pace. Some get up at the crack of dawn for tennis. Others take long walks on the beach. We give each other facials, manicures, and pedicures. There's no set time for meals or planned menus.

However, one night during the week, we don sundresses to show off our tans and dine at one of Destin's chic cafés, believing ourselves to be the cutest things around.

When the week is over and we have gone through the eternally long Creole goodbyes, we head to our respective homes.

It always seems too quiet in my car driving westward along the coast. To break the monotony and to give myself a sussie (a reward), I usually stop at a little seafood market in Biloxi to get some shrimp. The same fellow waits on me every year and knows to pack my purchase in a bag of ice so it will still be fresh when I get home.

After unpacking and shaking sand out of every article of clothing, I usually go into a small state of depression. I already miss the companionship of the previous days, and it's difficult to face a meal alone. That's why the shrimp treasure. I can always get out of depression by playing in the kitchen, rattling pots and pans. One experiment with my shrimp resulted in this recipe. Try it sometime when you're alone. It is fun to do, and I promise it will get you out of the doldrums.

BLEU CHEESE SHRIMP

Serves 1

1 pound jumbo shrimp, peeled and butterflied
1/4 teaspoon each of salt, cayenne pepper,
and garlic powder
several bacon strips, cut in half
3 ounces bleu cheese, softened to room temperature
1 egg, beaten and 1 cup milk, combined
3/4 cup yellow cornmeal
3/4 cup flour
oil for frying

Season shrimp with salt, cayenne, and garlic powder and let stand for a half hour. Then spoon a little of the cheese in the split of the shrimp, wrap the shrimp tightly with the bacon and secure with a toothpick. Dredge the shrimp in a mixture of cornmeal and flour, shake off the excess, then dip in egg and milk mixture, then again in cornmeal-flour mixture. In a deep pot, put enough cooking oil so that the shrimp can float and not touch the bottom. Be sure the oil is heated to 350 degrees. Fry the shrimp, two at a time, until shrimp pop up to the surface and are golden brown.

A simple potato dish goes well with the shrimp.

SCALLOPED POTATOES

Serves 4

2 large red potatoes, peeled and sliced thick
1-1/4 cup chicken broth
1/4 cup milk
salt and white pepper to taste
1/4 cup grated Romano cheese
1/4 cup grated sharp cheddar cheese

Simmer potatoes in chicken broth until potatoes get slightly tender. Drain and reserve broth. Place the potato slices in a small baking dish. Pour in the milk and sprinkle with salt and pepper. Add 3-4 tablespoons of broth, then top with the cheeses. Bake at 350 degrees for 30 minutes or until potatoes are tender.

I set myself a tray and sat under a whirring ceiling fan on the porch. I wondered what my friends were doing.

I thought about Judy who was with us on the trip. She loves to make sandwiches. My idea of a sandwich is a couple of slices of bologna and a dab of mayonnaise between two slices of white bread. On the other hand, Judy goes through great preparations for her sandwiches. Her enthusiasm and delight in making sandwiches can only be likened to someone writing a symphony.

She takes this business of making sandwiches very seriously. Watching her at work is like watching a symphony orchestra conductor. She wields her knife much like a conductor waves his baton. And she has to have just the right kinds of knives. One is for spreading on mayonnaise and mustard, another for skinning and slicing tomatoes, and still another is for slicing meats.

One year Judy, along with a couple of friends, joined me at the camp at Cypremort Point. The usual daily schedule was fishing and sunning on the pier until noon. Then we would retire to one air-conditioned room—the kitchen—for lunch and an hour or so of soap opera watching. Judy always volunteered to prepare sandwiches. While the rest of us huddled around the television with our glasses of lemonade, Judy set up her assembly line. It became a ritual. After a half hour, we would begin screaming and yelling for our sandwiches.

She coyly ignored us, and humming away she leisurely continued her work. Excuse me, her play.

Finally she delivered our plates and set before us sandwiches with as much aplomb as a waiter bearing Beef Wellington.

We all doubled over in giggles. How were we ever going to get them in our mouths? Her concoction consisted of mounds of baked ham, thinly sliced purple onions, chopped avocados, shredded lettuce, herbed mayonnaise, Creole mustard, and tomato on French bread.

But her all-time favorite is made with what she calls pepper beef. When she announces she's going to make pepper beef, you can see visions of lettuce and pickles dancing in her head.

Because Judy is as honest as the day is long, she is quick to tell you that her pepper beef recipe is not her own. She got it from her friend Dinky, who hails from north Louisiana but has assimilated into the Cajun culture quite well.

DINKY'S PEPPER BEEF

5-6 pounds boneless beef roast or
eye of the round, trimmed

First Day: (A friend of mine told me once that whenever she sees instructions that say "first day" she knows she's in trouble.)

Pepper Mix:
1/2 cup coarsely ground black pepper
1/2 cup poppy seeds

Place roast on flat surface. Rub pepper mix firmly into roast with the heel of your hand.

Marinade Sauce:
4 tablespoons catsup
1/2 teaspoon garlic powder
1/2 teaspoon onion powder

1 teaspoon paprika
1 cup soy sauce
3/4 cup white vinegar

Combine the above ingredients and pour over roast in a roasting pan. Refrigerate for 24 hours.

Second Day:
Remove the roast from the marinade and place on heavy aluminum foil. Pour marinade into a bowl and spoon about half of the marinade over the roast. Close foil tightly. Place in a baking pan and cook at 300 degrees for 2-1/2 to 3 hours. Do not overcook or the roast will crumble when sliced. When done, remove roast from foil and marinade and allow to cool. Reserve marinade.

Third Day: Slice the roast and pour the reserved marinade over the meat. Refrigerate and let stand for at least one day before serving.

During the first week of June, I begin stalking the stalls of the French Market in New Orleans, cruising slowly past the truck vendors and questioning neighborhood grocers. My mouth is primed for Creole tomatoes!

They're not real plentiful yet, and everybody wants to know, "What's the rush?" One year, I thought I was going to go into a panic when a friend called to say he had finally found some down in the Quarter.

I sped down there to be greeted by the sounds of machinery tearing up the street along the produce market. Parking was almost an impossibility, but I was willing to risk a parking ticket and the tow truck if I could get my hot little hands on some Creoles. I pulled alongside the broken up street and yelled to one of the workmen that I would only be a minute.

I dashed down the aisle shouting, "Who has some Creoles?"

I suppose the vendors have seen just about everything and were not shocked by my behavior. They didn't even look up or bat an eye. I guess they figured I was just another madwoman who had one too many Hurricanes at Pat O'Brien's.

Finally, after much waving and shouting, one gentleman looked up from his newspaper, pointed down the aisle, and said, "He has some, but not many."

I scooped up three baskets and dashed back to my car that was still sitting amid the rubble of the street. The workmen were not too happy with me, but what the heck, I had my Creole babies. On the way home, I held one in my hand, taking a whiff now and then. Oh, I couldn't wait to get home and eat them all.

The first thing I did was slice one, sprinkle it with salt and pepper, and savor every bite. Then I began to figure out how I could use them all up in one meal.

I had a Vidalia onion, so I sliced it along with two Creoles, poured some mint-flavored vinegar over them, and shoved the bowl into the refrigerator. While I had the fridge door open, I pondered what was available and at hand that could be used with my tomatoes. Ah, a luscious garden-grown zucchini, some sour cream, a pound of shrimp I had purchased earlier in the day, and various other tidbits. The first thing I came up with was:

SHRIMP AND CREOLES IN A MINUTE

Serves 2-4

1 pound shrimp, peeled and deveined
4 tablespoons butter
1 tablespoon cream sherry
1 tablespoon sour cream
1/4 cup chopped green onions
2 Creole tomatoes, peeled, seeded, and chopped
1 teaspoon soy sauce
pinch of dill weed
a couple of dashes of green hot sauce
salt to taste

In a heavy skillet, melt the butter and add shrimp. Gently sauté until shrimp turn pink. Raise the heat and add the sherry; stir for a minute or two. Reduce heat and add sour cream. Stir gently until the sour cream dissolves into the pan juices. Add green onions, tomatoes, soy sauce, dill weed, and green hot sauce. Cook for 2 or 3 minutes. Add salt to taste. I didn't pour it over pasta or rice. I devoured it with some hot French bread.

I also fixed something with the zucchini.

ZUCCHINI-TOMATO CASSEROLE

Serves 2-4

1 large onion, sliced
2 Creole tomatoes, sliced
1 medium size zucchini, sliced in rounds
3 tablespoons butter
1 tablespoon olive oil
salt and white pepper to taste
1/2 teaspoon basil
1/4 cup grated Romano cheese

In a large skillet, sauté onions and zucchini in butter and olive oil for 5 minutes or until onions just begin to wilt. Pour into a deep casserole dish and top with Creole tomatoes. Sprinkle with salt, pepper, and basil. Top with Romano cheese and heat in a 350-degree oven for 20 minutes.

Here's yet another Creole tomato recipe!

CREOLE TOMATO CASSEROLE

Makes approximately 4 quarts

4 tablespoons cooking oil
3 green onions, chopped
1 sweet green pepper, chopped
2 stalks celery, chopped
3 cloves garlic, minced
1 pound ground chuck or 1 pound shrimp,
peeled and deveined
6 medium Creole tomatoes, peeled, seeded, and chopped
1-1/2 teaspoons salt
1/2 teaspoon cayenne pepper
1 teaspoon basil
2 medium yellow onions, chopped
1 teaspoon chopped fresh mint (optional)
3-4 slices toasted white bread*

Heat oil in a large dutch oven. Sauté yellow onions, green pepper, celery, and garlic until they are transparent. Add the ground chuck and cook until browned. If you are using shrimp, do not add now or they will overcook. Add shrimp when dish is just about finished cooking. Add chopped tomatoes and seasonings; cook over medium low fire for 1 hour. Add green onions for the last 5 minutes. If you have some fresh mint in the garden, throw a few minced leaves in. Some people like fresh dill. Make this your very own dish.

*If you want to use this for a stuffing for tomatoes, sweet green peppers, or eggplant, add crumbled toast to absorb the juice.

Every summer, Mama is fortunate to receive from her gardener and farmer friends sacks of fresh corn, okra, and tomatoes. I remember her brewing up a pot of coffee for her visitors, and while they enjoyed the strong black liquid, they would talk about the year's crop. She herself had come from a farming family so she was well versed in agricultural "shop talk." After they left, she would stand in the middle of the kitchen and say, "O.K. everybody. Let's get to work and cook all of this to put in the freezer."

Nannan and Tante May, my two old aunts, were summoned from next door. Children who were old enough to wield a knife or spoon were kept home from swimming lessons, and before long the kitchen looked like a canning factory.

There were mountains of onions, bell pepper, and celery to be chopped. Corn had to be shucked and scraped. Okra had to be cut. (I used to pray I wouldn't be chosen to do okra because while I loved to eat it, I sure didn't like to fool with the slimy things.) Tomatoes had to be skinned and seeded.

Those who had been assigned corn would work at the old picnic table under the oak tree in the back yard. Before long, we had corn kernels on our faces and in our hair. Others, in the kitchen, would do their tasks sitting under the ceiling fan while they told stories of past canning days and gossiped about the neighbors. Soon we could smell the aromas of stewed okra and *maque-choux*. I can still see Mama at the stove showering the pots with salt, pepper, and other herbs and spices. She reminded me of the Wicked Witch of the West, standing there intent on her task with corn kernels still on the tip of her nose.

By the end of the day we had packed and labeled what seemed like hundreds of containers. The larder was stocked for the coming winter months.

While I'm not the recipient of sacks of corn and okra, I have my friendly roadside market to buy from. Early one morning while returning from my walk, I spied a sign announcing "fresh corn." In a few minutes I was the proud owner of a sack of corn and a basket of tomatoes. I couldn't wait to get home to put on a pot of corn soup.

Corn soup, you say, in the heat of the summer? My purpose for making soup is twofold. One, the aroma of the corn cooking brings back such wonderful memories and, two, I want something in the freezer to remind me of summer when the cold winter days are upon us.

CORN SOUP

Makes approximately 3 quarts

6 ears of corn, shucked and cleaned
1-1/2 quarts water
3 slices of bacon, cut into 1-inch squares
1/2 pound ham pieces, cut into 1/2 inch cubes
1 large onion, chopped
1 sweet green pepper, chopped
2 stalks celery, chopped
3 Creole tomatoes, peeled, seeded, and chopped
1 quart chicken broth
1 teaspoon basil
1 teaspoon tarragon
salt and pepper

Cut kernels from cob, scraping the cob to get the corn milk. Put cleaned cobs in 1-1/2 quarts of water and let simmer for 1 hour to make corn stock. In a large pot, cook bacon until it is brown but still soft. Add onions, green pepper, celery, and ham pieces and cook until vegetables become transparent. Add chopped tomatoes and cook for 10 minutes or until tomatoes begin to throw off juice. Add corn, 1 quart corn stock, and 1 quart chicken broth. If you have fresh basil and tarragon in your herb garden now is the time to use it. However, dried is alright, too. Season with salt and cayenne pepper. Simmer for 2 to 3 hours. Now you have a choice. You can have some for supper or you can put it in the freezer and serve it later in the year when everybody comes over to watch a football game.

Earthy Food

There's just something therapeutic about working in a garden, especially a vegetable garden. When we were children, Mama always had a big garden practically all year round. We had potatoes, okra, beans of all kinds, onions, tomatoes, cucumbers, eggplant, squash, and watermelons. Early in the morning and late in the afternoon, Mama would don her big straw hat, tie a scarf around her neck and with basket in hand, go "to check on the garden." She would hoe, weed, spray, and pick. It was her quiet time she said. Sometimes we were invited along. And, boy, it was great fun having her point out the blossoms, the new leaves, and the fruits of the harvest. You felt you could almost see things growing. The smell of the damp earth and the feel of the sun on your neck made you glad you were alive.

When the crops began coming in, Mama's kitchen along with Nannan's and Tante May's, was always busy with chopping, cooking and canning. Such wondrous smells! My sister and I would sit on the patio late in the afternoon, shelling peas and snapping beans. Edna would much rather have been frolicking with the dogs, but I loved it. I called it "mindless" work. It was a perfect time to "stare." I call it "staring" but it really is daydreaming and fantasizing. I still do it sometimes. I get a few pounds of beans at the supermarket, get a colander and sit on the patio in the late afternoon and snap beans. It clears the mind.

I had a glorious treat one time when I was visiting in Lafayette. Several of us were sitting around talking about the different kinds of peppers. Friends popped up and said they had several kinds (some I've never heard of) in their garden.

"What garden?" I asked.

Before I knew it, Ronnie was shoving me into his Jeep and we were off to see "THE GARDEN."

It was like stepping behind the garden wall into the magic land of all things good and green. There was that earthy smell I remember so well from my childhood. We ran up and down the garden rows. We were having a ball! We cuddled the squash and squeezed the melons. We dashed from row to row, then settled down and toured again at a leisurely pace. It was late in the afternoon, and a shower descended upon us, but we didn't care. With moisture on the tender leaves, the plants seemed to plump up as if they were preening. All we needed to complete our voyage into the magic kingdom was a rainbow!

With my arms loaded down with tomatoes, peppers, and zucchini, we headed to the kitchen.

That evening we had zucchini bread with dinner. It was so good we had it again the next morning for breakfast.

ZUCCHINI BREAD

Makes 2 loaves

3 tablespoons butter
3 eggs
1-1/4 cup oil
1-1/2 cup sugar
2 teaspoons vanilla
2 cups grated raw zucchini (unpeeled)
2 cups flour
2 teaspoons soda
1 teaspoon baking powder
1 teaspoon salt
2 teaspoons cinnamon
2 teaspoons cloves
2 teaspoons nutmeg
2 teaspoons ginger
1 cup chopped pecans or walnuts

Beat butter, eggs, oil, sugar, and vanilla until light and thick. Fold in zucchini. Sift together all dry ingredients and fold into the zucchini mixture. Add nuts. Pour into buttered loaf pans and bake at 350 degrees for approximately 1 hour and 15 minutes or until tester comes out clean.

Mama is a merliton freak. She likes them better than I like my Creole tomatoes. When it's time for them to come into season, she begins her hunt and usually finds someone to give or sell her a bagful.

If you're not familiar with merlitons, here's some information.

While they are sometimes referred to as vegetable pears, they are known by some other names. Merlitons are a member of the gourd family and are close kin to squash and cucumber. Their original home is Central America where they are called chayote. They are sometimes called cho-cho or mango squash and are found now on several other continents.

Some vegetable pears are pale green, while others are pearly white and can have smooth or prickly skin.

Being resourceful, the Creoles and Acadians have found numerous ways to prepare merlitons. I've always said that when in doubt, stuff 'em.

STUFFED MERLITONS

Serves 4

4 merlitons
1/2 stick butter or margarine
1 medium onion, minced
1 clove garlic, minced
1/2 cup chopped celery
salt and pepper to taste
1-1/2 cups cubed bread
1 egg
1 pound shrimp, cooked and peeled (or 1 pound chopped ham)
1/2 cup sharp cheddar cheese (optional)
buttered bread crumbs

Wash and cut the merlitons in half, lengthwise. Cover with cold water, bring to a boil and simmer about 30 minutes or until tender. Remove from water and allow to cool until they are easy to handle. Remove the seeds and discard. Carefully scoop out the pulp, leaving the skin intact. Set aside.

Chop the merliton pulp. Soak the bread in a little water or milk until soft, then squeeze out liquid. Melt butter or margarine and sauté the onion, garlic, and celery. Add the merliton pulp, soaked bread, egg and season with salt and pepper. Add the shrimp or ham and cheese, and any other seasonings you may wish. Cook for about 5 minutes. Remove from heat and carefully stuff the shells. Top with buttered bread crumbs and bake at 350 degrees for 20 minutes or until lightly browned.

My brother Bruce has an undying love for pickled merlitons. When Mama does these, she dares us to touch HIS jars and doesn't even offer us any.

"Those are for Brucie-Boy, so don't even think about taking any," she orders.

He's just as bad. He quickly packs them in his car and doesn't feel bad about being so selfish.

MERLITON PICKLES

6-8 merlitons, seeds removed and sliced like large French fries
2 large onions, sliced
2 large sweet green peppers, sliced like French fries
3-4 carrots, julienned
1 small head cauliflower, broken into flowerets
3-4 pods garlic, sliced
1/2 cup salt
1 scant cup sugar
1 tablespoon mustard seed
1 teaspoon tumeric
2-1/4 cups white vinegar
black, white, or red pepper to taste

In a large bowl, combine merlitons, onions, green peppers, carrots, and cauliflower. Cover with cold water and cracked or cubed ice. Let stand for 3 hours. Drain well. Boil remaining ingredients, then add vegetable mixture. Cook over low fire for 5 minutes. Pour into sterilized jars, filling jars with liquid.

They're wonderful to bring along on a picnic and I've been known to add them to a green salad, when I can snitch a few jars from Bruce's hoard.

When Mama is finished with her merlitons she starts on her figs. She watches her fig trees like a hawk and usually right around the Fourth of July, they're ready for picking.

She always says that you have to be on alert. If you don't get to them quickly, the birds will get them.

FIG PRESERVES, ACCORDING TO MAMA

First of all, the figs have to be washed. Fill the kitchen sink or a container large enough for the figs to be submerged. To this water add some salt or baking soda and with your hands, give them a good bath. Drain the water, then rinse again in clear water. Drain again. Then measure the figs, either in a large pot or measuring cup. One year, I had so many I had to use a large saucepan. Then it's "two of figs to one of sugar," for example, two quarts of figs and one quart of sugar. Place figs and sugar in a deep preserving kettle or pot and simmer. Stir gently as they begin to cook. Raise the heat when a syrup forms and allow it to come to a gentle rolling boil. Cook for 2 to 3 hours, or until "a foam begins to appear around the edges of the pot." Sterilize jars and caps. While the fig preserves are still hot, fill the jars, being careful to wipe the tops of the jars well to remove any syrup that may be on the area where the caps will screw on. Screw on the caps tightly and allow to cool to room temperature. Store in a cool place. Fig preserves are great with beignets, toast, biscuits, or cornbread, and they can be used to make fig cookies and cakes around Christmas time.

Holidays And Weekends

During the summer, every day seems like a holiday, and every weekend is like a vacation, but for some reason, I always look forward to the Fourth of July.

In my hometown of St. Martinville, there is still a parade and lots of family picnics. Old Glory waves from flag poles, balconies, and store fronts.

For many years, the Fourth of July was celebrated much like Christmas, save for the exchanging of gifts. Cousins came from up and down the bayou, and everyone gathered either at the camp at Catahoula Lake or in our backyard.

The feast lasted from morning until evening, with tables piled with barbecued chicken and brisket, fried chicken, salads of all kinds, and desserts for every one's sweet tooth.

One year, I was unable to make it to the family celebration, but wanting to keep up the tradition, I gathered some of my friends and hosted a glorious Fourth.

My houseguests began arriving a couple of days before the Fourth bearing bushel baskets of eggplant, tomatoes, okra, cucumbers, and squash. Out of their cars came an ice chest of strawberries, heavy cream, and champagne. Another friend emerged from her car with bags of sugar cookies and macaroons. Just when I thought my kitchen would burst at the seams, there came a pot of jumbo shrimp. Loaves of French bread poked out of picnic baskets. A watermelon was iced down on the deck. There was not a chance we would go hungry.

By the time everyone had gathered on that first day, we sounded like a bunch of chickens. We were all talking at once. We decorated the deck with tiny American flags and tried to determine where we would have our very own fireworks display. For a few days, we ate like kings.

On the big day, brisket topped the menu.

STUFFED BAKED BRISKET

Serves 10

First, make a marinade. This one is from Aunt Nan and can be used on chicken, rib racks, or thick pork chops.

2 cups liquid margarine
1 cup soy sauce
1 cup lemon juice
2 tablespoons garlic powder
2 tablespoons white or black pepper
1 tablespoon cayenne pepper
3 tablespoons ground basil leaves
1-1/2 tablespoons salt
1 tablespoon liquid smoke

This marinade can be made and stored in the refrigerator for several weeks. Mix all ingredients together and allow to stand at least 2 hours before using.

An 8-pound boneless brisket, trimmed
3/4 pound lean ground beef
3/4 pound lean ground pork
1 carrot, peeled and grated
5 large pitted green olives, chopped
1/2 teaspoon salt
1/2 teaspoon cayenne pepper
2 cloves garlic, minced

Have the butcher butterfly the brisket. Or, you can do it yourself using a sharp boning knife. Simply make a slit from end to end large enough in which to place the stuffing.

Make the stuffing by combining the ground meats, carrot, olives and seasonings, mixing well. Stuff the brisket with the mixture. Place the brisket in a pan with 2 cups of the brisket marinade and let stand for at least

4 hours. Baste occasionally with the marinade or turn the brisket over several times in the marinade. To bake, wrap the meat in heavy duty aluminum foil with the marinade and 1/2 cup water. Seal tightly and bake in a roasting pan at 275 degrees for 3-4 hours or until tender. After removing from oven, allow to cool slightly before slicing.

We also had these two wonderful desserts—

HUMMINGBIRD CAKE

3 cups flour
2 cups sugar
1 teaspoon salt
1 teaspoon baking soda
1 teaspoon cinnamon
3 eggs, beaten
1-1/2 cups oil
1-1/2 teaspoons vanilla
One 8-ounce can crushed pineapple, undrained
1 cup chopped pecans
2 cups chopped and mashed bananas

Combine dry ingredients in a large bowl. Add eggs and oil, stirring until moistened. Do not beat. Stir in vanilla, pineapple, pecans, and bananas. Spoon batter into 3 well-greased and floured 9-inch pans. Bake at 350 degrees for 25-30 minutes. Cool 10 minutes in pans. Then remove and cool completely on cake racks.

Frosting:
One 8-ounce package cream cheese, softened
1/2 cup butter
1 teaspoon vanilla
1 pound powdered sugar

Combine cream cheese and butter; cream together until smooth. Add sugar, beating until light and fluffy. Stir in vanilla. Spread the top of each layer slightly with frosting. Stack the layers and frost cake with remaining frosting. Top with crushed pecans.

CHOCOLATE CHEESECAKE

24 chocolate wafers
1/4 cup butter
1/4 teaspoon cinnamon
One 8-ounce package semi-sweet chocolate
1-1/2 pounds cream cheese
1 cup sugar
3 eggs
2 teaspoons cocoa
1 teaspoon vanilla
2 cups sour cream

Preheat oven to 350 degrees. Let cream cheese stand at room temperature to soften. Crush wafers in blender to make a little more than a cup. Melt butter and mix in crumbs and cinnamon. Press crumb mixture in bottom of 8-inch spring form pan. Then buckle sides and chill. Melt semi-sweet chocolate, stirring occasionally. In a large bowl beat the softened cream cheese until fluffy and smooth. Beat in sugar. Add eggs one at a time, beating well after each egg. Beat in melted chocolate, cocoa, and vanilla, blending thoroughly. Beat in sour cream. Pour all into spring-form pan. Bake 1 hour and 10 minutes. The cake will be a little runny but will become firm as it chills. Cool at room temperature, then chill for at least 5 hours; overnight would be better.

Summer weekends are perfect for fishing excursions.

One year I was invited on an adventure I will not soon forget. Here is my "fish story."

I've crossed it hundreds of times. I've walked along its banks and watched the ships ply its muddy waters. I've read Mark Twain's adventures of Huckleberry Finn. On a paddlewheeler I've travelled upriver and downriver, but I've never been to its beginning and only recently did I see where it ends. The Mississippi River is awesome.

As I travelled by car on the West Bank from Belle Chasse to Venice to meet up with friends, I noticed numerous roadside vendors stocked with Creole tomatoes, okra, bell peppers, corn, and eggplant. Citrus groves stretch from the road to the levees that contain the river. The land is flat and rich, and in a deep breath I smelled the combination of earth and water.

At Venice, where many Louisianians say the world comes to an end, I met my friends whose boat would take me on the final leg of my adventure.

Travelling through Tiger Pass, we encountered sleek Bertrams, armed with heavy duty rods and reels mounted like trophies on the stern. Shrimp boats draped with nets put-putted to their docks, and crew boats roared past on their way to rigs in the open water.

Our destination was the New Orleans Big Game Fishing Club, situated right beneath an old lighthouse and across from the now abandoned village of Port Eads in South Pass which was once the primary entrance from the Gulf of Mexico to the Mississippi River.

For two days we trolled the blue water of the Gulf, bringing in a Gulf tuna and a white marlin. Although the engines never stopped and the lines stayed in the water, we enjoyed brunch, lunch, and tea onboard. In the evenings, the Club crew served us hearty meals of red beans and rice, prime rib, meat loaf and mashed potatoes, rib eyes and baked potatoes, and for dessert, coconut pralines and

banana pudding. I wondered why we weren't having the catch of the sea until I learned that all edible fish had to be cleaned and packed for the anglers to take home for later use.

One evening as we sat on the porch in rocking chairs, with fiddler crabs scurrying across our feet, we watched a pink moon rise above the thick roseus, which are much like bamboo. The light from the lighthouse above our heads flashed its beacon to the incoming boats. People whispered in the darkness, and it was then I realized the magic of this great river.

On my way home I stopped and bought shrimp at Port Sulpher; tomatoes, corn, okra, and green peppers at Myrtle Grove. I had all the ingredients for a week of feasting. I pulled out a recipe given to me by an old co-worker at the *Times-Picayune* when we were on the staff of *Dixie*, the magazine section.

PANTRY SHELF PAELLA
Serves 4

1 chicken, about 3 pounds, quartered or cut into frying pieces
3 tablespoons butter or margarine
1 cup chopped onion
1 cup raw rice
1/4 cup tomato paste
2 cups water
1 pound peeled shrimp
1/4 teaspoon garlic powder or
1 pod of fresh garlic, minced
salt to taste
dash of cayenne
1 can of early peas (or beans of your choice)

Brown chicken in butter. Cook until almost done. Remove from pan. Add onion and rice. Cook 3 to 5 minutes. Combine tomato paste and water. Add to rice with shrimp, salt, garlic, and cayenne. Stir in peas or beans with their liquid. Return chicken to pot. Cover and cook for 25 minutes or until rice is done. Garnish with wedges of Creole tomatoes.

The following is a simple recipe for a light supper. Fresh shrimp is essential.

VERMOUTH SHRIMP

Serves 4

2 pounds peeled shrimp
4 tablespoons butter
2 tablespoons olive oil
1/2 teaspoon coarse ground black pepper
salt to taste
2 ounces dry vermouth
juice of 1/2 lemon
finely chopped chives or green onions to garnish

In a large skillet, heat the butter and olive oil. Add the shrimp and toss with the salt and black pepper. Cook until the shrimp turn pink, about 5 minutes. Add pepper, salt, vermouth, and lemon juice and toss again for about 1 minute. Serve on toast points or on pastry shells and garnish with chives or green onions.

To go along with the shrimp, serve thickly sliced Creole tomatoes layered with thin slices of green pepper, avocados, and onions sprinkled with crumbled bleu cheese and fresh dill. Garnish the salad platter with pickled okra.

The week after my fishing excursion, friends invited me on another boat trip to the Mississippi Gulf Coast. It was to be a leisurely weekend to include some easy fishing and island hopping, and of course good eating.

My friends do not consider ham sandwiches, boiled eggs, and soft drinks good shipboard fare.

They have developed a repertoire of divine boat food that can be easily prepared on a boat equipped with a two-burner stove and a refrigerator. These recipes are just as suitable for smaller boats equipped with only an ice chest and warm sunshine.

The common factors these dishes share is that they are easy to prepare—either before leaving the dock or on board—are tasty and imaginative, and above all, simple to serve and enjoy.

SOUTHERN SAUSAGE CAKE

Serves 8

This can be prepared well in advance in a disposable 9 x 9 x 2 baking tin and either frozen or refrigerated until time to be served. As it is best slightly warm or at "environmental" temperature, it is usually set in the sun for about 15 minutes. It can be just as good as a snack or an easy lunch. For an on board brunch, serve Bloody Marys and chilled white asparagus tips sprinkled with lemon juice.

1 pound hot bulk sausage
1/2 cup chopped onions
1 small chopped sweet red pepper
1 small chopped sweet green pepper
1/4 cup grated Parmesan cheese
1/2 cup grated jalapeño flavored cheese
1 egg, beaten
1/4 teaspoon Tabasco®
1-1/2 teaspoon combination of salt, black pepper, and garlic powder
2 cups biscuit mix
3/4 cup milk
1/4 cup sour cream

Brown vegetables and sausage, drain. Add cheeses, egg, and seasonings. Make batter of biscuit mix, milk, and sour cream. Gently stir sausage mixture into batter and put into greased baking tin. Bake at 350 degrees for 45 minutes and allow to cool to room temperature. At this point, it can be frozen for later use. To serve, cut into squares.

CEVICHE

Perfect for game fishermen, this recipe can be adapted to almost any firm seafood. In the Bahamas or southern Florida where lobster is plentiful, break the meat from the tails and cut into bite-sized pieces. Fresh tuna (from the ocean and not from the can) and fresh shrimp right from the net are also ideal. The beauty of this recipe is that it requires no cooking at all, and it is a delicious way to enjoy a "fresh catch." It does require time for marinating, approximately 6 to 8 hours, but that just builds the anticipation.

It can be served as an appetizer with crackers and is excellent as a summer salad with fresh greens. Everything can be prepared ahead of time and carried in an air-tight container. It is just as easy to prepare onboard.

3-5 pounds fresh firm seafood
juice of 10 limes (Bottled lime juice may be substituted.)
1 bunch green onions with tops, chopped
1/4 cup sliced jalapeños
3/4 cup good olive oil
1/4 cup lemon juice
fresh parsley
1/2 teaspoon oregano
1 teaspoon tarragon
salt and pepper to taste
1 cup sliced stewed tomatoes or fresh tomatoes, chopped

Mix all ingredients in container and marinate in the refrigerator for at least 6 hours. Mix every now and then to make sure everything marinates evenly.

When on a fishing tournament, plan ahead for a celebration dinner. After a few days of hard fishing, there is a certain ambiance associated with dining dockside amid all the activity going on around you.

Your neighbors will watch with envy as they chomp down their cold bologna sandwiches.

A nutritious but delicious menu could include the following:

ANTIPASTO SALAD

One 6-ounce jar of marinated artichokes
One 14-ounce can hearts of palm, drained and sliced
One 3-1/4-ounce can pitted ripe olives
1 small jar marinated mushrooms
1/2 cup sliced summer sausage

Mix, chill, and serve.

SUMMER SPAGHETTI

Prepare ahead of time and pack in air-tight plastic bags. Bring to room temperature before serving.

One 12-ounce bag spaghetti, cooked and drained
2 cans sliced stewed tomatoes
1 small onion, minced
1 tablespoon grated garlic
2 tablespoons chopped parsley
1/2 teaspoon basil
1/4 cup olive oil
a couple of dashes of tarragon vinegar

Mix all ingredients except pasta and refrigerate in air-tight containers. Before serving, bring pasta to room temperature, rinse in tepid water, drain and mix with sauce. Top with Parmesan cheese.

Make a fruit compote composed of canned mandarin slices with their juice, canned grapefruit slices that have been drained, and grated coconut. Chill and serve.

With some French pistolettes, you've got a meal fit for champions.

Too Hot To Move

It's just been too hot to move. It's absolutely stifling. Not only is it hot, but extremely muggy. It's like breathing soup when one walks out of an air-conditioned building. My eye glasses steam up when I get into my hot car.

Just about every August, I think of the term "the dog days of summer." There's not a breeze stirring under the oak trees late in the afternoon.

One August afternoon when I was living at Oak Alley Plantation, a transformer blew during a thunderstorm. A European guest staying in one of the cottages came to my door ranting and raving. In French he explained that he and his wife had been driving all afternoon in a rental car with no air-conditioning and had arrived to find his cabin in darkness. In my best South Louisiana French I explained that I had no control over lightning. And didn't they know about Acts of God? Didn't they have thunderstorms in France?

He didn't want to hear about Acts of God. He was hot, dripping with perspiration, and standing in a pool of water from the recent downpour.

I had to admit to myself I wasn't in such a good mood either. I had also been trying to keep cool, was worried about fifty pounds of shrimp that had been delivered that afternoon and stored in the cooler when the power went out. I had just returned from taking the shrimp out of the cooler, putting them in every ice chest I could find, and packing them in crushed ice. If the power went back on soon I would have to reverse the procedure. I eyed his poor wife in the car fanning herself with their road map. I had to act fast. I couldn't let them think that we had no Southern hospitality.

In my broken French I invited them in, offered them a glass of ice cold lemonade (I still had a couple of bags of ice in my ice chest) and inquired if they had swimsuits. They nodded and looked at each other quizzically.

In a minute, dressed in our suits, I led them out to the back yard where soon we were frolicking with my garden hose that has a wonderful nozzle with three speeds, much like a shower massager. I hung a large flashlight on a string in the trees and put a tape in my battery operated radio and hung it in the trees too.

The sun was setting and the electricity was still not back on so I figured I had to keep them entertained a while longer. I got out some old drink recipes, ran over to the shed and scooped up a couple of pounds of shrimp out of the ice chests and invited them to stay for dinner.

We were just going to have to make the best of it. While the shrimp were boiling (thank goodness the stove was gas), I made us a round of cool drinks.

GREEN COOLER

One 6-ounce can frozen limeade concentrate
One 6-ounce can filled with vodka
5 cans crushed ice

Put all ingredients in a blender for 15 seconds. Since we couldn't use the blender, I put everything in a big jar and shook it to the sounds of music.

STRAWBERRY EGG SHAKE

1/2 cup frozen strawberries (thawed) Well, that was no problem.
1 egg
1 tablespoon lemon juice
1 tablespoon sugar
1/2 cup crushed ice

Combine in a blender (again, I used my jar) and shake.

SCOTCH FROST

1-1/2 ounces Scotch whiskey
3/4 ounce lemon juice
1 cup crushed ice

Shake in a shaker (or blender) and serve.

RUM FLIP

1 teaspoon sugar
1-1/2 ounces light rum
1 egg
1/2 cup crushed ice

Shake or blend and serve sprinkled with nutmeg.

PINEAPPLE PASSION

One 13-1/2 ounce can pineapple chunks
1/2 cup light rum
1/4 cup lime juice
1 teaspoon grenadine
ice

I guess you're getting the idea now.

After the boiled shrimp cooled I served them in a tray covered with ice, and we peeled and dipped them in a sauce I had made with mayonnaise, Worcestershire, a little catsup, lemon juice, Tabasco,® and horseradish.

As we finished off our repast and licked our fingers, the electricity came back on. By the time I had walked them over to their cabin, it was cooling down. I gave them fans, the kind that are made of cardboard mounted on a stick, like the ones funeral homes used to give out at church, except these had Scarlett and Rhett faces on them.

I didn't see them the next morning at breakfast. Evidently they had gotten an early start. Hopefully, they had enjoyed the evening as much as I had.

It's not easy to be cool as a cucumber when the temperatures soar into the nineties and the humidity is knocking at 100 percent. The air is as thick as gumbo and just as hot. The only consolation I have when we hit the dog days of summer is that because of the moisture in the air, perhaps my skin won't wrinkle as quickly as our friends in Nevada. I knew it was some hot when, one day, as I sat in my car on the ferry crossing the Mississippi, my makeup dripped off my face and on to my freshly ironed white cotton dress.

Even the breeze off the river didn't help. As I exited the ferry, I stopped at my friendly vegetable vendor and quickly bought up his Creole tomatoes, cucumbers, and one big watermelon. With the car air-conditioner on full blast, I couldn't wait to get home to flop on an old canvas chair underneath a whirring ceiling fan. With a tall glass of lemonade garnished with fresh mint, I tried to get myself together before I entered my tiny kitchen. There was no way I could even think about turning on a burner on the stove, much less the oven. A nice cool supper was in order.

I am a fanatic for homemade MAYONNAISE. Anything with homemade mayonnaise is a treat. There are many ways to make the stuff. Some people still make it by hand, others do it in a minute in a blender or food processor. I happen to have one of those gadgets Mama called a mayonnaise machine. It's a jar, about quart-size, with a concave cap with a hole in the center through which a plunger fits. I've had the thing for years, and I don't know what will happen should I break it. This is the recipe for mayonnaise machine mayo:

MAYONNAISE

1 egg
2 tablespoons fresh lemon juice or vinegar
1 teaspoon dry mustard
1 teaspoon salt
1 teaspoon sugar
dash of black pepper or hot sauce
2 cups vegetable oil or olive oil

Chill the mayo machine and the egg, oil, and lemon juice, unmixed. Next, put the egg, lemon juice or vinegar, dry mustard, salt, sugar, and pepper into the jar. Screw the cap on with the plunger in place. Pour a little oil at a time into the concave cap. Beat with up and down motion while the oil runs down the stem of the plunger. Repeat steadily until all the oil is mixed thoroughly. Keep refrigerated until ready to use.

If you want to make mayonnaise by hand, use one raw egg yolk and one hard boiled egg, thoroughly blended, then add the dry mustard, salt, and sugar. Mix well. Slowly add a cup of oil, 1 tablespoon at a time, beating with a fork or wire whisk. Season with black or white pepper or a few dashes of hot sauce, according to taste.

BLENDER MAYONNAISE

1 whole egg and one raw egg yolk

Blend at high speed for 30 seconds. Add 1 teaspoon each of dry mustard, salt, and sugar. The sugar may be omitted if a tarter taste is desired. Add 1 to 1-1/2 cups salad oil or olive oil, in a steady stream while the blender is on a high speed. Finally season with black or white pepper or hot sauce and blend for just a few seconds more.

For different mayonnaise variations try these suggestions:

I. For cold fish, hard boiled eggs, or boiled shellfish, add to 1 cup of mayonnaise, 2 tablespoons anchovies, or 1 teaspoon shrimp or lobster paste, 1 tablespoon minced green onions, 1/2 teaspoon curry powder.

II. To 1 cup of mayonnaise, add 2 tablespoons each of chili sauce and chopped green onions, 2 teaspoons Worcestershire sauce, 2 peeled and seeded tomatoes, finely chopped, and a dash of dry sherry.

III. Try this on cold ham, pork, poultry, or game. To 1 cup of mayonnaise, add 2 tablespoons softened currant jelly, 1 tablespoon each of dry sherry, grated orange, and lemon rind. Use salt and pepper to taste.

IV. To 1 cup of mayonnaise, add 4 tablespoons whipped cream, 1 tablespoon Dijon or Creole mustard, and 2 tablespoons of vinegar.

V. To 2 cups of mayonnaise add 1/4 cup applesauce, 2 tablespoons horseradish, and 1 teaspoon grated lemon rind.

VI. On fresh fruit or green salads, mix together 2 cups of mayonnaise, and 1/2 cup each of sour cream and chopped walnuts or pecans, and 2 tablespoons of white wine or brandy.

VII. To 1 cup of mayonnaise, blend 1 cup of crumbled Roquefort or bleu cheese, 1/2 cup of sour cream, and 1 teaspoon of Tabasco.®

VIII. For cold beef and vegetables, add to 1 cup of mayonnaise pureed tomatoes, sliced pimientos, and 1/4 teaspoon minced garlic.

IX. I use the following as a dip for crudites of green beans, asparagus, broccoli, cauliflower, celery, and carrots: Add to a very thick mayonnaise, a puree of chervil, tarragon, watercress, and minced garlic. Dill is also good.

The variations are endless. Go ahead and make a couple of batches of mayonnaise and add your own herbs and spices.

For supper I had an assortment of cool vegetables with my mayonnaise and a sandwich, followed by a thick slice of cold watermelon.

I finally cooled down.

In August my garden is just about finished, and it's time to tear it down and plow it under. I'm going to miss it. I planted it in April and since then, I've visited it just about every day. I've weeded, watered, fertilized, sprayed, fought red ants, and run off birds and armadillos.

During May, June, and July, I've had tomatoes, cucumbers, eggplant, squash, zucchini, and fresh herbs. It's all coming to an end, and I'm sad.

With a basket in hand, I took a walk through the garden and gathered the last of the vegetables to prepare a memorial *ratatouille*.

Ratatouille is a wonderful melange of vegetables that can be a main course or a side dish. It shouldn't be overcooked. I like the vegetables to have a little crunch to them.

RATATOUILLE

Serves 4

2 tablespoons butter
1 tablespoon olive oil
1 cup coarsely chopped ripe tomatoes
2 cups sliced okra (optional)
1 cup coarsely chopped eggplant, peeled
1 cup chopped onions
1/2 cup chopped sweet green pepper
1/2 cup diced smoked ham (optional)
1/4 teaspoon black pepper
1/2 teaspoon salt
2-3 leaves fresh basil, finely minced

In a large skillet, sauté the onions and the diced ham in the butter and olive oil until the onions are well browned. Add the tomatoes, okra, eggplant, and green pepper and cook for 10 minutes, stirring frequently. Then add salt, black pepper and fresh basil and simmer for 10 minutes more. Adjust seasonings.

Another dish that is good for using up garden fresh vegetables is *caponata*, an Italian favorite usually served as an appetizer. With the addition of lean ground beef or ground veal, it can become an entree served *en casserole* with linguine or your choice of pasta.

CAPONATA

Serves 6

3 large eggplants, peeled and cubed
1/3 cup olive oil
2 large onions, chopped
3 ripe tomatoes, peeled and chopped
1/4 cup tomato paste
4 stalks celery, cut into 1-inch slices
5 cloves garlic, minced
1 cup pimiento stuffed green olives, sliced and drained
one 3-ounce jar of capers, drained
3 teaspoons salt
1/2 teaspoon black pepper
cayenne pepper to taste
1 pound ground beef or ground veal (optional)

In a large heavy pot, cook the eggplant in olive oil until eggplant wilts. Add onions, tomatoes, tomato paste, celery, garlic, salt, and black and cayenne peppers. Cook until mixture begins to bubble. Add the olives and capers. Cover and simmer for about 1 hour, stirring occasionally. Serve hot or cold with crackers or toasted slices of French or Italian bread. If you wish to add the ground meat, brown the meat in the olive oil before continuing with the recipe as described above. Prepare your pasta of choice, drain, and put into a buttered baking dish. Cover the pasta with the caponata, then sprinkle with grated Romano and Parmesan cheese and seasoned bread crumbs and bake at 350 degrees for 20 minutes before serving.

Mama found a treasure while cleaning the camp at Catahoula Lake in preparation for one of our Labor Day celebrations.

She was cleaning out closets and cabinets like a madwoman. Dust was flying, and she was mumbling to herself about how she hates this task. We tend to ignore her rumbling and mumbling, because once everything is gleaming, she's happy as a lark. She was attacking a small storage closet when she let out a yell. We all came running. I didn't know if she had hurt herself, found a snake (which she loves to do), a dead mouse, or if the mess was so great she had reached the end of her rope.

She had crawled into the closet on all fours, so we had to yank her out by her belt. She came flying out holding several black books we recognized as being her old travel diaries. Assured she was O.K., we left her sitting on the floor going through her little black books. We occasionally heard a chuckle, a sigh, and a few groans. We knew it was best to leave her alone with her memories.

A few days later, she handed a couple of the diaries over to me and told me to read them; she thought I might find her notes interesting.

The first one I chose to read was for the year 1969. I couldn't believe twenty years had passed so quickly as I began reading her notes.

Mama and Papa had just bought their first recreational vehicle, and the Toledo Bend Reservoir had evidently just been opened. They appeared to have burned up the roads between St. Martinville and the huge reservoir situated on the Texas-Louisiana border. I remembered that Papa was ecstatic when he learned that the large body of water had been well stocked with bass, perch, *sac-a-lait*, better known as white perch or crappie, and the other freshwater fish he so loved to catch.

Mama's notes indicate they tried just about every camp site, fishing spot, and park area. Paper clipped to the cover of her book are receipts from most of the places they stayed. Her observations include

descriptions of the area, names of people they met, a list of family and friends who joined them for weekends, and the food they cooked.

"Thursday, July 31. We're at Toledo Bend. Lois and children, Blackie and I, Brother and Pat and children are settled in. We've made ourselves a small compound with three camping trailers. All the children slept in ours. Mopped up fishing today and had fried fish, *courtbouillon*, potato salad and hamburgers. We were stuffed. No mosquitoes!"

"August 6. Multibreaker burnt. We were without lights, but still having fun."

On and on it went until June of 1970, because it was that summer we situated our camp at Catahoula on what Mama describes as, "Truly beautiful property. We are roughing it because as yet we have no electricity. We are anxious to really fix it up."

Her notes continued in much the same vain.

"Thursday, August 13. Fished all day. Caught 30 bream. No sac-a-lait. We cleaned them on the banks and then it began to pour down rain. A gang is coming to spend the day on Saturday. Hope to catch more fish."

A flood of memories came back to me. I remembered how Papa loved to fish in his beloved Catahoula Lake. He would spend hours in his small boat, paddling along the banks, stopping here and there, trying this and that for bait and coming back to the camp with a string of perch, green trout, and *sac-a-lait* trailing alongside the boat. He liked salt-water fishing, but freshwater was his forte.

And he was a mean cook. When he had a batch of catfish, he fried them to perfection. And while traditionally, *courtbouillon* is made with redfish, his version with bream and perch was a masterpiece. And sometimes, when he had an abundance of any kind of fish, he would poach them, pick off the meat and make a divine fish salad.

CATAHOULA LAKE FISH SALAD

Serves 6

12-14 bream or perch, scaled and cleaned
1 large onion, thickly sliced
6 cups water
2-ounce jigger of dry vermouth
2 lemons, sliced
1 teaspoon salt
1 teaspoon cayenne pepper

In a large pot, bring the water to a gentle rolling boil. Add the rest of the ingredients, including the fish. Cook for 10 to 15 minutes; remove the fish with a spatula or slotted spoon. Cool and pick off the meat from the bones. Then use your imagination. Papa mixed the fish with homemade mayonnaise, a little yellow mustard, chopped celery, chopped olives, sweet pickle relish, chopped hard-boiled eggs, minced parsley and minced green onions.

Serve your salad on a bed of lettuce. Papa liked to scoop his up with saltines. I prefer toast. Papa sprinkled his with hot sauce; I opt for a dash of peppered vinegar.

Since we're all looking for alternatives to redfish, you may want to try cooking your freshwater catches on the grill.

FISH IN A BAG

Serves 6

4-5-pound bass, dressed (or several small ones equalling 4-5 pounds)
1 sweet green pepper, julienned
1 large onion, thinly sliced
3 tablespoons butter or olive oil
1/4 teaspoon thyme

juice of one lemon
36-40 small shrimp, peeled and deveined
salt and cayenne pepper

On a large sheet of heavy aluminum foil, place the dressed bass. Fold the foil into a loose bag and before closing, lay all the other ingredients on top of the fish. Season with salt and pepper. Roll the bag closed and place on a moderately hot charcoal grill. Cook for 25-30 minutes. Fish should flake when prodded with a fork. This can also be done in a 400-degree oven. If you're not fighting cholesterol, you might also want to lay a couple of slices of bacon on top of the fish when cooking.

"Friday, September 11. We're at Cypremort Point, Vermilion Bay. No boat so fished off the wharf. Caught spade fish, small flounders and some croakers. Have enough for supper so we'll probably bake a few, fry a few and stuff a few."

And that's another story.

Summertime seems to go by quicker and quicker each year. Why, it seems I just returned from my four-day Memorial Day get-away. And although the Fourth of July weekend was a washout, I swear it was only yesterday. Can it be almost two months since, determined to spend the holiday at the camp, we withstood rain, rising water, and mud-caked children?

It was a holiday that I will long remember despite the hardships. There were twenty of us trying to keep things festive despite the dampening weather. We couldn't put the boats in the water because our wharves were under water. Children were underfoot simply because there wasn't anywhere for them to play except the rain-filled ditches. And we adults spent most of our time under the tin-roofed patio reminiscing about more pleasant fair-weather holidays.

But now we have Labor Day weekend fast approaching, and already Mama has sent word out that we are all expected again at the camp for our last full-fledged gathering before the camp is closed for the season. She's making her menu list for the three-day extravaganza and has given us each assignments.

Aunt Lois is bringing fixings for a barbecue. My Baby Brother Bruce has been hoarding fish from his fishing expeditions so we can have a big *courtbouillon*. A couple of the cousins have volunteered to make a big pot of jambalaya, and Mama has already put aside the allotment of *macque choux*, smothered okra, and eggplant dressing in the freezer. My sister and I are in charge of sweets and desserts. Knowing how tiny Mama's kitchen at the camp is and how many mouths there are to fill, I have already placed my order at the bakery for assorted cookies, fudge cakes, and eclairs.

I will also take a few homemade treats that are both cool and easy to prepare.

CRAZY CAKE

1-1/2 cups unsifted flour
1 cup sugar
3 tablespoons cocoa
1 teaspoon salt
1 teaspoon vanilla
1 teaspoon vinegar
6 tablespoons vegetable oil
1 cup water

Sift dry ingredients together into an ungreased 8 x 8 pan. Make 3 wells in the flour mixture. In one well, add 1 teaspoon vanilla. In the second well, put 1 tablespoon vinegar and in the third, 6 tablespoons oil. Pour 1 cup of water over the mixture and with a fork, blend all together. Bake at 350 degrees for 30 minutes. Put in airtight container and chill in the refrigerator. When serving top with whipped cream or a dab of cream cheese frosting.

For a new twist on an old favorite, bring along the fixings for Bananas Foster—brown sugar, butter, ripe bananas, cinnamon, banana liqueur, and rum. Heat the butter and add the brown sugar and cinnamon and blend together. Add sliced bananas, then pour in banana liqueur and rum. This can all be easily done in a large skillet and don't worry about trying to flame the liqueur and rum like they do at Brennan's. Make a big batch if you have a crowd. Then serve the warm bananas over pound cake.

POUND CAKE

A modification of the original pound cake in which a pound of each ingredient was used.

1-3/4 cups all-purpose flour
1 cup sugar
2 teaspoons baking powder
1 teaspoon salt
1/3 cup shortening or butter
1 teaspoon vanilla
5 egg yolks, unbeaten
3/4 cup milk

Heat oven to 350 degrees. Grease 9 x 5 x 3 loaf pan. Mix all dry ingredients together. Add shortening or butter, vanilla, egg yolks, and 1/2 cup of milk. Using an electric mixer, beat for 2 minutes on medium speed. Scrape sides and bottom of bowl constantly while mixing. Add rest of milk and beat 2 more minutes. Spoon batter into pan. Bake 60-70 minutes. Cool, then remove from pan.

I prefer pound cake a day old or even a bit stale. Then I cut it into slices and toast for a minute or so in the oven, then spoon the Bananas Foster over it. Of course, a scoop of vanilla ice cream on top makes it a true delight.

This next recipe is an old childhood favorite. My Nannan used to make a batch of this and put it into ice trays, then pop a couple of cubes out when we came to her back porch screen door begging for a treat.

FROZEN CREAM CHEESE

First of all, you can't use a product like regular cream cheese, it must be the old Creole cream cheese. It's available in some supermarkets. My method of making the frozen cream cheese is akin to that of the late Leon Soniat, a former *Times-Picayune* food columnist.

5 cartons of Creole cream cheese
1 quart of milk
1 quart of whipping cream
3 cups sugar
3 tablespoons vanilla

Mash the cream cheese through a colander to remove any lumps. Add milk, whipping cream, and sugar; mix thoroughly. Add the vanilla and stir. Freeze in ice trays or other container.

Nannan used to add chopped strawberries or crushed pineapple to hers. Use your imagination.

Labor Day weekend finds us all gathered at the camp for yet another festive feast.

Fall

Deep in the swamps and marshlands and along the bayous of south Louisiana, the leaves of bald cypress trees turn an earthy sienna and drop into murky waters. Spindly pecan trees that flourish in the humid flatlands begin to shed brittle leaves. Only the giant graceful live oaks retain most of their foliage while showering the earth with thousands of acorns. Hunters, fishermen, and trappers prepare camps for the coming season, clean and oil guns, ready their decoys, and work on boats. Flocks of water fowl fly overhead as they find their way from Canada to the warmer waters of Louisiana.

Here in the Deep South, where most Northerners believe there is little change between seasons, autumn is creeping on la prairie tremblante, along the banks of the bayous that reach out like many fingers toward the Gulf of Mexico and in the great Atchafalaya Basin surrounded by its miles and miles of levee.

The Hunt: A Male Rite of Passage

The millions of acres of marshland that comprise the coastline of Louisiana appear monotonous at first glance. The swaying marsh grass interspersed with serene water pools gives an illusion of sameness. The landscape is not broken by trees or solid ground. It's neither land nor sea, but a combination of both. An occasional whiff of sea salt and air wafts through as a gentle wind blows from the Gulf.

This seemingly desolate area lying between the swamps and the Gulf is actually a place of teeming wildlife—fish, crustaceans, and water fowl.

Long before the first brisk north wind of a cold front moves into these precious lowlands, avid hunters are preparing for the coming hunting season. Overhead, flocks of green-winged teal, mallards, and pintails can be seen flying in loose V formations. By the time the cold winter winds blow through south Louisiana, the ducks will be joined by honking blue and snow geese swooping down on the feeding grounds of the marsh.

To most men of south Louisiana, hunting is an important ritual of manhood. Even those who are not passionate about hunting will often find themselves part of a group that heads to the camp on any given Friday afternoon during the hunting season.

I have often wondered what is so magical about this time spent together in usually cold and primitive quarters. The lives of my father and brothers revolved around the duck camp. There seems to be a combination of special camaraderie and of sharing the spoils of the hunt in their somewhat makeshift kitchens. I have heard countless stories about the camp. The tales of the hunt and of the food prepared and eaten there are of equal importance. Gather together a group of men and listen to them tell their stories. It's entertainment of the highest form.

A young man once tried to explain to me his experience and I offer you his narrative.

There are several rites of passage that every young man in south Louisiana must go through en route to manhood. Eating raw oysters, killing a buck, and mastering the art of frogging are, of course, all part of that ritualistic experience. There is one ritual, however, that many consider to be the most sacred of all—cooking supper for a group of men at the camp. Unlike making love for the first time, if a south Louisiana boy fails this test, he may never be asked to do it again.

First, it must be understood that people in south Louisiana, myself included, tend to associate everything with food.

For example, I recently heard a television anchorman ask his audience if they could remember what happened on November 22, 1963. My answer immediately sprang to mind: that was the day that my Aunt Tootie made the best turtle sauce piquante that I've ever tasted. I was humbled when I heard the anchorman continue. It seems that November 22, 1963 was the day President John F. Kennedy was assassinated. I was a mere youngster then, so I forgave myself.

In case you haven't caught on to the food association game, let me further explain.

One day, a friend of mine came to my office to ask if I wanted to go goose hunting with him at "Shot's" camp in Lake Arthur. I was excited about the proposition, but rather than envisioning graceful flights of specks and snows, I wondered what we would eat the night before the hunt.

Being a stickler for details, I began to plan a menu.

First, I scanned my brain for a reference point. Like a newly-made slab of hogshead cheese, a thought congealed in my mind. I remembered back to that cold December night when I crossed the sacred bridge that separated men from boys. It was

at "Goat" Romero's camp in Kaplan. The men had gone out for an afternoon hunt leaving me, a fifteen-year-old boy, with two feathered French ducks with which to make supper. I poked around the ice chests and pantry searching for familiar ingredients to make a gumbo. I found all of the ingredients I needed to make the following:

DUCK, OYSTER, AND ANDOUILLE GUMBO

Serves 6

2 ducks, which I cleaned and plucked
salt, black pepper, and red pepper
1-1/2 cups flour
1-1/2 cups vegetable oil
3 sweet green peppers, chopped
3 onions, chopped
6 cups of hot water or chicken stock (approximately)
2-1/2 pounds andouille sausage, sliced into 1/4-inch pieces
2 dozen oysters and their liquor
1 bunch green onion tops, chopped

Cut up the ducks (as you would cut up a chicken for frying) and season well with salt, black pepper, and red pepper. Brown them in a small amount of oil in a big black iron pot, drain, and set aside. In the same iron pot, make a dark roux with the flour and oil. Once the roux is just the right nutty-brown color, add the onions and sweet green peppers and stir until they are wilted. Return the browned ducks to the mixture and slowly add enough hot water or chicken stock to cover the ducks. Add the sliced andouille sausage and cook on a very low fire for 3 hours. The oysters, their liquor, and onion tops should be added immediately before serving.

Before we left for the hunt, a reliable source told me that a meal is incomplete unless it includes at least four starches. With this in mind, I accompanied my duck, oyster, and andouille gumbo with rice, potato salad, hot crusty French bread, and baked sweet potatoes. For those of you who don't adhere to the four-starch philosophy, the potato salad can be omitted.

After the last bites of food were washed down with hearty burgundy (I didn't have any then, but I now recommend a Louis Jadot Macon Villages Beaujolais), I knew that the meal was a success and that I had entered the bonds of manhood, for Mr. "Goat" said out loud, "Leon, tu n'est pas un petit bébé. Tu es un grand homme maintenant."

❦

Oh, the sweet joys of arriving at manhood.

The young man's story did give me a clue to the mystery of the hunt. Not long after he told me his vignette, I woke one morning just as the fog was clearing from the nearby marsh. In the distance I could see figures clad in various types of garb, including but not limited to tattered jeans, boots of rubber and canvas, and caps and hats of all colors and design. There was a profusion of camouflage jackets and vests.

I ventured forth to investigate. I stepped lightly on the fallen brown weeds and approached the group. Calling out a warm greeting, I realized, when their surprised faces turned my way, that I was intruding on the ritualistic building of duck blinds.

They waved shyly and without a word, I retraced my steps. I felt like I had disturbed sacred ground.

On my walk home, I thought about these goings-on. These lusty men haul out mud boats, air and clean camps, and stock them with supplies. The old black iron pots used for cooking are oiled down. The various assortment of eating utensils such as plates, mugs, and trays—many of which sport a hunting scene, the face of a black lab, or at least a duck in flight—are dusted off.

Decoys are retrieved from canvas sacks, and then they are tied, weighted, and marked with the owner's identification. Shotguns are cleaned and oiled and a small fortune is spent on ammunition—shells are the preferred word, I think.

This sounds like a lot of work, but the guys seem to love it. The truth is, they probably love getting ready for the hunt more than the actual hunt. I will never understand how it could be fun to get up before dawn in an ice cold camp, walk through the wind, rain, and mud, then sit in a wet duck blind. I know for a fact that I would go into deep depression if, after doing all of the above, I wound up never getting off a shot, much less not bringing in a bird. Yet hordes of men go through this week after week during hunting season.

And if I've figured correctly, this is no cheap hobby. There's the gear, the guns, shells, licenses, decoys, the cost of the lease for the hunting land, boats, food and drink, and possible money losses at the card table. I'll bet many women have figured that the money spent on hunting season could very well pay for a full-length mink coat, a diamond necklace, or at least a trip to the Bahamas.

Of course, there is the enjoyment of the spoils of the hunt. I am one of the first to say there's nothing better than a roasted duck dinner or a good sausage and goose gumbo.

Because I come from a family of hunters I thought I'd had birds cooked just about every way possible until recently. An old neighbor who has always shared his catches from the sea—speckled trout, crabs, shrimp, flounder—stopped by the day after hunting season closed with a real treat.

When I opened the door to his grinning face, he was holding up a carefully wrapped package. I gleefully asked him what might be in this beautifully wrapped brown paper bag. With a great flourish he opened the bag and there between layers of wax paper were six fine duck breasts. I could see he had cut the breasts away from the bone as skillfully as a surgeon. In a minute he had taken over the kitchen, and I was directed to sit on a stool in the corner while he prepared our evening treat.

GRILLED DUCK BREASTS

Serves 2

6 duck breasts, removed from the bone and skinned
8 tablespoons butter
1 tablespoon Worcestershire sauce
1 garlic clove, finely minced
3/4 cup thinly sliced fresh mushrooms
salt, freshly ground black pepper, and cayenne pepper
6 strips of bacon

Melt the butter in a saucepan and add the Worcestershire sauce, garlic, and mushrooms; cook until mushrooms become slightly soft. Remove from heat. Light a fire in the barbecue pit and allow the coals to get glowing red hot. While you're waiting, rub the duck breasts well with salt, black pepper, and cayenne. Carefully wrap each breast with a strip of bacon, securing it with toothpicks. Let them stand at room temperature. You might want to take this time to fix a green salad with a creamy spicy dressing and some wild rice cooked with a handful of chopped roasted pecans. When the coals are ready, grill the breasts quickly, 3 to 4 minutes on each side if you like them juicy and with a little red in the meat; longer if you prefer your meat well done. Baste with the butter sauce. To serve, place the breasts on toasted slices of bread and pour the remaining butter and mushroom sauce over each breast. You've never tasted better!

While my friend and I savored our dinner and watched the coals die down, I reminisced about my father's craze for hunting.

During the season, my father was a madman. I remember many times when Papa arrived at home, rushing from his newspaper office, crashing through the kitchen door as though a herd of wild horses were after him, shouting with glee, "A cold front is on the way. Perfect duck hunting weather!"

We would all dash off in different directions. Papa would go directly to the hall closet for his camp suitcase. Mama would throw down mothball-scented blankets kept in an overhead storage closet. My brothers would gather shotguns and shells from the gun cabinet, and my sister and I would stuff the gear into the tattered "grip" (Louisiana for suitcase). By then, Papa was pulling on his longjohns with one hand and stuffing shotgun shells into his hunting jacket with the other.

In five minutes he was climbing into his old red pickup truck and with a grin on his face shouted, "I'll see ya'll when I see ya'll!"

That meant not to look for him until either he had shot his limit or the weather had turned into one of those clear bluebird days so common after a cold front moves through.

It was quiet in the kitchen after he departed. Mama would sigh and murmur, "Guess we'll be eating ducks and geese for the next few months."

It was a yearly ritual that announced hunting season was at its peak. I was always happy because I like few things better than the aroma of roasting ducks. Mama has a foolproof recipe. It's simple and can be cooked along with *topinambours*, otherwise known as Jerusalem artichokes, ground artichokes, or sun chokes. Her roast duck dinner usually includes potatoes of some kind and a Louisiana version of WALDORF SALAD. GATEAU DE SIROP, a syrup cake, is a must for dessert. It's a dinner she usually reserves for Sunday afternoon. While she performs her magic at the stove, family and friends enjoy a cold beer or chilled wine and a few bites of boudin—a Cajun sausage made with ground pork, rice, and spices, such as cayenne pepper, green onions, and parsley.

RHENA'S ROAST DUCK

Serves 4

4 teal ducks or 2 mallard or pintail ducks
3 large cloves of garlic, peeled and slivered
2 large sweet green peppers, coarsely chopped
2 large yellow onions, coarsely chopped
1/2 cup sauterne wine or dry sherry
flour
4 strips thickly sliced bacon
1 cup chicken broth or water
8 ounces of fresh mushrooms, sliced (optional)
salt and cayenne pepper to taste
1 pound *topinambours* (Jerusalem artichokes), skinned

The night before you want to cook the ducks, make slits in the duck breasts with a sharp knife. Insert the slivers of garlic into the slits. Rub the outside and the cavities of the ducks with plenty of salt and cayenne pepper. Don't be afraid to use a lot because game needs a liberal amount. Stuff the cavities with a mixture of the chopped green peppers and onions. Place the birds in a deep bowl or pan and add any remaining peppers and onions. Pour in the sauterne or dry sherry. Cover and refrigerate overnight. The next day, drain and reserve the marinade. Dust each duck liberally with flour and set aside. Cook the bacon in a large iron pot until crisp. Drain bacon on paper towels, set aside. Over medium heat, brown the birds in the bacon grease, turning often until they are evenly browned. Add 1 cup of water or chicken broth and cook for 10 minutes.

Add the reserved marinade (wine, peppers, and onions), cover, and bake in the oven at 350 degrees for 1 to 1-1/2 hours or until the ducks are tender. Baste occasionally with pan drippings and add more water or chicken broth if gravy becomes too dry. Add the *topinambours* and mushrooms, cover, and cook 30 minutes more or until sun chokes become tender when pierced with a fork.

CAJUN WALDORF SALAD

Serves 4

1 Granny Smith apple, cored and chopped, skin on
2 winesap apples, cored and chopped, skin on
1 cup seedless raisins
1/2 cup roasted and chopped pecans
1 tablespoon lemon juice
mayonnaise, just enough to lightly coat all ingredients.

Toss all ingredients together, add the mayonnaise, and serve on bed of shredded lettuce leaves.

GATEAU DE SIROP

1 large egg
1 cup cane syrup
2 cups flour
2 tablespoons butter
1 teaspoon baking soda
1 cup boiling water
1 cup pecan halves

Beat the egg, add syrup and flour. Mix well. Preheat oven to 350 degrees. Put the butter into a 7 x 11 x 2 pan; melt the butter in the oven. Remove pan from oven when the butter is melted and shake the pan to spread the butter evenly. Add soda to boiling water and then add to cake batter. Be sure to hold the cup of water over the cake batter bowl when the soda is added because it will bubble over. Pour the batter in the pan, cover the top of the mixture with pecan halves, and bake for 20 minutes. Serve warm with whipped cream.

By the end of the hunting season, which lasts into January, the freezer will be well-stocked with ducks and geese for gumbos, jambalayas, and who knows what else.

🍁

Ducks and geese are not the only flying fowl that please the palates of south Louisiana. During early fall, the highways between south Louisiana and south Texas are well-travelled as sportsmen head for annual white wing dove hunts along the Texas-Mexico border. They return with enough doves to last throughout the winter.

Each year, I anxiously wait for someone to share his cache. One year I almost waited in vain, but I did not go without, as I was lucky enough to be invited to dinner by an old beau. Since we had not seen one another in more than ten years, we had a lot of ground to cover and what better way, he said, than to really get into the nitty-gritty over dinner. It wasn't until we were about to end our telephone conversation and he began giving me directions to his home in Baton Rouge that I realized it was to be dinner *chez nous*, or at his house.

Because he was a single parent with a teenager at the time, he thought it easier (for him anyway) for me to go there.

I headed for Baton Rouge in the middle of Hurricane Juan and, while driving through wind and rain, I had visions of being drafted to cook dinner for the bachelor father and his son. When I arrived, they announced they had defrosted a dozen doves. Well, at least they had gotten that far. And before I could get out of my rain gear, they were propelling me to the car saying that we had to go to the grocery store to get the rest of the dinner fixings.

Oh, oh, I thought. I had done my own grocery shopping earlier that day and didn't think I could bear doing it all over again. But these guys had their act together. They told me that all I had to do was push the cart. To watch these two shop was

entertainment in itself. As I headed down the produce aisle they stood back and shook their heads with grins on their faces as if to say, "Poor thing just does it all wrong."

Back at the ranch, I watched them put everything away, something I hate to do. But father and son made a game of it. They played football with the groceries as they put things away. I was beginning to think we women just have the wrong attitude about domestic duties.

With that task out of the way, I was told to just sit back and relax. That sounded too wonderful to be true. My host handed me a drink, pulled out a chair, and I watched him as he chopped vegetables for salad and the dove dish. His son carved out a jack-o-lantern. The roles seemed reversed, but I revelled in this domestic scene. They even set the table. I was getting a bit restless so I volunteered to fix CORN PUDDING. I just had to show them that I, too, knew something about a kitchen.

I thought I had tasted these birds prepared in every possible manner, but my friend Rick pulled off the best dove dish I've ever had.

RICK'S DOVES

Serves 4

breasts of 1 dozen doves (hopefully without any shot still in)
6 tablespoons margarine or butter
3 tablespoons flour
2-1/2 cups chicken broth plus 2 cups water
1 bunch green onions, chopped
1 sweet green pepper, chopped
3 cloves garlic, thinly sliced
4 tablespoons Worcestershire sauce
2 teaspoons salt
1 teaspoon Cajun seasonings (He had his own special blend, but there are several brands available in most markets.)

1 tablespoon thyme leaves
1 teaspoon Chinese red pepper (or cayenne pepper)
2 bay leaves
1/2 cup cream sherry
1 pound whole fresh mushrooms

In a black iron pot, brown the dove breasts in the butter or margarine. Remove breasts. Add flour and blend well with butter or margarine. Add the chicken broth and water; bring to a rolling boil and cook until mixture becomes thick enough to coat a wooden spoon. Add the green onions, sweet green pepper, and garlic; cook for 5 minutes or until "it begins to smell good" (his words). Add the Worcestershire sauce, salt, Cajun seasonings, thyme leaves, red pepper, bay leaves, dove breasts, and sherry, lower the fire, and cover. Simmer for 40 to 50 minutes or until breasts become fork tender. The fire has to be high enough so that the gravy makes slow, tiny bubbles (again, his words). Then add the whole mushrooms, a dash more sherry, and cook for another 10 minutes.

While the guys dished up the doves, I pulled the corn pudding out of the oven.

GINJA'S CORN PUDDING

Serves 6

2 cups corn (canned or frozen)
8 tablespoons butter
3 tablespoons flour
2 tablespoons sugar
2 eggs
1 cup milk
salt and pepper to taste
a couple of dashes of Tabasco®
paprika

Melt the butter in a saucepan and add the corn. Cook for 10 minutes. Pour the cooked corn mixture into a blender and add the rest of the ingredients except for the paprika. Blend at medium speed for 30 seconds. Pour mixture into a 9 x 12 baking pan. Place the pan into a larger pan containing about 1 inch of water. Bake at 350 degrees for 45 minutes or until pudding sets. Remove and sprinkle the top of the pudding with paprika.

🍁

I also have a great fondness for quail. In fact, while I'm not so entranced about duck hunting, I think quail hunting is quite civilized. Watching bird dogs with their master "flushing quail" is fascinating. I had occasion, while living and working at Oak Alley Plantation, to become acquainted with yet another aspect of quail.

After I moved into my small cottage on the plantation grounds, I noticed that every afternoon, a pickup truck went slowly past my house on the gravel road. It stopped a few hundred feet away at a fenced-in compound consisting of several tin buildings. Out of the truck would emerge one, sometimes two or three ruggedly handsome men. For a week or so, I watched them from my screened front porch. They would reach into an ice chest in the back of the pickup and pull out ice cold cans of beer. I thought the scene would have made a great beer commercial.

I watched the dark-haired men unlatch the gate and head for the buildings. And for about an hour or so, they would work quietly, sometimes talking good-naturedly with one another. Occasionally I'd hear a great roar of laughter.

One day I couldn't stand it, I had to investigate. I carried a few cold beers with me as a friendly gesture. I tapped at the gate and called out a greeting. Three tanned, brown-eyed faces peeped out from behind one of the doors and beckoned me to come in.

I walked into a warm room where hundreds, no thousands, of tiny, tiny birds were contained in a low-fenced-in pen. My new friends, the Rodrigues, with great sweeps of their arms, introduced me to their newly hatched quail.

What a sight! The chirping chicks were so little, I could hold ten or so in my cupped hands. I leaned against the tin wall and watched these men gently

checking the feeders, the heat lamps, and watering troughs. I learned this was a hobby of the father and his two sons. They are all bird hunters, so naturally needed to work their dogs, and what better way than to have your own source of birds. They also supplied other hunters in Louisiana and Mississippi with birds with which to work their dogs.

Of course, too, when the quail are grown, the Rodrigues cleaned a mess of quail to bring home for supper. I was the lucky recipient of a few dozen several months later, and one of the sons gave me his recipe for preparing them.

KEITH'S SMOTHERED QUAIL

Serves 4

1 dozen quail, dressed
salt, cayenne pepper, and black pepper—
to taste. (Be generous.)
6 tablespoons butter or vegetable oil
1-1/2 cups chicken broth or water
3 onions, chopped

Season the quail well with the salt, cayenne, and black pepper. Brown them quickly in butter or cooking oil in a large iron pot. Add the water or chicken broth and onions. Stir, then cover and simmer for 2 to 3 hours. More broth or water may be added if the gravy becomes too dry.

Keith suggested serving the quail over rice, and I suggest having lots of hot French bread and cold beer to wash it all down.

You probably won't find too many south Louisianians who fry their quail, preferring to have a good gravy made by smothering the birds, but a friend of mine from north Louisiana served fried quail for breakfast once and when I have a few extra birds, I follow his recipe.

FRIED QUAIL

Serves 2

4 quail, dressed
4 strips bacon
2 cups milk
1/3 cup flour
1 cup cornmeal
1 teaspoon salt
1/4 teaspoon black pepper
1/4 teaspoon cayenne pepper
oil for deep frying

Wrap the birds with the bacon and secure with toothpicks. Soak the birds in milk for a couple of hours in the refrigerator. Remove from the milk and gently pat dry. Combine the flour with the cornmeal seasoned with salt, black pepper, and cayenne pepper.

Coat the quail with the dry mixture and deep fry until golden brown. Serve them on a cold winter's morning with biscuits, cane syrup, and hash brown potatoes spiced up with a few green onions. You've got a winner.

Fried quail are wonderful for breakfast, but they are also great when served for dinner and accompanied by special side dishes. I particularly like wild rice with birds and game. One of the best recipes I've ever tried was given to me by an excellent cook and a dear friend, Dick Torres. A whole head of cauliflower, baked with cheese, is a rich complement to the wild rice.

WILD RICE TORRES

Serves 8

2 boxes of wild rice mix, cooked according to package directions
1 pound pork breakfast sausage, or fresh pork sausage, or Italian sausage (If using links, remove casing.)
1/4 cup chopped green onions
1 cup raisins
1 cup coarsely chopped roasted pecans or walnuts

In a skillet, brown the breakfast sausage, or pork sausage, or Italian sausage and drain off excess fat. Add the sausage to the pot of cooked wild rice mix along with the green onions, raisins, and nuts. Mix thoroughly.

BAKED CAULIFLOWER

Serves 6

1 large head of fresh cauliflower, bottom trimmed
boiling salted water
8 tablespoons butter, melted
2 cups shredded Cheddar cheese
1/2 cup seasoned bread crumbs

Boil the whole head of cauliflower in salted water until slightly tender. Remove from water and drain well. Place in a shallow baking dish. Dribble the top of the cauliflower with the melted butter, then sprinkle with grated cheese. Top with bread crumbs. Place in a 350-degree oven for 15 minutes or until cheese melts and bubbles. To serve, cut in wedges.

One game bird we do not have in Louisiana is pheasant. A neighbor of mine in New Orleans hailed from upstate New York and was known as The Avid Sportsman. He hunted in just about every state of the union, fished from Tennessee to Colorado, and came home with everything from wild turkey to bass, including some things I never heard of.

His freezer was a sight to behold. One evening as I dug around trying to find a bag of ice in his oversize appliance, I was hit on the head by a package containing pheasants. As he administered first aid to the bump on my forehead and begged forgiveness, he offered to share the unfamiliar birds with me.

It was more like a challenge.

"Take the six pheasants. Make a grocery list of what we'll need to prepare them, and we'll invite some friends to share a meal with us."

With the cold pack still on my head, I stumbled home with my gift. It wasn't until I came to my senses the next day that I realized I had no idea what to do with these things.

I pulled out one of my James Beard cookbooks. Mr. Beard had a few recipes, but they didn't strike me right. Julia Child had a couple, but one called for the "plumage" which, of course, I didn't have. Nor did I have the right accoutrements to "serve under glass."

I got out my stack of treasured *Gourmet* magazines and began flipping through the pages, book after book, since I don't have the indexes for any of my ten-year collection. After skimming through several months, I decided this was, both literally and figuratively, for the birds.

I was getting a little frantic. I then attacked a stack of cookbooks I had shoved on the top shelf of the guest room closet. Ah! Bingo! I found my old Albert Stockli *Splendid Fare* which I remembered had a great venison recipe. Surely he must have a pheasant recipe. I turned to the index. Peas, pepper slaw, pepperoni, pheasant! Not one, but several recipes were listed. Broth, casserole, cream of—oh, please let there be the perfect one. My shaking fingers found "—with puree of chestnuts." Page 183. I turned the pages quickly—181, 182, 183— page 183 was torn in half. I had the ingredients but no directions.

Time was getting short. Guests were expected in four hours. My friend was at the door ready to go to the supermarket, and pheasants weren't the only thing I had to cook. Plus the table wasn't set. HELP!

"Marcelle," I said to myself. "You are going to have to wing it."

I jotted down a grocery list and shoved my friend out the door. I pulled myself together and eyed the pheasants lying in a pan on the kitchen counter.

"O.K. guys. You had better be wonderful."

The phone rang. It was my friend saying he couldn't find peeled chestnuts. To be honest, I wouldn't know one if I saw one. I told him to forget the chestnuts.

I then decided there wasn't anything mystical about pheasant. They were birds, had the appearance of large Cornish hens, and I felt that with my basic knowledge of game we would get through this together.

When my friend returned I gave him the tasks of setting the table, arranging some flowers, putting the wine to chill, and selecting music for the evening while I prepared my FRANTIC PHEASANT.

FRANTIC PHEASANT

Serves 12

Six 2-2-1/2 pound pheasants
salt
black pepper
cayenne pepper
3 tablespoons rosemary
12 slices of bacon
3 medium onions, sliced
3 stalks celery, chopped
1-1/2 cups chicken broth
3/4 cup dry sherry
1 cup heavy cream

Rub the pheasants generously with salt and both kinds of pepper. Sprinkle the birds with rosemary. Wrap two strips of bacon around each bird and place in a roasting pan. Dribble about half of the dry sherry over the birds and roast for 15 minutes at 450 degrees. Add the onions, celery, and chicken broth; reduce heat to 400 degrees. Roast for 45 minutes or until wings pull away from the breast. Take the pan out of the oven and remove the pheasants, keeping them warm on a platter in the oven. Place the roasting pan on top of the stove, add the rest of the sherry and heavy cream, and bring to a boil. Reduce the heat to simmer and allow the sauce to thicken, stirring constantly. Cut the pheasants in halves or quarters (depending on size) and pour the sauce over the birds before serving.

One of our guests brought some real honest to goodness wild rice which we served along with BABY LIMA BEAN PUREE.

BABY LIMA BEAN PUREE

Serves 6

1 cup chopped onion
4 strips bacon, cut into 1-inch pieces
1 pound dried baby green lima beans
6 cups chicken broth
1 cup sour cream
salt and black pepper to taste

In a 2-quart sauce pan, fry the bacon and onions together until they are wilted. Add the lima beans and chicken broth; cook over a medium fire until the beans become tender and creamy, or about 1-1/2 hours. Place the beans and sour cream in a food processor fitted with a metal blade and purée until smooth. Season with salt and black pepper to taste.

Dinner rolls with currant jelly and a slightly chilled Beaujolais rounded out our meal. I had become so frantic with the pheasants, I had no dessert, so we settled on a bag of Oreos. My friends are easily pleased.

My sportsman friend is really quite generous. Not too long after the pheasant escapade, I came home to find a message on my answering machine. He related, at the sound of the beep, that he was off to the wilds for a few days and he anticipated returning with heaven only knew what, and would I like several pounds of venison sausage that was in his gargantuan freezer, since he would need the space when he returned.

I knew where an extra key to his house was hidden, and I had the alarm combination. I felt like a burglar, armed with my paper sacks. Once inside I filled my sacks with the sausage, re-alarmed, and re-locked and ran home with my bounty.

The venison sausage would come in handy as I was expecting a house full of guests for the weekend and had been beating my brains as to what kinds of "pot" dishes I could dream up to feed the hungry hordes.

When the packages defrosted, I realized the sausage was not in links, but was simply the ground venison, seasoned, but not stuffed into casings. Not to worry, I could do lots of things with this. I had several pounds of lean ground beef so I decided to combine the two and make a couple of items that could be easily heated up during the weekend. As most of my friends know, I am a "red gravy" freak. Any sauce made with tomatoes makes my heart throb. The mere thought of having a pot of red sauce blurping on the stove is my idea of ecstasy!

VENISON SPAGHETTI

Serves 6

1 pound ground venison
1 pound lean ground beef
3 tablespoons olive oil
1 large onion, chopped
1 large sweet green pepper, chopped
3 stalks celery, chopped
6 cloves garlic, chopped
1 pound can whole tomatoes
One 6-ounce can tomato paste
One 8-ounce can tomato sauce
1/2 cup dry red wine
1/2 teaspoon oregano leaves
1/2 teaspoon basil
sprinkling of ground anise
salt
cayenne pepper

Brown the ground meats in olive oil in a heavy iron pot. Add the onions, green pepper, celery, and garlic; cook until vegetables are wilted. Add the tomatoes, paste, and sauce; cook about 20 minutes over fairly high heat, stirring to prevent sticking and burning. Add the wine and seasonings, reduce heat to simmer, and cook for 2 hours. Add a little water or beef broth if the mixture becomes too dry. Serve with your favorite kind of pasta.

I still had some venison left, so I kept going. I was on a roll!

VENISON CHILI

Serves 6

1 pound ground venison
1 pound lean ground beef
1/2 pound lean ground pork
vegetable oil for browning
1 large onion, chopped
2 fresh jalapeño peppers, seeded and chopped (wear
rubber gloves to protect your hands)
Two 15-ounce cans red kidney beans (purée some in the
food processor to give the chili a creamy richness)
1 pound canned whole tomatoes
One 6-ounce can tomato paste
2-3 tablespoons chili power—according to taste
(I had a small jar of piquante sauce hanging around
so I threw that in too.)
salt and cayenne pepper to taste

Brown the ground meats in a little vegetable oil. Add the onions and jalapeño peppers; cook for 10 minutes. Add the kidney beans, both whole and pureed, whole tomatoes, crushed and with their juice, and tomato paste. Season to taste with chili powder, salt, and pepper. Simmer for a couple of hours.

During the weekend, one of my guests got creative and poured the chili over a thick bed of large corn chips in a deep baking dish. Then he topped it all with a pound of grated cheddar cheese and more chopped jalapeño peppers. Not bad for a midnight snack. Not so good for your stomach.

La Roulaison

One fall night as I closed down the house for the evening, I heard the wind whistling as it raced through the narrow passageway between the patio and the hedges. Leaves whirled and bare branches clicked against the tin roof, making an eerie sound. I smelled the acrid smoke from nearby cane fields and in the distance I heard the churning sounds of the sugar mill. *La roulaison*, the sugarcane harvest, was in full swing in south Louisiana.

Early the next morning, at first light, I pulled on a warm-up suit and decided it was the perfect time to "make a little pass" through the countryside to investigate the harvest activity.

Workers were already in the fields. Cane trucks and wagons were being loaded to bursting with long stalks of cane. Men working the cranes warmed themselves by a small fire they built. Loaded trucks stood in line at the entrance of the St. Mary Sugar Co-op near Jeanerette. The smokestacks belched steam, and the sickly-sweet smell of the cane being processed made me remember the cold mornings I devoured biscuits, PAIN PERDU (lost bread), and COUSH-COUSH (fried cornmeal) drowning in dark, rich cane syrup.

I also remember coming home from school in the afternoons and sharing with Mama a small bowl of *la cuite* into which pecans had been stirred. Sometimes we stuffed the nose of a French bread with it along with a glob of sweet butter. Ah, the good old days before we had to worry about too much sugar and too many calories!

As I watched the activity at the mill, I decided it had been much too long since I had been inside a sugar mill. Years ago, Papa took me along on his weekly excursions to the St. John mill near St. Martinville where he would share a hot cup of coffee with the mill foreman while they talked about the year's crop. Sometimes, the men who fed the cane crushers would peel me a piece of cane to chew on while Papa went on with his business. After chewing the stringy stick of cane and rolling it around my mouth to get every drop of sweet juice, I spit it out like the men taught me. Mama would have rolled her eyes for sure if she knew Papa let me do this in public!

I called an old childhood buddy, Branan B. Beyt, Jr., "Burt," who is the general manager of the St. Mary mill. I asked him if he had time to take an old friend on a tour through the mill. He gladly agreed to meet me the next day. Before he hung up he reminded me to wear old clothes and old shoes.

Before we began our trek, he pulled out an illustration to show me on paper what we were to encounter. It is rather complicated, but basically what happens is this: The cane that is brought in from the fields is loaded onto a conveyor belt where it is literally ground with sharp cane knives, then dumped into a powerful shredder that extracts the juice. Hot water is sprayed over the crushed cane to extract every bit of the sweet juice. The juice is funneled into the evaporator tanks for processing. The fiber and pulp, called *bagasse*, is fed into furnaces to create the steam to run the turbines in the mill.

The raw juice heads for the clarification process. There, in huge tanks, it is boiled under pressure to separate the juice and any solids. The clear juice comes off the top and goes into an evaporator and is boiled again under extreme pressure. A thick syrup emerges. It is at this point that, in extreme vacuum heat, the sugar crystals are extracted, and the molasses is drained off. The raw sugar is carried off onto a conveyor belt to what Burt calls the "sugar palace," a building that can hold thirty-two million pounds of sugar. It was like walking through fairyland, because the mountains of light brown sugar sparkled and glistened as the natural light from the doors and windows bounced off the crystals. I wanted to jump right in. From the sugar palace, the sugar is dumped into barges which take it to refineries where it becomes what you use in your coffee, on your cereal, or to cook with.

As we walked away from the deafening noises of the mill, Burt remarked that I looked a sight. I had *bagasse* in my hair, my hands were sticky from running them through the slightly moist raw sugar, and syrup, and molasses dripped down my face. I almost had to be hosed down before I got into my car, but what fun it had been. I couldn't wait to get home to make a batch of something on which to put cane syrup, or find a way to use the wonderful *la cuite*.

I thanked Burt with a sugary handshake and drove off into the sunset, only to find myself behind a slow-moving, heavily-loaded sugarcane truck. For once I didn't mind being slowed down in the traffic. It gave me some time to think of all the things I could do when I got home to my kitchen. I made a stop at the grocery store to pick up several cans of that wonderful pure ribbon cane syrup made by the Steen family in Abbeville. I was even fortunate enough to find some of their *la cuite* which is only available in limited quantities. The next three recipes are Steen's classics.

GINGERBREAD

Serves 12

1/2 cup shortening
1/2 cup sugar
1 cup cane syrup
2 eggs
2-1/2 cups sifted all-purpose flour
1 teaspoon salt
2 teaspoons baking powder
1/2 teaspoon baking soda
1 teaspoon ginger
1 teaspoon cinnamon
1 cup hot water

Cream shortening. Gradually add sugar and cream mixture until fluffy. Blend in syrup. Beat in eggs, one at a time. Sift together flour, salt, baking powder, baking soda, and spices. Add dry ingredients to creamed mixture alternately with hot water. Turn into a greased and wax-paper-lined 9-inch square pan. Bake at 350 degrees for 40 minutes. Cool before cutting.

FRUIT CAKE

Makes 2 loaves

1/2 cup vegetable oil
3/4 cup *la cuite*
2 eggs
1-1/2 cups sifted all-purpose flour
1/2 teaspoon baking powder
1 teaspoon salt
1 teaspoon cinnamon
1 teaspoon allspice
1/2 teaspoon ground cloves
1/2 cup fruit juice (apple, pineapple, or orange)
1 pound (2 cups) candied fruit and peels
1 box dates, chopped
1 box candied pineapple, chopped
1/2 cup Muscat raisins
2 1/2 cups chopped nuts

Combine oil, *la cuite*, and eggs; beat for 2 minutes. Sift together one cup of the flour with baking powder, salt, and spices; stir into oil mixture. Add fruit juice. Mix remaining 1/2 cup flour with fruit and nuts. Combine with batter and mix thoroughly. Pour batter into loaf pans lined with wax paper. Bake at 275 degrees for 2-1/2 to 3 hours. When cool, the cake may be decorated with candied fruit such as cherries or pineapple.

BROILED GRAPEFRUIT

Cut grapefruit in half. Cut around each section, loosening fruit from membrane. (Do not cut around outer edge of fruit; cut only within the membrane of each segment.) Top each grapefruit half with 1 tablespoon of cane syrup. Place on broiler rack three inches from heat. Broil slowly 10 to 15 minutes, or until grapefruit is slightly browned and heated through.

The sun was setting as I finished my cooking project. I enjoyed my goodies as I listened once again to the churning noises of the nearby sugar mill.

The next morning I realized that I'd dreamed about sugarcane all night, so I decided to indulge myself by preparing my childhood breakfast favorites, PAIN PERDU (lost bread) and COUSH-COUSH (fried cornmeal). Heaven on a chilly morning!

PAIN PERDU

Serves 4

2 eggs, beaten
1 cup milk
1/2 cup sugar
1/4 teaspoon vanilla
8 slices of stale bread (I prefer French bread)
1/2 cup vegetable oil or butter, as you prefer

Blend the eggs, milk, sugar, and vanilla together in a bowl. Dip the slices of bread in the mixture and fry in the hot oil or butter, turning once, until golden brown.

You can be creative and top the *pain perdu* with powdered sugar, cinnamon, or honey. My friend Cathy used to put all of the above plus fig preserves on her lost bread. I think cane syrup is best!

COUSH-COUSH

Serves 6

1/2 cup vegetable oil (or bacon grease if you have it)
2 cups yellow corn meal
1-1/2 teaspoons salt
1 teaspoon baking powder
1-1/2 cups warm milk or water

Preheat oil or bacon grease in a large, heavy skillet. Mix corn meal, salt, baking powder, milk or water, and pour into the heated skillet. Give it a couple of good stirs, lower the heat, cover, and let it steam for 15-20 minutes.

My father loved his coush-coush with hot coffee-milk poured over it. Mama uses salt and black pepper, Tante May used to put fried eggs on top of hers, and me, well, I just drown my coush-coush in butter and cane syrup.

La Boucherie

Every year while my grandfather, whom everyone called Pop-Pete, was overseer at Burton Plantation near St. Martinville, Louisiana, he held a *boucherie*. Translated literally *la boucherie* means the slaughtering and butchering of animals, usually a pig which has been fattened for the kill. Sometimes there were several pigs to be slaughtered, and family members, friends, and workers on the plantation gathered early in the morning, prepared to work until dusk.

Either the night before or just before dawn, the men killed the animal, slit its throat and tied it up by its hind legs to allow the blood to drain out. The blood was saved to make *boudin rouge*, a sausage made with ground pork, seasonings, rice, and the blood. The pig was then shorn of its hair and cleaned well for the butchering.

The head and feet were kept to make *fromage de tête de cochon*, hogshead cheese. The fat outer skin was cut into dice to fry as *gratons* or cracklings. This was done in a large black iron pot under which a roaring fire was kept alive throughout the day. The cracklings were heavily seasoned with salt and cayenne pepper, and as soon as they were cool enough, everyone grabbed handfuls to gobble up while they went about their work.

The butchers, with their large, sharp knives, went about cutting out the roasts and pork chops, passing bits of meat on to the women who then made the *boudin rouge* and the *boudin blanc*. The intestines were cleaned and stuffed with ground pork, spices, and rice to make the spicy sausages so dear to the Cajun's heart. Even the stomach of the pigs was used to make *chaudin*.

One of my favorites of the *boucherie* was *reintier de cochon*, or BACKBONE STEW, which was served later in the day with rice, baked sweet potatoes, or smothered turnips.

Late in the afternoon everyone was given a share of the pig to take home. By the glowing fires, for most of the work was done outside on long wooden tables, everyone would linger for a while, relaxing while listening to the men who had brought along fiddles and accordions. Old French songs were hummed, and those with any energy left would do a few jigs in the dust under the oak trees.

You don't have to go through all the commotion of having a *boucherie* to have some of these delights. Take heart and don't worry about having to slay a pig. You can stir up a classic pork stew in the comfort of your kitchen.

BACKBONE STEW (REINTIER DE COCHON)

Serves 10-12

**One 6-pound lean pork loin, with bones, cut into
chunks**
1/2 teaspoon cayenne pepper
1-1/2 teaspoons salt
2/3 cup flour
1/2 cup oil
2 large onions, chopped
3 stalks celery, chopped
2 sweet green peppers, chopped
4-5 cups beef stock or water
1/4 cup chopped parsley

Season the pork chunks with the pepper and salt and
roll in the flour to coat them lightly. Shake off excess
flour. In a heavy black iron pot, heat the oil and brown
the pork chunks well, stirring frequently. Add the onions,
celery, and peppers; stir often, cooking until vegetables
are wilted. Then add the stock or water, bring to a boil,
stirring and scraping the bottom of the pot to get the
brown particles that make the gravy richer. Reduce to
simmer, cover, and allow to cook for about 2 hours or
until meat is tender. Serve over rice and sprinkle with
chopped parsley.

There are some camps that say a backbone stew
can be made like a *fricassée*. Make a roux with equal
parts of oil and flour (1-1/2 cups of oil and flour),
then add the vegetables (same amounts as above)
and beef stock. Some like a few slivers of garlic
thrown in.

If a backbone isn't available, thinly sliced pork
chops can be substituted. Add to roux and vegetable
mixture. Add 2-3 cups of beef stock or water and
allow to cook until meat is tender.

If you are really interested in preparing *chaudin*,
contact your butcher or slaughter house and ask for
a pig's stomach.

CHAUDIN

Serves 6

1 pig's stomach
2-1/2 pounds lean ground pork
1 large onion, minced
1 large sweet green pepper, finely chopped
2 pods garlic, minced
1 bunch green onions, finely chopped
**3 slices of bread, broken into pieces and soaked in a
little milk**
1 sweet potato, peeled and diced
1 stalk celery, chopped
1 whole egg, beaten
1/2 teaspoon cayenne pepper
1/2 teaspoon black pepper
1 teaspoon salt
3 tablespoons cooking oil
about 2 cups water

Clean the pig's stomach well, picking off any bits of fat
clinging to the lining or surface. Soak in enough cold
water to cover for 2 hours, then rinse and pat dry.
Combine all ingredients, except oil and water, in a large
mixing bowl.

Use your hands to mix the ingredients together. You
might want to fry a little of the mixture in a small skillet
with some oil to check for seasonings. Stuff the stomach
with the mixture. With a large needle and heavy thread,
sew up the openings. Place the stomach in a heavy iron
pot with the heated oil and brown quickly, turning it 2 or
3 times. Add the water and cook covered over low heat for
about 2 hours. Uncover and allow most of the water to
evaporate to allow the skin of the stomach to brown.
Remove the *chaudin*. Add a little cornstarch to the
remaining water to make a gravy. Slice the *chaudin*
along with the skin to serve. I suggest having some hot
crusty French bread around to eat along with it.

Louisianians are very particular about the pots
and pans they use for cooking, and they take special
pride in the heirloom cast-iron dutch ovens, skillets,
and griddles that are passed down in families from
one cook to another. I have a friend who came into
possession of his grandmother's seventy-five-year-
old "boucherie pot"—a large, three-footed cast-iron
cauldron used to make *gratons*, sometimes known
as cracklings or fried pig skins. The making of
gratons is becoming a lost art because fewer old-
fashioned boucheries are held in modern south
Louisiana.

The boucherie pot had been stored for many years
in a wash house where it fell prey to damp and rust.
My friend was determined to restore the valuable
pot. After many inquiries he found a sugarcane
farmer who also had a machine and welding shop,
and who agreed to clean the pot.

After the pot was cleaned, it had to be cured so
that it could be used for cooking. First it was rubbed
generously with mineral oil—mineral oil contains
no salt or impurities that can cause rusting. The
next step entailed collecting enough oak firewood to
make a large fire into which the pot could be placed
so that the oil could burn off. The pot was then
rubbed several times with more mineral oil applied
with Spanish moss. I recommended using the moss
because I remembered Papa curing his black iron
pots this way.

The only thing left to do was use the pot to make
gratons. My friend found a butcher who agreed to
cut up pork bellies into *graton*-sized pieces. We set a
date for the *graton*-making and invited friends and
family to come together in my front yard on the
banks of Bayou Teche. An old-timer heard about my
friend's project and came by that day. He brought
with him a gallon of rendered hog lard and some
advice. The day was gray, windy, and chilly—perfect
weather for gathering around an outdoor fire.

The work table in the cooking area held a large
pan filled with cut up pork bellies. Plenty of salt and

cayenne pepper was close at hand. A wheelbarrow lined with paper bags on which to drain the *gratons* stood nearby. The men built a fire, and we were ready to christen the boucherie pot.

GRATONS

*Do not attempt to prepare *gratons* on an indoor stove.

50 pounds of pork bellies, cut into 2-inch squares
1 gallon rendered hog lard
1 quart water
salt and cayenne pepper

Into the iron cauldron add the rendered lard, water, and pork bellies, stirring often with a large paddle to prevent sticking. When the *gratons* start to float and turn golden brown, quickly remove them from the oil with a large wire basket. Drain on brown paper bags and sprinkle generously with salt and pepper. *Graton*s are best served fresh, but they can be stored in a tightly-covered container.

We did not want to waste the hot oil, so into the pot were tossed ten pounds of thinly-sliced pork chops. They only took a few minutes to cook.

FRIED PORK CHOPS

15 pounds thinly sliced pork chops
salt, black pepper, cayenne pepper, and garlic powder

Season the chops generously and allow to stand for one hour. Add the pork chops to hot oil a few at a time. Remove and drain on paper bags.

Next we fried 15 pounds of skinned, thinly-sliced sweet potatoes. Drained on paper towels and sprinkled with cinnamon and sugar, the sweet potatoes were a great finale to a wonderful outdoor feast.

Because there is so much of it, pork is often seen on the Sunday dinner table and is used for seasoning vegetables and for making dressings. Pork is considered to be a great delicacy and is important to Cajun cooking.

Several years ago, after undergoing a series of dental surgeries, I longed for the time my mouth would be back in commission so I could chow down on a succulent pork tenderloin.

During the several months of painful trips to the chair, I though of nothing else. Everything that went into my mouth came through a straw or on a spoon. I didn't see a fork or knife at my table for weeks.

Mama, who stayed with me during my convalescence, tried to keep my mind off the pain. She put me to bed with ice packs wrapped in fluffy white towels. She propped me up with all the pillows in the house and even threw in a couple of my old Teddy bears. She brought me beautiful trays set with linen tea cloths, bud vases with tea roses from the garden, newspapers and magazines, and cups of broth or custard. She even put my milkshakes in fine crystal wine glasses. She fixed me creamed potatoes with cheese and soft poached eggs. As I got better, she pureed pizza and lima beans. But all I could think of was pork tenders. To get my mind off food, she entertained me with coloring books and paper dolls just like she used to do when I was little.

When I graduated to firmer foods, she took her leave. When I hugged her goodbye I begged her to come back in a few weeks to fix me that pork tenderloin. When she noticed the tears in my eyes, she promised to return when the dentist gave me a clean bill of health.

She kept her promise. A month later she returned with a pork tenders tucked in her basket. She had even brought the fixings for her famous CORN CREOLE and DRESSED UP RICE. I was in ecstasy as I gave her full run of the kitchen while I cut out a new batch of paper dolls she had brought with her.

PORK TENDERS ADELINE

Serves 6

2 pork tenders, about 1-1/2 pounds each
1 package dry zesty Italian salad dressing mix
2 tablespoons olive oil
1 tablespoon wine vinegar
2 tablespoons water
3 green onions, chopped

In a blender, mix the dry salad dressing mix, olive oil, vinegar, water, and green onions; blend for 1 minute. Pour over the tenderloins and allow to marinate for at least 1 hour. Grill over a slow charcoal fire for 25-30 minutes. Baste with marinade.

CORN CREOLE

Serves 6

1 large onion, chopped
1 large sweet green pepper, chopped
3 tablespoons bacon drippings
2 cups cream-style corn
1 beaten egg
2 cups milk
1/2 cup yellow corn meal
salt and cayenne pepper to taste
bread crumbs
butter

Sauté onions and green pepper in bacon drippings. Add the cream corn, beaten egg, and milk; cook for 5 minutes. Add the corn meal, stir, and allow the mixture to thicken. Add seasonings to taste. Pour into a greased baking dish, sprinkle with bread crumbs and dots of butter. Bake at 350 degrees for 1 hour or until it begins to bubble.

DRESSED UP RICE

Serves 6

4 cups cooked rice
2 stalks celery with leaves, chopped
1 cup crumbled bacon
1 cup sliced mushrooms
2 tablespoons chopped pimiento
1/4 cup chopped sweet green pepper
1/4 cup chopped green onions
1 cup pork gravy

Mix all ingredients together, adding the pork gravy until everything is well moistened. Sprinkle with freshly chopped parsley.

With my mouth in better condition than before the surgery, I went on an eating spree. All the weight I had lost was going to creep back on, but I didn't care. The holidays were approaching, and I cast my fate to the winds.

I was invited to a round of cocktail parties, wedding receptions, and open-house *soirées*. It goes without saying I ate hundreds of finger sandwiches, pastry shells filled with everything imaginable, and munched on mounds of chips smothered in a variety of dips.

It never fails to amaze me how we get through such affairs. While holding a glass of liquid refreshment, a purse, and a small plate of food, I continue to try to hook up a cracker with a chunk of cheese. I usually spill most of my drink, drop the purse, and never get the cheese to my mouth.

But with my mouth in such fine shape, I reorganized my party attitude for the next country wedding I attended. I found a hiding place for my purse. I bypassed the bar and headed straight for the buffet table. I loaded up my small plate with a little dab of everything and found a quiet place to sit down to enjoy what looked like real food. Everything was recognizable except for a richly-seasoned dressing-like item. It was easily the best thing on the plate. I determined it had bits of pork in it, but that was as far as I could go.

While I filled my plate with more of the delicious stuff, I asked one of the bridesmaids if she knew what it was. She answered nonchalantly that it was *fare*.

"*Fare?*" I never heard of it. "What's in it? How is it made and can I get the recipe?"

"Well," she told me, "my mother makes it all the time for weddings. You can make sandwiches with it too. You know, you can make a sandwich like this (she folded her hand like a pocket) or like this (she clapped both hands together)."

I caught her drift. I make bologna sandwiches with one piece of bread rolled in half. Major sandwiches I make with two slices of bread.

Anyway, I was enamored with this "*fare*." She promised to get me the recipe. In the meantime, I looked up the word in my Cajun-French dictionary and found it spelled "*farre*" and it referred to a stuffing of rice dressing used especially with fowl. However, in another section I looked up the word dressing and found it spelled "*fare,*" also meaning jambalaya.

When I questioned Mama, she said she remembered it being pork dressing. My sister-in-law Nancy also remembered the term and said her mother used to make it, and it was so good it rarely made it to the dinner table. She and her brothers used to make sandwiches with it. (I had heard this story before.) If and when it made it to the dinner table, rice was added and sometimes her mother used it for the stuffing of her boudin.

So, as far as I could determine, it can be a dressing, a stuffing, or a sandwich filler.

MOM'S DRESSING (FARE OR FARRE)

1 pound of lean ground beef
1 pound lean ground pork
1 whole fresh chicken, deboned and skinned
20 chicken gizzards, cleaned
1 pound chicken livers
1 bunch green onions
1 medium yellow onion, coarsely chopped
1 sweet green pepper, coarsely chopped
1 medium-sized raw sweet potato, peeled and chopped
1/4 cup oil
salt and cayenne to taste

Grind the chicken meat, gizzards, livers, onions, green pepper, and sweet potato in a meat grinder or food processor. Blend together well with ground beef and ground pork. In a black iron pot heat oil and add mixture, stirring until mixture begins to brown. When the mixture begins throwing off juice, cover and reduce heat to low. Season well with salt and pepper. Cook for 30 to 45 minutes until mixture is juicy-moist.

At the wedding reception, I had it without any rice added; however, you can add cooked rice for a rice dressing with a different taste. The sweet potato adds just a hint of sweetness. Be creative and try mixing it with smothered eggplant or use it for stuffing sweet peppers. Marvelous!

Festival Time

When my hometown newspaper arrives each week, I usually sit right down and read it from front page to last. Like most small town weeklies, it gives the news of who died, babies born in the parish, local football scores, who got married, and who visited with whom. The *Teche News* also holds a very special place in my heart because it's our family newspaper, started by my grandfather Lazaire in 1886. My father took over after Pop died, and now my brother Henri Clay is editor and publisher.

Many afternoons after school found all of us proof reading, folding, and updating subscriptions. This was where I learned to love the sounds of the presses rolling and how to use the linotype machine. I had ink in my blood!

One week, as I hungrily read each line, I came across some photographs of the annual *chariot* parade—pronounced "sha-ree-o."

The parade has been a yearly event for as long as I can remember and is usually held the last Sunday in September. This is how it works.

Children of all ages may participate, creating *chariots* in categories which include "fancy box," "plain box," and "floats." For weeks prior to the event children begin raiding their mothers' closets, the local grocery store trash bins, and dry goods stores storage areas, looking for just the right box.

Mama's closet always yielded those fanciful round hat boxes. You know the ones—they are covered or painted with pastel flowers and have silk or taffeta handles—very stylish. The grocery store had the big boxes, like the ones bathroom tissue comes in, or the funny boxes in which eggs are packed. At the dry goods stores, we sometimes found long flat dress boxes. The choices were endless. A regular old shoe box could become a box of enchantment.

Then, with the help of parents or older siblings, we would make cutouts on the sides, sometimes in the shapes of half moons, stars, flowers, you name it—whatever your heart desired. Then the cutouts were covered with crepe paper or colored cellophane begged from local florists. A candle was placed inside the box to illuminate the cutouts. Finally, we attached a ribbon or string to the box, enabling us to pull our creation along the sidewalk.

Older children, or children with clever parents, had more elaborate *chariots*. They were called floats. The creative ones would take little red wagons—you know the kind—the sort your parents put you in to go for a ride around the yard, and made them into floats, akin to the large floats usually seen in big parades. One year I made a float to look like one in the New Iberia Sugarcane Festival parade.

I dressed up all my dolls in evening gowns (made by Mama), then put a box over my wagon, decorated it with colorful crepe paper and small stalks of sugarcane, put a small pocket-size flashlight on each corner, and off I went.

The parade begins at dusk at the church square in the center of St. Martinville, and it is indeed a sight to behold. First of all, it's tricky to keep candles lit if it's a windy evening. Then, if someone doesn't know how to ventilate the boxes, your *chariot* goes up in flames. One year, all my sister had at the end of the parade was her string attached to a burnt piece of cardboard.

One year, a friend of mine, whose father was a general contractor, made an elaborate float. It was a *papier mâché* replica of "The Old Woman Who Lived in a Shoe," and all the children fell off along the parade route.

I was glad the tradition continued and I could read about it in the *Teche News* each year. One year the photographs made me laugh out loud. There was one of a float with what appeared to be a *papier mâché* replica of the Statue of Liberty, but I couldn't tell if the statue was really *papier mâché* or a real child atop the box!

When we were little, we would wait anxiously as the judges made their decision. It was rare that any of us came home with a prize, but boy, we sure had fun. After the winners were announced, Mama would pile us in the station wagon, along with what was left of our *chariots* and take us home for a late night supper.

While we discussed so and so's *chariot* and lamented that we didn't win, Mama turned on the stove, waved her hands like a bewitching sorceress and in a few minutes something piping hot was brought to the table.

One late night supper I remember well was welsh rarebit. I remember it because I recall my brother Henri Clay yelling that he wasn't going to eat any purple rabbit—you know—Welch rabbit.

After I finished reading the paper, I went in search of a recipe for welsh rarebit. I also had a great urge to make a *chariot*. I had a few shoe boxes hanging around my closet, so I set to work creating both a *chariot* and a comforting, satisfying meal.

WELSH RAREBIT

Serves 8

2 pounds grated American cheese
One 12-ounce can evaporated milk
2 cups white asparagus, drained and cut into 1-inch
pieces (If white asparagus is not available, green
asparagus may be used.)
salt and cayenne pepper to taste
saltine crackers or toast points

Melt the cheese in a double boiler. Add milk, a little at a time, stirring constantly until sauce is smooth and thick. Add the asparagus to the sauce and season to taste with salt and cayenne pepper. Spoon the mixture over crackers or toast points. Serve immediately.

If we weren't treated to welsh rarebit, it was vegetable soup that Mama had put on the stove to simmer earlier in the afternoon, and it was just about right when we got home from the parade. Mama often made cornbread to go with the soup, and it was a nice change of pace from French bread. We all fought over the chunk of homemade butter that sat on the center of the old cypress kitchen table. I still get an *envie* for homemade vegetable soup and cornbread when I think of the fun we all had together.

OLD FASHIONED VEGETABLE SOUP

Makes approximately 6 quarts

2 pounds of brisket, cut into 2-inch cubes
2-3 quarts of chicken broth
salt, cayenne pepper, and black pepper to taste
1/2 teaspoon basil

3-4 bay leaves
1 large onion, chopped
2 carrots, sliced
2 stalks celery, chopped
2 cups chopped fresh cabbage
1 cup cut green beans
3 cups canned whole tomatoes
6 ounces curly vermicelli (optional)

Place brisket in a large soup pot with salt, cayenne pepper, black pepper, basil, bay leaves, and chicken broth. Bring to a boil, lower fire to medium, and continue to cook for an hour or so, or until the meat becomes tender.

Add vegetables and cook until tender. Add the vermicelli and cook for 10 minutes more. If soup stock reduces too much, add more broth or water. Check seasonings and skim off any excess fat.

CORNBREAD

Serves 6

2-3 tablespoons bacon grease or shortening
2 cups yellow corn meal
1 cup flour
4 teaspoons baking powder
3/4 teaspoon salt
1 teaspoon sugar
1 beaten egg
1-1/2 cups milk

Sift dry ingredients together in a mixing bowl. Add the egg and milk; mix well. Melt bacon grease or shortening in a 9-inch skillet and pour in the batter. Bake in a 425-degree oven for approximately 25-30 minutes until golden brown.

And so it goes—each weekend throughout the fall there are festivals and celebrations. One of the festivals not celebrated in the cool autumn months is the Jambalaya Festival, held during the summer in the town of Gonzalez. But I always think of jambalaya during cool months because it's such a great "pot" dish, perfect for serving to the multitudes, thus being one of the favorite foods served at any of the festivals.

Jambalaya always reminds me of gatherings. Many times when my family gathers together for a project, such as cleaning up the campground, or when we're all in for a weekend to just be together, someone is bound to pull out our biggest black iron pot.

"Let's put on a jambalaya while we're doing what we're doing!"

The great thing about jambalaya is that you can make it with whatever is at hand. Like the Spanish *paella*, its basic ingredient is rice, which every good Cajun or Creole cook always has in stock. It's fun to see what can be added. Let's see. Ah, some chicken or duck. Oh, and maybe some smoked sausage and ham. What about some shrimp? You can use all of this, or you can be discriminating.

Just as everyone has his own version of gumbo, so too will you find no two jambalayas alike. Some will argue that jambalaya should be brown; while others will say no, it should be red, chock full of tomatoes. Of course, each is right. The type you prefer should be what your tastebuds tell you. I can assure you, both kinds are eaten with much gusto and there's usually not a grain of rice left in the pot when everyone is finished.

I like it most when it's cooked outdoors, but if you don't want to do battle with such an undertaking, at least take your plate of jambalaya outside, and sit under a tree in your back yard. The smells of any jambalaya seem to enhance the scents of the earth, and vice-versa. Eat it slowly and savor all the tastes that have come together in the pot.

I have my own version, just as everyone does. But be creative and take some initiative. Don't be afraid to add a little of this, a bit of that. Make it your very own.

JAMBALAYA—MY WAY

Serves 6

1/2 cup chopped green onions
1/2 cup chopped white onions
1 large sweet green pepper, julienned
1 cup chopped celery with leaves
1 teaspoon minced garlic
1/3 cup butter
1/2 to 1 pound raw shrimp, peeled and deveined
3 dozen raw oysters or 1 cup chopped ham
1 pound can whole tomatoes
1 cup chicken broth
salt, cayenne pepper, thyme, bay leaf, hot sauce
1 cup uncooked rice

Sauté onions, green peppers, celery, and garlic in butter until wilted. Add shrimp and oysters; cook for 5 minutes. If ham is used, add when rice is added. Add the tomatoes, chicken broth, and seasonings, which can be salt and cayenne pepper, a pinch of thyme, a couple of bay leaves and a couple of dashes of hot sauce. Add rice, stir a bit, and cover. Cook 25 minutes or until rice is tender. Add a little tomato juice or chicken broth if the jambalaya becomes too dry.

A mixed green salad or a salad of fresh fruit along with plenty of French bread are musts with this meal.

It seems that each year, a new festival is born. I've said it before and I'll say it again, Louisiana natives are always thinking of a new reason for a party. However, many of the festivals have been around for a while. The Sugarcane Festival and the International Rice Festival are legends. One of my favorites is the Crawfish Festival, created in the 1950s in Breaux Bridge to promote the lowly but tasty mudbugs that are now the toast of the country.

And there's not one, but several shrimp festivals. Probably the most well-known is the one held in Morgan City where Bayou Teche flows into Berwick Bay, at the mouth of the Atchafalaya River. Because of close access to the Gulf of Mexico, the fleet of shrimp boats that call Morgan City home is a large one.

Each Labor Day weekend, a crowd gathers in Morgan City for a round of merrymaking. The festival highlight is the blessing of the fleet by a priest who sprinkles holy water over the elaborately decorated boats as they chug along the waterfront on their way to the Gulf for a season of trawling. With poorboys (the southern version of a hoagie) piled high with shrimp, battered and golden-fried to perfection in hand, the crowds roar and wave as the gaily festooned boats pass in review.

It never fails to amaze me what wonderful things can be done with the succulent shrimp brought in from the Gulf. The shrimpers go through their catches, sorting them by size, for the market. The teeny, tiny ones are perfect for stews and gumbos while the medium-sized ones are great for frying.

The large ones are usually chosen for boiling or barbecuing. The latter treatment is a great delight, but actually the term is wrong, for the shrimp are never put on the grill.

BARBECUED SHRIMP

Serves 4

6 pounds large shrimp, heads on (Don't peel them.)
2 sticks butter
3/4 cups olive oil
1/4 cup Worcestershire sauce
juice of three lemons
1 teaspoon garlic powder
2 teaspoons paprika
2 teaspoons cayenne pepper
1 teaspoon freshly ground black pepper
1-1/2 teaspoons salt (or to taste)
1/2 teaspoon Tabasco® (or more, according to taste)
1 tablespoon rosemary leaves
1 teaspoon oregano leaves

Rinse the shrimp in cool water and drain. Spread the shrimp in a large shallow baking pan. In a saucepan, melt butter, then add the rest of the ingredients. Mix well. Pour sauce over shrimp and marinate for 1 hour. Bake at 325 degrees for 15 to 20 minutes. Stir a couple of times with a spatula. Do not overcook. Serve in a soup bowl with lots of hot French bread to sop up the sauce. Be sure to have some trays around on which to put shells and such. Be forewarned—this can only be eaten with your hands, and I would advise you not to wear your best outfit since it can get rather messy. I sometimes have plastic bibs for guests or, if nothing else, large napkins to tuck in the collar.

"Shrimp boats are coming. Their sails are in sight. Shrimp boats are coming. There's dancing tonight." So the song goes. But let me make one point— I've never seen a shrimp boat with sails where I come from. They do have large nets that when hitched up out of the water look like giant butterfly wings, which I guess gives them an appearance of having sails. And it's a wonderful sight to see the shrimp boats coming into port late in the afternoon, moving like giant insects across Vermilion Bay, silhouetted by the setting sun.

The scene is one I've enjoyed for many years. Aunt Eva and Uncle George have a camp at Cypremort Point, an area on Vermilion Bay that until recently was largely undeveloped. Many weekends have found us lounging on the large covered pier, fishing, crabbing, and waiting for the shrimp boats.

One Friday afternoon, I came home from work in New Orleans, dragging. I was beat up, tired, hungry, and in dire need of some fresh air. On the edge of a crying jag, I called Mama.

With a crack in my voice, I asked her if she would like me to come in for a visit. Could we coerce Aunt Eva and Aunt Lois to join us for a "just the girls" weekend at Cypremort Point?

I must have sounded bad because without missing a beat, she replied they would meet me there in a couple of hours. I think I even heard her say "poor baby" before she hung up the phone.

It was a crisp cool afternoon, and in a wink I was packed and humming along Highway 90. The sun was just going down when I arrived. The ladies were busy rolling up the bamboo shades on the large screen porch, icing down cold drinks and beer, and setting up my favorite cot with lots of pillows and cool sheets.

After our usual hugging and a fusillade of greetings, we pulled up the folding chairs to watch the last purple-golden rays of the setting sun. We could see the shrimp boats headed for the docks. I offered to go and bargain for a few pounds of shrimp. I was in luck. The captain of the first boat I boarded had a good day and agreed to part with five

pounds of his best.

By the time I returned, the ladies were chopping onions and had started a roux. We were going to have a rich stew.

SHRIMP STEW AT THE POINT

Serves 6-8

5 pounds shrimp
8 cups water
1 sweet green pepper, chopped
2 medium onions, chopped
2/3 cup cooking oil
2/3 cup flour
6-8 cups shrimp stock, see below
salt and cayenne pepper
2 boiled eggs, finely chopped
1/4 cup green onions, finely chopped

Peel the shrimp and reserve the heads and shells, being careful to keep the golden fat in the heads. Place the heads and shells with the fat in a large pot with 8 cups of water seasoned with a teaspoon of salt and a teaspoon of cayenne pepper. Bring to a gentle boil and allow to cook for one hour. In the meantime, make a golden roux with the oil and flour. Add the onions and peppers and cook for 15 minutes, stirring to prevent the vegetables from sticking to the bottom of the pot.

Meanwhile, drain the shells from the stock, pressing down on the shells to get all the moisture. Add the stock, a cup at a time, to the roux mixture. The stew should be thick enough to coat a wooden spoon. Simmer gently for 30 minutes. Then add the shrimp and cook for 10 to 15 minutes. Taste for seasonings. To serve, sprinkle with the chopped boiled egg and green onions. Traditionally, the stew is served with rice, but I like mine without. I want to savor the richness by itself.

After supper, the ladies refused to let me help them clean up the kitchen. I settled into my cot on the porch, and as I dozed off I could hear the lapping of the water underneath the camp. I knew my tired mind and body were already on the road to recovery.

The next morning my spirits were restored. I was ready to get into the "camp spirit," which generally means do anything you want, but don't strain too much. I planned to spend the day lolling around in the sun, watching the sailboats on the bay, and gossiping with Mama, Aunt Eva, and Aunt Lois. Naturally, food—what we were going to cook, when we were going to eat, how we were going to cook it—was an important topic. I was thrilled to learn that Mama had stopped at the fish market in St. Martinville for gaspergou, a fresh water drum with firm meat that is perfect for grilling. We were going to have the fish for supper along with smothered potatoes and bacon. I vowed I would never return to the city.

GRILLED GASPERGOU

Serves 4

One 4 or 5 pound gaspergou, or several smaller ones, deheaded, gutted, with the scales left on
salt and cayenne pepper to taste
1 stick margarine
3 ounces hot sauce
1 tablespoon Worcestershire sauce
2 cloves garlic, minced

Split the gaspergou in half lengthwise. Place the fish halves, scale sides down, on the barbecue grill over a medium hot fire. Season with salt and pepper. Make a basting sauce with the margarine, hot sauce, Worcestershire, and garlic. Baste the fish well, then close the lid of the pit. Allow the fish to cook for 20 minutes or until meat pulls away from the skin. Baste with more sauce and serve.

SMOTHERED POTATOES WITH BACON

Serves 4

6 strips of bacon, fried and crumbled
1 medium onion, thinly sliced
4 medium red potatoes, skinned and thinly sliced
salt and cayenne pepper to taste
1/4 cup chopped green onions

In a heavy black iron skillet, fry the bacon until crisp. Remove bacon and reserve. Add the potatoes and onions; season with salt and cayenne. Brown the potatoes, stirring often. The potatoes will break up and become slightly crispy. Reduce the fire, cover the pot, and allow the potatoes to continue cooking for 15 minutes or until they are done. Add crumbled bacon and a handful of chopped green onions.

In Thanksgiving

For many years, with a few exceptions, the whole family gathered at Mama's for all holiday meals. First of all, her house was the only one that could accommodate the brood. Even when my brothers and sister began having children of their own, she had room to expand. She has a large patio, a huge garage with a brick floor, and a yard that won't stop. She is also the only one who has a six-burner stove with double ovens. Mama has silver service for twenty-four, as well as enough matching china and crystal for all twenty of us. Mama also has a huge freezer where she can store the delicious goodies she prepares in advance.

But in the past few years, we children have come more or less into our own and have bravely offered to have some of the holiday celebrations at our humble abodes.

When I had a restaurant near Lafayette, I invited the whole family, plus a few friends, to join me at the restaurant (which I closed for a couple of days) for Christmas dinner. There was a huge Christmas tree, a large kitchen with plenty of cooking space, and a large commercial dishwasher that could handle the mounds of dirty dishes and pots in a matter of minutes. The walk-in coolers and freezers were perfect for storing pre-made delights.

As luck would have it, it was the holiday season that south Louisiana was locked into below freezing temperatures and an unforgettable ice storm. But we were undaunted.

Early Christmas morning, everyone cautiously drove from their homes to the restaurant and began lugging in bundles of gifts, trays of food, and children wrapped in blankets. We were well settled in when Baby Brother Bruce calmly announced that he had discovered the pipes were all frozen, and we had no running water.

At first, we thought nothing of it. We were all together, a pitcher of warm eggnog took the chill out of our bones, and we began to see about the business of getting dinner ready. It was only then that we realized the lack of running water might put a damper on our festivities.

But my family members are troopers. We've all been camping together many times under fairly primitive conditions. Papa was an old Boy Scout leader who trained us well. We just had to put our heads together and overcome a few problems.

Nancy, my sister-in-law, made the observation that we had tons of ice in the ice machine. She began melting ice in large pots so we could make coffee, cook rice, and wash dishes. We had a good laugh watching her stir the pots of ice on the stove.

Somehow we made it through the day, but as I hugged Mama goodbye, I suggested we keep with tradition and have Christmas dinner at her house from now on. She smirked but agreed it would have been a lot easier.

A couple of years later, I bravely invited the clan for Thanksgiving. I was living at Oak Alley Plantation, and the director kindly suggested that since the "big house" would be closed for the day, we could all have dinner there. What an invitation. The house is one of the loveliest on the Great River Road, and the old kitchen was more than adequate to handle the crowd. And what a setting for the children to play football and ride bikes!

For days preceding turkey day, I had visions of what a grand day it would be to have a memorable dinner in the historic, gracious home.

It was memorable all right. The day dawned gray and wet. There went the idea of seating the children at a large table on the veranda. While the table in the grand dining room was large, it could hardly accommodate all of us.

I quickly reorganized and soon had my brothers hauling folding tables and chairs to the Big House. At first, the teenagers thought this quite an adventure, but after getting soaked to the skin, they went in search of a portable radio and huddled on the front gallery.

In the meantime, Mama and I were trying to get dinner together. For the first time in years, the ovens went on the blink, so for the next hour we transported dishes that had to be warmed to other available ovens on the grounds, then brought them back to the Big House. We lost Mama's creamed spinach casserole in the melee.

The music emanating from the portable radio seemed to get louder and louder. The drawer containing the silver serving pieces was locked, and we couldn't find the key. I became a nervous wreck watching small children running around the 150-year-old mansion filled with family heirlooms.

But somehow we got it all together and sat down to dinner. Brother Henri Clay had just finished saying the blessing when we heard voices at the front door. Lost and weary travellers had seen a light and heard voices. They were in search of a place to have a warm meal. I had no choice but to invite them to join us. We found more folding chairs and place settings. As I watched everyone chow down, I realized I was probably the only one who didn't think all of this was the cat's meow. I was close to tears and having *gros coeur* when a child seated next to me looked up and winked, whispering to me about how much fun he was having. I finally realized that my family can put up with anything and have a good time at it.

Later in the day, when all of us were cleaning and sorting things out in the kitchen, my sisters-in-law and I said at the same time, "Don't you just love the *grimilles*?"

One of the guests overheard our comment and questioned, "What is a *grimille*?"

We explained that it was the crumbs, or tiny bits of anything. In this case, it was the pieces of pork roast and turkey at the bottom of the pans. We told her how wonderful the *grimilles* are for sandwiches or just for picking at the next day.

Early the next morning as I bade everyone *au revoir*, Mama told me that she had put the *grimilles* in a container in the back of the fridge for me to enjoy after everyone was gone.

That evening the quiet was deafening but not unpleasant. I poked around in the fridge looking for leftovers and discovered the *grimilles*. I decided to amuse myself and make a gumbo. I even had the turkey carcass to make a rich broth. I instinctively knew this was going to be one of the best gumbos I ever made. I was right. It was hearty and nourishing—perfect for a lonely rainy evening meal along with reheated dinner rolls and leftover fruit salad.

GRIMILLE GUMBO

Serves 8-10

Roux:
1 cup oil
1 cup flour
2 cups chopped onion
1 cup chopped celery
1/3 cup chopped sweet green pepper

2-1/2 cups of *grimilles*, cubed turkey, or chicken
6-8 cups turkey or chicken broth
salt and cayenne pepper to taste
pinch of thyme
minced parsley
1 bunch green onions, chopped

I usually make my roux in the traditional manner—combining flour and oil in a heavy iron pot, and over a moderate fire, stirring slowly until the roux reaches a rich golden brown, then adding the vegetables for a few minutes. But being a bit weary from the past few days' activities, I proceeded to make a roux in the microwave.

In a 4-cup measure, mix oil and flour. Microwave on high for 6 to 7 minutes. Stir and return to microwave for 30 seconds to 1 minute until roux reaches a dark brown color. Add the onions, celery, and bell pepper. Slowly add warm water to bring the mixture to the 4-cup mark. Stir. Put roux into a large heavy pot.

I had about 2-1/2 cups of *grimilles*, but you can substitute the same amount of cubed turkey, chicken, or whatever your heart desires. Then add 6 to 8 cups of turkey or chicken broth—more if you want a thinner gumbo. Add salt, cayenne pepper, and a pinch of thyme. Simmer for 1-2 hours. Sprinkle with minced parsley and green onions; serve over steamed rice.

Pour yourself a glass of *Beaujolais nouveau* and you will have a meal to warm the body and soul.

You would think I had learned my lesson about having the family for Thanksgiving, but I was determined to have a holiday meal that went smoothly and was enjoyable for everyone, so I tried again the following year.

I was amazed when everyone agreed to come. I was warned, however, that the teenagers seldom travel without friends these days, so I was to prepare for a few extras.

As for the Thanksgiving menu, I thought I was being real cute when I saw a menu for a Creole Thanksgiving dinner in a copy of a food magazine. I made a couple of changes. Instead of stuffing a turkey with jambalaya, I thought it would be fun to stuff Cornish hens instead. I would allow one little bird per person. Having the jambalaya would eliminate Mama having to make her rice dressing with oysters. I would make oyster tartlets which would take the place of our usual giant oyster pie. We would have pumpkin peanut butter pie and praline ice cream rather than our regular plain pecan pie.

I made copies of the food article and sent copies along with typed memos to those who had volunteered to bring dishes. The same day I mailed the memos, I purchased twenty-five Cornish hens. I was very pleased with myself. Everything was being well organized to make the day a pleasurable one.

Two days later I had a rash of phone calls. My sister-in-law informed me that her children do not eat carrots and brussel sprouts and asked if I minded if she made a sweet potato casserole instead.

My brothers let me know very diplomatically that they weren't coming if Mama wasn't making her oyster dressing. My sister asked if it would be O.K. to have pecan pie AND pumpkin peanut butter pie.

Mama called and told me to buy a few more hens because the football player nephews would probably eat two instead of one each.

So much for trying to be cute and innovative.

Since my family prefers traditional fare, I'll share with you the dishes we prepared.

BAKED CORNISH HENS

Serves 6

3 Cornish game hens, about 1 pound each
salt and freshly ground black pepper
4 tablespoons orange marmalade
3 tablespoons soy sauce
6 strips bacon
3 tablespoons olive oil
3/4 cup water or chicken broth
1/2 cup dry sherry
3 tablespoons minced parsley

Rinse the hens in cool water and pat dry. Season each hen well with salt and black pepper. Set aside. Mix the orange marmalade and soy sauce together. Rub the hens with this mixture and wrap each bird with two strips of bacon. Place hens in a roasting pan and dribble with olive oil. Place in a 350-degree oven. When the hens begin to brown, add water or chicken broth to the pan. Loosely cover pan with foil. Baste occasionally with pan juices and cook for 30-40 minutes or until the wings pull away easily from the body. Remove hens from pan and set aside on a platter to keep warm. Remove any excess oil from baking pan. Place the roasting pan on top of stove over medium heat. Add dry sherry to the pan juices and allow to reduce by one-fourth. Cut hens in half; spoon pan gravy over the top of each hen. Garnish with minced parsley.

OYSTER RICE DRESSING

Serves 6-8

4 tablespoons vegetable oil
4 tablespoons flour
2 large yellow onions, finely chopped
1 large sweet green pepper, finely chopped
3 cloves garlic, minced
1/2 pound chicken livers
4 chicken gizzards
1 cup water
2 pints raw oysters with their liquor
3 cups cooked rice
salt and cayenne pepper to taste
1/4 cup finely minced parsley

Make a roux with the oil and flour and cook to a dark brown. Add the onions, peppers, and garlic; cook for 5 minutes. Grind the livers and gizzards in a food processor or meat grinder. Add water to roux mixture and simmer for 1 hour. Add oyster liquor and cooked rice. Season with salt and cayenne pepper, being careful not to use too much salt if the oysters are salty. Add oysters and mix into rice mixture. Add minced parsley and cook for 10 more minutes until oysters are just done. If mixture becomes too dry, add a little warm chicken broth.

RUM GLAZED SWEET POTATOES

Serves 8

3 pounds sweet potatoes, pricked several times with a fork
3 Golden Delicious apples, peeled and cut lengthwise
1/4 cup fresh lemon juice
1 cup roasted pecan halves
1 stick of unsalted butter
1/2 cup firmly packed light brown sugar
1/2 cup honey
2 tablespoons dark rum
1/2 teaspoon cinnamon
1/4 teaspoon ground ginger
1/4 teaspoon ground mace

Bake sweet potatoes in preheated 400-degree oven for 45 minutes or until tender. Let cool and then peel. Cut the potatoes into round slices. Toss the apples in the lemon juice. Arrange the sweet potatoes and apples in a buttered baking dish. Sprinkle with the pecans. In a saucepan combine butter, brown sugar, honey, rum, cinnamon, ginger, and mace; cook mixture over moderate heat, stirring until sugar is dissolved. Spoon the syrup over the potato and apple mixture and bake for 30 minutes in a 400-degree oven, basting occasionally with the pan juices. Place under broiler about 4 inches from fire until edges of potatoes and apples are slightly brown.

That holiday went quite smoothly except for a small child's mishap—he fell into a sewerage ditch.

Which brings me to the problem of children and holiday food.

Have you ever tried to serve a ten-year-old a plate of food from the Thanksgiving table?

"Cher, would you like turkey or roast?"

"Turkey, I guess."

"White or dark meat?"

"Maybe a drumstick."

The turkey, as we all know, has only two drumsticks, so if you're late going through the line around the table, the kid is out of luck.

"How about some cauliflower *au gratin*?"

"Can you take off some of that white gook?"

"Ah, here's *grandmere's* specialty, oyster dressing. How about a little of that?"

"Can you take out the oysters?"

Sometimes you can pass off the cranberry sauce by telling the child it really is strawberry preserves. And if you're lucky, he might take a shot at the ambrosia if you pick out the grated coconut. French bread is usually a taker, but forget the giblet gravy.

Many times, I've seen a child's plate with nothing on it but a slice of turkey, bread, and white rice with a lump of butter.

They'll sometimes take a slice of pumpkin pie, but they want to know why it's such a gross color. Any apple or cherry pie around? What would children really like to eat on Thanksgiving? I gathered my twelve nieces and nephews recently and took a poll.

This is what is acceptable:

Chicken, baked or fried. Creamed potatoes, or some kind of sweet potatoes. One five-year-old said pigs-in-the-blanket would be great. Vegetables are questionable. They just don't want gook on them. The want to be able to determine what they're eating. Hot apple pie with ice cream got the most votes for dessert.

So here goes for the children.

For the pigs-in-the-blanket, use canned flaky biscuits for the dough. Break each biscuit in half and roll each piece thinly on a floured board. For adult tastes, put a dab of Creole mustard on the rolled dough; it's best to leave them plain for children. Wrap the dough around two-inch pieces of wieners or smoked mini-sausages. Pinch closed and bake at the temperature recommended on the biscuit can.

A fruit salad may be made with drained pineapple chunks, mandarin slices, apple slices, and whatever fresh berries that can be found at the market. Sprinkle the fruit with fresh or dried mint leaves and stir in plain yogurt. If you want to sparkle some up for the adults, splash in some light rum.

Just about everyone can bake a chicken. I like to add a little oregano and paprika to softened margarine and rub the bird well with this. Add a cup of chicken broth to the roasting pan along with some chopped green onions or sliced yellow onions. Baste with pan juices. Kids love this gravy with plain old white rice.

And for the adults, a holiday twist for duck.

BAKED DUCK WITH JALAPEÑOS

Serves 4

2 wild ducks, dressed
2 teaspoons salt
1 teaspoon cayenne pepper
1 teaspoon black pepper
2 tablespoons olive oil
2 fresh jalapeños, seeded and cut into slivers (When handling fresh hot peppers, be sure to wear rubber gloves.)
4 strips of bacon
2 tablespoons flour
3 tablespoons vegetable oil
4 cups chicken broth
1/4 cup dry sherry
2 cups sliced fresh mushrooms
1/4 cup chopped parsley

Rub the dressed birds with salt, cayenne pepper, black pepper, and olive oil. With a sharp knife, make slits in the breasts and stuff with slivers of fresh seeded jalapeños. Wrap each bird with two slices of bacon. Sprinkle the birds with flour; shake off excess flour and brown them in hot vegetable oil (preferably in a black iron pot). Turn the breast side of each duck up and add the chicken broth and dry sherry. Cook slowly, covered, on the top of the stove or in a 350-degree oven for 2 hours or until the birds are tender. Just before serving, add the sliced mushrooms and chopped parsley to the pot; cook for 10 minutes.

This next dish is the star of Thanksgiving dinner, liked by both children and adults.

SWEET POTATO PONE

Serves 6

1 egg
1 cup sugar
1 stick margarine
2 cups grated raw sweet potatoes
1/4 teaspoon salt
1/2 cup milk
1 cup chopped pecans

Beat egg with sugar and softened margarine. Mix together with grated sweet potatoes, salt, and milk. Pour into a buttered casserole and bake at 325 degrees for 30 or 40 minutes. Sprinkle with chopped pecans and return to oven for 30 minutes or until it sets.

While we're on the subject of sweet potatoes, I feel it is necessary to discuss Mama's addiction to them.

I ate so many sweet potatoes as a child, my nickname was *patate douce*. Mama was to blame. She was fanatic about sweet potatoes any way they were prepared. Just about every day during the cold fall and winter months, she would put several potatoes in the oven to bake, and in the afternoon she and I would snack on them.

We would carefully pull off the skins and then douse the soft orange pulp with melted butter and cane syrup.

Sometimes, we plopped them into a bowl of chicken and sausage gumbo. When pork was on the menu, sweet potatoes were the inevitable side dish, sliced, French fried, and sprinkled with sugar and cinnamon.

If a few somehow remained in Mama's sack under the sink and began to sprout, she would put them in jars filled with water and soon we would have a sweet potato vine framing the kitchen window.

She was an absolute diehard about the darn things. We knew we were in trouble especially around the holidays. She would pull out the recipe box and go through her collection of sweet potato recipes.

I once had a request for a sweet potato dish that was "different." My quest for yet another way to serve sweet potatoes led me to the source: I didn't have any new recipes, but I was sure Mama did.

So I called Mama. After I hung up the phone, I knew she was already hot on the trail. Sure enough, a few days later, she called up with this unusual recipe.

NUTTED SWEET POTATOES

Serves 6

4 cups canned yams, drained
1/2 teaspoon salt
1/8 teaspoon cayenne pepper
1/4 cup miniature marshmallows
4 tablespoons melted butter
1/3 cup honey
1 1/2 cups chopped pecans

One day before serving, mash yams well, and add salt, pepper, marshmallows, and 1 tablespoon of butter. Form into 12 balls, the size of a small orange. Place in a covered container and refrigerate for 24 hours. The next day, preheat oven to 350 degrees. Heat honey and 1 tablespoon of butter. With 2 forks, roll each yam ball, first in honey, then in chopped pecans. Place the yam balls in a baking dish. Spoon 2 more tablespoons of melted butter over the yams and bake for 15 minutes.

I thanked Mama for her research and was about to hang up when I realized she had begun to dictate more sweet potato recipes. I dutifully copied down a few, and then made my excuses. I had to get off of the telephone. Mama was still talking when I hung up. She probably didn't even notice.

Sweet Treats

I love desserts just as much as the next person, but I'm terrible at preparing them. My cakes don't rise, cream won't whip, and soufflés simply flop. I made Floating Islands one time, and the islands sunk. I tried a can't miss lemon pie which turned out beautifully except that I forgot to add the lemon juice. One of my nieces called it "Nani Celle's Neuter Pie."

However, there are a few little Cajun desserts that I have mastered, probably because I literally learned them at my mother's knee—or rather, stove. They are simple, but quite tasty. I wouldn't recommend them for one of your five-course, *haute cuisine*, candlelight, black tie affairs. Rather serve them at family dinners when the north wind blows and a pot of soup is simmering on the stove, or when dear old friends are coming for a weekend stay.

One of my favorites is *les oreilles de cochon* which literally translated means "the pig's ears." But they are really deep fried pastries dipped in cane syrup and sometimes sprinkled with chopped pecans. If you have a child who likes to play with a rolling pin, ask him to help. They're fun to do.

LES OREILLES DE COCHON

Makes approximately 1 dozen pastries

1 cup all-purpose flour
1/4 teaspoon salt
about 1/4 cup water
vegetable oil
One 12-ounce can cane syrup
1/2 cup finely chopped pecans

Combine flour and salt. Stir in enough water to make a stiff dough. Divide dough into 12 equal parts and roll each into a ball. Roll out the balls of dough very thin on a lightly floured surface. Pour about 2 inches of oil into a heavy, deep frying pot. Heat oil to 350 degrees. Drop the pastry into hot oil and using a long-handled fork, stick the tines into the center of the pastry and twist quickly. Hold fork in place until dough sets. This will give it the appearance of a pig's ear. Cook until golden brown and drain well on paper towels. Repeat procedure with remaining pastry. Bring syrup to a boil in a heavy sauce pan and stir until it reaches the ball stage (as in making candy). Dip each pig's ear in the syrup, coating well. Sprinkle with chopped pecans and lay on buttered wax paper. They're great warm or at room temperature.

This next little dessert can be used for breakfast as well and is the Cajun's version of tea cakes.

CROQUIGNOLES

Makes 1 dozen pastries

3 eggs
1/2 cup sugar
1 tablespoon butter, melted
2 tablespoons water
1 teaspoon baking powder
Approximately 3 cups of sifted flour, sufficient to make a stiff dough
1 tablespoon vanilla
powdered sugar
cinnamon

Beat eggs. Add sugar and melted butter, then water. Add flour with baking powder sifted together. Add vanilla. Roll out and cut into triangles about 3 inches long and 2 inches wide. Slash in center with a sharp knife and fry in deep fat. Sprinkle with powdered sugar and cinnamon.

A fresh batch of *croquignoles* can perk up a dreary November afternoon, especially if you have a nice hot pot of spiced tea to wash them down. Pull a chair up to the kitchen table and take a break from life's troubles.

SPICED TEA

Serves 4

juice of 2 lemons
juice of 2 oranges
1/2 cup sugar
4 cups boiling water
1/4 teaspoon cinnamon
4 whole cloves
5 small tea bags (an orange pekoe blend will do just fine)

Dissolve the sugar in 1/2 cup of boiling water. Add the juice of the lemons and oranges, cinnamon, and cloves. Pour the remaining 3-1/2 cups of boiling water over the teabags; allow to steep for 5 minutes. Remove the teabags and add the tea to the lemon and orange flavored syrup. Serve immediately.

Bread pudding is a staple dessert in south Louisiana, but rice pudding is seldom seen anymore. Mama used to make it for us with leftover rice since nothing went to waste in her kitchen.

BAKED RICE PUDDING

Serves 6

1-1/2 cups cooked rice
4 cups milk
4 eggs, slightly beaten

3/4 cup sugar
2 teaspoons vanilla
1 cup raisins (optional)
1 teaspoon nutmeg mixed with 1 teaspoon cinnamon

Grease a 2-quart casserole. Scald the milk and gradually add the beaten eggs, stirring constantly. While stirring, add the sugar, vanilla, rice, and raisins. Pour into casserole and sprinkle with cinnamon and nutmeg mixture. Set casserole in a large baking pan which has about 1 inch of hot water in it. Bake uncovered at 350 degrees. After 15 minutes, stir pudding with a fork. Bake 25 minutes longer or until a knife inserted in the center of the pudding comes out clean.

When we returned home each afternoon after school, we always had a treat waiting for us. Sometimes it was a piece of French bread spread with homemade butter and topped with cane syrup and pecans. Sometimes it was condensed milk that had been cooked six hours in the can until it caramelized. Or maybe, just maybe, Mama would have a batch of silky-smooth egg custard waiting for us—a delicacy she called Burnt Cream.

BURNT CREAM

Serves 10

1 quart heavy cream
8 egg yolks
1 cup sugar
1 tablespoon vanilla extract

Preheat oven to 350 degrees. With a whisk or electric beater, beat the egg yolks and 1/2 cup of sugar together in a mixing bowl for 3 or 4 minutes or until the eggs are thick and pale yellow. Heat the cream in a heavy saucepan until small bubbles begin to form around the edges of the pan. Pour the cream in a slow stream into the egg yolks, beating constantly. Add the vanilla and

strain the mixture through a fine sieve into a baking dish that is at least 2 inches deep.

Place the dish in another shallow pan and pour enough boiling water into the pan so that the water comes halfway up the sides of the custard dish. Bake for 45 minutes or until a knife inserted in the center comes out clean. Remove the custard dish from the pan of water and cool to room temperature. Refrigerate for at least 4 hours.

About 2 hours before serving, preheat the oven broiler to its highest temperature. Sprinkle the top of the custard with the remaining 1/2 cup of sugar; coat the surface as evenly as possible. Slide the dish under the broiler about 3 inches from the heat; cook for 4 or 5 minutes or until the sugar forms a crust over the cream. Watch carefully for any signs of burning. Allow the cream to cool again and refrigerate before serving.

I often wish I could come home from work and a treat would be waiting for me. A friend told me what he sometimes does. He's a grown man but still remembers his after-school treats and so shared this divine sweet with me. Make yourself a batch today and tomorrow, you too can have a sweet treat.

CRACKERS AND CREAM

2 packages of unsalted soda crackers (approximately 84 crackers)

Cream Sauce:
1 quart milk
One 12-ounce can evaporated milk
2 eggs
1 cup sugar
4 tablespoons cornstarch dissolved in
6 tablespoons of water
2 tablespoons vanilla

Dissolve the cornstarch in water. Cook milk and evaporated milk until the mixture begins to simmer. Add cornstarch and stir for 15 minutes or until milk mixture begins to thicken. Add beaten eggs and sugar; cook for 2 more minutes. Cool and add vanilla.

Butter the crackers on one side and sandwich them together. Arrange the crackers in a large square glass baking dish. Pour hot cream sauce over the crackers and allow the crackers to absorb all the cream.

🍁

I have always loved October because it means Halloween, and that means carving jack-o-lanterns. Apparently this love is a family trait, because one year my nephew Nicholas, then aged five, called me on the telephone. He said, "Nani Celle, let's go to the pumpkin stand. It's almost Halloween, and we don't want to be without a jack-o-lantern." Because I am a wonderful aunt, I agreed to take Nicholas into the country in search of the perfect *feu follet*.

We found that perfect pumpkin and were soon back on my patio, spreading out newspapers to work on. I cut out the face; Nicholas scooped out the pulp with a spoon. We created one of the ugliest, scariest, most wonderful jack-o-lanterns ever made, and we

had *lagniappe* from our efforts. We saved the pulp to make PUMPKIN CAKE WITH CREAM CHEESE ICING.

PUMPKIN CAKE

4 eggs
2 cups sugar
1 cup vegetable oil
2 cups flour
2 teaspoons soda
2 teaspoons cinnamon
1/2 teaspoon salt
2 cups of cooked mashed pumpkin (canned may be used)

Cream the eggs and sugar together until light and well blended. Add the oil, continuing to beat. Sift the flour, soda, cinnamon, and salt together. Alternate adding the dry ingredients and the pumpkin to the creamed mixture. Pour into a greased and floured 9-inch tube pan. Bake at 350 degrees for 55 minutes or until a straw or toothpick inserted into the center comes out clean. Let the cake stand in the pan for 10 minutes, then turn out onto a rack to cool.

CREAM CHEESE ICING

3 ounces cream cheese
1/2 cup butter or margarine
1 pound box of confectioner's sugar
1 teaspoon vanilla
1 cup chopped pecans

Have the cream cheese and butter at room temperature. Combine them, and add the sugar and vanilla, beating until very smooth. Stir in the chopped pecans and spread on the cooled cake.

When we were children, we all participated in making the sweets for Halloween night. Nannan, Mama's aunt, joined us to make *tac-tac*, or popcorn balls. While we worked, Nannan told us scary stories. She would put a candle in the window over the sink and light several kerosene lanterns to get us in the mood. She had to set the stage, so to speak. One of her favorite tales was about the burning scarecrow that haunted the old barn near her house. She liked to tell us, too, about the old bald lady who gathered Spanish moss from the trees to make her wigs. Oh, how we would laugh and be scared at the same time. And while we howled and she cackled, she would pop the popcorn and cook syrup for the popcorn balls. Then all was dumped into a huge wash tub on the back porch, and there we would sit and make our *tac-tac*.

POPCORN BALLS

Makes approximately 3 dozen popcorn balls

1/2 cup sugar
2/3 cup cane syrup
1/3 cup water
1 tablespoon vinegar
1/3 teaspoon salt
1 tablespoon butter
1/8 teaspoon baking soda
3 quarts of popped corn

Combine sugar, syrup, water, vinegar, and salt; stir until sugar dissolves. Cook mixture until it reaches a light "crack" stage, about 270 degrees. Remove from heat and add butter and baking soda, stir well. Pour over popcorn. Then comes the fun part. Butter your hands to form the mixture into balls. Wrap the popcorn balls individually in wax paper.

Nannan was also a firm believer in picking pecans. She cracked and peeled them for sweet treats throughout the year. I think of her when pecan season rolls around in the fall.

Ping! Crash! Roll! Rat-tat-tat!

The noise on my roof early one morning woke me up out of a sound sleep. Clutching my robe around me, I slowly opened the patio door and looked up. I was promptly struck on the head with what felt like a big rock. What was going on? The sky was clear, and no one was in sight. Then I spied several squirrels scampering around looking much like Mardi Gras revellers scooping up doubloons and beads. Ah, they were gathering pecans!

The brisk north wind that ushered in the cool front was shaking loose the fruit of the trees, and everywhere I looked were pecans—big fat round ones and some that were long and narrow. In a second, I joined the squirrels. On my hands and knees, I gathered up a few handfuls within a matter of minutes. The pockets of my robe were soon filled and were akin to the puffed cheeks of my squirrel friends.

I pulled out a paper bag, retrieved my nut cracker from the back of the kitchen drawer, and was soon cracking and munching away.

I thought about the many times years ago that Papa, Mama, and my old aunts would walk in a line through the yard scrambling for pecans. It was like finding gold nuggets. We had sacks, paper bags, cans, anything in which to put our nuts. Nannan fashioned herself a great tool so she wouldn't have to bend down because she had a bad back. On the end of a shortened broom stick, she had attached a small can with a nail. Her can acted like a scoop with which she could pick up several pecans at a time. Of course, along with her pecans she could not help but pick up a few leaves and twigs. Her sack was always a mess!

At the end of the day, Papa would take our sacks of pecans to Foti's Store where they would be weighed and we would be paid. I was allowed to keep my money to do with as I pleased. Oh what mad money it was! I could treat my friends to Grapettes at the drug store, go to the movies, or to the football games. I was one of the last of the big spenders.

As the pecan season drew to a close, Papa would keep the last sack to crack and peel for our use. He sat for hours in the garage, cracking pecans and putting them in a large tray. On Saturday, he positioned himself in front of the television and while watching football games he contentedly peeled pecans.

Mama's freezer looked like a squirrel's storehouse. She kept a ledger of sorts, designating so many bags for Christmas goodies, so many for roasting, and a few to give to various less fortunate relatives.

Here are a few tips for storing pecans that you gather yourself or receive as gifts.

As soon as they are thoroughly dry, pecans should be stored in airtight containers in a cool, dry, dark place. Pecans are rich in oil and will become stale or rancid quickly if not stored properly. Shelled or unshelled nuts will stay fresh for about a year stored in airtight containers in the refrigerator, or for several years in the freezer. Unbroken kernels stay fresh longer than broken pieces. Keep in mind that about 2-1/2 pounds of pecans in the shell yield one pound of shelled nuts, or about four cups. Now you can use them in recipes.

TOASTED (OR ROASTED) PECANS

3 cups shelled pecans
salt
1/2 stick margarine

For each 3 cups of shelled pecans, melt half stick margarine in shallow baking pan. Stir in pecans, coating with margarine.

Roast in a slow 275-300-degree oven for about 45 minutes to an hour, or until desired degree of toastiness is reached. Stir at 15 minute intervals. When done, drain on absorbent paper; salt while warm. Be careful not to over toast. Smaller pecans cook faster, and the amount of moisture in pecans affects cooking time. Store in airtight containers.

Pecan pie is a fixture on holiday tables in Louisiana. I've tasted many versions of the delicacy, and this is absolutely the best. The secret is the dark corn syrup.

PECAN PIE

Makes 1 pie

3 eggs
1/2 cup sugar
1 rounded tablespoon flour
1-1/2 cups dark corn syrup
1 teaspoon vanilla
1 cup pecans

Beat the eggs. In a separate bowl, mix the sugar and flour together; be sure to mix well. Add the sugar mixture to the eggs. Add the corn syrup and vanilla. Add the pecans; fold carefully into the rest of the mixture. Pour into an unbaked 9-inch pie shell and bake for 45 minutes to 1 hour, or until filling is set. Do not overcook. This recipe makes a very full 9-inch pie.

SKILLET COOKIES

2 egg yolks
1 stick butter or margarine
1/2 cup sugar
1 cup pecans, chopped
8 ounces dates, chopped
2 cups rice krispies
shredded coconut

Cook first three ingredients in skillet for 5 minutes. Add dates and pecans. Cook 5 minutes longer. Remove from heat. Add rice krispies and mix well. Cool enough to handle, then shape into small balls and roll in coconut.

The squirrels and I are going to have a ball for the next few weeks!

Winter

    ***J**ust as the last leaves of autumn stop falling, winter comes barreling through Louisiana fast on the heels of the first cold front that sweeps in from the west. Great storm clouds filled with torrents of rain burst open over the low-lying terrain. With harvesting done, it's time for the people of south Louisiana to gather around stoves and kitchen tables and prepare for holiday feasts. Papa Noël is on his way and Le Petit Bonhomme Janvier will be right behind. Then it's time for one of the favorite of all Louisiana celebrations—Carnival. Weeks of parades, balls, and galas culminate with Mardi Gras—Fat Tuesday. Following Mardi Gras are the forty days of the Lenten season of penance, fasting, and abstinence in preparation for the coming of Easter. As Easter approaches, the bleakness of winter begins to disappear, and the warming days of March herald the coming of spring.*

Cold Nights, Warm Food

I'm not particularly fond of winter in the South. The sun sets earlier, and I no longer have my quiet time watching the sun go down. If I want quiet time, I have to get up earlier and watch the sun come up. My lush, semi-tropical plants must be moved indoors, and my lawn furniture finds a new home in the shed, away from the elements.

But I like to think that I'm flexible, so I've learned to make the best of the shorter, colder days. When I'm up earlier I have time to linger over a cup of coal-black coffee and have a leisurely breakfast while catching up on my reading. In the evenings, I eat earlier and find that I want a sweet snack before I bury myself in the heavy quilts of my bed.

While my tiny kitchen is a bit too warm in the summer, it's a cozy place to spend some time in the winter. Preparing a snack in my warm kitchen is a great way to end a winter day, and a snack that is close to my heart is FRIED SQUAW BREAD.

FRIED SQUAW BREAD

Makes approximately 24 pastries

1-1/2 cups sifted all-purpose flour
1/2 teaspoon salt
1-1/2 teaspoons baking powder
1 tablespoon sugar
1/2 tablespoon melted butter
3/4 cup water
vegetable oil for deep frying
powdered sugar
Squaw Bread Syrup (recipe follows)

Sift dry ingredients together. Add melted butter and water. Mix thoroughly. Drop tablespoons of the batter into the hot oil. Cook for 2 to 4 minutes until golden brown. Drain on paper towels; sprinkle with powdered sugar. Serve hot with syrup.

SQUAW BREAD SYRUP

1 cup light brown sugar
2 cups light corn syrup
2 tablespoons cooking oil
1 tablespoon maple flavoring

Put all ingredients in a saucepan and heat to the boiling point, stirring constantly. Dribble over bread.

To go along with this snack, I like spiced coffee (if you must, use decaffeinated).

SPICED COFFEE

In a 4-cup coffee pot, put 4 rounded tablespoons of ground coffee. Sprinkle the ground coffee with 1/2 teaspoon cinnamon, 1/4 teaspoon nutmeg, and a few dashes of ground cloves. Drip coffee as usual. Top each cup of hot coffee with whipped cream.

Although winter days are short, they tend to seem long when they have to be spent indoors. To wile away the hours, it's best to put a pot of soup or gumbo on the stove to simmer while wind and rain rattle the windows.

I remember waking one morning to the sounds of the north wind shaking the shutters and roaring through the lonely patio. In my centrally-heated home I was as warm as toast, but I thought about the countless mornings of my childhood when the mere thought of getting out from beneath the mound of quilts and blankets struck fear in my heart. Suppose my slippers weren't right where I left them and I had to put my feet on the cold floor? And what if the Boogey Man had come during the night and confiscated my chenille robe because he didn't have a warm quilt like mine? Even the thought of moving my feet from their warm nest to the other side of the bed made me shudder.

But here in my present warm abode, I didn't have to worry. If my slippers had been kicked under the bed, I knew the warm carpet awaited my feet. Once up, I peeped through the window. Yes, it was one of those cold, gray days, a perfect day for making a gumbo. I made a grocery list. I needed a hen. Mama always says that a hen makes a better gumbo. I pulled a package of andouille sausage out of the freezer and added oysters to my list, along with French bread.

I braced myself against the wind and headed for my car. There wasn't a leaf left on the trees and dark clouds were rolling in from the west. A real gumbo day indeed!

CHICKEN, ANDOUILLE, AND OYSTER GUMBO

Serves 6

One 3-4 pound hen, cut into frying pieces
salt and cayenne pepper
1 cup oil
1 cup flour
2 medium onions, chopped
1 sweet green pepper, chopped
2 stalks celery, chopped
10 cups chicken broth
2 bay leaves

1/2 teaspoon thyme

1 pound andouille, cut into 1/4-inch slices

1 pint of oysters with their liquor

Season the hen well with salt and cayenne pepper. In a heavy black iron pot, make a dark roux by slowly browning the oil and flour, stirring constantly. When I attempted to make my first roux years ago, I remember calling Papa and asking him how long it would take and he told me, "The time it takes to drink two beers." Not being a beer drinker, I had to come up with my own system. I put on two record albums, and when they have played out, my roux is usually just about right.

When the roux is the color of a pecan, add the onions, sweet green pepper, and celery; cook until vegetables are wilted, about 10-15 minutes.

Add the chicken broth. I usually warm it up in a pot just a bit before adding it to the roux mixture. Next, add the chicken. There are those who will tell you to brown the chicken first, but I throw it in raw. Add the bay leaves and thyme. Cook over medium heat for one hour. Add the andouille and cook for at least another hour or until hen is tender. Check seasonings. A few minutes before serving, add the oysters and their liquor; simmer just until the oysters curl. If the gumbo becomes too thick during cooking, simply add more chicken broth or water.

Following a blustery storm we are sometimes blessed with a gorgeous bluebird day. The sky is a deep blue and save for a few evergreens, it provides the only color in the landscape. A bluebird day is a great day for a trip to the country to see Mama.

With a couple of quarts of chicken, andouille, and oyster gumbo packed in an ice chest in the trunk of the car, I forsook the interstate and opted to travel the back roads to St. Martinville. At the time, I was living at Oak Alley Plantation, which is located upriver from New Orleans, below Baton Rouge. My usual route to St. Martinville, because it was the quickest, was Interstate 10, although it did mean that I had to cross the mighty Mississippi not once, but twice.

But that particular day, I wasn't in a hurry, so I decided to drive along Highway 1 from Donaldsonville to Port Allen, thus eliminating any crossings over the Mississippi River. This route would allow me to drive through several small towns along the river, with a change of scenery for the first fifty or so miles of my trek.

The sugarcane harvest was just about at its end, and I watched the mills along Highway 1—St. James, Cinclare, and Cora Texas—belching white-gray smoke and emitting the sweet-sour odors of processed cane.

At Port Allen, just across the river from the state capital of Baton Rouge, I turned west on to Interstate 10, a ribbon of concrete and steel that took me through the heart of the Atchafalaya Basin, which at this time of year was clothed in drab winter dress. On this day, the dancing rays of sunshine bounced over the quiet waterways, making the noble cypress trees look like soldiers guarding the sleeping land.

When I arrived at Mama's, she had a pot of coffee brewing and a tray of her treasured demitasse cups set on the breakfast table. She had just poured our coffee when my brother-in-law Al came rushing in, looking for her big gumbo pot.

His wife, my sister Edna, has a cold weather ritual. She says that to keep warm and cozy, all one has to do is keep a pot of gumbo simmering at the back of the stove all day while baking bread, muffins, and biscuits. Like a squirrel, Edna hordes all the necessary ingredients for these items in the back of her freezer and pantry, and when cold weather strikes, she is Boy Scout prepared.

As Al banged the screen door shut, he hollered to us to come join them for gumbo later. Mama and I wondered if it was going to be a seafood gumbo, or perhaps chicken and okra, or might it be a chicken and sausage gumbo?

We were on our second cup of coffee when the telephone rang. It was Maria, my sister-in-law, calling to invite us for a gumbo dinner the next day.

Mama's eyes rolled as she accepted the invitation. She said we were going to be gumboed to death. After hanging up the phone she admitted that she had given some serious thought earlier in the day of making a shrimp and okra gumbo. It was then that I confessed that in my ice chest in the car was a chicken, andouille, and oyster gumbo. We howled. We agreed that we would eat them all. We would lunch on mine, have supper with Al and Edna, and enjoy Sunday dinner with Maria and Henri Clay.

The day after my gumbo treat, I thought about oysters, those salty, delectable bivalves that are a favorite treat among Creoles and Acadians alike.

During the cool months of fall and the cold ones of winter, oyster luggers can be seen following the jagged shoreline of the Gulf of Mexico and the neighboring bays, harvesting the oyster beds.

Many days find New Orleanians standing elbow to elbow at marble counters behind which shuckers pry open oysters to fill the many orders during the noon hour.

"Joe, give me the biggest ones you have," says a hefty dock worker.

"Mister, I like the small ones, if you please," squeaks a fragile dowager.

Purists slurp the oysters straight out of the shell with no adornments. Others prefer them doused in a sauce that is custom-made by each consumer. In a small paper cup, ketchup, hot sauce, a splash of olive oil, and a hefty dab of horseradish is stirred around and used for dipping the ice-cold oysters. Some people make a big "to do" about squeezing lemon juice over their oysters, and crackers, more often than a cocktail fork, are the vehicles by which the oysters get from tray to mouth. Cold beer is the accepted liquid accompaniment.

While I didn't experience the oyster bar concept until I was well into my teens, many a late Friday night, upon returning from a high school football game, I found Papa, my uncles, and their cronies sitting at the kitchen table slurping down raw oysters.

Earlier in the day, Papa would have visited his old friend, Mr. Frank "Banane" Foti who had a stand in St. Martinville where one could get roasted peanuts, fresh vegetables, and freshly shucked oysters. Mr. Banane packed the oysters in little white cardboard boxes with wire handles (what we know now as "takee-outee" containers) which Papa would then store in the refrigerator for the Friday night feast.

I was allowed to put my stool next to Papa and watch the ritual of the men mixing up their cocktail sauce. On the table was a large bottle of ketchup, a jar of horseradish, several wedges of lemon, hot sauce, and olive oil. Each man had his own cup, and with great vigor they would stir up their own concoctions according to individual tastes. A big basket of saltine crackers was also on the table. The white containers of cold oysters were passed around and around as the men jabbed the oysters, dipped them in sauce, and threw them down their throats.

I watched in amazement. I was not quite ready to put the gray, slimy mollusks in my mouth. Papa sometimes gave me his cup of sauce into which he poured a little oyster juice; I would break up a couple of crackers in it and thought that was quite acceptable.

It wasn't until college that a sophisticated upperclassman took me out to Poor Boy's Riverside Inn in Lafayette for dinner and asked if he could order for me. I of course thought that this was just the cat's meow. But lo and behold, as a first course he ordered a dozen raw oysters on the half shell. I dared not refuse to eat them. As I mixed up my sauce he told me he was a purist and didn't need all that razzmatazz. Somehow, with enough crackers, I was able to eat them all. And from that night on, I was an avid raw oyster fan.

When oysters are at their peak, it's a perfect opportunity for an oyster *soirée*.

If you have friends who will volunteer to shuck, get a sack of oysters in the shells. Or, if that seems like too much work, a couple of gallons of shucked oysters will do.

Allow for some to be eaten raw, on the half shell. The rest may be used for a variety of delectable dishes that should satisfy the craving of even the most insatiable oyster lover.

OYSTER AND ARTICHOKE CASSEROLE

Makes 12 appetizer portions

6 whole fresh artichokes
8 tablespoons butter or margarine
3 tablespoons flour
2/3 cups finely chopped green onions
1 teaspoon minced garlic
1/2 cup finely chopped parsley
1 pint oyster liquor
pinch each of ground thyme, ground oregano, and marjoram
salt and pepper to taste
6 dozen oysters
thinly sliced lemons sprinkled with paprika for garnish

Boil the artichokes in unsalted water until tender; cool. Scrape the tender pulp from the leaves. Clean the hearts and mash together with the pulp. In a skillet, melt the butter or margarine and stir in the flour slowly and constantly until smooth and well blended. Add the green onions and garlic; cook until slightly wilted. Add the oyster liquor, thyme, oregano, marjoram, parsley, salt, and pepper.

Simmer for 15 minutes. Add the oysters and cook slowly until edges curl. Add the artichoke mash and blend into the mixture. Spoon the mixture into individual casserole cups or shells; garnish with lemon slices. This filling may also be put into small pastry shells, heated, and served as hors d'ouevres.

There are some cooks who will tell you that OYSTERS CASINO is made with a tomato-based sauce. This version was created by a chef friend who prepared it at my restaurant, Chez Marcelle, which I operated during the early 1980s near Broussard, Louisiana. It has not a bit of tomato in it, but it is a superb dish that can be served as an elegant appetizer or as a late Sunday afternoon repast. It's perfect for a cold evening spent in front of a blazing fire with lots of hot French bread and a chilled bottle of white wine.

OYSTERS CASINO

Serves 4 as an appetizer or 2 as a main course

1/3 pound Italian sausage, removed from casing and crumbled
1 cup finely chopped sweet green pepper
1 cup finely chopped white onion
1/2 cup chopped pimiento
1 teaspoon minced garlic
salt and pepper to taste
3 tablespoons olive oil
1/2 cup cream sherry
1 cup half-and-half
1/2 cup flour
1 cup melted butter
1 pound grated sharp Cheddar cheese
1 dozen freshly shucked oysters
4 slices cooked bacon

Sauté the vegetables and sausage in olive oil until meat has browned. Add sherry and half-and-half; cook for 10 minutes, stirring constantly. Thicken sauce with flour which has been dissolved in melted butter. When sauce has thickened, add grated cheese. Season to taste. Remove from heat and allow to cool to room temperature; then chill in refrigerator until firm.

Place 3 oysters on a scallop shell or in a ramekin and bake in a 350-degree oven for 5 minutes, or until edges of the oysters curl. Top the oysters with chilled sauce and a half slice of cooked bacon. Return to oven and cook until sauce bubbles, or about 15 minutes.

Everyone has heard of Oysters Rockefeller, the famous dish created at Antoine's in New Orleans and named after one of the wealthiest men in the United States, John D. Rockefeller. Antoine's recipe has never been disclosed, but there are many versions served in and around New Orleans. Brian Richard, the same chef who created OYSTERS CASINO for my restaurant, came up with a rich soup which he dubbed OYSTER ROCKEFELLER SOUP.

OYSTER ROCKEFELLER SOUP

Serves 8

1 cup minced yellow onions
1 tablespoon minced garlic
1/2 cup minced celery
3 cups chicken stock, divided
2 cups cooked and drained spinach, pureed in a food processor
2 pints oysters and their liquor
2 pints half-and-half
3/4 cup freshly grated Parmesan or Romano cheese
1/3 cup cornstarch dissolved in 1/2 cup Pernod
salt and cayenne pepper to taste
1 tablespoon anise seeds

Cook onion, garlic, and celery in 1 cup of chicken broth for 10 minutes or until slightly tender. Add spinach puree and simmer for 5 minutes. Add remaining chicken stock and liquor from the oysters. Slowly add half-and-half and blend well. Cook for 10 minutes, stirring constantly. Add cheese, whisking well. Thicken with cornstarch dissolved in the Pernod. When soup is thick and hot, remove from heat and add drained oysters. Add anise seed and season to taste with salt and cayenne pepper. Garnish each bowl of soup with lemon slices.

When they are at their peak, freshly shucked oysters invariably find their way into the pots of creative south Louisiana cooks. These innovative cooks give birth to a new oyster dish practically every day of the season. This was the case when I came home one late afternoon with a small carton of oysters, swimming in their delicate liquor.

A golden moon was on the rise, glowing just above the horizon. There was a chill in the air, but it wasn't so cold that I couldn't grill outdoors. I had two nice, thick pork chops and some sweet potatoes. With a little ingenuity, I could have myself a delightful evening. A small banquet for two seemed to be in order. A neighbor accepted my invitation for dinner and came over with a good bottle of red wine.

While the charcoal was getting hot, I put lighted candles all around my deck. I took out a couple of old hurricane lanterns and set them on the patio table. While my neighbor and I exchanged local gossip, I created an oyster dressing for the pork chops.

STUFFED PORK CHOPS WITH OYSTER DRESSING

Serves 2

2 center-cut pork chops, 1-1/2 inches thick
1 pint oysters, drained
2 tablespoons butter or margarine
3 green onions, finely chopped
1 sprig parsley, minced
1 tablespoon finely chopped sweet green pepper
1 egg, beaten
seasoned bread crumbs
salt, cayenne pepper, and garlic powder

In a skillet, melt the butter and cook the oysters until the edges begin to curl. Add the green onions, parsley, and sweet green pepper. Cook for 2-3 minutes. Add the beaten egg and enough bread crumbs to thicken the mixture. Season to taste with salt, pepper, and garlic powder. Allow the mixture to cool to room temperature. While the dressing cools, prepare the pork chops.

Place the chops on a cutting board so that the bone is away from you. At the narrow tip end of the chop, insert the point of a stiff-bladed knife and push it in along the underside of the back fat, all the way up until you make contact with the bone. Be careful not to cut through the membrane that separates the back fat from the meat—that's what holds the dressing in.

When you have made contact with the bone, cut along it through the meaty part of the chop from right to left to form a pocket. Season the chops well with salt, cayenne pepper, and garlic powder. Spoon in the stuffing, pressing it in firmly. Rub the chops with a little cooking oil. Grill on a medium fire for 30 minutes or until juices run clear when pierced with a fork. If you don't want to butterfly the pork chops yourself, your butcher can do it for you.

While the chops were on the grill, I spied some fresh mint growing near the deck. I chopped up a few leaves, added two tablespoons of vinegar and a teaspoon of sugar and brought all to a boil in a small saucepan. I boiled the sauce briefly, then let it stand for a few minutes before pouring it over the grilled pork chops. The sweet potatoes had been baking slowing in the oven and were done to a turn when we sat down to dinner.

The moon was high when we settled down for our evening repast. It was quite an enchanting evening and as we chatted I reminisced about an oyster soup Mama used to make on chilly winter nights.

OYSTER SOUP WITHOUT MILK

Serves 6

3 tablespoons vegetable oil
3 tablespoons sifted flour
1 large onion, chopped
4 sprigs of fresh parsley, minced
1 quart of boiling water
4 dozen oysters and their liquor
1 tablespoon of butter
salt and cayenne pepper to taste

Heat the vegetable oil in a large, heavy pot. When the oil is hot, add the flour and make a light brown roux, stirring constantly to avoid burning. When it has reached a light brown color, add the chopped onions and minced parsley and continue to stir. Strain the oyster liquor from the oysters and add it to a quart of boiling water. Pour the liquor/water mixture into the roux slowly, stirring constantly. When it begins to come to a boil, reduce to a simmer, add the oysters and the butter, and cook until the edges begin to curl. Season to taste. Serve with crackers or toast points. If a thicker, heartier soup is desired, milk may be substituted for the water.

On cold nights after football games, Mama sometimes had hot oyster pies waiting for us. They were warm and spicy and took the chill off the bones.

OYSTER PIE

Serves 6

Two 9-inch pie crusts
4 slices of thick bacon
1/4 cup chopped onions
1/2 cup chopped green onions

1/4 cup chopped parsley
1/2 teaspoon cayenne pepper
salt to taste (the oysters may be salty enough)
1 quart oysters, drained
melted butter

Preheat oven to 375 degrees. In a skillet fry the bacon until crisp; drain and crumble. Set aside. Add onions to the bacon drippings in the skillet and cook until onions are wilted. Add the parsley and cayenne pepper. Remove from heat and scrape the mixture into a mixing bowl. Add the oysters and toss gently. Brush the pie crust with a little melted butter and pour in the oyster mixture. Check for seasonings. Top with the other pie crust and prick with a fork. Bake for 30-40 minutes until the top crust is golden brown.

Joyeux Noel

The stoves and ovens of south Louisiana rarely get cold at any time of the year, but during the weeks between Thanksgiving and Christmas, kitchens are frantic with preparations for the holidays.

Just about every day of the week finds Mama and Aunt Lois whipping out batches of fudge, pralines, and yummy lizzies for gift-giving and for family consumption. As a child I was sometimes put to work in what we all called "the candy factory." Pecans had to be chopped, pots had to be stirred and watched closely, and festive cans and jars had to be tied with ribbons and labeled before delivery was made to friends and relatives. I can't say I minded. After all, I got to lick the spoons, taste the crumbles, and I was always rewarded with a little stash of my very own.

My Aunt Grace, otherwise known as Cina by her many nieces and nephews, is the queen of pralines. Cina has a special pot in which she makes these delightful candies. There's really nothing special about the pot, other than it is a heavy black iron pot, but it is the designated praline pot.

CINA'S PRALINES

Makes approximately 2 dozen pralines

1 pound light brown sugar (or 3 cups)
1/8 teaspoon salt
3/4 cup evaporated milk
1 tablespoon butter
2 cups pecan halves

Mix sugar, salt, milk, and butter in a heavy pot. Cook over low heat, stirring all the while, until sugar is dissolved. Add pecans and cook over medium heat to the soft ball stage. Remove from heat. Allow to cool for 5 minutes. Stir rapidly until mixture begins to thicken and coats the pecans lightly. Drop by teaspoons onto aluminum foil or onto a lightly buttered baking sheet. When the candy has cooled, gently lift from surface and store in airtight container.

Note: If candy becomes too stiff, add a few drops of hot water to the mixture.

I have another praline recipe I learned when I was living at Oak Alley Plantation. Princess Margaret of Great Britain was visiting New Orleans and asked to be shown a plantation. Thus it came to pass that she came to Oak Alley for coffee, or tea, if you prefer. From our collection of old plantation recipes came this classic.

ALTHEA'S PRALINES

1 cup buttermilk
2 cups sugar
1 teaspoon baking soda
a large pinch of salt
2 teaspoons vanilla
1/8 pound butter
2 cups pecans

Stir the buttermilk and sugar together with the soda and salt in a deep, heavy pot. Stir constantly until mahogany brown in color. Add the vanilla and butter, and beat until the mixture begins to thicken. Add the pecans and drop by tablespoons onto a marble slab or waxed paper. Allow to cool.

We knew they were fit for a princess when she sent one of her ladies-in-waiting to the kitchen for the recipe and a box of the delicacies to take with her.

Mama is an absolute fanatic about fudge. At Christmas time she makes so much that we laugh at the number of tins she stashes. One year, several months after the holiday season, we came upon a couple of tins hidden in her armoire. We asked her if she hid those for her own snacking when no one was about! Her most special fudge is not chocolate and is called RUSSIAN TAFFY.

RUSSIAN TAFFY

Makes approximately 24 pieces of candy

3 cups sugar
1 cup milk
One 14-ounce can sweetened condensed milk
1-1/2 cups chopped pecans
4 tablespoons butter
1 tablespoon vanilla

Combine sugar, milk, and condensed milk. Cook until mixture forms a soft ball in a cup of cool water. Remove from heat and add pecans, butter, and vanilla. Beat until it becomes thick. Pour into a buttered 9 x 12 pan. Cool and cut into 1-inch squares. This can become chocolate fudge by the addition of 1/2 cup cocoa when mixing the sugar, milk, and condensed milk.

My sister Edna and I always volunteered to make SANDIES, or COCOONS as they are sometimes called. For every one of these cookie-like confections that made it into the candy tin, we ate two.

SANDIES (COCOONS)

Makes 4 dozen

1 cup butter
1/3 cup sugar
2 teaspoons water
2 teaspoons vanilla
2 cups all-purpose flour
1 cup chopped pecans
confectioner's sugar

Cream the butter and sugar. Add the water and vanilla; mix well. Add the flour and pecans. Chill the dough for 2-3 hours. Shape the dough into small balls. Bake on an ungreased cookie sheet in a 350-degree oven for about 20 minutes. Cool slightly and roll in confectioner's sugar.

Lizzies, which are little fruitcake cookies, were the specialty of Mama's good friend, Miss Do. She had no children, but many of us were like her adopted nieces and nephews. Each Christmas season she brought us each a box of lizzies, and we treasured them dearly.

LIZZIES

Makes approximately 2 dozen

2 tablespoons margarine
1/2 cup plus 2 tablespoons brown sugar
1 egg
3/4 cup flour plus 1/4 cup in which to dredge fruit
1/4 teaspoon baking soda
1/4 teaspoon cinnamon
1/4 teaspoon cloves
1 tablespoon buttermilk
1/4 cup bourbon
1/4 pound red candied cherries, chopped

1/4 pound green candied cherries, chopped
1/4 pound dark raisins
1/4 pound white raisins
2 cups chopped pecans

Cream margarine and sugar; add egg and mix well. Add 3/4 cup flour, soda, cinnamon, cloves, buttermilk, and bourbon. Dredge raisins, pecans, and cherries in 1/4 cup of flour. Add to first mixture. Mix well. Form tablespoon-size balls and bake on a greased cookie sheet at 300 degrees for 15 minutes.

Unfortunately I never knew either one of my grandmothers. One died before I was born and the other when I was a little baby. However, every time we have a Bienvenu family gathering, everyone talks about how good a cook "Mrs. Lazaire" was. Her name was Leoncia, but my grandfather's name was Lazaire, and back then people called them Mr. and Mrs. Lazaire.

Leoncia's family had a hotel and restaurant in St. Martinville, and that is where she learned her magic cooking secrets.

Most of Leoncia's eight daughters are pretty good cooks, and they all have their specialties. Aunt Taudie makes incredible pies. Aunt Taye is known for her divinity fudge, and Aunt Jenny makes *daube glacé* or *daube froide*, if you prefer.

Aunt Jenny usually makes *daube* during the holidays, and every time she does I make her promise to give me the recipe. Aunt Jenny always says, "Mais, cher, I don't have a recipe. I do it from memory and you'll just have to come watch me do it."

So that is exactly what I did. Be forewarned. This is not a dish you can whip up in an hour. Reserve an afternoon for this one.

AUNT JENNY'S DAUBE GLACE

3 pound round rump roast, boneless
1 teaspoon salt
1/2 teaspoon cayenne pepper
3 tablespoons vegetable oil
3 cups chopped onions
3 cloves garlic, minced
2 cups carrots, thinly sliced
equal parts of water and beef consomme
2 pigs feet, cut in half, lengthwise
water
1/2 cup dry sherry
2 bay leaves
1/2 teaspoon thyme
2 envelopes gelatin
pimiento strips
parsley leaves
green olives, sliced
several slices of carrots

Rub roast with salt and cayenne pepper. In a large, heavy pot, brown the roast in hot vegetable oil. Add the onions, garlic, carrots, and enough water and beef consomme to cover the beef. Cover and simmer slowly for 2-3 hours until the meat is tender. Add more liquid if necessary to keep meat covered.

In another pot, place the pig's feet (secured in a net bag), bay leaves, thyme, enough water to cover, and sherry. Boil for 2 hours until meat falls off the bones.

When the roast is tender, remove from pot. Strain cooking stock in a sieve, mashing the vegetables well to remove all liquid. Set aside. Remove pigs feet and pick off the meat. Strain the stock in which the pigs feet were cooked. Add meat from pigs' feet to stock; stir in gelatin and dissolve. Combine the roast stock with the pigs' feet stock, skimming off the fat that rises to the top.

Place the roast in a 4-quart mold or bowl. (The roast can be cut in two, and two small molds can then be made.) On the bottom of the mold or bowl, place pimiento strips, several leaves of parsley, sliced olives, and sliced carrots and pour a little of the combined stock over the vegetables. Place in refrigerator and allow the stock to congeal. Sliced lemons and sliced hard boiled eggs can also be used to garnish the bottom of the mold or bowl.

Remove from refrigerator. Place the roast on top, then gently add the stock to cover the meat. Allow to cool. Return mold or bowl to refrigerator and chill for at least 10-12 hours. Before unmolding, scrape off any fat that has floated to the top. Run a knife around the edges of the mold or bowl, then dip the bottom of the mold or bowl in hot water for a few seconds. Place an inverted plate or platter over the bottom of the bowl, and grasping the plate and mold together firmly, turn them over. Rap bottom of mold of bowl sharply on a table or counter. The jellied beef should slide out easily. Refrigerate until ready to serve. Slice thinly.

In the old days, the sliced daube was served for a meal along with boiled new potatoes or fresh green beans. If you wish to serve it for a cocktail party, slice the jellied meat into smaller pieces so guests can place it on toast points, crackers, or toasted croutons.

The holidays are indeed a very special time in Acadiana. Not unlike the rest of the world, there's much visiting between friends and families. Gifts are bought or made, wrapped, and delivered. Small children are urged to be very, very good because *Papa Noël* is watching to see who has been naughty or nice. There are tree-decorating parties and yes, even yard-decorating *soirées*.

Because of the many bayous and streams that wind through south Louisiana, a great many homes are located on some body of water. In St. Martinville and Lafayette, for example, residents along Bayou Teche and the Vermilion River erect extravagant Christmas scenes that can be viewed from the water. These range from *Papa Noël* being pulled in his sleigh by festive alligators, to humble nativity scenes. Many a night before Christmas, boats loaded with children and adults who are bundled warmly against the cold night air, putt-putt along the waterways observing the sights.

Children hum Christmas carols in between stops along the bayou to see friends and relatives. Cups of eggnog and trays of num-nums are passed around. It's a time of celebration and goodwill.

CELEBRATION EGGNOG

Makes 8-10 cups

6 eggs, separated
1 cup sugar
1 pint bourbon
1 quart heavy whipping cream
nutmeg

Beat egg yolks until they are light yellow. Add 2/3 cup of the sugar and beat well. The yolks should be beaten until they are thick and lemon-colored, no matter how much your arm aches for relief. Slowly add the bourbon, beating all the time. When this much of your task is done, set aside the egg and bourbon mixture and turn your attention to the egg whites. Beat the egg whites until they are stiff but not too dry, adding the remaining 1/3 cup of sugar, beating it as you would for meringue. Then slowly pour the sugar-bourbon-egg yolk mixture into the egg whites, folding it in ever so gently. Next, whip the cream and fold it into the other mixture. Even if you have been doing this by hand, you will not be too exhausted to stand back and admire the bowl of fluff you have produced. Warm just a bit before serving. Serve in cups and sprinkle with ground nutmeg. This may also be served chilled.

The eggnog is especially good accompanied by fig cake. It's a perfect opportunity to use some of the fig preserves that were put up the previous summer.

VICKY'S FIG CAKE

2 cups sugar
3 eggs
1 cup vegetable oil
1 cup milk
2 cups flour
2 teaspoons cinnamon
1 teaspoon salt
1 teaspoon soda

2 cups mashed fig preserves
1 cup pecan pieces

Cream the sugar and eggs. Add vegetable oil and stir well. Add milk and mix well. In a separate bowl, combine the flour, cinnamon, salt, and soda. Add to first mixture and then add the pecans and figs. Stir again to combine. Pour into a 12-cup bundt pan; bake at 350 degrees for 1 hour. Cool before slicing.

A favorite num-num of mine is little sausages smothered in a sweet and sour sauce. These are easily stabbed with toothpicks for munching.

SWEET AND SOUR SAUSAGES

2 pounds smoked cocktail sausages
One 6-ounce jar yellow mustard
One 10-ounce jar of tart jelly, such as currant

Slowly heat the mustard and jelly and stir until all is well mixed. Add the smoked sausages and cook for 10-15 minutes. Serve in a chafing dish and let guests pick them up with toothpicks.

From the time I was a toddler until I was eight or nine years old, my great-aunt Isabelle, fondly called Nannan by all of her family and friends, lived next door to us and always walked through the backyard to join us for libations early on Christmas Eve.

We would gather in the living room where the Christmas tree and the *crèche* were the focal point. While Bing Crosby and Gene Autry sang Christmas songs on the radio, Mama would bring in a silver tray set with her best crystal. We all had a thimbleful of cherry bounce and got to open ONE present—just one, mind you.

More often that not, Mama made sure my sister and I opened the boxes that held our red Christmas nightgowns. They were always bedecked with lace ruffles and tiny silk ribbons, and I thought they were much too pretty to sleep in. It wasn't until I got older that I realized the gowns were handmade by Nannan and her sister Tante May, and thus they became even more special to me. I still have a couple of them wrapped in tissue in my treasure trunk. The boys, my two brothers, received warm plaid flannel pajamas which I thought were rather plain but sensible.

Then we were all packed up to bed to dream about what *Papa Noel* was bringing to us. The boys were settled into their knotty pine-paneled room which was decorated with plaid curtains and blankets (to match the pajamas). My sister and I were buried under piles of quilts in Mama and Papa's room since we had to vacate ours to make room for Nannan, who always spent the night. She stayed with us while Mama and Papa went to midnight Mass.

Every Christmas morning I awoke to the smell of Mama's pork roast (which she had put in the oven when she returned from Mass), blended with the scents of brewing coffee and re-heated cinnamon rolls purchased the day before from Mr. Jack's Bakery on Main Street.

The doors to the living room remained closed until everyone had eaten breakfast and Tante May had been fetched to join us. Then with great ceremony, Papa opened the doors to wonderland. Bikes, dolls, footballs, stuffed animals, and baskets of gifts were everywhere!

The next few hours were complete pandemonium, with treks to church, the arrival of aunts and uncles, cousins and friends, and the exchanging of gifts. It usually wasn't until mid-afternoon that we calmed down enough to have Christmas dinner, a combination of dishes prepared by the numerous aunts and highlighted by Mama's pork roast, sometimes a turkey, or perhaps baked capons.

MAMA'S STUFFED PORK ROAST

Serves 12-14

One 10-12-pound pork butt roast
1 large onion, finely chopped
1 large sweet green pepper, finely chopped
10 cloves garlic, thinly sliced
3 teaspoons salt
3 teaspoons cayenne pepper
1 teaspoon black pepper
vegetable oil
2 cups water

Set the roast on a large cutting board or platter. Then, in a small mixing bowl, combine all of the seasonings. Typical ingredients of Cajun cooking, referred to as "seasonings," are chopped onions, sweet green peppers (called bell peppers in Louisiana), salt, red pepper, and black pepper.

With a sharp boning knife, make several deep slits in the roast spaced several inches apart. Using your index finger, stuff the seasoning mixture into the holes. Pack the stuffing firmly. Season the outside of the roast generously with salt and cayenne pepper. Rub the roast lightly with vegetable oil. Place the meat in a heavy roasting pan, put it in a preheated 450-degree oven, and allow it to brown well. When the bottom of the roasting pan begins to sizzle, add the water. More water can be added if the pan becomes too dry. This will mix with the roast drippings and make a dark gravy that can be used now for basting the roast, then later to pour over steamed rice.

When the roast is well browned, reduce heat to 350 degrees, cover, and cook for 3 to 4 hours or until juices run clear when roast is pierced with a fork.

Remove from oven and allow to cool before carving.

Although most side dishes varied from year to year, Mama's roast, her rice dressing, and chicken and oyster patties bought from Aline Garrett (whose recipe was never given out), were always on the menu.

By the way, we never called rice dressing "dirty rice." I never heard that term until I was older, and then it was called such by people who weren't natives.

The rice dressing is always made a day or two in advance to allow the flavors to mix.

RICE DRESSING

Serves 10

2 tablespoons vegetable oil
2 tablespoons flour
1 pound lean ground pork
2 tablespoons vegetable oil
1 cup chopped onion
1/2 cup chopped sweet green pepper
1/2 cup chopped celery
1 pound chicken gizzards, cleaned
water
4 cups cooked rice
1/4 cup chopped parsley
1/2 cup finely chopped green onions
salt and pepper to taste
1 pint raw oysters (optional)
1 cup canned sliced mushrooms (optional)

In a small, heavy saucepan, make a dark brown roux with the oil and flour. Set aside. In a large, heavy skillet, brown the ground pork in vegetable oil. When the meat is brown, add onions, sweet green pepper, and celery;

cook until vegetables are tender. In the meantime, place the cleaned gizzards in a pot with enough water (about 3 cups) to cover the gizzards; boil until tender. Drain the gizzards and reserve the stock. Grind the gizzards in a meat grinder or food processor. Add this to the pork mixture along with the roux. Mix together the gizzards, pork, roux, reserved stock, and seasonings; simmer for 1 to 2 hours. Immediately before serving add the parsley and chopped green onions. Add the rice and mix gently but thoroughly. Adjust seasonings. If you like oysters in your dressing, 1 pint or so can be added in the last 5 minutes of cooking time. A cup of canned sliced mushrooms may also be added with the oysters.

There were many sweets at the Christmas table—remember the fudge, pralines, and lizzies? Aunt Eva could always be counted on to bring a cake of some sort. Her *pièce de résistance*, though, was coconut cake that always appeared to me to be too pretty to cut.

COCONUT CAKE

Cake:

2-1/4 cups flour
1-1/2 cups sugar
3-1/2 teaspoons baking powder
1 teaspoon salt
1/2 cup softened shortening
1 cup milk
1 teaspoon vanilla or almond extract
4 egg whites, unbeaten

Heat oven to 350 degrees. Grease and flour two 8-inch layer pans or a 13 x 9-1/2 x 2 oblong pan. Measure flour and blend with sugar, baking powder, and salt. Add shortening, 2/3 cup of milk, and extract. Beat with a mixer for 2 minutes at medium speed. Scrape sides and bottom of bowl constantly. Add the rest of the milk and egg whites. Beat for 2 more minutes, scraping bowl

frequently. Pour into pans. Bake the layer cake 30-35 minutes and the oblong cake for 35-40 minutes. Cool on wire racks.

Cream Filling:

1/4 cup sugar
1 tablespoon cornstarch
1/4 teaspoon salt
1 cup milk
1 egg yolk, slightly beaten
1 tablespoon butter
1 teaspoon vanilla

Mix sugar, cornstarch, and salt in saucepan. Gradually stir in milk. Bring to a boil over medium heat, stirring constantly. Boil 1 minute. Remove from heat. Stir at least half of hot mixture into egg yolk, then blend egg and milk into remaining mixture. Boil 1 minute more. Remove from heat. Blend in butter and vanilla. Cool, stirring occasionally. If making a layer cake, spread cooled filling between the two layers. Then top with icing.

Fluffy Icing:

1/2 cup sugar
2 tablespoons water
1/4 cup light corn syrup
2 egg whites
1 teaspoon vanilla

Mix sugar, water, and corn syrup in a saucepan. Cover saucepan and bring to a rolling boil. Remove cover and cook until a temperature of 242 degrees has been reached on a candy thermometer, or until syrup spins long threads. Beat egg whites until stiff enough to hold a point. Pour hot syrup very slowly in a thin stream into the beaten egg whites. Continue beating until frosting holds peaks. Blend in vanilla. Spread on cool cake and decorate with flaked coconut. Chopped pecans or almonds may be sprinkled on top.

After the dinner table was cleared and the good silver and china had been washed and put away, it was time to bid everyone a long Creole good-bye. Some of us would be seeing one another again on New Year's Day, but there were always a few relatives who had come a long distance, so it might be another year before we would see them again. It was a sad-happy time for me, but I was always comforted by the fact that I could put on my red lacy gown and that my new doll for the year could sleep with me.

The week between Christmas and New Year's has always reminded me of a lull in a storm—a break between the Christmas feasting and the New Year's toasting. But it has also been a time to visit with friends who are in town for the holidays. In recent years, I have made it a tradition to have an elegant dinner party at which we can all have an opportunity to dress up. What better time for the men to sport new ties or a cashmere jacket and the ladies to show off their baubles and beads?

And too, it gives me a chance to use some of the treasured old china and silver pieces that have been handed down in my family from generation to generation. Among these heirlooms are several hand-painted oval fish plates, along with slender fish knives with curved points, designed to be used to pick the bones out of a whole fish.

In genteel New Orleans homes of days gone past, it was not uncommon to have fish for breakfast and again as a course for dinner. More often than not, either small whole fish or fish steaks, with bone in, were served, rather than the fillets in vogue these days. The fish were served alone, with perhaps a sprig of parsley and a wedge of lemon, on colorful fish plates.

Also in my possession are several ornate bowls with six compartments known as oyster plates—perfect for serving fresh-from-the-sea cold oysters. Instead of serving them on the half shell, the plates are ideal for a formal dinner party when the oysters can be plopped into the compartments, dabbed with cocktail sauce, and served with a wedge of lemon.

In my antique collection is an elegant set of pear-shaped glasses I recently learned were used for serving syllabub, a drink made with sweetened milk or cream mixed with wine or cider. I've been known to also use them for *parfaits* and *frappés*.

Probably my most treasured pieces are *café brûlot* cups designed in the late nineteenth century by the proprietor of Antoine's Restaurant, Jules Alciatore. These fanciful cups feature a devil holding the bowl part of the cup.

Now on to dinner. I believe I'll serve the following dish on my beautiful fish plates.

BROILED SPANISH MACKERAL

Serves 4

4 tablespoons butter
1 tablespoon fresh strained lemon or lime juice
1/2 teaspoon anchovy paste
1/8 teaspoon cayenne pepper
1/2 teaspoon salt
Four 6-ounce Spanish mackeral fillets, skinned
1 tablespoon vegetable oil
lemon or lime, cut lengthwise into 4 or 8 wedges

Preheat the broiler to its highest setting. Melt the butter in a small saucepan. Remove the pan from the heat and stir in the lemon or lime juice, anchovy paste, cayenne pepper, and salt. Set the sauce aside. Pat the fillets completely dry with paper towels. Then, with a pastry brush, spread vegetable oil evenly over the grid of the broiling pan. Arrange the fillets side-by-side on the grid, and brush them with about 2 tablespoons of the butter sauce. Broil 4 inches from the heat for 4-5 minutes, brushing the fillets once or twice with remaining butter sauce. The fish is done when the tops are golden brown and firm to the touch. Transfer fillets to fish plates and garnish with lemon or lime wedges.

Keep the meal light and serve with boiled new potatoes seasoned with a bit of dill and dribbled with butter.

For dessert, I'll make the syllabub, which can also be served in wine goblets or *parfait* glasses.

SYLLABUB

Serves 8-10

2 cups whipping cream
1/4 cup brandy
1/4 cup dry sherry
1/4 cup sugar
1 tablespoon vanilla
2 lemons

Whip cream until stiff and fluffy. Add brandy, sherry, sugar, vanilla, and the juice and grated rind from the lemons. Mix well until blended. Spoon into dessert glasses. Garnish with a pirouette cookie and a few chocolate sprinkles, or with grated lemon rind.

After dessert, and before my guests depart, I must serve coffee in my treasured *brûlot* cups.

CAFE BRULOT

Serves 4-6, depending on the size of cups used. If you don't have brûlot cups, demitasse cups may be used.

Peel of 1 orange, cut into 1-by-1/8-inch strips
Peel of 1 lemon, cut into 1-by-1/8-inch strips
3 sugar lumps
6 whole cloves
2-inch cinnamon stick
1 cup cognac
1/2 cup curaçao or other orange liqueur
2 cups fresh strong black coffee

Light the burner under a *brûlot* bowl or chafing dish and adjust the flame to low. Drop the orange and lemon peel, sugar lumps, cloves, and cinnamon stick into the bowl or pan, pour in the cognac and curaçao, and stir to dissolve the sugar. When the mixture is warm, ignite it with a match. Stirring gently, pour the coffee into the bowl in a slow, thin stream; continue to stir until the flames die out. Ladle into *brûlot* cups or demitasse cups and serve at once.

Bonne Année et Le Petit Bonhomme Janvier

Christmas has come and gone. The presents have all been opened. All that is left of Christmas dinner is the turkey carcass. The Jolly Old Man has returned to the North Pole and Johnny Mathis has gone hoarse on the holiday music tape. The lights on the Christmas tree seem to have dimmed, and all there is to look forward to are endless football bowl games over New Year's.

But, if you believe in Acadian folklore, legend tells of *Le Petit Bonhomme Janvier*, the little man of January, who visits the homes of good little children (and adults) on New Year's Eve and brings small sacks of treats filled with such things as oranges, pecans, candy, coloring books, and crayons.

I learned about this little man one New Year's Eve when we children were farmed out to Nannan's so Mama and Papa could have a night on the town. We were all still young, and we were allowed to bring one Christmas gift to Nannan's to play with. I had my Toni doll, Henri Clay had his electric football game, Edna had her blackboard and chalk, and Baby Brother Bruce had his white fuzzy stuffed lamb.

Nannan had laid down quilts over the cold, hard wooden floors and turned up the gas heaters which burned brightly in the living room, where the only other light came from the Christmas tree. No television then. Nannan had tuned to WWL radio where music was coming "live and direct" from the Roosevelt Hotel's Blue Room in New Orleans.

Because it was a special night, we were allowed to stay up late because Nannan had promised us a treat. Then we were going to be sent off to the big four poster beds to sleep so that *Le Petit Bonhomme Janvier* could "make his pass" with his goodies.

I remember thinking, "Adults always think of a way to make us go to bed." But I trusted Nannan.

This was our first treat.

On a huge tray lined with her best linen napkins, Nannan brought out coffee cups filled with

steaming hot chocolate thickened with lots of marshmallows and flavored with a bit of strong coffee, and plates of cheese toast.

Then it was off to bed to wait for that little man who comes only after children are asleep. I had full intentions of playing possum, but alas, my body wasn't willing.

Early the next morning, hung on the posters of the beds, was a colorful sack for each of us, filled with sussies of all kinds—apples, oranges, mandarins, candied pecans, little dolls made out of clothespins, and pralines wrapped in red cellophane paper tied up with gold ribbons.

I had a new hero! It is a tradition that is still practiced and even now, as an adult, I can't wait to make and receive bags of goodies from the Little Man of January.

After I was grown, New Year's Eve remained a special night of parties and great celebration. Elegant evenings out on the town became part of my holiday traditions, as they had been for my parents, so many years ago.

After they deposited us safely with Nannan, Mama and Papa would head out for a round of parties held in private homes and at public watering holes. One of their favorite nightspots was Toby's Oak Grove, the "in spot" and ultimate dinner club in Lafayette. Toby's holds a special place in my heart, for once, a long time ago, my parents took me there for an evening I'll never forget.

Mama was decked out in a sleek black silk crepe dress over which she draped her fur wrap. Papa,

with a smart bow tie and double-breasted suit, was quite dapper. The hair style for women then was the chignon, a bun caught at the nape of the neck. Mama's thick black hair was done just so, and she had ebony chop sticks with dangling rhinestones stuck in the bun that were absolutely chic. I thought I was pretty smart in a navy velveteen affair with a sterling silver barrette holding my pageboy hairdo to one side.

After we were seated, the waiter took our cocktail orders, and although I thought myself a bit old for a Shirley Temple, at least it was brought to me in a highball glass. Mama simply ordered a martini, dry, up. Daddy had his usual bourbon on the rocks with a splash.

When our drinks arrived, I watched as Mama sipped her martini from the frosted stem glass, her red fingernails gracefully wrapped round the stem. Then I noticed the red lipstick mark left on the glass and I thought that most intriguing.

It was then that I decided that once I was old enough, I too wanted to always have red nails and red lipstick, and I would have a martini, dry, up.

Through the years I have been fascinated when people make or order a martini. It's a very personal matter, like your choice of a brand of toothpaste. If it's not just like you want it, it's not pleasurable.

At the Fairmont Hotel in New Orleans (many of us still call it the Roosevelt), I once observed a gray-haired, smartly dressed gentleman who came up to the bar, and who, with a nod to the bartender, was brought a small tray. On the tray was a silver shaker and strainer, a small glass ice bucket, a frosty stemmed glass, a thin sliver of lemon peel, a bottle of good gin, a bottle of dry vermouth, and a glass stirrer. With great aplomb, the gentleman made his very own martini. His recipe was three jiggers of gin gently poured over a few cubes of ice in the silver shaker, a whisper of dry vermouth, which was then gently stirred, then strained into the stemmed glass. The lemon peel was passed around the top of the glass, then dropped in the cold liquid. With great relish, the gentleman sipped and smiled. He made

another, and while sipping the second, you could almost see the strain of the day slip away. Ah, what pleasure he had.

I had an aunt and uncle who had a nightly ritual. They had no children, lived in a gracious home, and were devoted to each other. Every evening, when my uncle got home from work, he and my aunt would sit in the parlor where the butler would set up a martini tray from which they would make their drinks. He would put a few chips of ice in a small glass martini pitcher, add several jiggers of iced vodka, a couple of drops of vermouth, give the liquid a swirl, and pour out the ice-cold martinis. Their preference was olives rather than lemon peel. The olives had to be the large Queen olives which were speared on sterling silver monkeys that hung over the rim of the glass. How absolutely civilized.

When the New Year dawns in south Louisiana, pots are simmering on stoves, filled with the traditional black-eyed peas (for good luck) and cabbage (to ensure monetary success).

To get the juices flowing before embarking on a day-long feast (particularly if the New Year's Eve celebration included martinis!), an ice-cold MILK PUNCH or a tangy, spicy BLOODY MARY is in order.

MILK PUNCH

Makes 1 gallon

This drink is quite popular in old New Orleans restaurants and is a favorite during the winter holiday season. It is a soothing, pleasant drink after a night of partying.

1 (4/5-quart) bottle of bourbon (brandy may also be used)

3 quarts half-and-half
4 tablespoons vanilla extract
simple syrup (recipe follows)
ground nutmeg

Combine the bourbon, half-and-half, and vanilla in a 1-gallon container; add simple syrup to attain desired sweetness. Chill thoroughly. Serve in a chilled glass (not over ice) and sprinkle with ground nutmeg.

Simple syrup:
1 cup water
1 cup sugar

Combine sugar and water in a small saucepan; boil until sugar dissolves and liquid becomes slightly thick. Cool completely before using.

BLOODY MARY

Makes four 8-ounce cocktails

This is a real eye-opener when spiced up with Louisiana's own Tabasco.®

4 cups good quality, thick tomato juice
1 teaspoon salt
1 teaspoon black pepper
1/2 teaspoon celery salt
1 tablespoon Worcestershire sauce
8 dashes of Tabasco®
2 teaspoons fresh lime juice
4-5 jiggers vodka
lime wedges to garnish

In a large pitcher, combine all ingredients and chill for at least 1 hour. Stir again before serving. Pour into tall glasses over chipped ice; garnish with lime.

To make the day last as long as possible, it is usually my choice to serve a brunch in late morning or early afternoon and keep the peas and cabbage for later in the day.

One of my all-time truly great breakfast dishes is GRILLADES (pronounced gree-yahds) and BAKED GRITS. Besides such traditional Acadian-Creole favorites such as jambalaya, gumbo, and red beans and rice, grillades is the epitome of what Southern cooks can do with simple ingredients to make a dish that will wake up your taste buds, warm your soul, and excite your heart! It is all in the way it is seasoned, cooked with patience, and served with great flair.

GRILLADES

Serves 8-10

4 pounds boneless beef round steak (approximately 1/2-inch thick)
1 tablespoon salt
1 teaspoon cayenne pepper
1/2 teaspoon black pepper
1/2 teaspoon garlic powder
approximately 1/2 cup flour
1/2 cup vegetable oil
2 cups chopped onions
1 cup chopped sweet green pepper
1 cup chopped celery
3 cups whole canned tomatoes, crushed, with their juice
2 cups water or beef broth
2 bay leaves
1/2 teaspoon tarragon
1/2 teaspoon basil
hot sauce to taste
1 cup finely chopped green onions
1/2 cup finely chopped parsley

Remove and discard fat from meat. Cut into 2-inch squares. Then combine the salt, cayenne pepper, black pepper, and garlic powder in a small bowl. Have flour at hand. Lay several pieces of the beef on a cutting board and sprinkle with seasoning mix and a little flour. Then with a meat pounder, pound each piece of meat until slightly flattened. Flip pieces over and repeat. Do this with all of the beef. Now, in a large, heavy pot, add the oil and brown the meat on both sides. Add the onions, sweet green peppers, and celery; cook until tender, stirring to prevent sticking. Add the crushed tomatoes and their liquid; reduce heat to moderate. Add rest of seasonings, water, or beef broth and cook for 1 to 2 hours, or until meat is tender. If gravy becomes too thick, add more water or broth. Check for seasonings and add more salt and pepper if necessary. Add hot sauce to taste. Right before serving add chopped green onions and parsley. Serve over baked grits.

BAKED GRITS

Serves 10-12

2 cups grits (not the instant kind) prepared according to package directions
3 eggs, beaten
1/2 pound grated cheddar cheese
1 cup milk
8 tablespoons butter

Cook the grits. Add the beaten eggs, grated cheese, milk, and butter to cooked grits; stir until all is blended and cheese is melted. Pour into a 2-quart baking dish and bake at 350 degrees for 45 minutes to 1 hour.

If you are an egg lover, you may want to opt for egg dishes at your brunch. I was introduced to the following potato omelet by my childhood friend Beau, who loves to cook almost as much as he loves to eat. He says this omelet was one of his mother's specialties.

FRENCH FRIED POTATO OMELET

Serves 1

1 russet potato, skinned or unskinned (your choice), cut as for French fries
vegetable oil
3 eggs
2 tablespoons cold water
salt and pepper
Tabasco®

Fry potatoes in enough oil to deep fry. When potatoes are golden brown, remove and drain on paper towels. In a small bowl, beat the eggs with water and pour over potatoes in a hot, oiled skillet. Give it a couple of stirs and fold over. Season with salt, pepper, and Tabasco.®

Beau also parted with another egg dish which is luscious.

EGGS BEAUREGARD

Serve 2-4

1-1/2 cups chopped celery
1/2 cup chopped sweet green pepper
4 tablespoons butter or margarine
1-1/2 cups heavy cream
4 eggs
1 cup grated cheese such as Cheddar, Swiss, or Colby
salt and pepper

In an 8-inch skillet, sauté the celery and sweet pepper in butter until transparent. Spread the vegetables evenly on the bottom of the skillet. Pour in the cream, but do not stir. Allow cream to set. Drop whole eggs a couple of inches apart and let them poach in the cream. When the eggs are cooked to the desired doneness, sprinkle with grated cheese. Cover the skillet and let cook for a few more minutes, or until the cheese has melted. Season with salt and pepper. To serve, cut pie-shaped slices, making sure to have one egg in each slice.

A similar egg dish which is great when you have guests is something I call skillet eggs. A friend of mine and I created this dish when we were testing a set of pots I had given myself as a birthday present. It is a dish that is as good as your creativity and imagination. It's akin to creating your very own pizza.

SKILLET EGGS

Serves 2, but it can be made for as many as 12 with ease. Adjust amounts accordingly.

1-1/2 teaspoons olive oil or vegetable oil
1/2 sweet green pepper, coarsely chopped
4 eggs
4 fresh mushrooms, thinly sliced
1/2 cup chopped cooked asparagus (or squash or green beans or tomatoes. You get the idea.)
1/4 cup shredded cheese of your choice
salt and pepper to taste
dill

In a skillet, sauté the green pepper in oil. Do not over cook; you want them to be a bit crunchy. Add the mushrooms and whatever vegetables you've gathered and lightly sauté them. Spread the vegetables evenly over the bottom of the skillet. Drop whole cracked eggs into the pan a couple of inches apart. Top with shredded cheese. Cover and allow eggs to poach to desired doneness. Remove the skillet from heat and cut into pie-shaped pieces. Season to taste and sprinkle with dill. Serve with hot French bread.

You can also add chopped shrimp, diced ham, or smoked sausage. The list is endless. You can top the eggs with hollandaise, béarnaise, or even marchand du vin sauce.

See what I mean about being creative?

If you have any leftover rice, let me introduce you to a very thrifty egg dish that Cina always served on Sunday nights. It is also perfectly fine for brunch, served along with LIGHT-AS-A-CLOUD BISCUITS, homemade butter, and fig preserves.

RICE AND EGGS

Serves 4

2 cups cooked rice
2 eggs
2 tablespoons vegetable oil or margarine
1 tablespoon each of chopped green onions and parsley
1/2 cup diced ham or crumbled cooked bacon
salt and pepper to taste

Heat the oil or margarine in a heavy skillet. Drop in the eggs and with a fork, stir the eggs around gently for a minute or two. Add the cooked rice and blend with the eggs. Add the green onion, parsley, ham or bacon, and seasonings.

LIGHT-AS-A-CLOUD BISCUITS

Makes 24 good-sized biscuits

4 cups biscuit mix
1 heaping tablespoon sugar
1 scant teaspoon salt
1/2 teaspoon cream of tartar

1 teaspoon baking powder
1 cup shortening
1-1/2 cups milk

Sift all dry ingredients together into a large bowl. Drop the shortening into the middle of the dry ingredients and pour the milk over it. With your hands, not with a spoon, pastry knife, or anything else, mix everything together, working in the dry ingredients. Keep going until the dough has formed a nice, slightly sticky ball. If you want to roll the biscuits, dust a pastry board well with flour, roll the dough out to about 1/4-inch thickness, and cut with a biscuit cutter. Otherwise, make drop biscuits by dropping a tablespoon of the dough on an ungreased cookie sheet. Sometimes I dust my hands well with flour and pat out little rounds. Bake at 400 degrees for 12-15 minutes or until golden brown. By the way, the uncooked dough can be frozen.

Now, you say, how can one possibly think about eating for the rest of the day? Never fear. Come six or seven o'clock there are bound to be a few requests for something to eat. At least that's how it is down South. Besides, one could not think of letting New Year's Day go by without eating at least a small helping of black-eyed peas, a dab of cabbage, and for lagniappe, a thick slice of baked ham, eaten alone or rolled inside a fistful of French bread. It wouldn't be proper.

I will admit right here and now, I don't cook black-eyed peas from scratch. I can't find anything better than Trappey's Black-Eyed Peas with Jalapeño, canned in New Iberia, Louisiana. I have been known to doctor them up a bit, but the Trappey's company seems to have the secret to producing the peas cooked whole, yet swimming in a creamy sauce that's perfect for mixing with steamed rice.

BLACK-EYED PEAS

Serves 8

1 pound smoked sausage, cut into 1/4-inch slices
1/2 pound diced ham
2 tablespoons vegetable oil
1 cup chopped onion
1/2 cup chopped sweet green pepper
One 15-ounce can black-eyed peas with jalapeño
salt and black pepper to taste
Have hot sauce on hand for those who wish to spice
them up more!

In a heavy saucepan, brown the smoked sausage and ham in vegetable oil. Add the onions and sweet pepper and cook until wilted. Add the black-eyed peas and simmer for 30 minutes. Add seasonings and cook for 10 minutes more. Serve over rice. Or, better yet, make a jambalaya of sorts by mixing the pea mixture with about 4 cups of cooked rice. If it is too dry, add a little beef or chicken broth to moisten.

SMOTHERED CABBAGE

Serves 6

1 large head of cabbage, cleaned and chopped
1 cup chopped ham
1 tablespoon vegetable oil
1 cup chopped onion
1 teaspoon sugar
salt and black pepper

In a large Dutch oven, cook the ham pieces and chopped onion in vegetable oil for 5 minutes. Add the chopped cabbage and seasonings; cover and cook for 30 minutes or until cabbage is tender. Stir occasionally during cooking.

I simply adore baked ham. I don't care that sometimes a baked ham can last for several days. Plus there's always the ham bone—a prize with which to make soups or bean dishes.

GLAZED HAM

Serves 12-14

One 8-1/2 pound ham shank
whole cloves
1 cup port wine
1 tablespoon dry mustard
1-1/2 tablespoons dark brown sugar
1/2 cup ginger ale

Most people prefer to remove any of the skin remaining on the ham, but I like to keep it on. Once the ham is cooked, the skin provides delightful tidbits to munch on.

Score the skin and/or fat by making long vertical and horizontal cuts. Bake the ham at 300 degrees for 30 minutes. Remove the ham from the oven and place a whole clove in the center of each scored square; return the ham to the oven for another 30 minutes, basting with 1/2 cup of port.

In the meantime, mix the dry mustard, brown sugar, and the rest of the port together in a small bowl. Remove the ham from the oven once again and spread the sugar/mustard/port sauce over the whole fat side of the ham. Pour the ginger ale into the bottom of the pan. Raise the oven temperature to 450 degrees and return the ham to the oven. Baste every 10 to 15 minutes with pan juices. Continue to bake for 1 hour more. Loosely cover the ham with aluminum foil for this last hour of cooking. If you need more basting liquid, add some port and ginger ale.

Most folks are fairly tired of fancy eating after the Christmas and New Year holidays. If you have saved the ham bone from your holiday ham (and no self-respecting Louisiana cook would throw such a thing out), now is the time to stock up the freezer with humble but delicious bean dishes. Here are two of my favorites: WHITE BEAN SOUP and RED BEANS, MY WAY.

WHITE BEAN SOUP

Serves 8

1 pound Great Northern beans
4 quarts water or chicken broth
1/2 pound salt pork or ham pieces (a leftover ham bone
may be used)
1 medium onion, chopped
1 medium sweet green pepper, chopped
2 ribs celery, chopped
One 16-ounce can whole tomatoes, crushed, with their
juice

Soak the beans overnight. Before cooking, drain and sort out any bad beans. Place the beans in a large soup pot or kettle along with water or chicken broth, onions, green peppers, celery, and salt pork, ham pieces, or ham bone. Bring slowly to a boil, then allow to gently boil for about 1-1/2 hours or until the beans are tender and can be easily mashed with a spoon against the side of the pot. Check for seasoning. Since the salt pork or ham may have made the beans taste salty enough, you may need to add only a little black or red pepper. Papa liked to eat his white bean soup with a couple of spoonsful of rice, a fistful of finely chopped green onions, and a generous dousing of hot sauce.

Just like gumbo, everyone in south Louisiana has his very own recipe for red beans. I've listened to people argue if they should have smoked sausage and ham, or either one or the other. Some like to use only ham hocks. Others like the red beans served along with a fried pork chop.

I'm not a purist when it comes to red beans. Do it any way you like. The following recipe happens to be a combination of Mama's way and my way.

RED BEANS, MY WAY

Serves 8

1 pound red kidney beans
2 quarts water
1/2 cup beef broth
3 tablespoons margarine or vegetable oil
2 medium onions, chopped
1 sweet green pepper, chopped
2 stalks celery, with leaves, chopped
2 cloves garlic, minced
1 pound smoked pork sausage, cut into 1/2-inch slices
1/2 pound ham pieces
3 bay leaves
2 pinches of thyme
salt, black pepper, and cayenne pepper to taste

Soak beans overnight. Place the beans in a large soup pot or kettle along with the water and beef broth; bring to a gentle boil. In a large skillet, heat the margarine or oil and sauté the onions, green peppers, celery, garlic, and sausage or ham. Brown well on a fast fire. When the beans have come to a boil, add the vegetables and meat mixture. Add bay leaves, thyme, salt, and peppers. Reduce heat to a high simmer and cook for 2-3 hours until beans have become tender. I like my red beans a little creamy, so I remove 2 or 3 cups, purée them in a food processor or blender, and return them to the pot. Serve the red beans over rice topped with a sprinkling of minced green onions.

Mardi Gras Beads

While the rest of the country is taking a much needed break from festivities once the holiday season comes to a close, the people of south Louisiana are moving quickly into one of their favorite seasons—Carnival.

The Carnival season officially begins on Twelfth Night, and from New Orleans to Lake Charles, there will be countless balls, parades, and *soirées*. The round of parties will continue until Mardi Gras Day, which is also known as Shrove Tuesday or Fat Tuesday. The Carnival season ends at midnight on Shrove Tuesday, ushering in the somber Ash Wednesday morning and the Lenten season of penance and abstinence.

But until midnight on Fat Tuesday, the prevailing attitude is *laissez le bon temps roulez*!

Every year about this time, when everyone begins making plans for Mardi Gras, I hear the lament, "Gosh, Mardi Gras is early this year!" Or, "Gee, Mardi Gras is certainly late."

I've never heard anyone say, "Boy, Mardi Gras is right on time."

In 1970, it was on February 10. That's early. In 1973, it was on March 6, so that's real late. In 1974, it was on my birthday, February 26, and I remember we all thought it was mighty late too.

In 1989 Mardi Gras fell on February 7—very early. In the year 2000, it's going to be real late, on March 7. And it won't be until 2009 that Mardi Gras will fall on my birthday again!

Mardi Gras is celebrated in a variety of ways all across south Louisiana. Sure, most people in the United States have heard about the New Orleans Mardi Gras—a big-city party with big-city traditions. Most people aren't aware of the country-style Mardi Gras I grew up with in St. Martinville. We didn't have king cakes, elaborate parades, or krewes. Our Carnival traditions were a little less formal, but fun nonetheless.

On the Sunday before Mardi Gras, the St. Martinville Lion's Club always sponsors the Children's Carnival. For weeks mamas piece together crepe paper, bits and pieces of net and ribbon, cardboard—anything at hand—and create a bit of mythical wonder for the children of the town.

The night before Mardi Gras is reserved for adults when the Rotary Club presents a magnificent tableaux and dance. I've often said that the costumes outshine those I've seen at most balls in the city. Since my father was a charter member of the St. Martinville club, my brothers, sister, and I have run the whole gamut from being pages, entertainers, maids, dukes, captains, and queens.

For weeks before the affair, the women, and yes, many times the men, can be found bending over tables and work benches, beading, spray painting, sewing, and building sets in preparation for the big event.

I'll never forget the year I was queen. During the week before Mardi Gras, everyone ran around like chickens with their heads cut off. There were teas, receptions, and last minute dashes to Lafayette for more beads and long white gloves. I can still smell the scents of velvet, starched net, and glue.

On the magical day, those without hangovers would march down Main Street attired in makeshift costumes, banging on tin cans shouting, "Mardi Gras Chick-a-la-Pye, Run Away and Tra-la-la." Sometimes, if Mama and Papa could handle it, we would drive to Lafayette to see a parade. There were no doubloons, beads, or ladders back then. The float riders threw candy, bubble gum, and whistles. The big hoorah were the costumed horses and riders from neighboring towns. Even the hooves of the horses were painted and glittered.

If time warranted, we drove to Church Point and Mamou to see the *courir de Mardi Gras* (the running of the Mardi Gras). The men of the rural communities, dressed in colorful costumes, gather on horseback. The maskers visit farm houses along a planned, or sometimes unplanned, route. At each stop, "Le Capitaine" asks for a donation. Sometimes the donation is a bag of rice, a small fat hen, or other ingredients for a big gumbo. Sometimes the maskers thank the farmers and their families by performing dances and singing Cajun songs. At the end of the day, they ride back to town, shouting invitations along the way, telling everyone to come to the town hall where the cooks prepare a big gumbo, and a *fais-do-do* is held. Here is a recipe for a traditional gumbo much like the one which might be prepared in Mamou or Church Point on Mardi Gras Day.

CARMEN BUILLIARD MONTEGUT'S CHICKEN AND OYSTER GUMBO

Serves 8

3/4 cup vegetable oil
3/4 cup flour
1 large onion, finely chopped
8 cloves of garlic, minced
1 large hen, cut up as for frying
salt, cayenne pepper, and black pepper
3 quarts of water, more if the chicken is not tender
1 pint oysters with their liquor
filé powder
chopped parsley
chopped green onion tops

Make a roux by heating the oil, adding the flour, and blending until smooth. Cook over low heat until the roux is golden brown. Add onions and garlic. Season the chicken with salt, cayenne pepper, and black pepper. Add the chicken to the roux and cook until oil comes out around the edges of the pot, about 1 hour. Add warm water and cook slowly until the chicken is tender, about 2 hours. Add the oysters and their liquor 5 minutes before serving. Serve with rice. To each serving of gumbo add a small amount of filé powder to taste. Garnish each bowl with parsley and chopped green onion tops.

Once I moved to New Orleans as a young adult, I was introduced to a whole 'nother kind of Carnival celebration. There were before-parade parties, during-parade parties, and after-parade parties. There were weekly king cake parties and parties before balls and parties after balls.

I quickly got the hang of it, and during the several years I lived in the French Quarter, my apartment became the meeting place for all of the above.

Not to be outdone by my new group of friends, I broadened my cooking repertoire to include not

only gumbos, jambalayas, and *etouffées*, but also simple but good hors d'ouevres that could be put out for the hungry hordes that stopped at my door.

SAUSAGE CHEESE BISCUITS

Makes about 6 dozen

1 pound extra-sharp Cheddar cheese, shredded
1 pound spicy bulk pork breakfast sausage, crumbled
3 cups buttermilk biscuit mix

Melt cheese in the top of a double boiler. Add sausage and cook for 20 minutes or until sausage browns, stirring constantly. Transfer mixture to a large mixing bowl and allow to cool just a bit. Add the biscuit mix and mix well. Shape dough into 1-inch balls. (The dough may be frozen at this point.) Place balls on ungreased cookie sheets and bake at 450 degrees for 15 to 20 minutes or until golden brown.

If Mardi Gras season is late and crawfish are beginning to show up at the market, mini crawfish pies are also good finger food.

MINI CRAWFISH PIES

Makes 4 dozen bite-sized pies

8 tablespoons butter
1 cup finely chopped onion
1 sweet green pepper, finely chopped
1/2 teaspoon cayenne pepper
1/2 teaspoon white pepper
1/4 teaspoon black pepper
1 teaspoon salt
2 tablespoons tomato paste
1 teaspoon paprika
2 tablespoons cornstarch dissolved in 1 cup water
1 pound crawfish tails
1 bunch green onions, finely chopped
2 tablespoons minced parsley
4 dozen bite-sized, pre-baked patty shells

Sauté onions and sweet green peppers in melted butter over medium heat. When tender, add salt and peppers; lower heat. Simmer for 10 minutes. Add tomato paste and paprika and let the mixture bubble for a few minutes. Add cornstarch dissolved in water and cook until a fine glaze appears on the mixture. Add the crawfish, green onions, and parsley. Cook for about 20 minutes. Adjust seasonings to taste. Spoon mixture into pre-baked patty shells and bake for 5 minutes at 350 degrees.

I am also a firm believer in finger sandwiches that are filling and easy to make. For Mardi Gras, I usually opt for a great ham salad spread on hearty rye bread.

HAM SALAD

Makes 20 finger sandwiches

3 cups diced ham
1/4 cup minced green onions
1/4 cup minced celery
1/4 cup minced black olives
2 tablespoons minced pimientos
mayonnaise
Creole mustard
hot pepper sauce
Worcestershire sauce
10 slices of rye bread

Chop the ham up very fine in a food processor. In a mixing bowl, combine the ham with green onions, celery, black olives, and pimientos. Blend with mayonnaise, Creole mustard, hot pepper sauce, and Worcestershire to taste. Spread on slices of bread and cut each sandwich into quarters.

The final hurrah of Carnival (which translates from the Latin as "farewell to the flesh" is Mardi Gras Day. Even before dawn on Fat Tuesday,

inhabitants of New Orleans and south Louisiana are crawling out of warm beds to pull themselves together for the last wallop of festivities. Even with hangover headaches pounding at their temples, revelers are bristling with excitement.

Parade riders, armed with costumes, beads, and doubloons, are winding through the streets heading for krewe dens and other designated meeting places, where they will board their assigned floats.

Members of marching bands have one more practice session as they line up in the streets. Horseback riders give their mounts one more brushing. Maskers add the final touches to costumes before taking to the streets. Families load up station wagons and vans with ladders, picnic baskets, and folding chairs. It's going to be a long day and everyone will need sustenance for the action-packed festivities. Knowing that the day after Mardi Gras is Ash Wednesday, which opens the Lenten season of forty days of penance and abstinence prior to Easter, everyone is prepared to fill their tummies with all the good things they love.

In rural communities, pots of gumbo—both seafood and sausage—*sauce piquantes*, and possibly *fricassées* are bubbling on stoves long before the sun comes up. After all, there will be aunts, uncles, many cousins, and friends who will be dropping by in the late afternoon after much dancing in the streets to play *bourrée* (a popular card game) and enjoy a hearty meal.

For those who will ensconce themselves along parade routes, picnic hampers and small ice chests are the order of the day.

A couple I know always goes to parades in style with a couple of bottles of good champagne, caviar and all the fixings, a stash of STEAK TARTARE, and an assortment of good breads. A bowl of strawberries rolled in sour cream and sprinkled with brown sugar will be for later in the day, along with a thermos of coffee and brandy. A tin of PECAN LACE COOKIES are brought along for good measure.

An Uptown New Orleans family who lives right off St. Charles Avenue gathers together each Mardi Gras Day, and in between parades, they warm themselves up with hot, thick SPLIT PEA SOUP. Food tables are laden with finger food and decorated with piles of doubloons, beads, and tiny handmade flambeaux figures. A huge king cake is the traditional dessert. Children fill up on hot dogs and hamburgers. At the house next door, guests enjoy chicken galantine, pistolettes, MARDI GRAS PASTA SALAD, and MINIATURE CREAM PUFFS. The choice of food that can be served on Mardi Gras Day is endless and only limited by your tastes and imagination.

Whatever you should choose to serve, use the colors of Mardi Gras—green, gold, and purple, symbolizing Faith, Power, and Justice. It is traditional to decorate homes with yards and yards of bunting. Carnival flags fly from balconies, and vases and baskets are filled with purple and yellow tulips. Bouquets of balloons are sometimes tied to parked cars and serve as markers for family members who may stray from the group. Green, purple, and gold frostings are used on cakes and cookies. And those who may not choose to mask should at least wear Mardi Gras colors.

It's a time for frivolity. That's what it's all about. We say eat, drink, and be merry because for the next six weeks of Lent, we must pay for our sins.

STEAK TARTARE

Serves 2-4

1 pound beef tenderloin or sirloin, freshly ground
2 teaspoons capers, mashed
6 anchovy fillets, mashed
1/2 cup minced onion
1/4 teaspoon black pepper
2-3 dashes of Tabasco®
3/4 teaspoon salt (or to taste)
2-3 dashes Worcestershire sauce
4 tablespoons dry red wine (optional)
1/2 teaspoon Dijon or Creole mustard
1 teaspoon brandy
2 eggs, separated

Mix all ingredients together except egg yolks; blend well. Just before serving, break egg yolks into the mixture and blend with a fork. It's best served at room temperature or slightly chilled. Serve on assorted thinly sliced breads.

PECAN LACE COOKIES

Makes about 2-1/2 dozen cookies

6 tablespoons softened butter
4 tablespoons plus 1/2 cup unsifted flour
1 teaspoon double-acting baking powder
a pinch of salt
2 cups sugar
2 eggs, well beaten
1 teaspoon vanilla extract
2 cups coarsely chopped pecans

Preheat oven to 400 degrees. With a pastry brush, spread 2 tablespoons of the softened butter over 2 large baking sheets. Sprinkle each sheet with 1 tablespoon of flour; distribute evenly. Shake the sheets to remove any excess flour. Combine 1/2 cup of flour, the baking powder, and salt; sift them together in a bowl. Set aside.

In a deep bowl, cream 2 tablespoons of softened butter until light and fluffy. Add the sugar, beat in the eggs and vanilla, and stir the flour mixture into the dough. Add the pecans. Drop batter by heaping teaspoons onto the baking sheets, spacing the cookie dough about 3 inches apart. Bake for 5 minutes or until the cookies have spread into lace-like 4-inch rounds and have turned golden brown. Allow the cookies to cool for a minute or so and then transfer them to wire racks to cool completely. Allow baking sheets to cool before dropping the next batch. Repeat the process until all the dough has been used. Store in airtight containers.

An old New Orleans drink, popular during Carnival, is an OJEN (pronounced oh-hen) COCKTAIL. Ojen is short for Bobadillojean, a Spanish liqueur that is difficult to find. However, anisette or any other anise-flavored liqueur may be substituted.

OJEN COCKTAIL

Makes 1 serving

1-1/2 tablespoons anisette
3 dashes of Peychaud bitters
2-4 cubes of ice

Combine the liqueur, bitters, and ice in a mixing glass and place a bar shaker on top. Shake vigorously. Remove from shaker and strain into a chilled cocktail glass.

SPLIT PEA SOUP

Serves 8-10

1 pound dried split peas
1 ham bone, 2 ham hocks, or 2 cups diced ham
3 quarts beef broth (If using canned, dilute and use only half broth and half water to make 3 quarts.)
1 cup chopped celery
1 cup chopped onions
1 cup coarsely chopped carrots
1 teaspoon ground thyme
1 bay leaf
salt and black pepper to taste
1 cup dry sherry

Bring all ingredients, except sherry, to a boil in a large soup pot. After it comes to a boil, reduce to simmer and cook for 2 hours. Add sherry and cook for another 20 minutes. Adjust seasonings to taste.

MARDI GRAS PASTA SALAD

Serves 8

1 pound pasta, your choice—capellini, vermicelli, or fusilli
1 cup shredded purple cabbage
1 cup whole kernel corn, frozen or freshly cut from the cob
2 tablespoons butter
1 bunch green onions, finely chopped
about 1 cup mayonnaise
1 teaspoon Dijon mustard
1/2 teaspoon basil
salt and freshly ground black pepper to taste

Cook pasta in boiling salted water according to package directions. Drain thoroughly and place in a large mixing bowl. In a skillet, sauté the corn in butter for 2-3 minutes. Drain. Add the corn, purple cabbage, and green onions to the pasta and toss with mayonnaise. Add the mayonnaise a little at a time until the pasta is lightly coated. Add mustard, basil, salt, and pepper; toss gently. Serve at room temperature or slightly chilled.

MINIATURE CREAM PUFFS

Makes 24 pastries

Pastry:
1 cup water
1/2 cup butter or margarine
1/4 teaspoon salt
1 cup all-purpose flour
4 eggs

Combine water and butter in a medium saucepan and bring to a boil. Add salt and flour; stir vigorously over low heat until mixture leaves the sides of the pan and forms a smooth ball. Remove and cool slightly. Add eggs, one at a time, beating well after each addition. Beat the batter until smooth. Drop batter by rounded teaspoons, 3 inches apart, on to a greased baking sheet. Bake at 425 degrees for 15 minutes or until puffed and golden brown. Remove to wire racks and allow to cool. Cut tops off of the puff pastries; pull out the soft inside dough and discard. Fill bottom halves with cream filling, replace tops, and spread with frosting. Serve slightly chilled.

Cream Filling:
3-1/2 tablespoons all-purpose flour
1-1/3 cups sugar
dash of salt
3 egg yolks, beaten
3 cups milk
1 teaspoon vanilla extract

Combine flour, sugar, and salt in a heavy saucepan. In a separate bowl, combine egg yolks and milk, mixing well. Add egg yolks, milk, and vanilla to dry ingredients and cook over medium heat, stirring constantly, until smooth and thickened. Chill thoroughly before filling puffs.

Frosting:
1/2 cup softened butter or margarine
2 tablespoons plus 2 teaspoons milk
4 cups sifted powdered sugar
green, purple, and orange paste food coloring

Cream butter, then add milk, mixing well. Gradually add sugar, beating well. Divide frosting into thirds. Add food coloring to each portion until you have attained the desired color. Spread over cream puffs after they have been filled and topped.

Lenten Fare

The Catholic religion is deeply rooted in the hearts and souls of Acadians. The French peasants who made Acadie (now Nova Scotia in Canada) their New World paradise were expelled from the colony in 1755 when they refused to pledge allegiance to the British.

During the *grand dérangement*, families were separated, and many wandered along the eastern seaboard of what is now the United States before finding their way to New Orleans, where they could speak their language and practice their religion among fellow Frenchmen. The city was not for hunters and trappers, however, and they soon spread out into the countryside, settling along the bayous, in the swamps, and on the fertile prairies.

Religious faith was very important to the Acadians who came to Louisiana from Acadie, and it remains an integral part of the lives of modern Acadians. Feast days of the Church are honored with tradition all across south Louisiana.

So it is that on Ash Wednesday, the Catholic Creoles and Acadians descend upon the many Catholic churches to receive ashes, a reminder of their mortality (or immortality). Ash Wednesday is a solemn day, and the foreheads of the faithful are smudged with dark ashes, giving witness to their belief in penance and abstinence for the six weeks that precede Easter.

One Ash Wednesday morning, I slowly opened my eyes and thought, "I've made it through the siege."

I now had some idea of what it must have been like on Sherman's march through Georgia. I had begun my trek during the Christmas holidays, then went on to New Year's and the Sugar Bowl, plowed through Super Bowl week, and stood my ground during Mardi Gras.

Why in the last four days I had joined the throngs along parade routes, attended two balls, climbed on reviewing stands, and watched the Krewe of Gabriel parade in Lafayette. I then sped down the back roads to Mamou to watch the running of the Mardi Gras—eating all the while.

Ah, but that was all behind me now. It was the first day of Lent and I was eager to get my ashes at church. Just as it was a time to cleanse my soul, it was also a time to cleanse my body.

Some people choose to give up something they especially like—sweets, soft drinks, whatever. Others pledge to attend daily Mass, Way-of-the-Cross services, or to spend more time in meditation. The nuns always impressed upon us "to offer it up" to the Lord whenever we had a sacrifice to make, such as being quiet or giving our candy money to the poor box in church.

Mama's Lenten tradition was to eat light and clean. No heavy, festive meals, save for perhaps on Sunday, and of course, there was no snacking between meals. If nothing else, we were healthy for at least forty days of the year. Because of certain Lenten rules, there was less eating of meat and consumption of seafood was up. Shrimp, crabs, crawfish, and fish were on just about every table, which didn't seem like penance to me. Sometimes we had dishes made with canned salmon or tuna. With a deft hand Mama was able to stretch the salmon or tuna into absolute delights.

SALMON CROQUETTES

Serves 4
If formed into tiny balls, these may be used as hors d'ouevres; yields about 2-1/2 dozen

1 egg, beaten
1 cup mashed potatoes
One 6-1/2-ounce can salmon (or same amount of tuna), drained and flaked
1 tablespoon chopped pimiento
1 tablespoon minced onion
1/4 teaspoon salt
dash of black pepper
dash of cayenne pepper
1/4-1/2 cup dry unseasoned bread crumbs
1 egg slightly beaten
1/2 cup seasoned bread crumbs

Mix the first 10 ingredients in a bowl, adding enough bread crumbs so that the mixture can be handled and is not too sticky. Pat the mixture into hamburger-sized patties, or if you prefer, into balls the size of a large egg. Dip into the second slightly beaten egg and roll in seasoned bread crumbs. Place on a platter lined with waxed paper and chill for 1 hour. Fry in deep, hot oil for about 5 minutes or until golden brown. Drain on paper towels. Croquettes may be served with tartar sauce or a mayonnaise-mustard sauce.

MAYONNAISE-MUSTARD SAUCE

2/3 cup mayonnaise
2 tablespoons prepared yellow mustard
2 tablespoons capers
1 teaspoon lemon juice.

This next dish is also a good *Carême* (Lenten) dish. Although it is not a seafood dish, it is one Mama often served to us during Lent because it was a meal in itself and could be made with chicken or turkey leftovers.

CHICKEN (OR TURKEY) TETRAZZINI

Serves 6

5 tablespoons vegetable oil
3 tablespoons flour
1/4 teaspoon salt
1-1/2 cups chicken broth
2 cups cooked chopped chicken or turkey
One 12-ounce package spaghetti, cooked and drained
1 cup grated Cheddar or American cheese
One 4-ounce can sliced mushrooms, with the liquid
1/4 cup unseasoned bread crumbs

In a large saucepan, blend 3 tablespoons of vegetable oil with flour over medium heat until smooth. Add salt and broth. Continue stirring until sauce begins to thicken. Add the mushrooms and their liquid. Oil a 2-quart casserole dish with 1 tablespoon of vegetable oil. Alternate layers of turkey, spaghetti, cheese, and mushroom sauce. Top with bread crumbs sprinkled with remaining tablespoon of oil. Bake at 275 degrees for 25-30 minutes until sauce begins to bubble.

With either of these dishes, Mama served a salad that we children thought rather odd, but we never turned it down.

PERFECTION SALAD

Serves 6

2 envelopes unflavored gelatin
1/2 cup sugar
1 teaspoon salt
1-1/2 cups boiling water
1-1/2 cups cold water
1/2 cup vinegar
2 tablespoons lemon juice
2 cups finely shredded raw cabbage
1 cup chopped celery
1/2 cup chopped sweet green pepper
1/4 cup chopped pimiento

Mix together the gelatin, sugar, and salt. Add boiling water and stir until all is dissolved. Add the cold water, vinegar, lemon juice; mix together. Add the cabbage, celery, green peppers, pimiento, and mix gently. Chill until set and serve.

During my years in New Orleans, Lenten Fridays found me in line at the seafood market checking to see what was fresh off the boats. Sometimes it was redfish or trout. If I had a few extra dollars, I purchased fish AND a pound or so of shrimp. If I had to abstain from meat, no one said I couldn't enjoy my seafood meal.

TROUT WITH SHRIMP PROVENÇAL

Serves 4

4 trout fillets, about 6 ounces each
1 cup milk
1 teaspoon salt
1 teaspoon cayenne pepper
1/2 cup flour
8 tablespoons butter or margarine

Dip trout fillets in milk seasoned with salt and pepper. Dredge in flour. Heat the butter in a 10-inch skillet and brown fillets on both sides. Remove from skillet and drain on paper towels. Keep warm.

Sauce:
4 tablespoons butter
2 tablespoons olive oil
1/4 cup finely chopped green onions
1/4 cup finely chopped sweet green pepper
1 clove garlic, minced
2 cups peeled and deveined shrimp
2 tablespoons brandy
1 cup peeled and chopped fresh tomatoes
salt and cayenne pepper to taste

In a large skillet, heat the butter and oil together. Add the onions, sweet green peppers, and garlic; stir fry for a minute or two. Add the shrimp and stir for 5 minutes. Pour in brandy and shake the pan. Add the tomatoes and seasoning and shake the pan again. Place the fillets on a serving plate and top with sauce.

I'm not usually real crazy about casseroles, but this SPINACH BAKE is perfect with seafood.

SPINACH BAKE

Serves 6

Two 10-ounce packages frozen chopped spinach
4 tablespoons butter or margarine
1 cup onions, chopped
1 cup celery, chopped
salt, cayenne pepper, garlic powder to taste
8 ounces cream cheese
1 pint sour cream
1 cup canned sliced mushrooms, drained
grated Cheddar or Mozzarella cheese
paprika

Cook the spinach according to package directions and drain well. Melt the butter or margarine in a large skillet and add onions and celery; cook until wilted. Add salt, cayenne pepper, and garlic powder to taste. Add the cream cheese and sour cream, and with a fork, cream together with vegetables. Add the mushrooms and spinach; mix well. Spoon into a buttered casserole dish and sprinkle with grated cheese and paprika. Bake in a 350-degree oven for 15-20 minutes or until cheese is melted and bubbly.

In keeping with simplicity, for dessert whip heavy cream, slice some fresh peaches, and chill together. Sprinkle with a little cinnamon sugar.

♣

St. Patrick's Day and the feast of St. Joseph usually fall right smack dab in the middle of Lent. These religious feast days are grandly celebrated in New Orleans with parades (whenever New Orleanians can parade, they do), feasting (never mind Lent for a couple of days), and or course, some praying.

Every year around this time, I wish I had some Irish blood running through my veins because I sure like their style. They're flamboyant, like to sing, love good food, and even mourn well. Definitely my kind of people. Red hair is also associated with the Irish, and I have a particular fantasy about red hair.

Since I was a child, I have prayed that my hair would one day turn bright red, or at least strawberry blonde. Coming from south Louisiana where there aren't too many redheads, I thought having titian hair would make me magic. Papa added fuel to the fire. When I was little, he allowed me to visit with him while he was shaving in preparation for an evening out. It was my job to stir up the soap in his mug; then after he shaved, I got to splash with Old Spice along with him.

I always knew when he and Mama were going out because his best suit and bow tie were laid out on the bed along with a starched white shirt. We would then play a little game.

"Where ya'll going, Papa?"

"Well, I don't know about your Mama, but I have a date with a redhead." I knew he was teasing, but I often wondered why he always talked about a redhead.

Even Mama would play along.

"And Blackie, just where are you going to find you a redhead?"

And Papa would wink at me and grin.

Yes, I definitely wanted to be a redhead and have emeralds dripping from my neck and ears. I've finally given up. I've come to terms with the fact that I will go through life as a brunette. And anyway, emeralds are not so bad on brunettes.

But back to St. Patrick's Day.

While living in New Orleans and working for the Brennan family at Commander's Palace, I quickly learned how to be Irish for at least one day out of the year. I make CABBAGE ROLLS and toast my Brennan friends with one of their very own St. Paddy's day desserts, AVOCADO CREAM.

CABBAGE ROLLS

Makes approximately 20-24 rolls

1 large head of cabbage
1 cup raw rice
2 pounds lean ground beef
2 cloves garlic, minced
2 medium onions, finely chopped
1 sweet green pepper, finely chopped
salt and cayenne pepper to taste
One 6-ounce can tomato paste
Four 15-ounce cans tomato sauce
2 cans of water measured in tomato sauce cans

Boil the whole head of cabbage until tender; drain well and allow to cool. In a large bowl, mix raw rice, ground beef, garlic, onions, sweet green pepper, salt, and cayenne pepper. Add tomato paste and mix well. Separate cabbage leaves. Spoon 2-3 tablespoons of meat mixture into the cabbage leaves and roll up. Be sure to tuck in the ends so that the filling won't fall out. In a large roasting pan or pot, make a layer of rolls, then one of tomato sauce, seasoning with salt and pepper as you go. Continue to layer cabbage rolls, tomato sauce, and seasonings. Pour in water, cover, and cook over low heat for about 1 hour or until rice is thoroughly cooked.

AVOCADO CREAM

Serves 4

1 ripe medium-sized avocado
1-1/2 tablespoons fresh lime juice
6 tablespoons granulated sugar
1/2 cup heavy cream
1-1/2 teaspoons vanilla
4 cups French vanilla ice cream

Peel and slice avocado. In a blender or food processor purée avocado with lime juice, sugar, cream, and vanilla. Blend well. Then, in a large mixing bowl, blend softened ice cream with the avocado mixture. Spoon into *parfait* glasses, cover, and freeze until serving time. Garnish with a slice of lime.

I've wanted to be Italian just as often as I've wanted to be Irish. I can eat pasta any time of the day and tomato sauce on anything.

On the feast of St. Joseph, an altar is laden with dishes that the Italian community spends weeks preparing. This happens not only in New Orleans, but in towns and cities all over Louisiana. When I have the opportunity to visit such an altar, I always make sure to taste the stuffed artichokes and grab a few lucky fava beans.

Artichokes were not part of my childhood. It wasn't until I was a working woman straight out of college, living in New Orleans, that I was introduced to a fresh artichoke. I was acquainting myself with a large supermarket when I spied these fabulous light green globe-like objects in the produce section. Just about everyone who passed them grabbed a few and chunked them into their baskets. I followed suit. I eyed the sign over the bin. It read ARTICHOKES.

The only artichokes I had ever tasted were those in jars, packed in oil. All I could figure out was that the tiny artichokes must grow up and become these wondrous things.

I quickly got over my timidity and asked my neighbor, an old-time New Orleanian, what to do with these artichokes I brought home. She was amused. "And I thought you Acadians knew everything about cooking!"

STUFFED ARTICHOKES

Serves 4 as an appetizer, 2 as a main course

2 large artichokes, trimmed, washed, and drained
1 cup seasoned bread crumbs
1/2 cup grated Romano or Parmesan cheese, or a combination of both
3 green onions, finely chopped
1/3 cup finely chopped ham or shrimp
1 clove garlic, minced
3 teaspoons olive oil
juice of 1/2 lemon
1 teaspoon salt
1 teaspoon black pepper
pinch of oregano leaves

In a small mixing bowl, combine the bread crumbs, cheese, green onions, ham or shrimp, and garlic. Add 1 or 2 teaspoons of olive oil to moisten mixture. Stuff each leaf. Place the artichokes in a deep Dutch oven or heavy pot with about 1 to 2 inches of water. Season water with salt, black pepper, the rest of the olive oil, oregano, and lemon juice. Cover and let water come to a boil. Reduce to simmer, cover the pot and cook for one hour or until leaves pull away easily. If water evaporates, add a little more water to the pot.

Following the short break in Lent for the celebration of the feast days, solemn Holy Week services are observed in anticipation of Easter Sunday.

Church altars are stripped bare and ceremonies commemorating the last days of Jesus Christ on earth are held in the grandest cathedrals and the most humble chapels. Many hours are spent in meditation and prayer by the faithful. Perhaps the most solemn day of Holy Week is Good Friday, when customs regarding food, drink, and behavior are strictly observed.

As I have noted before, there are many types of gumbo in south Louisiana. They can be made with everything from chicken, turkey, seafood and yes, even sometimes rabbit or squirrel. But there is one gumbo that is truly the king of them all—*gumbo aux herbes* or *gumbo z'herbes*.

This unique gumbo is said to have been originated by the superstitious Creoles especially for Good Friday when, it was believed, you would have good luck for the coming year if you ate seven greens and met seven people during the day. Some folklore has it that for every green that was put into the gumbo, a new friend would be made during the coming year. Since it was to be eaten on Good Friday, no meat was added. Oysters were sometimes used.

In Acadiana, it was not the traditional Good Friday meal, since there *gumbo z'herbes* is usually prepared with salt meat or ham. However it is a hearty gumbo often prepared by Cina when the hordes of aunts, uncles, and cousins flock to her house on weekends.

In addition to the controversy regarding the inclusion of meat in *gumbo z'herbes* is the debate about whether or not it should be made with a roux. Here then are two versions, one made with a roux and one without. If you can find fresh greens, I highly recommend using them, but if not, frozen will suffice.

GUMBO Z'HERBES (WITHOUT A ROUX)

Serves 10-12

1 pound collard or mustard greens
1 pound spinach
1 pound turnip greens
1 pound green cabbage leaves
1 large bunch fresh watercress (optional)
1 large bunch fresh parsley (optional)
the tops of 6 carrots (optional)
the tops of a large bunch of radishes (optional)
1/2 teaspoon cayenne
1/2 teaspoon black pepper
2 bay leaves
1/2 teaspoon ground thyme
1/4 teaspoon allspice (optional)
1 pound salt meat or ham, cut into 1/4-inch cubes
3 tablespoons shortening
1 bunch green onions, finely chopped
1 cup chopped yellow onions
1 clove garlic, minced

If using fresh greens, trim and wash well. Put greens in a large, deep pot and cover all of the greens with water. Add cayenne, black pepper, bay leaves, thyme, and allspice. Boil until greens are tender. Drain and reserve cooking liquid (you should have about 3-4 quarts of liquid). After the greens are well drained, chop them up fine, either by hand or with a food processor. If you are using frozen greens, cook according to package directions with spices, drain, and reserve the cooking liquid.

In a skillet, melt the shortening and brown the salt meat or ham, yellow onions, and garlic. Return the greens to the reserved liquid, add the sautéed onions, meat, and chopped green onion, and simmer for 2 hours. Some people add a couple of teaspoons of white vinegar during this cooking time. Correct the seasonings to taste. When it is prepared in this manner, you can choose to eat the gumbo with or without rice. If it is to be a Lenten dish, substitute 2 pints of oysters and their liquor for the salt meat or ham.

GUMBO Z'HERBES (WITH A ROUX)

Serves 10-12

Use the same ingredient list as above, with this addition:
1/2 cup vegetable oil
3 tablespoons flour

Make a small roux with the oil and flour. When the roux is a warm brown color, add the yellow onions and garlic; cook until onions are wilted. Add the salt meat or ham and cook for a few more minutes. In a large soup pot, combine the roux mixture with the cooking liquid from the greens, add chopped green onion, and cook for 30 minutes. Then add all of the greens. Continue to simmer for 2 hours. The only step omitted from the first recipe is the browning of the onions and salt meat in the shortening.

Papa liked to douse his bowl of gumbo and rice with a homemade vinegar in which Tabasco peppers had been steeped.

On Holy Saturday preceding Easter Sunday, while eggs were being dyed and the final touches were given to our Easter bonnets, there was one final meatless supper. It was a simple but delicious repast.

SHRIMP CREOLE

Serves 6

4 tablespoons butter or margarine
2 tablespoons flour
1 cup chopped onion
1 cup chopped sweet green pepper
2 stalks celery, chopped
3 cloves garlic, minced

1 pound can whole tomatoes, crushed with their juice
2 bay leaves
2 cups shrimp stock or water
3/4 teaspoon salt
1/2 teaspoon cayenne pepper
2 pounds medium shrimp, peeled and deveined
parsley

Melt butter in a deep black iron pot. When butter begins to foam, add flour and whisk quickly to make a light brown roux. Be careful not to burn the roux. Add onions, sweet green peppers, celery, and garlic; sauté for a few minutes, just enough to wilt the vegetables. Blend the tomatoes and their juice into the roux. Add the bay leaves and shrimp stock or water, blending well. Add salt and pepper; simmer gently for 30 minutes, stirring occasionally. Add shrimp and cook for 15 minutes. Be sure not to over cook the shrimp or they will be tough. Just before serving add chopped fresh parsley. Serve over steamed or boiled rice.

BAKED MACARONI

Serves 6

12 ounces elbow macaroni
4 tablespoons butter
One 12-ounce can evaporated milk
3 eggs, beaten
One 8-ounce block of American cheese, cubed
salt and cayenne pepper to taste

Cook macaroni in boiling water until just tender. Drain and rinse in warm water. Place macaroni in 9 x 13-inch baking dish and add butter; stir to allow butter to melt thoroughly. Add milk and beaten eggs; mix well. Add cheese and mix again until cheese is slightly melted. Season to taste with salt and cayenne pepper. Bake at 350 degrees for 45 minutes.

Fried catfish, crisp and well seasoned, is the perfect complement to baked macaroni. The secret to this catfish recipe is the marinade.

ROGER'S CATFISH

Serves 4

1 pound catfish fillets, cut into 1" x 3" strips
1/2 teaspoon salt
1/2 teaspoon black pepper
1 cup milk
2 tablespoons yellow mustard
juice of 1/2 lemon
a few dashes of Tabasco®
2 cups corn flour
1 tablespoon cornstarch
Shortening for frying

Season the fish with salt and pepper. Place the strips in a bowl with the milk, mustard, lemon juice, and Tabasco®; refrigerate for several hours.

Put the corn flour and cornstarch into a brown paper bag. Remove the catfish from the marinade a few pieces at a time, allowing the milk marinade to drain off a bit. Put the strips in the bag and shake well to coat each piece. Heat the shortening to 350 degrees and drop a few pieces of fish at a time into the hot oil. You must use enough shortening to deep fry. When the fish pieces rise to the top and are golden brown, remove and drain on a brown paper bag.

Recipe Index